浙江省百项档案编研精品

英文文献中的"温州"
资料汇编（1876-1949 年）

THE COMPILATION OF
MATERIALS ON WENZHOU
IN ENGLISH LITERATURE
(1876-1949)

《北华捷报》
温州史料编译

温州市档案馆

【第四辑】

（1916—1935年）

译　编

THE COMPILATION AND
TRANSLATION OF MATERIALS ON WENZHOU IN
NORTH-CHINA HERALD (1916-1935)

社会科学文献出版社
SOCIAL SCIENCES ACADEMIC PRESS (CHINA)

目录
Contents

第二部分　英文文献

第三部分 专有名词

《北华捷报》
简介与本书编辑说明

英国商人亨利·奚安门（Henry Shearman）于 1850 年 8 月 3 日在上海英租界创办周报《北华捷报》（*North – China Herald*）。1856 年后，随着商业广告增多，《北华捷报》开始增出英文广告日报《每日航运新闻》（*Daily Shipping News*），1862 年后该刊更名为《每日航运与商业新闻》（*Daily Shipping News and Commercial News*，又译为《航务商业日报》）。

自 1859 年起，《北华捷报》被英国驻沪领事馆指定为公署文告发布机关，得到上海工部局的资助和优先刊载工部局文告及付费广告的特权，因而它在一定程度上也反映英国政府的观点，被视为"英国官报"（Official British Organ）。1864 年 7 月 1 日，《北华捷报》将《每日航运与商业新闻》改为综合性日报，独立出版。这时，该报馆改组为字林洋行，因而当时的中国人将这份 *North China Daily News* 英文日报译作《字林西报》。《字林西报》创刊后，《北华捷报》成为《字林西报》的星期日附刊，继续出版，其地位与影响力日益下降，1867 年 4 月 8 日后其增加商情并易名为《北华捷报与市场报道》（*North China Herald and Market*

Report），继续出版。1870 年 1 月 4 日，《北华捷报与市场报道》增出《最高法庭与领事公报》（*The Supreme Court and Consular*），不久后两报合并，更名为《北华捷报及最高法庭与领事馆杂志》（*North China Herald and Supreme Court and Consular Gazette*），继续出版，并一直出版到 1941 年 12 月。

为便于表达，本书将以《北华捷报》统称该报纸。本书是《英文文献中的"温州"资料汇编》系列第二辑（1876 ~ 1895 年）与第三辑（1896 ~ 1915 年）的后续编译，选取的是 1916 ~ 1935 年该报纸有关"温州"（Wenchow）的主要新闻报道和评论，并按照编年顺序加以编辑和翻译。

另外，需要特别指出的是，《北华捷报》在这一时期的报道，大量涉及有关温州的革命史，尤其是有关红十三军的内容。在国民革命时期，"非基督教运动"进入高潮，全国各地教会学校都遭受巨大冲击。在此背景下，温州教会学校艺文学堂甚至关闭，而《北华捷报》在温州的许多新闻通讯员，如蔡博敏等人，本身就是教会或教会学校中人。且《北华捷报》的新闻通讯员多数是英国人，他们会天然地将对苏联与第三国际的怀疑与厌恶移植到温州革命运动上，因此《北华捷报》这一时期的报道在立场上往往对本地共产党员与国民党左派持负面与敌视态度。该报纸对金贯真、胡公冕等革命先烈记述颇多，有一定史料价值，但也不乏污蔑与偏见，我们对其不少观点与立场并不赞同，在翻译时以尽量保持史料真实性为原则，对一些极端用词做适当处理，在此特作说明。

中文
翻译

junks cruising after pirates along
-Ché sea coast, it seems that th
of Fukien and Taichow are sti
erous and as savage as ever.
d its consort bound from Ningpo t
w laden with rice and sundries wer
attacked near Wênchow by a cow
irates, who boarded the merchant
ving ransacked everything of valu
e latter, left them with twenty-five
nd seriously wounded Stri
have been issued by the Governo
, T'an, for the capture of the pirate
te a large fleet of war junks is not
t it seems to be the universal opinio
.... will be unsuccessful

xpression, spread himself out over the
whole subject of the health, pestilence
amines, and topography of the place
Thirty-six closely printed pages have
not sufficed to relieve him of his whole
burden of knowledge, for at the begin
ning of his paper he says that he reserve
he medical ....
occasion; but ....
f which he h ....
nally have the
hat we sho
uch a trifle
aply :
l rigl He begins v
spec district in wl
o gre and passing
other ....

During a fierce gale which raged at Wen
chow about a fortnight ago, several seriou
disasters occurred, attended in many case
with lost of life. Four large junks, lade
with poles, were upset and many other
dragged anchor or sustained other injuries
whilst a great number of small fishing craf
suffered a worse fate. The villagers on th
coast showed great barbarism. Instead o
ffording succour, they busied themselve
with picking up wreckage thrown ashore
In the worst cases they even wrested th
poles away from the shipwrecked people
who in their exhausted state were made t
yield the logs to the merciless people
Owing to the unusually cold weather a
Wenchow there is considerable suffering
amongst the poorer classes, who are no
provided with extensive wardrobes, and
specially amongst those who have a pre
....

e sent to Ta-c
Yo-ching-hsien
pirate-robbers
used considerat
es of both this
now. Some tim
oes plundered two
the Yu H'uan Bay
e) which caused the
to order one of his
against them. On
of the bay the office
vessel decided to an
ed a party of soldier

Yungning, from Wênc
d here on Saturday, b
ulars of a riot which had
how on the night of the
rst intimation of this ri
ed up from Ningpo from informatio
ed by the Yungning on arrival a
ort, though efforts had been made b

(FROM A CORRESP
Notice to mariners, also
ad to feminine sphere-
emarkable Peak on the
avigators see on their f
Wênchow, having only
ad never named, has no
he denizens of Wênchow
Hart's Peak," in recogn
ices which the Inspecto
mperial Maritime Custo
y illuminating the coa
formal recognition of the
y the Wênchowese, in pic-nic assembled
n the 22nd March, and that being th
irthday of the Emperor of Germany, nea
o the celebration of the Queen's Jubilee
nd within measurable distance of th
atal day of President Cleveland, th
ealth of those estimable rulers was dran

which a reference to Mr. Don
's table on the opposite page rend
ent. My views elsewhere publis

ichow as its Consul on the 12th inst.,
Parker taking leave on a new de-
ure, having first secured the last instal-
t of the indemnity that the authorities
ed to pay for losses sustained by
iguers in the recent disturbances. To
be Mr. E H. Parker's success in giving
ral satisfaction to foreigners and native
orities in regard to the questions raised
ie riot to good luck, would be unjust to
accomplished officer. It was tact that
ted an amicable settlement

ng-nang, running as she n
rt of the most influential
fter trip with improved
esults, seems now to have
o that point where if more
of necessity become m
g superfluity. As has bee
the impetus given by
y means of shipment has
nt export of al
spects for tea
for the Sh

To the Editor of the
NORTH-CHINA DAILY NEWS.

IR,—Although the subject of r
China was ably discussed at a late
of the Shanghai Literary and De
iety the question was not so exha
reated as to preclude me from o
nall contribution, assuming that
be unacceptable to those who
ary (but not

(UNRATED.)

vastation that met on
e river of Wênchow wa
les and miles the countr
vast expanse of wate
teads and graves, an
nds crowded with cattle
frowning background
a most depressing an
We passed too quickl
by the pen. Women an
roups, doubtless talkin
sses, while the men we
ay in their boats. In some places wher
he bridges were still standing only th
pper portion of their arches was visibl
oking like mirages—water above, belo
nd around them! Great indeed mu
ave been the downpour to have caused suc
n inundation. It was a comforting chang
o turn one's gaze from the immerse
ountry to the numberless fishermen pur
uing their calling as if no such thing
ome troubles existed. The flooded cou
....

Macgowa
ow recen
put down
sumption
outhwaite
ld be tra

bitants of the so-called "Ca
ave put away their store-clo
ar. The rejoicings were co
uietness and decorum, the
of nastiness was eaten,
ount of tomtomming and fi
ulged in; in fact, everyth
accordance with "olo cu
Year's Eve most of the
cipal thoroughfares were
ted with coloured lamps, a
re lighted in nearly all the
ty and suburbs. That this
isement did not result in a
onflagration is simply miraculous,
mmunity is by all right-thinking
tributed to the special interve
en Tien Ta Ti, the great Lord of
leaven, or some other benevolen
hough here, as elsewhere, scoffers
und who point to the saturated con
verything or to some other such c

ically, it m
think the
mature, tha
where it m
needed; f
northern Ch
courses, and
is doubtful
ccessfully c
It was urge
yed by an it
of China,

R OWN CORRESP
ing, on enter
d some straggl
trawropes, the

that were d
ut the enemy'
ng. ... they resisted th
would have been as useless
A proposition that was mad
channel has been abandoned
a panic was created by a p
quiring every family to brin
darins a basket of stones,
as secure as if they had
protection; the authorities
solicitous for their safety. S
threw missiles, and others er

《温州街道的闸门：一种旧俗与目前堪忧的局势》，《北华捷报及最高法庭与领事馆杂志》，1916 年 1 月 15 日

温州街道的闸门：一种旧俗与目前堪忧的局势

（本报记者报道）

数天前，这里的每个本地人和外国人都惊讶地看到，在几乎所有主要街道的路口都建起了超过 10 英尺高的厚重木门。在一些长街，不仅在路口设门，在路中也置有门禁。城门外人口稠密的郊区同样照此办理。这实际上是快被废止 20 年的、称为"冬防"（tung voa）① 的旧习俗的重现。

人们认为，在漫长的冬夜，应该做好更充分的准备以应对盗贼。但过去 10 年的经验表明，没有恢复这种旧制的任何特殊需要，我们必须从其他地方找原因，我们的印象是这些路障实际上并不是用于表面目的，而是为了在宣布变更国体后，防止出现人群聚集和暴动。

在过去的几天里，城市弥漫着一种等待的氛围。衙门已经做好准备，并且每天都在等着共和国总统紫袍②加身。这里普遍的观点是，温州以及浙江其他地方都将接受君主制，即使不鼓掌赞成，也只能顺从辞职，但有相当多的学生阶层相信云南、四川、贵州、广东和广西 5 地将宣布独立。（温州，1 月 4 日）

---

① 清代为了防止冬季年关盗案的发生，主要依靠保甲加强相关防务，谓之"冬防"。民国以后，冬防政策得到延续。1915 年 12 月 12 日，袁世凯称帝，全国一致反对，故各地在当年特别强化了冬防。参见《中央：讨论冬防计画》，《兵事杂志》1915 年第 20 期，第 4 页。

② 在古罗马时期，紫袍是皇帝的象征。

《温州：瓯柑产季与财富》，《北华捷报及最高法庭与领事馆杂志》，
1916 年 3 月 31 日

温州：瓯柑产季与财富

（本报记者报道）

当前瓯柑产季快要结束，出口状况也是出奇地好。虽然去年的出口不超过 1 万箱（主要是因为减产），但自今年 11 月的第一个星期开始，每名商人的商船都会运走 2500 箱至 4000 箱，仅数周时间总出口量就达到 7000箱。这些瓯柑大部分会被运往上海，然后转运到天津与北平。

瓯柑很特别，与中国其他任何果蔬品种都不同。瓯柑果实硕大，皮厚而松软，很多人对它的喜爱是慢慢养成的，一旦尝过以后，其滋味就无可替代。也许值得一提的是，这种对瓯柑的喜爱让人想起"塞维利亚橙"，因此瓯柑可能是制作"橘子酱"的最佳选择。① 至于其大规模生产是否能够成功，还有待进一步观察。

温州另外一种可资利用的产品是生姜，温州生姜的产量很大却不用于出口，本地姜加工后与广州的品种很类似。

据报道，在今年的茶季中，采购商很可能会放弃从当地茶商手上采购，这是由于去年发生了史无前例的掺假事件。多年以前，温州茶叶一向美名在外，其大部分被运往汉口进行茶叶拼配②，但由于前述原因，如今温州茶的出口量已经逐年降低。从商业的角度看，温州茶商们显然没有意识到他们正在腐败中自取灭亡。

温州以南 30 英里处的平阳县的明矾产量正稳步增长，随着今年价格的

---

① 西班牙塞维利亚橙，也被称为苦橙，其橙皮可以被用来制成最好的橙子酱。参见图林、桑切茨《香水指南》，南海出版公司，2013，第 319 页。

② 所谓茶叶拼配，即将不同种类与等级的茶叶进行拼配、分装，以提高其经济价值。参见陈宗懋编《中国茶叶大辞典》，中国轻工业出版社，2000，第 513 页。

大幅增长，这项贸易获利丰厚。一般明矾都是由帆船运到温州，然后再由轮船转运出口，每艘船能够装运数千包。

温州是一个非常守旧的地方，铜分在最近几个月才开始流通。据说多年来，由于当地银行和钱铺的阻挠，人们一直在抵制这种有用的硬币。至于抵制的原因很难搞清楚，但现在障碍已经被清除，市场流通中的铜圆①数量正在迅速增加。

电灯在温州似乎已经永久扎根。这座新建立的工厂②成立于约两年前，在过去的 12 个月中几乎没有发生故障。管理层现在完全掌握在中国人手中，值得我们为其高效的服务而祝贺。温州夜晚共有超过 4000 盏电灯在使用，虽然电厂还能提供更多电力，但公司无法提供更多的安装服务。

除了已经存在的温州师范外，人们建议当地政府重组一所一年制的学校。③ 这所新学校过去被称为省立附属高等小学校——现在被称为国民学校，其目的在于培养和提供教师，这显然对学生不公平，这种新冒险只是在糊弄学生的需求而已。这种“快速获得文凭”的弊端太过于明显，实在不值一评。（温州，3 月 21 日）

---

① 据张棡记载，20 世纪 20 年代，温州大洋一元可兑铜圆 168 片，或兑小洋 11 角加铜圆 8 片。参见温州市图书馆编《张棡日记·第六册》，张钧孙点校，中华书局，2019，第 2664、2672 页。

② 这里指的是普华电灯公司。

③ 这所小学最早在清代宣统三年二月创办，是温州师范的附属小学校。民国二年改为省立，但并未获得省资助。民国六年，改为省资助，并由此改名为“浙江省立第十师范附属高等小学校、国民学校”。参见《教育部视察浙江省立第十师范附属高等小学校、国民学校报告》，载陈元晖主编《中国近代教育史资料汇编：普通教育》，上海教育出版社，2007，第 626 页。

《温州：税收纠纷》，《北华捷报及最高法庭与领事馆杂志》，1916
年4月22日

温州：税收纠纷

（本报记者报道）

楚门（Tsumen）是一座建有城墙的城市，坐落在海岸线上，有1万名居民，位于温州和台州的中间。在过去18个月里，此地在征收盐税问题上遇到了极大困难。

楚门城外的村民大多数从事制盐业，其中最突出的是外塘村（Whadoa），此地大概有1500名居民。盐税官员在去年告知当地居民，官方将会收购所有的盐，并且禁止私人直接贩盐。当盐价是1元2角时，官员们以1元的价格购入；当盐价是8角时，官员们会以1元卖出，这样就可以获得50%的利润。当地民众认为这是当地官员另一种形式的"压榨"，因此拒绝将盐卖给盐务局，并纷纷直接到周围市场私自销售。盐务局官员试图阻止民众购买私盐，因此激怒民众，在后续双方冲突中有2名盐务局职员被杀死。这件事似乎没有立即被报到杭州，所以几个月后当省府得到消息时，省府没有采取任何行动。

今年当局已经采取了新的税收办法，但人们相信或者说掩耳盗铃地认为不会再有高级官员被派来收取盐税。当新官员①来到楚门时，他得到了省城50名士兵的支持。当局的新计划是从买家而不是从盐户手上征税。买家每购买价值8角1分的盐，就要支付5角的盐税。当地人拒绝了这项计划，因为他们认为按照此条款根本无法做生意。盐务官员随即咨询了玉环

---

① 这里指的是两浙缉私统领蔡竹贤。由于玉环县在楚门征收盐税屡办屡辍，当局准备改设北盐场兼收盐税，同时派遣官兵与役夫34名以备镇压（注：史料记载有出入，原文如此）。参见《查缉浙东盐枭》，《申报》1916年3月1日，第10版；《游缉队调往楚门》，《申报》1916年3月21日，第10版。

（Yuhuanting）知事，① 这名知事于是逮捕了外塘村的两个主要头目。外塘村村民在一两天后展开报复，也逮捕了玉环知事的两个手下，并将其带到玉环，希望与当局交换人质。近 1000 个村民在被鸣枪警告后，仍拒绝后退——在这种情况下知事认为同意交换人质才是明智之举。村民们随后安静地返回家中，但他们担心军队会回来报复，所以村民向一群土匪寻求帮助，在后续的一系列小冲突当中，有一名士兵和几个村民被杀死。

楚门市面已完全失序，所有妇女、幼童和富人都逃往安全地方避难 。我得到的最新消息是，160 名土匪袭击了楚门城，共计有 70 栋房屋被烧毁，20 人丧生。附近乡下地区都陷入了恐慌。（温州，4 月 14 日）

---

① 这里指的是新任玉环县知事不久的秦联元。

《温州独立》，《北华捷报及最高法庭与领事馆杂志》，1916 年 4 月 29 日

温州独立

（本报记者报道）

　　在广东宣布脱离中央政府独立的消息传来温州之后，人们普遍认为浙江很快也会随之独立。果然在 4 月 14 日下午，温州军事长官戴任（Dai Ning）① 接到了台州镇守使张载扬（Chang Tse－yang）的电报，对方劝告戴任，说目前台州、宁波、嘉兴和绍兴都已宣布独立，因此要求戴任与其他温州官吏商量后加入独立队伍。当日下午，温州所有主要官员齐集海关监督衙门开会。参会人员一致认为，目前维持温州秩序最好的办法就是遵从张载扬的建议。

　　但温州官员也很谨慎，他们向省长拍发了电报以寻求意见。当天没有收到任何回复，但夜间水警部门的长官陈先生收到了来自杭州军界的消息，杭州方面明确表示已正式脱离袁世凯政府并宣布独立。温州方面随即感到事不宜迟，应立刻宣布独立。次日清晨，城中共和旗帜随处飞扬，学校放假一日，以志庆贺。

　　温州官员办理此事极为迅速，对于保障本地当前之和平极有益处。仅仅在布告张贴不久，即有各地革命党人聚集到温州准备举事。普遍观点认为，如果当局行动迟缓让这批革命党发现温州没有宣布独立的话，他们一

① 戴任，原名学礼，字立夫，号石渠，永嘉城区人，国民党左派，一生坚定追随孙中山的革命事业。戴任原本担任浙江警备队总稽查职务，在 1915 年接替梅占魁担任温州第六区警备队统带职务，在 1916 年至 1917 年间掌握温州地方军事权力。皖军入浙后，戴任被迫出走。参见《地方通信：温州》，《申报》1915 年 4 月 3 日，第 7 版；游寿澄《戴立夫事略》，载温州市鹿城区委员会文史资料工作委员会编《鹿城文史资料·第四辑》，1989，第 134～136 页。俞雄《戴任史事补遗》，《温州会刊》2000 年第 6 期，第 17～19 页。

定会制造大麻烦，所幸现在这个不受欢迎的团体几乎立刻离开了城市。

商会诸人与城内士绅拟组建地方议会，襄助官吏共同管理城市。他们认为这样一个代表机构能够做许多工作以保障和平。但地方道尹①表示，杭州方面已来电明确表示，以他目前的处境不得建立该新机构。② 但道尹还是向省长拍发电报，以候裁示。（温州，4 月 17 日）

---

① 即瓯海道尹陈光宪。

② 1911 年，最后一任温处道道台兼海关监督离开温州后，海关监督衙门被梅占魁占据为司令部。1914 年袁世凯任命新的文官职务瓯海道尹，取代过去的道台职务，以管理温州 2 府 16 县。在反对帝制运动当中，瓯海道尹的职务被废除，这可能是杭州方面拒绝陈光宪组织新机构的原因。参见中华人民共和国杭州海关译编《近代浙江通商口岸经济社会概况：浙海关、瓯海关、杭州关贸易报告集成》，浙江人民出版社，2002，第 445 页。

《温州：对公立学校的控诉》，《北华捷报及最高法庭与领事馆杂志》，1916 年 5 月 27 日

温州：对公立学校的控诉

（本报记者报道）

圣道公会①艺文学堂（United Methodist Mission College）② 校长，理学硕士蔡博敏（T. W. Chapman）先生（有时他也会担任本报记者职务）今天已经离港，前往英格兰度假。蔡博敏夫妇收到了许多精美礼物，可以看出其学生、同事、邻居与地方官员对他们的感情与尊敬。

上个星期五，在艺文学堂的基督教青年会（Y. M. C. A.）③ 举办了一场大型聚会，以向蔡博敏先生告别。大家纷纷演讲并朗诵诗歌，以感谢他的工作。蔡博敏先生起身答话，大家报以热烈掌声。

在这些演讲中，其中有一位的演说内容可能超出了当地的情况。这位演说者是一名 20 岁的青年，他曾有一两次因为其热情演讲而引起人们的注意，他应邀在集会上发表演说，他对公立学校管理的严厉批评引起轰动。他说艺文学堂是公认的整个地区教育机构的领先者。他和他的同学们都感谢校长，因为在这所学校，通过校长的良好的管理，讲师总是守时，并保

---

① 偕我公会于 1857 年创办，1907 年改名为圣道公会，1932 年改名为循道公会。参见沈迦《寻找苏慧廉》，新星出版社，2013，第 10 页。

② 1879 年传教士李庆华创办艺文男塾。1897 年苏慧廉扩大男塾，在瓦市殿巷创办艺文书院。1902 年艺文书院改名为艺文学堂，并由苏慧廉夫人路熙到英国筹款，在海坦山麓建立新校舍。参见浙江省温州市鹿城区慈善总会编《温州市鹿城区慈善志》，方志出版社，2018，第 134 页。

③ 1914 年在裴德士的鼓吹之下，温州艺文学堂模仿山东广文学校青年会，建起了自己的青年会，从相关文献来看，温州的青年会具有很强的宗教性。参见《温州艺文学校青年会成立》，《青年》1914 年第 8 期，第 189 页。

证课堂全勤。此外，由于艺文学堂的教师比较固定，学生得以接受连贯性的学习。

在其他学生鼓掌之后，这名演讲者继续说道：

"但是如果我们在杭州或其他公立学校学习过的话，我们就会知道它们是怎么样的。首先，公立学校的老师会迟到。然后，他会上半小时课并自以为满意，接着就下课。这还不是全部。你原本跟随一位老师学习了不长时间，突然这位老师就离职了，换了一个新老师过来，学习的连贯性完全被摧毁了。"

在思考这件事时，我认为虽然由于年轻人说话往往在情感上过于冲动，他们的话也应该打一个折扣来听，但仍能看出两点事实。第一，虽然公立教育工作取得了巨大进步，但西方学校生活的基本要求，如守时和工作的连续性，在中国的学校中还没有普及。第二，西方在华所开展的教会教育或其他教育的特征是，彻底忠于原则且不尚浮华，以便最大限度地帮助改善中国的教育生活。这种特征需要被强调，才能使中国从学者之乡变为学校之乡。（温州，5月14日）

《一名中医医生治疗伤寒》，《北华捷报及最高法庭与领事馆杂志》，
1916 年 11 月 4 日

一名中医医生治疗伤寒

（本报记者报道）

今年初秋，温州以北的许多村庄时疫暴发，根据病症判断，这很有可能是伤寒。身强力壮的患者还有可能康复，但老人与小孩难以抵挡这种疾病。

某人染病后，请了一位本地医生为其治病，这名医生决定舍弃折中的保守疗法。为了让病人降温，医生用湿冷毛巾敷在病人头上，同时在病人腹部盖上厚厚的泥土，并不断灌凉水使病人保持舒适和凉爽。同时在一天之内，病人服用了 12 银圆的犀牛角，病人随后得以康复。

现在伤寒疫情已经结束。

持续 4000 年的收获方式

最近水稻正在收割。粮筐会放在田里，或是放在临近工人的路边，工人们一边割稻穗，一边立刻脱粒。汉字"谷"指的是没有去壳的稻米，谷子会被放进筐里，稻秆则被堆在田边。

"我想中国人使用这种相同的农作方式已经数百年了，"一位老实的当地人如是说。"数百年了，"他很快接着说道，"我不知道为什么有人要把这种农作方式上溯到神农时期（公元前 2700 年）。"这种生产方式也许不会出现在那么久远的年代，但无论如何，它们确实存在了相当长的一段时期。但西方人不知道自己最该感到惊讶的，到底是这种生产方式持续了千百年而不变，还是这种古老的系统在 20 世纪的今天还能解决数百万中国人的吃饭问题。（温州，10 月 24 日）

《温州鸦片泛滥》，《北华捷报及最高法庭与领事馆杂志》，1916年12月2日

温州鸦片泛滥

（本报记者报道）

温州大约有8万人口，据说仍有数千人吸食鸦片。现在县知事①正大力惩办这些烟客。在发现张贴告示，以及在报纸上发公告对制止这种非法行为无济于事后，知事决定逮捕并监禁一批烟客。此外，从衙门中流出的小道消息说，吸食鸦片者如果在新年期间被发现就会被枪毙：若用雷霆手段清除掉一两颗老鼠屎，则能保住一锅粥！

阿歧森先生②退休

11月12日，前瓯海关税务司阿歧森（James Acheson）已经离开港口前往英格兰。阿歧森先生在温州待了两年半，受到外侨社区与当地华人的尊敬。他从1874年进入海关，如今正式退休。值得一提的是，在19世纪80年代早期，阿歧森先生曾徒步穿越西伯利亚，返回家乡。带着中国各港口朋友们的美好祝愿，阿歧森先生开启了最后一次的返乡旅程，这些朋友们都相信他能拥有一个漫长愉快的退休生活，这也是他应得的。（温州，11月20日）

---

① 此时任职永嘉知事者为郑彤雯，可以看到在当年报纸上永嘉多处百姓状告永嘉县借禁烟勒索金钱、鱼肉乡里的情况。民国初年，温州借禁烟勒索更为出名的是郑彤雯的前任刘强夫，刘强夫上任后派警察四处缉拿有钱烟客，温州乡下地主如茶山诸岩松、霞坊叶玉周等都遭其勒索，每人罚金800元至1000元不等，刘强夫因此被当地人称为"刘强盗"。参见《请看永嘉县渔田警察之鱼肉乡民》，《申报》1916年8月9日，第四版；戴冀席《解放前温州的鸦片流毒》，载《温州文史资料·第四辑》，浙江人民出版社，1988，第211~219页。

② 阿歧森，爱尔兰人，1874年进入中国海关，曾经两次在温州任职，1916年11月在温州税务司任上退休。转引自詹庆华、冯雪松编《全球化视野：中国海关洋员与中西文化传播（1854—1950）》，中国海关出版社，2008，第506页。

《温州的红衣大炮：明朝旧物当废铁卖》，《北华捷报及最高法庭与领事馆杂志》，1917 年 1 月 27 日

温州的红衣大炮：明朝旧物当废铁卖

（本报记者报道）

　　来到温州的游客们，一定不会对温州的许多老旧大炮感到陌生，其中一些大炮被安放在旧堡垒里防卫河口，一些被用来装饰城墙，另一些则被闲置在城市中的荒地里。在温州，像这样各类大小型号的大炮，总计大概超过 1000 门。根据杭州方面督军①的命令，所有这些无用旧物都应尽可能变卖。② 这一大批旧物都被按照每 1 钱重量折成 1 文钱的价格售卖。工人们将大炮敲成小块，这些小块由两名苦力就能搬运，每艘驶离港口的船都会装运这些小块。

　　这些旧炮都有它们的故事。其中最后一批大炮，是在太平天国时期被安放在温州的。曾经的温州府历经千辛万苦才买到这些大炮，当这些大炮抵达温州时，人们为它们感到自豪。所以少数还知道当年情形的人说："可耻，可耻！想想看，我们花了这么多钱买来的大将军炮，现在就要从我们身边被夺走了，而且还是当废铁卖——一钱只卖一文！"

　　更古老的大炮可以追溯到康熙时期，当时明朝的残余势力仍在，整个国家仍未安定下来。在那些年月，这些加农炮被称为"红衣大将军"，他们是"将军"，身着红袍，充满力量，在呼吸间就能带来火焰、浓烟和死亡。人们抚今追昔，不禁回想起这些大炮当年参与战斗的情景，这些大炮

---

① 这里指的是浙江督军杨善德。

② 1917 年杨善德裁撤炮台的范围，除温州外，还包括定海、乍浦。除将一些旧炮变卖外，另将一些送往上海兵工厂修理。参见《杭州消息》，《民国日报》1917 年 4 月 27 日，第 3 版；《旧枪炮修竣运浙》，《申报》1918 年 8 月 6 日，第 10 版。

曾对三角门外山麓附近的起义军大肆屠戮。① 那是一次著名的胜利，水渠里都流淌着鲜血，其中一条水渠后来被改建为"得胜路"（The Way of the Golden‑Victory），这个名字一直延续到今天，以铭记过去战争年代的历史。

致命的爆炸

上述法令除了允许销售旧炮外，也授权地方当局处理其他老旧无用的军需储备。因此大批存储的旧子弹被售卖，在此期间还发生了意外。需要指出的是，这些旧货是当地士兵所能用到的最好的后膛来复枪子弹。

苦力们负责将子弹敲碎，并将黄铜、铅和火药进行分离。他们第一天的工作地点实际是在军火库！第二天，他们将工作地点迁到了远一点的地方。第三天他们离得更远了一点。星期五早上，也就是在第五天，城西七圣庙②的老门卫惊讶地发现一群苦力扛着一堆旧子弹进到了庙里。门卫问这些苦力将子弹搬进庙里干什么，这些苦力回答说："晒太阳！"目前共有18个人在工作，他们先将子弹分开，然后将黄铜分成一堆、铅分成一堆、火药分成第三堆。

这项工作需要承担一定程度的风险，但他们可以获得3天1银圆的高工资，同时还可以得到大米！一名妇女负责给他们做饭。其中有一个人起初是挑水的，后来他找到另一个人顶替自己挑水，然后在第三天改为做更赚钱也更轻松的拆子弹工作。可惜，他现在既干不了辛苦的挑水工作，也干不了轻松的拆子弹工作了。

12 人遇难

到了星期五晚上，金属废料和火药已经堆积到相当规模，但仍有许多子弹未被拆解。只听到"哒——哒——哒——砰"的声音，一个弹药筒爆

---

① 三角门即来福门，也被民间称为山脚门或生姜门，1862 年太平军曾先后六次攻打温州府城，最后被击退。参见浙江省温州鹿城区委员会文史资料工作委员会编《鹿城文史资料·第五辑·温州城区近百年记事（1840—1949）》，1990，第 16 ~ 17 页；温州市测绘志编纂委员会编《永嘉城池坊巷图（1882 年）》，《温州市测绘志》，上海三联书店，2019，第 470 页。

② 七圣庙，原址在今温州市区七圣殿巷。庙神姓薛，宋咸淳间赐额，封孚惠侯。转引自陈瑞赞《东瓯逸事汇录》，上海社会科学院出版社，2006，第 702 页。

炸了，一堆火药被点燃，这些可怜的苦力用尽了不久前值得庆幸的好运，他们将面对烧伤和残疾。可能有 3 人当场死亡，其他人冲出正门跳进了庙前的水渠，另一些人冲出侧门满地打滚，试图扑灭身上的火焰。目前在现场仍能看到当时可怕场景的残迹。

包括天主教会（Roman Catholic Mission）附属建筑①在内的附近房屋，都在爆炸中受到震动。火势仅局限在七圣庙内，剩余的子弹已经被紧急搬走。虽然在七圣庙的墙上可以看到弹孔，但所幸没有人被子弹击中。大多数伤者被送到圣道公会医院（United Methodist Hospital)②，第二天医院里来了许多访客，修女们正在尽最大努力为病人疗伤。一些人的烧伤很严重，当晚有 3 人不治身亡，此后又有 6 人去世，这场事故总共造成 12 人遇难。（温州，1 月 13 日）

---

① 周宅祠巷天主教堂由意大利神父董增温建立，1888 年教堂开始动工，是温州第一座哥特式风格建筑。参见金丹霞、周红《温州老城印象：讲述温州城的陈年旧事》，浙江古籍出版社，2011，第 44～54 页。

② 即白累德医院。

《旅沪温州人：遭遇诈骗团伙的故事》，《北华捷报及最高法庭与领事馆杂志》，1917 年 8 月 25 日

旅沪温州人：遭遇诈骗团伙的故事
（本报记者报道）

上个月底，一名温州有钱人刚抵达上海就遇到了陌生人，这名陌生人告诉他，他的一位数年前离开温州的老朋友现在就住在上海孟德兰路（Mandalay Road），想与他叙旧。这毫无疑问是个诈骗的老把戏，在全世界任何国家的任何大城市里，都会看到类似的针对乡下人的诈骗，这些老把戏的历史与城市历史本身一样古老，[1] 但这名初到上海的温州人对此闻所未闻。

这名温州人陪着陌生人来到孟德兰路，马霍路（Mohawk Road）跑马场（Race Club）入口的对面，他在那里受到了另外一名陌生人的热情接待。温州人被告知，他的朋友碰巧外出了——如果可以的话，他可以坐下来一边喝点新茶一边等待。当时正是炎热的七月底，茶自然可口，既让人感到清爽，又让人宽心。事实上，温州人在喝完饮料后很快就舒服地睡着了。

他在昏迷后被捆绑着送上了一辆人力车，当他再次醒来的时候，好像前一刻才刚喝过茶一样，但已身处卡德路（Carter Road）的一栋房子里。他看了看房间，发现周围全是陌生人，这才意识到所谓"温州老朋友"全是谎话。绑架他的人向他们的这位受害者保证，他没有获救的希望，然后对他进行压榨，并威胁说，除非付清赎金，否则绝不允许他回到温州。

温州人口袋里总共有 169 银圆，他把这笔钱全交了出来，以为绑匪会满意，并且表示没有更多钱了。但是绑匪很了解他们的受害者，要求他交

---

① 关于此类西方城市的经典诈骗，14 世纪薄伽丘的《十日谈》里有大量案例。

出更多钱来。他们捕到了一只稀有的“鸟”，因此在决定放掉它之前，一定要拔光它每一根亮丽的羽毛。首先绑匪强迫温州人写一封信，要求（家人）立刻寄来 1000 银圆钞票。这封勒索信随后被送到受害者在上海的寓所，绑匪很快拿到了这笔钱。紧接着，绑匪强迫受害者签了 4 张 500 银圆的支票，支付日期定在 8 月 17 日，在此之后受害者才被释放。所有这些事情，都发生在受害者被绑之后的三天之内。

8 月 3 日，也就是绑架事件发生数天后，此事被报告给中央巡捕房，后者立刻开始调查。上海展开此类调查一般进度较慢，但肯定能破案。与其他国家城市相比，上海追回赃物以及逮捕罪犯的可能性更高。8 月 16 日，一名新闸巡捕房的华探逮捕了两名涉案诈骗犯，并在其中一人身上搜出两张支票。在上个星期五，也就是支票应该兑现的日子，两名诈骗犯被送到了会审公廨（Mixed Court）进行听证，之后将被还押，择日再审。

《温州觉醒：一座不为人知的繁荣城市》，《北华捷报及最高法庭与
领事馆杂志》，1917 年 9 月 29 日

温州觉醒：一座不为人知的繁荣城市

（本报记者报道）

　　温州作为区域中心，大概有 200 万人口，[①] 它虽然距离上海的南部只
有两天航程，但并不为人所重视。这可能是温州商业不像其他城市那样繁
盛的缘故，但最近我们可以在温州发现一些进步的信号。

　　温州最近最显著的进步是安装了电灯。主路的街道现在看起来更为
热闹，但还会有一些犄角旮旯一片漆黑，说明这些地点的公共精神缺乏，
未能足额缴纳电费。电灯很少会出意外状况，它们是如此可靠，我们应
该感谢许经理（Mr. Hsu），[②] 同时我们还发现使用电灯比旧煤油灯便宜
多了。

轮船服务的改进

　　在美好的旧时光里，"普济号"（Poochi）是温州唯一的定期客轮，每
十天有一次航班，现在则又新增了"广济号"（Kwangchi），这两艘船都属
于轮船招商总局（C. M. Co.），此外还有两艘属于其他公司的轮船也开通了
航班。航班的增加看起来将会刺激贸易，目前客运量与货运量都在增长。

　　瑞安县（Juean）是这个区域的第二大城市，大概有 3 万人口，有运
河相连，每天有两班轮船，开销之外仅能略有盈余。目前美孚石油公司
（Standard Oil Co.）和亚细亚石油公司（Asiatic Oil Co.）都进驻该地，美
孚石油公司有 2 名美国代理商。英美烟草公司（Anglo – American Tobacco

---

① 　这里可能是把整个温州府的人口都囊括进来了。

② 　此处指许仲贤，但许担任的是工程师职务，并不是经理职务。

Co.）在温州也有 1 名代理商。胜家缝纫机公司（Singer's Sewing Machine Co.）在温州主路上建立了商店，这家公司看起来真的就好像家一样。①

新产业

温州最近引进了制袜机器，从事此业者日渐增多。

上海一家著名公司，也将织窗帘花边机器运到温州，招人工作，计件付酬。这是一项新兴产业，可以雇佣很多工人。

一家小型玻璃吹制厂最近开业了。有一天我们去参观，看到他们在制作灯罩。价格比进口的便宜很多，因此这个行业很有发展前途。

不久前还新开了一家蒸汽锯木厂，可惜最后没有成功。这可能是由于购买设备的经验不足，也可能是由于管理不善。无论如何，温州有大量木材运往上海，于适当监管下在温州建立一个这样的锯木厂，极有可能获取巨大成功。

今年温州甲种商业学校（Commercial School）② 即将开学，这无疑将帮助这座城市的年轻人找到更好的职位。

---

① 可以清楚地看到，这一时期外国资本在温州份额的变化，在一战期间，美国工业产品迅速取代英国占领了温州市场。

② 温州甲种商业学校由余朝绅建立，年预算6000元，有学生80人，教师12人，但其建立的年份存在争议，大概有三种说法。第一种说法，按照1917年《字林西报》与《海关贸易报告》的记录，该校建于1917年；第二种说法，1940年《温中校刊》只是模糊提到该校是在民国初年建立，这种说法后来被1990年出版的《温州城区近百年记事》所继承；第三种说法则来自冯坚在1989年撰写的文章《温州府学堂首任总理余朝绅》，这篇文章认为该校建立于1914年，这种说法目前流传最广，后续持此说文献皆本于此。但综合来看，第一种说法是当年记载，后两种说法皆为后出，因此在进一步发现更多关键史料之前，笔者认为温州甲种商业学校最有可能建立的年份应该是在1917年。参见中华人民共和国杭州海关译编《近代浙江通商口岸经济社会概况：浙海关、瓯海关、杭州关贸易报告集成》，浙江人民出版社，2002，第447页。朴垞《第一任校长：余筱泉先生》，《温中校刊》1940年第7期，第2页；浙江省温州鹿城区委员会文史资料工作委员会编《鹿城文史资料·第五辑·温州城区近百年记事（1840—1949）》，1990，第64～65页；冯坚《温州府学堂首任总理余朝绅》，《温州文史资料·第四辑》，浙江人民出版社，1988，第40～43页。

　　城市中所有现代与进步的新造建筑物，可以视为一个额外的证据，证明这里的人们日益富足。温州最奢华的建筑是最近新建的绸布公会（Clothiers' Guild），其附近几乎所有店铺都是洋楼样式，有些高达三层。①

当地艺术品

　　温州人有两个产业可以大力发展，一个是青田石（soap stone）② 雕刻，另一个是竹嵌木雕。

　　青田石需要从 50 英里外的山上采得。一些温州人去欧洲时会随身带一块青田石，我们在青田山村碰到一个村民甚至曾去过遥远的巴黎。如果上海的一些公司有办法在温州采购青田石的话，一定能够获取厚利。

　　温州的竹丝镶嵌产业同样大有可为。我们已经将一些样品送往英格兰，在那里这些物件珍贵异常。温州人制造了诸如可拆散出口的小桌子、相框、托盘、裁纸刀等物品，其中许多会有很高利润，而且肯定会卖得很快。我们听说上海有个人最近从温州最好的雕刻师那里订购了价值 400 银圆的木雕。

　　温州正在觉醒，虽然它的贸易潜能还没有完全被激发出来。但对于那些把握时势的人，无论是外国商人还是中国商人，都有许多途径来促使中国进步，从而使资本和劳工共同受益。（温州，9 月 23 日）

----

① 温州"许云章"的老板许玉漱将店面从曹仙巷迁往五马街，购地新建三层大洋楼，其规模之大、花色之多、装饰之摩登，独步浙江各县。参见计和立、邱百川《温州绸布店盛衰及其公会组织经过概况》，《温州文史资料·第二十三辑》，浙江南方印业，2008，第 85~86 页。

② 本义为皂石，依据石头形态以及后文文意判断，此处应指青田石。

《温州独立三日》，《北华捷报及最高法庭与领事馆杂志》，1917 年
12 月 15 日

温州独立三日
（本报记者报道）

前几日，南方革命党从宁波派来小群党人①劝说温州加入独立阵营。②
这些党人首先找到负责军队的营长（Yingchang）③，让他们加入，然后又
接近统领（Tungling）④，统领随后与其他官员协商后同意加入自主运动。
据说戴统领反对加入，但是从宁波来的党人威胁，如果没有得到满意答
复，将会视其为北方敌人，以炸弹来解决问题。

因此，11 月 30 日，温州加入了南方，并且宣布从北方阵营中独立出
来。然而在 12 月 2 日，温州人听说南方党人在宁波战败了，于是便立刻撤
销了独立的决定，一切又恢复原样。据说一名劝说温州独立的南方党人已
经被逮捕。⑤

现在城市已经完全恢复安宁。（温州，12 月 5 日）

---

① 据《张棡日记》记载，是夏观天游说戴任独立。夏观天，青田人，革命党人，1912
年曾加入黄兴发起的陆军将校联合会。参见温州市图书馆编《张棡日记·第四
册》，张钧孙点校，中华书局，2019，第 2001 页。

② 浙江"丁巳自立"运动，除了有南方护法运动反对北方的大背景外，更有深厚浙人
治浙的地方背景，从这篇报道来看，显然外人对于中国政治时局的认识还仅停留在
南北之争的层面，故评论多为皮相。参见傅璇琮主编《宁波通史·民国卷》，宁波
出版社，2009，第 46 ~ 50 页。

③ 即浙江第一师营长杨三，温州参与自主运动时任第一梯团长。

④ 即戴统领，戴任。戴任主导了这一次的温州自主运动。

⑤ 据《张棡日记》，被捕的共有两人，分别是瑞安士绅子弟伍井和乐清人李成民。因
此可以知晓，这篇报道里提到的南方从宁波派来的党人，起码有夏观天、伍井和李
成民三人。参见温州市图书馆编《张棡日记·第四册》，张钧孙点校，中华书局，
2019，第 2001、2003 页。

《"普济号"失事：温州一片悲痛》，《北华捷报及最高法庭与领事馆杂志》，1918 年 1 月 19 日

"普济号"失事：温州一片悲痛

（本报记者报道）

"同华号"（Tungwah）昨天已抵达温州，据说船上运回了最近海难当中遇难的十余名死者的棺木。之前已经报道过，徐定超（Hsu Ting-chao）① 先生也是这次船难的受害者。他是一名温州人，是当地最有名望的人，曾考取过进士。徐先生原本登上了救生艇，但因为其他人抢着往艇上冲，最后小艇倾覆致其丧命。今天早上我在港口看到了其家人为徐氏夫妇准备的巨大棺木，徐先生的家属会将棺木运到上海并希望能打捞起遗体。如果不能发现遗体的话，他们将会依照中国习俗，在空棺材里放上木雕假人和丧服，然后带回家乡的祖坟安葬。

新任的警局长官也在船难中丧生。

有 4 人在船难中爬上桅杆，后被招商局船只"新丰号"（Hsinfung）所救。有一名招商局职员的儿子也在海难中丧生，他原本是为了回家给父亲庆祝 50 岁生日。

据说有一家当地公司原本在船上委托托运了一批价值很高的布料。毫无疑问，许多店主将在这场船难中损失惨重。

"普济号"的沉没如同一个老朋友的逝去，这艘可人的小船，对于我们的意义正如"江天号"（Kiangteen）对于宁波的意义一样。在许多年里，

---

① 徐定超，字班侯，温州名宿，戊戌变法失败后在政治上失势，辛亥革命成功后再次活跃于浙江政治舞台，1915 年任浙江通志局提调，参与了 1917 年的浙江自主运动以及宁波被攻占后的劝和运动。参见徐逸龙《浅议徐定超对民国浙江的贡献》，《浙江方志研究论坛第二届学术研究会论文集》，浙江人民出版社，2008，第 259~269 页。

它几乎是我们与外部世界的唯一联系，因为那时我们还没有电报。每隔十天，我们在温州听到最甜美的音乐就是"普济号"的汽笛声，它意味着英国本土（Home）① 的邮件已经送达。

船长弗洛伯格（Froberg）可能是与"普济号"联系最紧密的人，他驾驶这艘船的时间是如此之久。在完成了 300 次航行之后，这位船长曾获得招商总局颁发的锦旗。

1900 年 7 月 8 日，在温州发生义和团运动时，所有外国社区人员，包括领事和海关税务司都是乘坐"普济号"避难的。当时我们在头一天晚上匆忙上船，离开码头后在江中抛锚，在甲板上放了一长排来复枪，以备不时之需。第二天早上我们决定乘"普济号"离开温州，并在江口位置碰到一艘援助我们的英国炮艇，但我们仍决定前往宁波。

很难想象这是"普济号"最后一次旅程，像她的许多勇敢船员一样，这也是她最后一次"越过沙洲".② 外国社区因为失去很多成员而感到悲伤，死亡的外国人当中，船长马基（Mackie）最为知名，他的离世使我们都陷入巨大悲痛之中。

航班时刻调整

在这场灾难发生后，有人建议应该调整上海与温州之间航班的时刻表，航班离开上海时应该尽量选在白天。我不知道其他港口的情况是什么样的，但作为一名温州的老居民，我知道上海到温州的航班总是在半夜出发。考虑到诸多因素，航班不妨改到第二天清晨出发，同样可以在抵达温州时赶上涨潮。

昨天驾驶"同华号"抵温的罗斯（Ross）船长，选择的就是完美的时间表。他在星期三的白天离开上海，然后在星期四早上抵达宁波；同日白天又离开宁波，随后在昨天上午跟着潮汐进入瓯江，这与他提早 7 个小时半夜从上海出发效果相同。更改时刻表的好处是，能够尽量在

---

① 那时，身处海外的英国人常用大写的 Home 指代英国本土，香港人在 1997 年之前常将其翻译为"祖家"。通过这则新闻，可以判断出记者的国籍身份是英国。

② 这里是借用英国诗人丁尼生（Tennyson）的诗歌，名句是：I hope to see my Pilot face to face, When I have crost the bar，借指平静地接受死亡的来临。

白天驶离危险区域。船员得到应有的充分休息，同时也不会耽误潮汐。因此，我们诚恳地建议温州船只在非绝对必要时不宜在夜间出发，而应等到白天，这样可以降低事故发生的可能性。（温州，1月12日）

《温州地震》，《北华捷报及最高法庭与领事馆杂志》，1918 年 3 月 2 日

温州地震

（本报记者报道）

对于整个县城，乃至于整个温州府来说，2 月 13 日绝对是难忘的一日；[①] 这一天发生的地震同样也让我们印象深刻。我看到电线猛烈晃动，水渠里的水以怪异的方式前后波动，整个大地如海上之船一样颠簸。一名外侨看到教堂的一块岩石竟然在令人震惊地从东至西移动。另一名外侨则听到巨墙倒塌的轰鸣声，并亲眼看到一棵大树被震得乱晃，但他说在大街上走倒也不觉得有大碍。在这场地震中，温州的许多旧墙坍塌了。

在第一波地震过后，平阳县（Pingyang）在下午 4 点也发生了轻微地震。当地人说 8 年前曾发生过一次小规模地震，50 年前曾发生过一次大规模地震，规模都比这一次要大。

南下的军队

在经历地震之前，温州人还经历过一次较轻微的震动，一艘搭载 500 名士兵的军舰抵达温州，随后有一艘同样搭载 500 名士兵的军舰抵达温州。他们的目的地相当模糊，只说是"温州南方的某座城市"，其战略目标是在抵达后防御南方可能的朝温州方向的进攻。[②]

如果南方军队真的要取道温州进攻，那么无疑将是对这座城市的忠诚

---

① 这次地震范围遍及东南沿海各省，震中在广东汕头，据闻沸水热气自地喷发，华界房屋全毁，死者千余人。参见《香港电》，《申报》1918 年 2 月 17 日，第 3 版。

② 同为皖系的浙江督军杨善德派遣童保暄军取道温州援助福建李厚基，主要是为防备驻扎在潮汕准备征闽的陈炯明护法军。参见段云章、沈晓敏编《孙文与陈炯明史事编年》，广东人民出版社，2012，第 201 页；《中国大事记》，《东方杂志》1918 年第 5 期，第 215～216 页。

的再一次考验，但所幸我们已经学到了许多在南北之间见风使舵的本事，我们有理由相信即便身处尴尬境地，我们轮船招商总局"广济号"的安全也可以得到保障。

轮船招商总局"广济号"

昨天我又得到一个令人震惊的消息，邮政通知说"广济号"原本应返回上海，现在被改派到了福州。至于原因，我找到两个：首先，温州本地商人认为"广济号"太小，他们想要一艘大船；其次，当地人恼怒于"广济号"没有打捞穷人遗体。但是"广济号"前往打捞遗体时，海上波涛汹涌，船长已经做了最好的选择，如若不然，我们将会失去更多生命。①

虽然当地有这样的需求，但是招商总局很难派一艘更大的船来温州，因为大船在其他航线可以赚到更多钱。（温州，2月22日）

---

① 船难发生后，徐定超遗族认为船难是船只老化所致，招商总局又派旧船"广济号"接替瓯沪线，徐定超遗族不服，与招商总局发生冲突，徐定超子徐翰清身死，招商总局只能改派"同华号"来代替。参见张恩骏《本局编年纪事》，《国营招商局七十五周年纪念》，美灵登有限公司，1947，第67~68页。

《温州大冰雹》，《北华捷报及最高法庭与领事馆杂志》，1918 年 5 月 4 日

温州大冰雹

（本报记者报道）

三天前，我前往乡村地区时遇到了相当惊人的暴风雨，我的帽子和斗篷都被吹走了，唯有雨伞苦苦支撑，最后也完全被毁——就好像兰斯大教堂（Reims Cathedral）① 一样，伞面已经没了，只有伞架还立着。但与温州城里人所遭的罪相比，我的烦恼也就算不得什么。这场暴风雨抵达温州的时间，大约是黄昏时分，它已演变成一场猛烈的冰雹。这场风暴自西北方向而来，因此城市西北损失最大。

很难确定冰雹的确切大小，因为冰雹看起来大小各异，后来我在询问时各人说法不尽相同，但在冰雹下了 12 小时后，我在大街上看到了约长 1.5 英寸、宽 1 英寸的冰雹。因此我相信某人对我所讲的话，他说冰雹如鸡蛋般大小。这场冰雹，就如同一个飞行中队对一座城市发起的低空轰炸。

至于这场天灾所造成的破坏，虽然没有房屋被完全摧毁，但许多房屋的墙壁和屋顶遭到损毁；碎裂的房瓦和窗格玻璃不计其数。

圣道公会医院有大约 300 块窗格玻璃被砸毁，学校遭到损毁的数量更多，教堂约有 200 块，加上其他房屋，圣道公会总计有超过 1000 块窗格玻璃被砸坏。如前文所述，城西是受灾最严重的地区，位于城西的内地会教堂已经完全倒下。

目前城内对玻璃和房瓦的需求量很大，尤其是后者。其价格已显著上涨，且很难降下来。商贩甚至会在收取定金后，再把房瓦转卖他人。即便是工人现在也要收取双倍工资。昨日下了一天雨，雨水落在没有房顶遮盖

---

① 兰斯大教堂位于法国香槟区巴黎北部，与巴黎圣母院一样古老，建筑采用哥特立式结构，这里大概是指雨伞被吹得如教堂般立起来。

的床上，或流进厨房，人们忍受的痛苦远超我们的想象。最糟糕的是，在这场天灾里有人丧命，风暴来时一名船老大正在岸边吃晚饭，他的船正停在温州码头附近，结果船遭倾覆，十多人因此丧命。

目前正在调查城市在这场冰雹中所遭受的损失程度，据估计在 10 万银圆左右。（温州，4 月 25 日）

《温州来信：美孚石油公司的新产业》，《北华捷报及最高法庭与领事馆杂志》，1918 年 7 月 6 日

温州来信：美孚石油公司的新产业

（本报记者报道）

去年纽约的美孚石油公司在离温州 4 英里的地方买了一大块土地，位于河的下游北岸。这是因为官员不允许在太过靠近城市的地方建立油栈（Oil Tank）①，以免引发火灾。所购土地约 20 亩，也有可能更多，前有河流经过，一座优良码头现已拔地而起，并配有两个泊位。

目前已经建起一座大油栈，还准备建一座小油栈，并配建一座仓库以及其他附属建筑，此外还准备建一座洋房给美国代理商居住。油轮能够开到码头，这样火油就能直接注入大油栈，然后再转注入供油漕。工程已经进行了好几个月，但还需要更多时间才能彻底完工。整个工程将花费一大笔钱，但公司自然希望最终能收回这笔钱。这些新式改良设施，无疑将会促进该地区贸易的增长。

我还不敢肯定大油栈的建成是否会导致火油价格的下降，目前火油价格是过去的 2 倍，而空油罐的价格是过去的 4 倍。一个空油罐的价格已经达到 35 分，这是由于大量猪油被制成罐头运往上海，有人告诉我共有 2000 罐之多。

上海，我们这里说的可是上海，它不仅进口温州的猪油，还进口大量薪柴和不计其数的鸡蛋，这自然导致了温州当地消费品价格的上升。如果不是严格禁止，大米价格也会上涨，而鱼和鸡，甚至是本地土豆价格都已

---

① 也被翻译为"火油池"或"火油池栈"，1917 年所建油栈在今永嘉县梅园，二战时被日军炸毁。参见温州市土地管理局编《温州市土地志》，中华书局，2001，第 191~192 页。

经大幅上涨，工资增长速度很难跟上生活费用增长的速度，人们发现越来越难以维持收支平衡。

水文变化

最近瓯江里的沙洲发生了很大变化，使得轮船更加难以驶入。出现了一个长条状的沙洲，甚至在低潮之前，有些沙洲的高地也可以用作耕地。

有时沙洲会突然出现，温州共有三家小轮船公司，其中一家建起了一座码头，并配有浮桥。可浮桥还没有建成，在附近就突然形成了一个沙洲；浮桥也被从码头上冲走。现在沙洲已经消失，我们希望浮桥能够重建，但未来何时重建尚不确定。属于上游另一家公司的浮桥也被冲走，现在正在维修中，这条河的水文状况实在令人难以捉摸。

每周4艘轮船往来

除了多年来没有竞争对手的招商总局外，温州还有另外三家小轮船公司，这三家公司每周都有一次航班。我不想在这里点名，但有一艘船存在倾斜，且倾斜程度很不寻常。我并不是一名职业水手，但我见过无数船只的两舷，我从没见过如此倾斜的船，我只希望在未来不会出现厄运。有一名外籍职员告诉我，这艘船头重脚轻，迟早会倾覆。我认为应该保证每艘客轮在获准进入商埠之前，都接受检查并获得证明。

但让我感到高兴的是，有关当局已经对这艘特别船只进行了检查，并且感到满意，认为它是一艘安全的、适于航海的船。（温州，6月25日）

《瓯海道尹》，《北华捷报及最高法庭与领事馆杂志》，1918年8月3日

瓯海道尹
（本报记者报道）

　　人们阅读报纸时总能频繁看到针对中国官员的负面批评，我不能说他们不应受到如此批评，但我们应该公平地记住，有一些人，我们希望更多的人，正在真诚地为他们所关心的人民的最大利益而献身。我们很高兴地说，现在就有一位这样的好官员，他就是瓯海道尹黄先生。①

　　他的父亲是50年前上海教会医院里的第一位华人医务助理，即便不是第一，也是最早的那批之一。

　　毫无疑问，早期家庭生活的启蒙影响，帮助他建立起更加清晰的自觉意识，并促使他忠诚地履行高官的职责。

　　他发布了一份公告，指出早婚的不可取和杀婴的害处。他赞成妇女放足，并希望阻止这一地区一项令人反感的社会习俗，即温州流行的临时借贷，它指的是把一个人的私人财产在一定期限内以约定的数额暂时借给另一个人。②

　　黄先生正在着手对城内的育婴堂进行改革，这是一个纯粹的中国机构。许多弃婴被交给住在育婴堂外的养母抚养，养母每收养一个小孩，每月可收到1200文的津贴，对于幼儿来讲这笔钱可能尚且宽裕，但对于年长

---

① 即黄庆澜，字涵先，上海人，在任仅一年，在任期间在温州发起了广泛的改良运动，时人记载“一人提契于上，各属风从于下，一时吏治几有蒸蒸日上之势”，胡珠生在《温州近代史》中对其评价极高。胡珠生：《温州近代史》，辽宁人民出版社，2009，第270~275页。

② 指的是温州民间借贷方式“同人集”，清末已开始流行于瑞安地区。大概的运作方式为同人每年各出5银圆，分为10分，定期抓阄轮收，具体办法详见温州市委员会文史资料委员会编《记同人集事》，《温州文史资料·第八辑·陈虬集》，浙江人民出版社，1992，第200~201页。

的孩子来讲可能略有不足。

但这种外包制度很容易被滥用，因为很难找到合适的督察员，婴幼儿的死亡率异常高，所以黄先生希望能建造更多适合孩子居住的育婴堂房屋，以方便院内抚养，也有助于更有效地监督。

最近瓯海道尹的母亲68岁生日，他采取了一种有益社会的方式为母亲庆生。他准备了大量用于治疗痢疾、夏季热病和其他疾病的药包，这些药材被分发给城里的穷人；据说这份礼物的总费用相当可观。这种医疗救助并非偶一为之，事实上他在衙门里专门开设了一个诊所，他的儿子是诊所的负责人，他的妻子在这项事业上也耗费了许多心力。

黄先生请了两到三名中医医生，他们每天轮流来到诊室为病人看病。诊所并不负责当场赠药，医生会为每位病人写出药方，然后由病人拿着药方前往城内指定的两到三家药房抓药，这些药房会免费将药物送给病人，账单则寄给黄先生。

据说，到他衙门看病的人，平均每天在200人左右，药费和医生的工资每个月在1000银圆左右。

据了解，他在上海有私产，使他有能力将钱花在温州穷人身上。但如果他不慷慨地使用这些财富，这笔财富也无法发挥其造福群众的作用，因此人们很高兴有机会赞美这位中国官员。他在行政上的智慧，以及他对人民的关心和慷慨，都使他有资格得到这一赞扬，也展现出他是一名开明、仁慈的官员，他是其人民真正的"父母官"（Father）。（温州，7月27日）

《温州邮局盗案》，《北华捷报及最高法庭与领事馆杂志》，1918 年
10 月 26 日

温州邮局盗案
（本报记者报道）

前几日，"广济号"从上海驶来，准备停靠，船上有一人已准备好登岸，但他不知道的是一群警察已在岸上埋伏好，只等他自投罗网。这名罪犯刚完成了一次短暂但无疑成功的上海之旅，在上海他试图将价值 1700 银圆的邮票兑现。这些邮票是他和其他 3 名同伙从邮局里偷出来的，一同失窃的还有大约 100 银圆。这 4 人当中，有 3 人都是邮局现雇员，另一个是前雇员。尽管邮票还没有追回，但 4 个劫匪已经全部归案，说明这个城市的侦破力量非常出色。而邮票的追回无疑还需要很长时间，这需要带着邮票窃贼再次前往上海追赃。

第一艘油船

美孚石油公司的"美南号"（str. Meinan）已经行驶在瓯江上，它是在这条江上航行的第一艘油船。既然这家公司在温州有了新财产，我希望我们能经常看到这艘整洁的小船，一艘油船的到来标志着这个城市的发展又向前迈进了一步。（温州，10 月 14 日）

……

《浙江学生风潮：全校学生被开除》，《北华捷报及最高法庭与领事馆杂志》，1918 年 11 月 16 日

浙江学生风潮：全校学生被开除[*]
（本报记者报道）

温州这片区域有很多疾病，不幸的是一名男孩患病了，疾病蔓延到了温州市的中学，这所学校大概有 400 名学生。这些年轻人当中有一人患病，据说他向监学寻求帮助，监学带他去看校医，但校医当时不在学校，据说校工也忽视了他。

当这名学生病情恶化时，他被转移到另一栋楼居住，其他学生认为该地不适合让一名年轻的病人居住，结果小伙子病死在了这栋楼里。

据报道，他在临死前告诉了至少一名同伴，希望其他学生为其报仇，由此其他学生的怒火被彻底点燃。

依照中国风俗，对于没有好好对待他们同伴的学监，这些学生开始回忆，或者说是开始"创造"这名学监平时的黑材料。根据报道，这些学生指责学监盗卖校产以自肥，不仅偷运学校粮食，还侵占学生伙食费。

学生们还向另一名学监表达了不满，他们甚至注意到这两名学监与校长是同乡。有人认为这绝对不是巧合。

最终，道尹和县长来到学校。两名官员在接受少年中国学会（Young

---

* 据温州中学（也被称为"省立十中"或"温州十中"）校长刘绍宽日记所述，整个风潮皆因校中教员崔陈鸿（字涤泉）与郑济（字式钦）不和所致。由于校内吴姓学生病故，而校长刘绍宽正好不在校内，崔陈鸿乘机发难，鼓动学生闹事。最后风潮以革去教员 3 人、处理学生 80 名、刘绍宽自请辞职收场。参见温州市图书馆编《刘绍宽日记·第二册》，方浦仁、陈盛奖整理，中华书局，2018，第 659 页。

China)① 采访时讲，他们的责任是管理城市而不是处理学校事务，但他们会很乐于看到记者的调查结果。学生们随后在大门口设立纠察队，以阻止老师的朋友进入学校，同时还对老师信件实施审查。

最后意想不到的事情发生了：几天前杭州来了一封电报，说所有的学生将被赶出学校。为了公义，这群年轻人自己把电报译出，学生们不想继续在这样的机构学习，所以他们将返回家，但事实是大约 360 名学生已离开，学校关闭了。如此退出，相比原计划和安排来说，听起来比被迫离开要体面。他们中的许多人一直待在城内的餐馆，玩得很开心，但当他们的钱花光时，他们最终还得回家面对父亲的裁决，他们的父亲也曾叛逆，但他们可能已淡忘了。

学校共有 4 名学监，情况更加困难，因为 2 名与此前 2 名不同乡的学监据说对学生表示同情。然而这 4 人的职务都已经被终止，校长也将被替换，其他教师也将停课一年，这些教师在风潮过后将会被重新聘任。

当学生们听到必须离校的消息后，都想从母校带走一些纪念品，为了不与其他人重样，一双双强壮的小手几乎拿走了所有能拿走的东西，甚至电灯、地球仪、书籍、家具都被搬走或破坏。

我被告知大约 40 名男孩将受到惩罚，不准他们回来，但如果其他人愿意的话，他们将被允许返校。

但在 40 名学生当中，据说有些可能是无辜的，而真正犯错的学生可能并不在惩罚名单之列。可以肯定的是，那些被认为是无辜的学生的家长一定会有话要说，而有人声称，一些被开除的学生会尽其所能劝说大多数男孩不要回来，从而试图让当局让步。

美妙得难以置信

几天前，一位在中国待了 30 多年的外国人告诉我，大约两周前，从杭

---

① 英文名称与"少年中国学会"英文名相同，该学会于 1918 年 6 月开始筹备，1919 年 7 月 1 日正式成立，是新文化运动时期的重要组织，出版专刊《少年中国》。至于少年中国学会在温州的联络人与记者到底是谁，待考，推测可能与温州新学会有关。参见《少年中国同学会消息：会务消息》，《少年中国》1919 年第 1 期，第 34 页；《本会通告》，《少年中国》1919 年第 1 期，第 43~44 页。

州到温州的铁路扩建合同已经签订了。它将由一家美国公司承造，铁路线不是沿海岸而是沿内陆建造，我想这是一条支线，以连接温州和南行的铁路干线。①（温州，11 月 6 日）

①　1916 年中美签订条约，允许美国裕中公司出资 1 亿美元铺设杭州至温州铁路，此后美国将上述权利转让给国际新银团。参见《美银借款内容益形复杂》，《申报》1931 年 2 月 19 日，第 4 版。

《置身温州》，《北华捷报及最高法庭与领事馆杂志》，1918 年 11 月 30 日

置身温州

（本报记者报道）

　　11 月 16 日，道尹与交涉员（Official for Foreign Affairs）① 邀请了外国社区成员以及大约 70 名中国官绅来参加庆祝停战茶会，其间人们致了贺词。11 月 21 日，外国社区又为温州官员和部分士绅举办午宴。这次午宴由瓯海关税务司谭安（M. Tanant）在圣道公会艺文学堂的大厅举办，大厅装饰得很雅致。宴会主人首先向中国客人宣读了欢迎词，感谢中国在战争中提供的帮助，并阐明了对德立场，击败德国的意义是明确的。宴会结尾主人再次致辞，表达了同盟国对于中国走向繁荣的美好祝愿。（温州，11 月 21 日）

---

① 这里指的应是瓯海关监督兼交涉员冒广生，因为海关监督在名义上仍是海关税务司的直属上级，所以民国时期一般都由海关监督兼任交涉员，专门处理地方对外交涉事务。

《温州记事》，《北华捷报及最高法庭与领事馆杂志》，1919 年 2 月 22 日

温州记事

（本报记者报道）

　　春节期间，温州及该地区遭遇了异常寒冷的冬天。

　　新年的曙光降临在这座白茫茫的城市，雪有 4 英寸深；白天，雪继续下个不停。28 年来，这座亚热带港口第一次碰到如此严寒的天气。民国八年的第一天，温州犹如死城，居民那么安静，街上行人也那么少。直到第三天，这座城市才开始被唤醒，鞭炮声、锣鼓声努力补偿着大雪和严寒造成的压抑。温州人热爱旧俗，人们用无数的鞭炮辞别旧岁，并在主要街道的中央点燃数百堆松木篝火。（温州，2 月 10 日）

　　……

《温州与世界和平》，《北华捷报及最高法庭与领事馆杂志》，1919
年3月15日

温州与世界和平

（本报记者报道）

星期天晚上，在圣道公会艺文学堂校长理学硕士蔡博敏先生的家里举行了一次特别重要的会议。这是最近成立的组织"中外英语会话交流协会"（The Society of English Speaking Chinese and Foreigners）举办的第一次会议，该协会旨在增进会员彼此间的了解，并就工业、社会、文学和科学问题，以及所有大家共同关心的问题进行坦率的交流。该协会计划每两周宣读一次论文，并不时就大家关心的世界问题安排辩论。

周三晚上演讲的主题是"永久实现世界和平的方法"，温州盐税总局局长李文彬（Li Ung－bing）[1] 和传教士谢道培（W. R. Stobie）[2] 分别作了演说。出席会议的有中国人、日本人、英国人和法国人。这两个演说都引起了人们极大的兴趣，接着又进行了一场同样有趣的讨论。

李先生针对当今的远东问题发表了看法。李先生是商务印书馆的前董事，同时他还是英文《中国历史大纲》以及其他著作的作者，这些著述代表了中国对上述问题的看法，值得详细介绍。

以下节选自李先生的话：

> 世世代代都没有战争肯定是一个美好的梦想。但这真的有可能实现吗？答案应该是肯定的。人们普遍认为，这场即将结束的战争是由一个人的意志——前德国皇帝的意志——带来的，如果一个人的意志

---

[1] 李文彬在1914年出版了英文专著《中国历史大纲》，根据这篇新闻所记载的李文彬讲稿看，李氏应受过良好的精英教育。其更多行迹，待考。

[2] 在晚清即来到温州传教的偕我公会传教士。

足以使世界陷入战争，所有文明国家的意志加在一起，就足以给世界带来和平，只要世界存在，和平就会持续下去。我们这样说并不是说这是一项容易的任务。相反，它是非常困难的，而且可能是人类迄今为止所面临的最大困难。

我们不应让我们久经考验的外交官和国际专家继续单独从事这项工作，因为如果他们的工作没有得到他们所代表的不同人民的帮助，就达不到我们所设想的目的。我们面前的问题是一个全世界都关心的问题，每个个体都应发挥自己的作用。因此，现在让我们看看，我们在温州能做些什么，来帮助实现一个甜美而富有成果的理念——世界的永久和平。

我认为，和平的基础是国家之间的良好感情。没有什么比这更重要的了，没有这一点，巴黎和会的工作以及按照威尔逊总统建议的方针建立的国际联盟都将是徒劳。我认为，本协会的推动者说他们希望通过英语这一媒介，促成中国和外国人之间有更好了解时，他们所谈到的实际上是实现普遍持久和平的基本原则。巴尔干半岛将不再扮演它们在第一次世界大战前在世界政治中扮演的角色，它们的位置很快将被中国和远东所取代。在中国说英语的中国人和说英语的外国人几乎是一体的。让我们永远为人类事业大声疾呼，让我们永远携手努力，消除对国家间成功与和平交往如此有害的各种误解。国家可能继续是竞争对手，一切问题、争端和争议可能像过去那样继续出现；但请允许我说，这些问题应以和平方式解决，通过谈判、仲裁，通过任何可能的方式解决，战争手段除外。如果远东没有巴尔干半岛，战争就不可能发生。在这方面，我们能做的不多，但是，我们所取得的每一点成功，都使我们更接近实现我们的伟大目标，即实现永久和平。

因此，在场所有人都应该支持我们的社会。我们支持它，不是在促进我们自己的利益，而是在促进人类和文明的利益。

（温州，2月27日）

《温州邮局：令人满意的进步纪实》，《北华捷报及最高法庭与领事馆杂志》，1919年5月3日

温州邮局：令人满意的进步纪实

（本报记者报道）

在过去的15个月里，这个城市和这个地区的中国邮政服务有了很大改善，办公效率和公共便利性预计还会进一步提高。

温州邮局总局①一直位于朔门外的瓯海关内。就邮局本身而言，它的位置非常方便收发邮件，但对一般公众来说并不算方便。在城市商业中心设立的邮政分局在满足公众需求方面起了很大作用，特别是在戒严期间，城门很早就会关闭。

新邮政局屋计划②

目前当局正计划在城市中心位置创建一个新的总部，它将设有最新的职位，以处理不断增长的中国邮政业务。建筑工程将耗资约1万银圆，预计将在今年年底前完工。

前段时间，为了满足东门外每周有三艘轮船航班的邮政需求，特地开办了一个新的邮政支局。我们的现任邮政局局长邓永愚（Deng Yong–yu）先生有远见卓识，该支局的设立相当合理。邓先生以其一贯的礼貌和对追求公众最大利益的热情，为推广中国邮政服务已经做了很多，现在正在做更多。

---

① 1919年正式名称为"永嘉一等邮局"。参见吴炎主编《温州市交通志》，海洋出版社，1994，第284页。

② 1918年9月30日，邮局方面在温州城内北大街招贤巷口（今温州墨池荣庭酒店）购得临街土地1213平方米，拟自建邮政局屋，但因故一直拖到新中国成立后仍未建造。参见温州市邮电局编《温州市邮电志》，人民邮电出版社，1996，第70页。

大约 20 个月前，当邓先生初来温州市时，这个城市的邮箱每天只收取 2 次邮件。现在他们已经宣布每天收取 5 次邮件。同时，每天递送邮件的次数也增加到 4 至 6 次。今年年初，邮局开通了乡村邮递服务（周日除外），并将其扩展到温州附近 40 里的范围，使许多乡民了解到这种廉价、高效的服务。像邓先生这种类型的人，与旧的保守政权没有任何关系，是少年中国最好的代表。

胆大包天的盗窃

去年秋天，在邮政总局发生了一件令人不快的事情。当时总局正在进行修缮工程，匪徒在一个风雨交加的夜晚胆大包天地实施了盗窃，盗案金额高达 1877 银圆。

邮局局长迅速采取行动，逮捕了 4 个人，其中一个是邮递员。然而，这次盗案的策划者是一个名叫程罗尚（Dzang Lo-shang）的本地人，他在几年内从一个苦力迅速暴富。今天，人们都知道他的大部分钱是通过非法的鸦片走私得来的。他为什么要冒着失去地位的风险洗劫邮局，这个问题目前仍悬而未解。当地法官认定这 4 个人都有罪，判处程某 18 个月监禁，并退还 1877 银圆。该邮递员也被判 18 个月监禁，第三个人被判 14 个月监禁，第四个人被判 1 年监禁。另外，这 4 人都被剥夺了选举权。

富有的罪犯随即提出上诉，但省法院认定地方法院判决有效。他又上诉到北京最高法院，最终判决在最近刚刚公布，最高法院已确定下级法院判决有效。（温州，4 月 21 日）

《温州局势》，《北华捷报及最高法庭与领事馆杂志》，1919 年 6 月 14 日

温州局势

（本报记者报道）

温州人正在认真推行抵制日本的运动，通过积极宣传，抵制日本的口号已经遍及老城，并且每天都有人到附近村、镇和市集进行宣传。

这场运动非常严肃且持久，这对中国人来讲是一次全新的经验。与过去历次运动的喧嚣相比，到目前为止，此次运动组织性更强，更具有自制力。用一句"哦！这只是一个学生的事情"，无疑将错误理解许多显而易见的事实的意义。我们研究这里的人民和他们的语言已有多年，发现很难嘲笑"学生罢课"，与大多数城市一样，温州也发生了罢课行动。这场运动除了抵制日货之外，所有措施都尽量避免冲突。温州官员证明自己是明智且冷静的，他们不认同这场运动，并采取一切措施防止和平遭到破坏。

虽然目前的抵制运动很可能会像以往那样结束，但它将成为中国历史和演进的一个"里程碑"。（温州，6 月 7 日）

《祈禳霍乱鬼：温州大办神会》，《北华捷报及最高法庭与领事馆杂志》，1919 年 11 月 1 日

祈禳霍乱鬼：温州大办神会
（本报记者报道）

昨晚温州举办了多年以来最大规模的迎神赛会。即便对于一个长期居住在这片既充满变数又一成不变的土地上的人来讲，这也是一种奇异而美妙的景象。

和中国其他地方一样，霍乱在去年夏天也曾在温州流行。此外，最近城市里出现莫名的火灾，各种关于怨灵攻击城市的神秘故事甚嚣尘上。

为了安抚导致火灾与疾病的"鬼怪"，并诱使它们离开城市，人们花了数千银圆购买"鞭炮""蜡烛"等物，1 万多名男子和男孩护送着几个最重要的神像穿过主要街道。人们建造了一艘特殊的竹纸船来抬不受欢迎的访客（恶灵），人们在退潮时将纸船送入江中，纸船会顺流而下。人们兴高采烈地回来了，希望由于他们的热情，他们的命运将得以改善。

抵制、大米和罢工

在温州人看来，这是一个令人兴奋而有趣的夏季。首先是抵制运动，这不仅受到了学生们的热烈欢迎，也受到了普通民众的欢迎。直到今天，人们依旧平静而忠诚地推行这一运动。

随后出现了反对非法出口大米的抗议活动。大量大米被偷运出这个港口和地区是事实。那些被召集起来进行抵制的组织开始关注大米偷运的问题。他们与市当局进行了激烈的斗争，市当局起初拒绝了控制大米出口的要求。

然而城内商户的罢市行动为人民赢得了胜利，人们撑着巨大的灯笼游行以庆祝胜利。在这些运动中没有人受伤，人民似乎已经意识到，只要他

们团结一致，遵纪守法，他们就能掌握权力。

由于人口的增长，对于居住在这座城市的中国人来说，住房日益成为一个非常现实的问题。目前已经很难买到土地，与前几年相比，土地价格已经上涨了100%至200%。

各种繁荣迹象

这座城市呈现出各种贸易繁荣的迹象，在城市的各个角落都可以看到半洋房风格的新屋。

5艘轮船发现定期开往这个港口是有利可图的——其中2艘来自上海，3艘来自宁波和其他中国港口。

今年秋稻收成的前景是多年来最好的，丰收将十拿九稳。

瓯柑的收成不会达到过去两年的水平。然而这并没有对农民造成困扰，他们说三年中有一年歉收是正常现象。（温州，10月22日）

《温州火灾》，《北华捷报及最高法庭与领事馆杂志》，1920 年 1 月 10 日

温州火灾

（本报记者报道）

　　昨天温州发生了多年以来最具破坏性的一次火灾。在大火肆虐的 2 个小时中，100 多家店铺和一些私人房屋被焚毁。

　　至少有 250 个家庭无家可归，损失一定非常惨重。

　　另一场大火于午夜发生在城市的东南部；而在南部郊区，大火又烧毁了 9 座房屋。

　　到目前为止，我们经历了异常干燥的秋冬。城市的运河和水井几乎都干涸了。因此，与火焰搏斗几乎是无望的。火灾能局限在这样小的范围，已经让人惊奇了。（温州，12 月 31 日）

《温州忙碌的劳工：一座港口及其未来》，《北华捷报及最高法庭与
领事馆杂志》，1920 年 8 月 3 日

温州忙碌的劳工：一座港口及其未来

（本报温州记者报道）

温州开埠已有 43 个年头，但很少有人能说清这座港口的主要产业是什么，如果问他这座港口的特产贸易是什么，被问人多半会感到茫然。温州的特产贸易虽然规模很小，但却给这座港口与区域带来鲜明的个性特征。

在开埠初期，温州在商业上似乎有可能取得成功，但到目前为止仍不尽如人意。造成温州商业相对失败的主要原因有许多，其中几个原因包括：（1）航运公司有在温州港口采取垄断保护政策的倾向，缺乏远见、效率和雄心；（2）城中社区所谓的"商人"阶层严重与世界脱节；（3）缺少一些真正大富之人来组织贸易渠道以获取商业成功。

虽然预言未来是一件危险且靠不住的事情，但只要决心去除上述三个缺陷，人们就可以大胆地认为，温州在未来 10 年将取得比过去 40 年更大的进步。

温州的贸易是多元的。在旧温州府时代，你可以找到该地的出口商品有茶叶、丝绸、瓯柑、棉花、小麦、糖、鸡蛋、猪油、樟脑和明矾。现在矿产时代已经来临，无数双眼睛正在这个地区的崇山峻岭中寻找埋藏已久的宝藏，而且已经有证据表明，这种勘探不会白费功夫。

温州还有一些独特的地方行业，这不仅为许多人提供了生计，同时也是这个社会的某些阶层具备进取心与技艺的充分证据。

在此简要介绍几个产业。

青田石刻画

青田石开采和雕刻早已闻名于世，在第一次世界大战之前青田石就已在

许多西方国家热销。在过去的 10 年里，某些特定等级的青田石被用于制作描绘中国历史和民间传说的场景画板。各种颜色的青田石薄片被镶嵌在深红的木材上，这需要非凡的技巧和艺术品位。此外青田石的浮雕效果更佳。

猪皮与皮革

温州的猪皮箱产业已经有了很大发展，客户仍主要局限于中国买家，这些昂贵的旅行箱值得引起外国客户的注意。这些箱子装有篓状的箱盖，以铰链连接，可以完全免去开合的麻烦。经过油漆描绘后，这些箱子外观漂亮。我已经带着箱子去过 4 次欧洲，并且仍像新的一样适合再次伴我前往。这种箱子最好的款型只要 5 银圆，并不算贵。最近还推出了一种新款，已被证明非常成功。我有一只用上等皮革做的箱子，配上国外进口的锁具与皮带，总共只需要 7.5 银圆。

方竹

只有少数人知道，方竹在温州是可以买到的。① 它轻巧独特，是一种理想的手杖。在过去的日子里，英国海军偶尔会有一艘炮舰来温州，他们一直是方竹的最佳客户。

椅子

温州另一种迅速发展的现代贸易产业，是制造各种类型的椅子。其中有全木型、藤椅和靠背型，此外还有皮革座椅。它们适用于餐馆、大厅、卧室、办公室、花园等场所。

摇椅和婴儿安全高脚椅的出口数量也相当可观。一般来说它们是不涂漆出售的，买家可以根据需要决定是否涂漆。

雨伞

总的来讲中国人使用的雨伞都是本地制造，但也仍有机会寻找外地市场。

---

① 温州方竹，产于乐清雁荡山，适合制手杖，明代已有记载。转引自李振南《雁荡山的方竹》，《温州日报》2012 年 8 月 8 日，第 16 版。

造纸业

以稻草与竹子为原料的造纸业为当地许多人提供了就业机会。

温州山区生产有大量木炭，主要用于出口。

《温州台风：特大暴雨和洪水》，《北华捷报及最高法庭与领事馆杂志》，1920 年 9 月 25 日

温州台风：特大暴雨和洪水
（本报记者报道）

　　9 月 3 日至 6 日的台风在温州造成的损失仍难以估计。洪水已将平原淹没，直至山脚下，城市的四面八方已被洪水包围。幸运的是惊人的降雨量主要集中在江河下游流域，否则 1912 年灾难性的洪水很可能会重演，那将造成更严重的后果。

　　毫不夸张地讲，当人们注意到第 24 号台风头三天的降雨量时就已经意识到会出现这样的结果。第一天的降雨量为 10 英寸，第二天为 7.5 英寸，第三天为 6.5 英寸。

　　土豆作物受灾严重，幸运的是第二季水稻收成没有受到太大影响。

教会财产受损

　　英国圣道公会教堂的财产损失惨重。截至撰写本文时，有报道称有 3 座乡村教堂被完全摧毁，有几座教堂的墙体部分倒塌。几个村庄遭受了巨大的财产和生命损失，但目前还不清楚详细情况。北部的楠溪江（Nan Ch'i Creek）在人员方面似乎损失最大，报告估计有 800 人到 1500 人丧生。我希望在两三天内发送更详细的报道。（温州，9 月 11 日）

《客轮相撞：有乘客在慌乱中身亡，事故绝不是意外》，《北华捷报及最高法庭与领事馆杂志》，1921 年 1 月 22 日

客轮相撞：有乘客在慌乱中身亡，事故绝不是意外

周四上海有报道描述了两艘中国轮船相撞的细节。事故发生在温州与宁波之间的航线，永川轮船局（Yungchuan Steam Navigation Co.）① 的"湖广号"（Hukuang）客轮被撞出一个大洞，船只在乘客被转移后搁浅。

报道称，15 日上午 7 点，"湖广号"客轮从温州出发驶往宁波，船上载有 300 多名乘客。午夜后不久，它在越过台州附近平礁（Pingchai）洋面时，与另一艘从上海开往宁波的轮船"永安号"的船头相撞。"湖广号"前舱左舷被撞出一个大洞。

水立刻涌了进来，乘客们惊慌失措，惊恐地大喊："救命！救命！"

"永安号"没受什么损伤，并未施救。不久，另一艘船"永川号"碰巧经过，听到求救信号后立即驶往现场。救援工作随即展开，300 名乘客全部获救。然而在这场恐慌中，1 人死亡，4 人重伤，据说还有 10 人受了轻伤。

---

① 宁波商人林希恒创立，永川轮船局旧址在今鹿城区江滨街道行前社区，现已被公布为省级文物保护单位。参见浙江省文物局编《浙江省第三次全国文物普查新发现丛书：近现代建筑》，浙江古籍出版社，2012，第 116~117 页。

《温州赈荒：本城缺粮仍愿提供帮助》，《北华捷报及最高法庭与领事馆杂志》，1921 年 5 月 14 日

温州赈荒：本城缺粮仍愿提供帮助

（本报记者报道）

在中国各城市为援助北方饥荒地区所做的许多努力中，温州的努力是值得被记录的。

在这里，我们看到了一个地区在自身缺粮的情况下，却响应了北京国际统一救灾总会（United Inernational Famine Relief Committee）① 的号召。

一个由官员、士绅、商人和代表团组成的委员会组织本次运动。在中国基督徒的大力支持下，以露天演讲和传单的形式进行宣传。由于当地的条件，这项工作并不容易，经常有人问工作人员："你们为什么不帮助温州人呢？"

目前还不清楚为北方筹集到的确切救济总额，但据我所知，瓯海关外交专员兼财务主管已经自信满满地向我保证，足足有 4000 银圆可资使用。这是一个穷人帮助穷人的例子，因为善款绝大多数是由铜分和 10 分银圆构成！

粮价飞涨

温州目前的情况是自去年秋季歉收以来，已经进口了 22 万多袋大米。这个港口历史上从未进口过如此数量的大米。温州在正常情况下是能够自

---

① 该组织是华洋义赈会的前身，1920 年北方 5 省出现旱灾，全国相继建立 9 个华洋义赈组织，其中以"北京国际统一救灾总会"的实力最为雄厚。1921 年 11 月 16 日，这些分散在全国的组织集中在上海，成立了统一机构"中国华洋义赈救灾总会"，简称"华洋义赈会"。参见刘峰、吴金良主编《中华慈善大典》，浙江工商大学出版社，2017，第 199~200 页。

给自足的，而且一般还会有多余的粮食来出口。去年的台风和洪水改变了这种状况，附近许多村庄正在承受巨大的不幸和苦难。再加上几个县小麦歉收，情况更是雪上加霜。

现在还需要等三个月第一季水稻才能收获，许多人读到温州进口大米的报道就以为饥荒会得到缓解。

然而，另一个因素也需要考虑，在许多地方粮价比一年前已高出一倍。现在许多人依靠吃土豆为生，但土豆价格也上涨了4倍。

许多农民的房子在洪水中被摧毁，土地因为沙石无法耕种，存粮在洪水中也没了，现在成千上万的农民既没有现钱，也没有途径借钱购粮。在今后的三个月里，许多体面的家庭将不得不放弃尊严去当乞丐。

政府救济

永嘉县知事正在免费发放价值5000银圆的大米，其他县也在做同样的工作。

天主教会已经分发了几百袋大米，许多个人也正在出力帮助穷人。

在过去五年担任瓯海关税务司的谭安先生于4月28日（星期四）开始休假。他准备经由福州和南方港口，在香港搭乘 M. M. 邮轮回乡。

阿拉巴德（E. Alabaster）① 先生最近结束休假，并接替了税务司的职务。随他一起回来的还有阿拉巴德夫人，对这个小型的外国社区来讲，这可是一件令人高兴的事。（温州，4月30日）

---

① 英国人，1921年4月25日至1922年5月8日任职于瓯海关税务司。1928年至1930年任职于北京，在推动华人员工出国学习海关知识方面贡献不少。参见詹庆华《中国海关洋员与中西文化传播》，中国海关出版社，2008，第507页。

《温州的政治：道尹与督军斗争后离开》，《北华捷报及最高法庭与
领事馆杂志》，1921年8月27日

温州的政治：道尹与督军斗争后离开

（本报记者报道）

昨日8月10日，道尹①已经乘坐"嘉禾号"离开港口，他的离去是被
迫的，因此也就没有大官离任时的喧闹风光。

在这个地区经历了最艰难的粮荒期间，林道尹向温州人民表示了自己
改善他们生存条件的决心。

自去年秋季以来，温州进口了70多万袋大米，防止了失序和暴乱的
发生。

林道尹一直是当地赈荒委员会的积极成员，在上海华洋义赈会的资助
下，该委员会已经帮助了几万户贫困家庭。

然而，政治优先于官员的能力，我们的道尹是省长的朋友，这导致他
被驱逐出温州并一度受到逮捕威胁。

违抗督军命令

事情的起因是林道尹在沈省长的授意下开展省议会选举，但卢督军反
对进行选举，因为卢督军想要推动浙江省的自主运动，事实上他已经开始

---

① 林鹍翔（H. E. Ling）是以省长公署秘书的身份代理瓯海道尹，同时林鹍翔与省长
沈金鉴一样，都是在直皖战争结束后，北京政权插入皖系的钉子，因此林、沈二人
与浙江督军卢永祥的关系势同水火。卢永祥想要在浙江推行自主运动，并禁止开展
第三届浙江省议会选举，这就成为林鹍翔与卢永祥矛盾爆发的导火索，最终卢永祥
指令温州驻军团长兼司令王国梁派兵驱逐了林鹍翔。参见谢仲伟《1921年省议会
选举亲历记》，载温州市政协文史资料委员会编《温州文史资料·第七辑》，1991，
第222~226页。

起草浙江省宪法。

林先生认为，推迟甚至禁止省议员选举是直接违反《省议会议员选举法》的行为，并决心按照相关法律继续进行选举。

这导致了军方与文官政府的冲突。随后戒严令被颁布，道尹被禁止进行选举，否则将被逮捕。林鹍翔并没有被吓倒，虽然他得到了人民的同情，但还是不得不离开温州，目前很难预测下一步会发生什么。

第一季水稻已收获。虽然收成不错，但并没有使得粮价下跌。目前急需雨水，否则会影响到今后的收成。（温州，8月11日）

《温州火灾：消防队供应商的时机——缺水》，《北华捷报及最高法庭与领事馆杂志》，1921 年 12 月 24 日

温州火灾：消防队供应商的时机——缺水

（本报记者报道）

    这座城市自从 7 年前有了电灯以来，直到今年秋季，公益事业毫无进展。温州目前亟须办两件事，一是需要更好、更现代化的消防设备，[①] 二是为城市人口提供充足的水源，但迄今为止我们还没有看到当局做出任何改善的努力。

    一旦火灾发生，许多财产会被焚毁，但在许多情况下，如果按照最适当的路线重新组织和装备消防队，这些财产原本是可以挽救的。通过商户捐献，再加上政府拨款，相关费用问题很容易就能解决。

    因此上海的一些公司调查和推荐一些适合消防队使用的发动机、水泵等设备是很值得的，这是一个能够扩展到省内其他城市和大型城镇的潜在市场，更不用说全国市场。今年秋季，是多年以来火灾最严重的一个时期。最近一场大火发生在圣道公会东院墙外，如果不是近 20 支"火龙队"在与教会毫无瓜葛的几位外国绅士的指挥与协助下集中救火，教会的三座住宅必定会被焚毁。

缺水

    第二个需求是家庭用水的供应问题，日日夜夜的缺水状况在最近愈发严峻。自 9 月中旬以来，温州几乎没有下雨，大多数井干涸了。目前只剩

---

① 清光绪年间，就可以看到温州设立民间水龙（也被称为"义龙"）的记载，一直到 20 世纪 20 年代，温州灭火主要仍依靠各处水龙救火。参见温郡筹防编《温州》1884 年 8 月 13 日，第二版；《地方通信：温州》，《申报》1920 年 1 月 20 日，第二张第七版。

下一两口井还有水，人们不得不买水喝，通宵排队买水都不算稀罕事。

我需要再次强调，自流井①不仅能保证这座古城的供水，还能减少疾病发生，挽救生命。

这座城市群山环绕的自然条件为自流井的开凿提供了成功的希望，也是在为企业提供商机。

人民愿意接受改革并承担其费用。

一条省道

与此同时，一条伟大的道路正在建设中，这将使那些在两三英尺宽的高速公路上旅行多年的人感到震惊！据报道，这将是一条"省道"，北至台州与宁波，南至福建。从过去几周已经开始修建的工程来看，这将是一项进步而具有雄心的计划。这条省道经过温州东门外的河岸，为南北走向，共有30多英尺宽。到目前为止，公路工程还没有受到坟墓和房屋的阻碍，在获取土地问题上也没有遇上大麻烦。

当地官员已同外国社区取得联系，要求外国社区同意将一些15平方英尺的外国墓地移交绐道路委员会（Road Commission），以便满足其调查和筑路计划的需要。同时他们会提供一个更好的新墓地，并承担所有迁葬费用！

外国居民正在认真考虑这件事，但还没有做出明确决定。（温州，12月7日）

---

① 1929年永嘉县即提倡私人投资兴办自来水厂，后因花费巨大而作罢。1935年永嘉县估计全城需要开凿10口自流井，当年即决定先开5口，由宁商洁丽公司承建，第一口自流井位置在府头门钟楼旁，井建好后居民需要购专门竹签挑水，每支竹签零售铜圆2枚。参见李定荣《温州第一口自流井开凿始末》，载温州市鹿城区委员会文史资料委员会编《鹿城文史资料·第九辑》，1995，第266~268页。

《好博逊先生讣告》，《北华捷报及最高法庭与领事馆杂志》，1922
年4月22日

好博逊先生讣告

据报道，退休前曾担任过中国海关高级税务司职务的好博逊（Herbert Elgar Hobson）① 先生，已于2月25日在英国什普罗郡艾恩布里奇（Iron Bridge，Shropshire）去世，享年78岁，他是萨默塞特郡威灵顿（Welling-ton，Somerset）已故罗伯特·霍布斯（Robert Hobson）的长子。

1861年8月，好博逊来到上海并进入海关工作。第二年冬天，太平天国军队包围了上海，像其他欧洲居民一样，他加入了志愿军。1863年他去了北京，在太平天国军队首领被斩首后不久，他被任命为戈登将军的见习翻译，直到1864年太平天国运动结束。由于他的贡献，他被授予金宝星勋章（Gordon Campaign Medal）②。随后，他重新进入海关，以数种身份服务过18个以上的中国通商口岸。因此，好博逊先生在中国有着丰富而独特的经历。

好博逊先生在1877年负责筹建瓯海关，1890年负责筹建重庆关，1900年又负责筹建云南腾越关，此外他还在西藏边境的亚东待了3年。他最后于上海江海关任上结束了自己在中国的职业生涯，在那里所有与他打过交道的人都喜欢他。

---

① 好博逊18岁进入海关，曾担任过戈登的见习翻译，在担任江海关税务司期间威望极高，是赫德选择继任者的四个候选人之一。参见方德万《潮来潮去：海关与中国现代性的全球起源》，山西人民出版社，2017，第203~204页。

② 晚清金宝星勋章最早是崇厚于天津模仿印度1861年勋章款式所造，由于最早受颁勋章的是戈登，所以外国人也将该勋章称为"戈登勋章"。同治四年（1865年）正月二十九日，李鸿章命令苏松太道仿造天津样式，为戈登所率领常胜军的洋员颁发勋章。勋章一共分为三等，一等又分为两品，分别为一等一品重一两四钱金宝星，以及一等二品重一两二钱金宝星；二等为重一两金宝星，三等为银牌。共计98名洋员获勋章。好博逊获得的是一等二品重一两二钱金宝星。参见《洋弁请奖片，附清单》，《李鸿章全集·2》，安徽教育出版社，2008，第18~19页。

《温州纪事：海关人事变化与传教代表团来访》，《北华捷报及最高法庭与领事馆杂志》，1922 年 4 月 22 日

温州纪事：海关人事变化与传教代表团来访

（本报记者报道）

我们的小社区在听说海关税务司阿拉巴德先生将被调往镇江后，都感到很遗憾。

阿拉巴德先生只在温州待了 12 个月，但在此期间，他身为赈荒救济委员会主席做出了杰出的贡献，并随时准备帮助这个小外国社区。阿拉巴德先生及其夫人将在 5 月底搬家，他们会带着许多美好的祝福离开。

一个成功的教会

英国布里斯托尔的巴特勒夫妇（Mr. and Mrs. Butler）最近来到我们的港口，他们与宣教总秘书（General Missionary Secretary）斯凯德福德牧师（Rev. C. Skedeford）组成了一个圣道公会代表团，并将陆续前往云南、浙江、山东和直隶的宣教区。

阅读过《中国传教纪事》（A Mission in China）① 的读者应该都知道，虽然圣道公会人手严重不足，但该教会是传教事业最成功的教会之一。圣道公会共有 276 座教堂，超过 1 万名成年教徒和慕道友（inquirer）②，附属学校已经培养了超过 170 名学生。多年以来，圣道公会医院始终在这项伟

---

① 1907 年苏慧廉撰写的作品，目前已有中译本，也被翻译为《晚清温州纪事》。参见 W. E. Soothill, *A Mission in China*, Edinburgb and London：Olphant, Anderson & Ferrier, 1907。

② 按照苏慧廉的说法，慕道友是圣道公会入教准备阶段的称呼，还不是正式教徒。参见 W. E. Soothill, *A Mission in China*, Edinburgb and London：Olphant, Anderson & Ferrier, 1907, p. 48。

大而有益的事业中扮演着核心角色，它大大减轻了广大中国人民的诸多病痛。医院仅在去年就接待了 35000 人次门诊病人和 800 多名住院病人，这些人数也说明了此项工作的艰辛。迄今为止，一名外国医生在没有外国护士帮助的情况下独挑大梁，同时他还担任着海关医官的职务。

我们要恭喜西德福特（Shedeford）医生，一名专业的英国护士波尔（L. Ball）小姐将在今年秋季抵达温州，同时曾经在温州服务多年的包莅茂（W. E. Plunmer）医生也将回来与其共事，包医生曾因为工作过度而暂时离职。

英国商人的支持

英国商会联合会（Associated British Chambers of Commerce）① 的慷慨同情和支持，可能会刺激教会的教育和医疗传教工作，并使之更为有效。有英国商人在前所未有的贸易萧条中仍准备提供援助，教会也不会缺乏信心或胸襟。（温州，4 月 12 日）

---

① 该商会成立于 1860 年，对英国政府和议会具有重要影响力，在 20 世纪 20 年代对庚子赔款、治外法权、租界、海关税等涉中国事务都有发言权，同时明确反对英日同盟。参见《侨华英国商会联合会》，《顺天时报》1923 年 2 月 25 日，第二版；John Turner, *Businessmen and Politics: Studies of Business Activity in British Politics, 1900 - 1945*, London: Heinemann, 1984, p. 5。

《温州纪事：中国内地会荣女士去世》，《北华捷报及最高法庭与领事馆杂志》，1922 年 7 月 1 日

温州纪事：中国内地会荣女士去世

（本报记者报道）

6 月 17 日，周六，天还没亮，温州社区一位受人尊敬的老成员去世了，她就是中国内地会（China Inland Mission）的荣女士（F. A. M. Yong，也称"荣姑娘"）①。荣女士享年 40 岁，她曾在英国公务员体系中担任要职，后接受内地会的邀请参与传教工作。

在传教过程中她克服了语言上的障碍，并在 23 年中主要担任一所男子寄宿学校的校长②职务。在过去的 6 个月里，内地会已经失去了 3 位宝贵而勤勉的工作者。王廉（F. Worley）③ 牧师亲自主持了荣女士的葬礼，外国社区表达了深切的哀悼，华人也对这位已故的女士表达了深切敬意。

监狱改革

负责该地区的司法官员正在努力改善囚犯的生活与居住条件。为此最近在旧监狱中新建了一个试验区，并已开始建造一个全新的模范监狱，总

---

① 内地会荣女士 1899 年来到温州传教。参见黄光域编《基督教传行纪念（1807—1949）》，广西师范大学出版社，2017，第 204 页；吴百亨《经营百好炼乳厂的回忆》，载温州市委员会文史资料研究委员会编《温州文史资料·创刊号》，1985，第 46~47 页。

② 即温州崇真小学，前身是曹雅直所创办的男子义塾。注释同上。

③ 内地会的王廉 1911 年来到温州平阳传教，后接任崇真小学校长职务，1925 年五卅运动期间因为王廉反对学生上街，学校爆发学潮并走向自治。参见黄光域编《基督教传行纪念（1807—1949）》，广西师范大学出版社，2017，第 368 页；《温州电》，《申报》1925 年 6 月 11 日，第四版。

花费估计为 3 万银圆。

县知事最近在衙门举办了一次晚宴，邀请了几位重要的外国公民领袖，包括罗马天主教以及英国圣道公会的负责人，目的是获取他们的同情与帮助，为监狱改革计划筹措资金！宴会结束后，知事分发了认捐簿，并要求外国客人去找他们的朋友帮忙，以便为犯罪分子的新家园改造做贡献。其中一位受邀的外国人指出这样的请求很不寻常，在所有外国国家提供监狱住宿都被认为是国家应尽的义务，教会事实上已经在医院、学校等许多方面为改善中国民众福祉做出巨大努力。无论如何，我们还是要表扬这位知事，无论他的上级是否拨款，他都渴望改善监狱条件，我们只能祝他能够成功。

没有绝对的坏事

我们目前正在经历"梅天"（梅雨）季节，外国人普遍感到无力和倦怠。

然而，中国人满怀希望地期待着今年水稻的丰收。第一季的收成看起来很好，如果我们没有遭受过去两年的洪水和台风，那么今年有充分的理由期待好收成。今年的瓯柑果实累累，瓯柑业公会（Orange Guild）① 的成员预测，今年秋天的瓯柑收获量将是去年的两倍多。（温州，6 月 20 日）

---

① 宁波商人杨正裕在光绪年间于五马街创立"五味和"蜜饯店，杨正裕 50 岁去世后由其子杨直钦继承，杨直钦在温州有瓯柑店铺十余家，瓯柑远销京津一带。杨直钦被推选为瓯柑业公会会长职务，至于该公会具体成立时间待考。参见张叔震《百年老店五味和》，载浙江省新闻出版局编《温州文史资料·第六辑》，1990，第 247～250 页。

《温州纪事》，《北华捷报及最高法庭与领事馆杂志》，1922年9月2日

温州纪事

（本报记者报道）

第一季水稻已经安全收获，来自周边地区的报告显示，收获情况比前两年要好。农民们感到高兴的是，台风没有像过去两年那样摧毁他们的庄稼，他们希望第二季收成能远远超过夏收。然而，尽管获得了丰收，大米的价格仍没有下降，反而上涨了。百姓将矛头指向官员允许大米出口。18个月前，温州为了缓解粮荒曾进口超过60万袋大米。人们不禁感到困惑，为什么要在今年全部收获前就出口成千上万袋大米。温州从来就不是大米的出口地，人们怀疑这是为了供给军粮，而不是为了满足中国其他地区的饥荒需求。[1]

今年温州幸运地躲过了台风的蹂躏。在8月时，4场台风在温州附近的东部、北部和南部肆虐，但除了两三天的大雨和降温，以及平原与山谷地区被淹了两天外，我们没有遭受任何损失。

今年夏季是数年来最为酷热的一年，少数幸运儿已经可以住在城市对面的山上。虽然山只有海拔1200英尺，但阴凉处的最高气温也只有86华氏度，这让许多居住在北方气温更高港口的人感到惊奇。（温州，8月20日）

---

[1] 1922年浙江省以浙西缺粮名义，颁发给平阳王理孚运米执照，粮食后被运到上海销售，遭到温州旅沪同乡会激烈反对，指斥王理孚为"著名贩米之奸商"，温州人一向痛恨大米出口，将其称为"漏海"。参见《温州旅沪同乡会致浙省长电》，《申报》1922年8月15日，第15版。

《温州风灾：六间教堂和许多房屋被夷为平地，江面损失惨重》，
《北华捷报及最高法庭与领事馆杂志》，1922 年 9 月 23 日

温州风灾：六间教堂和许多房屋被夷为平地，江面损失惨重
（本报记者报道）

周一，本地年龄最长的居民所见过的最具破坏性的台风以惊人的速度袭击了这个港口，因为电线是南北向，温州与外界的一切联系都被切断，直到今天，从福州来的"遇顺号"（Yushun）轮船离港时，电线还没有修好。

9 月 10 日，星期日，是一个晴空万里的好日子，没有发生风灾的任何预兆。但在周一下午 2 点，一场猛烈的台风开始明显向温州方向移动，当时气压下降得很快，气压计读数是 29.556。到晚上 8 点 30 分，已降至 28.56，这座城市和附近地区已成为一片废墟。据官方计算，台风以 24 小时 500 英里的速度向温州移动，且台风眼已经过去了，即便台风眼没有扫过温州，也一定离我们很近。

"飞鲸号"逃过一劫

从晚上 7 点到午夜时分，是台风最猛烈的时刻，江面船舶损失惨重。招商局的"飞鲸号"（Feiching）却在这场灾难中避开了损失，她能逃过这一劫，无疑是船长和船员们最大的荣耀。当时船员们将船系在一个大浮桥上，用锚和链条牢牢拴住，但在晚上 8 点到 8 点 30 分之间，整个浮桥被吹断，船在浓重的夜色里被冲走，随即撞上了河边的房子，不幸的是房子被毁了，但短暂的撞停使船员有时间重新控制船只。后来调查显示，撞船的地方水深已有 47 英尺，可谓险矣。

一艘载有 30 人的官办船只就没有那么幸运了，她一头撞上了沿江石

墙，这导致船只顷刻沉没，这艘船是从亚细亚石油公司租借的。幸亏有亚细亚石油公司代理鲍威尔（Powell）先生及其仆人伸手援助，船上共有28人得救。此外还有一艘轮船覆没，溺毙者5人。

据华人统计，大概有100艘帆船及数艘大帆船沉没，一般舢板小船损失在1000艘左右，人命损失无法估量。

黑夜中的浩劫

在岸上，砖墙和房屋像纸牌一样倒塌，暴风雨早将路灯吹坏，漆黑一片的城市，呈现满目疮痍的景象，仿佛受过炮火猛烈轰炸。晚稻收成大受损失，瓯柑树木也大受破坏。

英国圣道公会也遭受重创，城内附属的学校、医院和教堂都惨遭损毁。根据报告，城外乡村已有6座精美教堂被夷为平地，该教会损失总计高达2万银圆。（温州，9月16日）

《温州风灾损失：堪比轰炸，教堂与教会损失惨重》，《北华捷报及最高法庭与领事馆杂志》，1922 年 9 月 30 日

温州风灾损失：堪比轰炸，教堂与教会损失惨重

（本报记者报道）

9 月 16 日，海和德（J. W. Heywood）牧师夫妇①离开了温州，两人的健康状况都很差，牧师是由于积劳成疾，其夫人则是因为疾病需要回英国本土进行外科治疗。32 年前，海和德先生来到这个港口，直到近 11 年前，他在中国服务的一半时间是在宁波度过的。在过去的两年里，由于缺乏人手，他不得不监管温州的传教工作。他不仅要管理温州的 150 个教堂，同时还要应付宁波教会的一般工作，对于一个在最近几年冬季反复发作支气管炎而虚弱不堪的人来说，担子实在太重了。由于温州实在过于缺乏人手，海和德先生将原定去年春天的假期拖延到了今年。

可怕的破坏

9 月 18 日（周一）晚上的台风对这座城市及其周边地区造成了史无前例的破坏，这让我陷入无与伦比的悲痛之中。在城市附近，有数十艘大、中型帆船和 70 多艘小帆船沉没，此外还有一艘日本轮船与一艘小轮船，以及数百艘舢板船被毁坏。还有一些人因为房屋倒塌或山体滑坡而丧命，这场风灾中的生命损失无法估量。在温州的一起山体滑坡事故中，5 座房子

① 海和德夫妇于 1891 年来到温州协助苏慧廉进行传教工作，直至 1929 年退休回国，中途多次回国述职并休假，海和德夫妇与瓯海关监督冒广生及其母亲私交甚好。参见沈迦《冒广生的旧照》，载冯克力编《老照片·第 87 辑》，山东画报出版社，2013，第 154 ~ 159 页。

被压垮，27 人因而丧命。

在德国人轰炸哈特尔普尔（Hartlepool）后，我和我的家人在斯卡伯勒（Scarborough）的第二次轰炸中遭到炮火袭击，当时一艘德国潜艇向这个城镇发射了大约 30 枚炮弹。今天温州所呈现的浩劫景象，就像被轰炸了100 次的哈特尔普尔。城市与郊区的损失绝对在 100 万银圆以上，更不用说农村地区的损失了，农村的房屋、树木、大豆、玉米、棉花几乎全被摧毁，土地和稻谷也被洪水淹没。

许多教堂被毁

据报道，截至目前，仅温州圣道公会教区就有 10 座教堂全部倒塌，其他许多教堂的墙壁部分倒塌，需要重新铺装房瓦，瓦匠和烧瓦工肯定能大赚一笔。以前 1 银圆能买 600 块至 700 块瓦，现在只能买到 150 块瓦，工价也比之前要高出很多。温州圣道公会至少需要 2 万银圆或 3000 英镑用于修缮和重建。在城外 4 英里的地方，有一座小教堂被摧毁了，这座教堂在12 年前或 15 年前建起来时只花了 450 银圆，但今天要重建需要超过 1200银圆。目前按照类似大小和风格建造其他教堂，预估容纳 400 人至 500 人，花费也多半在 1200 银圆左右。艺文学堂、教会大院的墙都倒了大半，城里可以容纳 1000 人的大教堂现在也因为损毁严重而无法使用。

不幸的是，教会手头的资金不足以应付这种规模的灾难，我们贫穷的信徒，他们在平时都很慷慨，但在此时此刻，他们也要面对房屋、土地被毁的困境。尽管如此，我们的华人牧师和信徒已经筹建了一个调查与善后委员会，以便在当地寻求帮助。我们的一位华人妇女信徒从她每月 5 银圆的工资里向我们捐献了 2 银圆，另一位信徒从她 6 银圆的工资里拿出 3 银圆帮助我们。

一艘中国商轮如何渡过难关

据刚刚从温州港口抵达上海的"飞鲸号"船员说，9 月 11 日台风的突然袭击造成了温州沿岸大量的生命和财产损失。尽管周一下午气压下降得很快，但预计风暴会在 24 小时后才抵达温州，因此"飞鲸号"一直在载货，直到下午 5 点。当时正下着暴雨，天气也很恶劣，涨潮异常剧烈，大风使江水猛涨了一段时间。

7 点 55 分，台风突然来了。"飞鲸号"的前系泊处从浮桥上脱离，船随之转动，但尾部系泊处仍牢固地拴着。后风向随之转变，没有什么能与台风对抗，尽管船还系在浮桥上并下了重锚，但船和浮桥还是一起被吹了出去。

天漆黑一片，不可能展开救援工作。"飞鲸号"最后救起了两名紧紧抓住散落在江里帆船桅杆的水手，另外还有两名水手爬上了浮桥才获救。

遇难记述

江上仍漂浮着尸体，直到人们将尸体打捞上岸装进棺材摆在江边。共计有 1000 多所房屋被毁，据估计有 58 艘帆船幸存下来，但损失总数难以估计。共计损失了约 150 艘货船，有一艘日本轮船失事，造成 15 人丧生，一名幸存者靠着一小片轮船残骸漂到岸上，这说明巨浪在席卷甲板后导致所有船员落水。涨潮淹没了城市，站在船只甲板上可以看到河岸已与屋顶齐平。洪水退去时，一艘帆船被发现搁浅在一所房子的屋顶上。

当"飞鲸号"再次返回温州停泊时，数小时内甚至找不到一艘舢板船，因为所有小船都正忙着打捞江里的财物。当地官员正在尽最大努力开展救灾工作，并且已经向北京请求援助。（温州，9 月 21 日）

《温州惨状：台风后的暴雨，城镇与农村遭到大范围破坏》，《北华捷报及最高法庭与领事馆杂志》，1922 年 10 月 14 日

温州惨状：台风后的暴雨，城镇与农村遭到大范围破坏

（本报记者报道）

　　自 9 月 21 日我发出温州发生风灾的通讯后，这座城市和附近地区又出现了洪水，大大增加了财产损失与人民痛苦。城中屋宇，前因风灾损毁者现多崩塌。人民遭此两重浩劫，不胜绝望。一些房屋尽毁的人呆立在旷野瓦砾中，任凭暴雨无情吹打，显然已经忘记还需要遮风挡雨，他们现在就像石头一样绝望。

　　城中传说，在温州西部约 100 英里处一座拥有数千居民的小镇，已被洪水冲没。今天我又听说此间南方平原广袤的平阳县，积水已达 5~7 英尺深，人已经无法徒步行走。一名传教士原本计划在那里停留 3 周，但由于洪水的原因，他不得不折返。一位年轻的华人牧师被派去调查他所在教堂的财产受损情况，他谈到他所访问的县的收成已在洪水中全部被毁。①

　　府中最高官员今天一直在拜访外国人，在向我发出呼吁后，他们向我解释了其任务是重建华洋义赈会（R. C. Mission），随后他们找到瓯海关税务司，并寻求与外国人的合作，就像去年在水灾和饥荒期间所做的那样，成立一个联合委员会，审议救济措施，并讨论分配物资的组织方式。

　　目前街上正在用大木桶施粥，极贫之人可以获取粥食。寺庙里挤满了来自城市和乡村的难民，人们最近经常听到某小康之家彻底破产，只能托

---

① 据张棡记述，赵岩下庄收谷，租子只能收上四成，张棡侄子醒同家里 150 亩地仅收谷 1500 斤。张棡认为"如此灾歉，真数百年所未见也"。参见温州市图书馆编《张棡日记·第六册》，张钧孙点校，中华书局，2019，第 2612 页。

庇寺庙的事情。

城里有一棵大树被吹倒，倒塌时毁了一幢房子，隔天有人以 17 银圆买下了这棵树。此人又花了 90 银圆把树锯成木材，现在还不确定他是否还有钱把木材运回家。

招商局的"飞鲸号"上次因为台风在温州被困了 16 天，这次因为水灾又将被困 8 天，预计 3 天后才能起航。它的锅炉整日都在烧，显然它需要螺旋桨不停地旋转来抵抗巨大的水流，更重要的是，就如同梦魇一般，它的船舷这次可一定要拴牢浮桥。（温州，10 月 5 日）

《温州台风：洪水与海盗使风灾更重》，《北华捷报及最高法庭与领事馆杂志》，1922 年 10 月 28 日

温州台风：洪水与海盗使风灾更重
（本报记者报道）

目前温州最紧要的新闻仍与风灾有关。人们还不能忽略这些新闻，温州的许多地方还有故事可讲。就在昨天，一位老相识从洞头黑牛湾（Bullock Harbour）附近的外海岛屿来看望我，他告诉我说岛上最近发生了猛烈的洪水，除非是潮汐，否则那种规模的洪水只有在大陆上才能发出如此大的声响。在岛上的某个村子里，由于水涨得太高，村民不得不躲到房顶以策安全。这场天灾似乎导致该地区岛屿和台州地区的海盗数量急剧增加。

在最近一次的华洋义赈会委员会会议上，永嘉商会（Wenchow Chamber of Commerce）会长唐先生[1]和当地的另一位商人被派往宁波，与那里的行政官员商议救灾措施。随后华人和外国人都聚集在前统领衙门开会，报告当地的组织、资金以及农村的受灾情况，并讨论了未来救灾的物资分发问题。（温州，10 月 21 日）

---

[1] 唐先生即唐伯寅。温州商会创立于晚清时期，任会长者多为官员或有功名者。民国以后，温州商会改名为永嘉商会，先后任会长的叶维周、杨雨农、唐伯寅等都是单纯的商人出身，商会有较强的自治能力。参见郁建兴、江华、周俊《在参与中成长的中国公民社会：基于浙江温州商会的研究》，浙江大学出版社，2008，第 39～40 页。

《温州贸易的航运利益：更多船只停靠港口，日本通商意愿强烈》，
《北华捷报及最高法庭与领事馆杂志》，1922年11月4日

温州贸易的航运利益：更多船只停靠港口，日本通商意愿强烈

（本报记者报道）

最近来此港口的轮船数量显著增加，除每周有3艘小轮连通海门（Haiman）、舟山（Chusan）和宁波外，招商局的"飞鲸号"每周也会来往于瓯沪之间。此外最近温州又多出了"广华号"（Kuang Hua，华船）连通上海，"云海丸号"（Unkai Maru，日船）连通横滨，另外还有一艘小轮船。日本人似乎想要和温州开展更多贸易。我们听说南门外开了一家日本松脂厂，有一艘三桅机帆船来往于温州与南部厦门之间，据说是中国船只，但实际挂着日本国旗。还有一艘在风灾中沉没的日本船"汉阳丸号"，① 原本是经营温州附近的内河客运的。相较而言，"云海丸号"看起来更加野心勃勃，这艘船满载着木炭运往横滨，② 连甲板上也堆满货物。

每周前来温州停靠的帆船与老闸船的数量在以肉眼可见的速度增长，来去如飞的较小木船与舢板同样也在增多。岸上木匠正在赶工，许多从前的砖墙现在被改造成了木板墙。寺庙忙碌不已，无数以乞讨为生的难民现

① 1921年日本商社新泰洋行在温州经营"汉阳丸"，此船吨位仅19吨，主要跑内河客运运输。参见周厚才《温州港史》，人民交通出版社，1990，第110~113页。

② "云海丸"是一艘专门运输木炭的货船，温州木炭质量优良，从晚清开始即大量出口至日本。仅1922年1月至11月间，温州就有大概16万担木炭出口到日本。日本在温州从事木炭生意的商社主要有岩井、三井、藤末、东美等，日商大量高价收购是温州木炭价格上涨的主要原因。参见《行业要讯》，《申报》1922年12月28日，第13版；夏超群《温州木炭业盛衰记》，载浙江省新闻出版局编《温州文史资料·第六辑》，1990，第79~85页。

在以寺庙为家。寺庙忙碌的另一个原因是无数善男信女前往供奉，最受欢迎的庙宇是建在山上的东瓯王庙（Temple of Neptune）①，此庙周围有城墙，并且能够俯瞰江海。另外招商局希望能在两个月内修复浮桥。（温州，10 月21 日）

---

① 如果直译，应译为"海神庙"。查温州东瓯王即东海王驺摇，东瓯王庙在华盖山，且周围有城墙，山顶能够俯瞰江海，符合文义。

《温州纪事：一系列事故：海上爆炸与瓯江贸易》，《北华捷报及最高法庭与领事馆杂志》，1923年1月20日

温州纪事：一系列事故：海上爆炸与瓯江贸易

（本报记者报道）

在过去的数月当中，这座城市及其邻近地区发生了一系列意外事故。温州最好的街道发生了大火，好几处房屋被焚毁，其中包括一家颇具现代风格的鞋店。不久前，一所房屋内发生火药爆炸，造成数名居民以及一名路过的女孩罹难。在另一场爆炸中，据说一名男子的头被炸飞。此外大约在一周前，一艘轮船在沙洲搁浅，也有人说是在江中抛锚，其乘客被转移到另一艘船上。结果这艘搭载自身乘客和转运乘客的船不幸倾覆，造成12人溺亡，船员也在失踪名单中。

温州的内河与海上贸易正日益繁荣，这从轮船数量的增长就能看出来。上周，日轮"大新丸号"（Daishin Maru）运走了一批木炭，中国船"胜利号"（Shengli）也来了一次。昨天来了一艘日本轮船，今天又来了两艘小轮。温州与宁波之间固定有三艘轮船往来，其中一艘轮船的华人船长在两周前去世了。由于浮桥在上次风灾中被吹走，三个月以来这些轮船只能停在江中卸货和上下乘客。浮桥已被翻新，已再次使用。这三艘定期往来宁波与温州之间的航班，中间会停靠几个港口，与往来伦敦与英国东海岸的定期客轮很像，我听说外国旅客更愿意在海门登上去上海的轮船，这些轮船能为外国人提供与常规轮船一样好的住宿，且票价更为合理。

亚细亚石油公司的兰伯特（Lampert）先生离开了温州。内地会刚来了一位新成员，她就是伊宝珍（Eynon）小姐，当她休假归来，内地会就可以增加外国职员人手。圣道公会的山尔曼（A. H. Sharman）在离开三年半后，也将在数星期后回到温州。（温州，1月5日）

《惊险遭遇海盗：警方智破海盗，海盗船一沉一擒》，《北华捷报及最高法庭与领事馆杂志》，1923年2月17日

惊险遭遇海盗：警方智破海盗，海盗船一沉一擒

（本报记者报道）

离开温州许久的老居民如果重新回到这座港口，只要看到日益增长的轮船数量，马上就可以判断出这个地区的贸易必定有了相当大的增长。在某日清晨，我看到港内至少停着7艘轮船。在这7艘船中，3艘是日船，其中"大新丸号"和"马勒号"（Ralph Moller）悬挂英国国旗，"广华号"和"升利号"（Sing Li）悬挂中国旗帜。此外，最近中国警船"永平舰"（Yung Ping）① 在鸡冠山（Chinhoi）外海② 捕获了一艘海盗船，13名海盗同时被捕。③

"永平舰"在离开时突然发现有4艘伴行的帆船十分可疑，它们似乎想抵近侦察，后发现它们果然是海盗船，"永平舰"展开行动时，海盗船员被安排在船侧，随后撞沉了1艘海盗船，并俘获了1艘，另外2艘逃跑，还有许多海盗跳船逃生。"永平舰"在行动期间遭到了海盗炮击，一块价值高昂的指南针被严重损毁。随后"永平舰"押着13名海盗驶往温州，据消息人士透露，这些海盗看起来都是吸大烟的人，外貌皆不似善类。

对于温州轮船数量增多的原因，有一种解释认为是去年风灾摧毁了太

---

① "永平舰"隶属浙江外海水警第二巡队，专门负责抓捕海盗工作。参见《杭州快信》，《申报》1923年1月31日，第10版。

② 乐清鸡冠山外海，也被称为凤凰洋。凤凰洋是清代与民国常见温州地名，以海盗出没著称。

③ 《民国日报》记载，生擒7人，击毙10余人，匪首名叫尹老五。参见《外海水警又获海盗》，《民国日报》1923年1月30日，第8版。

多帆船，现在轮船公司正在趁机夺占港口的贸易份额。最近"恒利号"
（Kenli）① 从芜湖驶回温州，运回了 1.1 万袋大米，在一定程度上平抑了
温州的粮价。

庙会

在过去的三四个月中，中国人花了大量金钱来修复城中被破坏的庙
宇。其中海坛山的寺庙②格外受人欢迎，为此中国人花费了 5000 银圆来进
行扩建与美化。这些钱财来自居住在北门附近吴家的一名成员的捐赠，这
位先生为了恢复民众的信仰，还捐资复建了附近的佛寺。据说士绅参与这
些公益活动，是由于他们被寄予期望，如果他们拒绝的话将是对发起者的
极大冒犯。另外，宣讲也是公益活动中的重要组成部分。

在东瓯王庙重新开放后的许多天里，可以看到很多人参观庙宇，特别
是在开放的当天，可谓人山人海。晚上山上放起烟火，全城各处都能看
到。火神庙山脚下连续一个多月都在演戏，戏台就搭在户外，在天色好的
夜晚看戏的群众尤其多。③

城市对面的"江心屿"在风灾期间遭到部分损毁，如今也已修缮。另
外我们要感谢海关港务长（Harbour Master）克里斯托弗森（Christophers-
en）先生的能力与倡议，他使粮商同意将从芜湖买来的大米储存在江心屿
的寺庙里。（温州，2 月 7 日）

---

① 永济公司轮船，其航线由沪开轮赴芜，由芜运米至温，再由温运货至沪。参见《永
济公司恒利快轮开往温州芜湖露布》，《申报》1922 年 12 月 26 日，第 1 版。
② 应指海坛山杨府庙，旧址即今山元道观。
③ 根据张棡的记载，当时温州露天流行的戏曲是台州乱弹"一品玉"。参见温州市图
书馆编《张棡日记·第六册》，张钧孙点校，中华书局，2019，第 2628 页。

《温州纪事：心怀旧俗，新人事，日本贸易增长》，《北华捷报及最高法庭与领事馆杂志》，1923 年 4 月 28 日

温州纪事：心怀旧俗，新人事，日本贸易增长

（本报记者报道）

温州是一座平静祥和的城市，它几乎没有变化，即便有也是缓慢、渐进的变化。一方面温州正在响应充满活力的时代的影响，另一方面可以明显看到来自古代的旧俗与旧信仰正在复兴。摩登的学生们在外国老师的影响下，会试图摆出一副目空一切的怀疑论者的架子来，① 但商人以及其他一般老百姓，仍热衷于在清明节涌向寺庙，并到祖先坟墓祭拜。旧秩序已经改变，并且让位于许多新事物，这的确是事实。但是许多旧秩序仍牢牢统治着人们的内心与生活，而对于任何承诺保留旧信仰和古老习俗的东西，人们仍然愿意慷慨解囊。一户吴姓人家，不久前捐款数千元翻修寺庙，该工程已竣工。庙宇附近山上的那条蜿蜒曲折的林荫道，由一位瑞安的女士慷慨捐助，山路用精美的花岗岩铺设，现在已经铺到了半山腰。

最近海关的外勤人员发生了人事变动，在韦斯特（West）先生前往牛庄后，备受尊敬的港务长克里斯托弗森先生也将要离开温州，他将会前往美国和伦敦度假，他的假期已经延期两年。

人们对此都感到很惋惜，因为过去的三年任期，是克里斯托弗森先生第二次在温州任职，他赢得了社区真诚的赞誉和尊重。在继韦斯特先生和赖登（Ryden）先生后，卡瑟尔（Coxall）先生带着他的妻子，成为克里斯托弗森先生的继任者。卡瑟尔先生在足球方面很在行，希望他能教导艺文学堂的学生，孩子们富有锐气，但他们正急需一个教练。

---

① 指的是 20 世纪 20 年代盛行的"疑古"风潮。

日本轮船仍继续在温州从事贸易，贸易内容主要是木炭，几乎每个星期都能看到日本船停靠在温州城。据报道，温州的日本居民人数超过 50 人，另一份报道则说大约有 100 人。在东郊，日本人正在建一座工厂，即便不是日本人亲自建也是日本人的厂。工厂仍在建造中，共有三栋房，第一栋是单层，第二栋是双层，第三栋是粉刷过的整洁小木屋，配有砖制柱子，这栋房屋是给来自福建的林经理（Mr. Ling）居住的。据相关人士透露，前两栋建筑用来生产牛肉、羊肉、杨梅和枇杷罐头，以出口为目的。当被问及这家工厂是否有日本背景时，消息人的回答是"与日本人没关系，这家工厂是由福建人和温州人开的"①。工厂和房子都靠近新公路边，公路则靠近河岸。（温州，4 月 21 日）

① 这家公司并不是日本人的厂，而是来自厦门的淘化公司，它于 1922 年在温州设厂，经理为林子达，工厂产品主要销往南洋一带。参见彭一万《发源于鼓浪屿的淘化大同公司》，载鼓浪屿申报世界文化遗产系列丛书编委会编《鼓浪屿文史资料》（下），2009，第 19~20 页。

《温州坚决抵制日货：学生出动检查行李，海关抗议，校长的智慧》，《北华捷报及最高法庭与领事馆杂志》，1923 年 5 月 5 日

温州坚决抵制日货：学生出动检查行李，海关抗议，校长的智慧

（本报记者报道）

　　本周温州许多学校和学院的学生都积极参加了抵制日货的运动。在 4 月 15 日（周日）下午，在温州商会大厅召开了一个 1000 人的大会，会后又举行了 500 人的集会，参加集会的大多数是学生，也有商人和一些其他人。事实证明，虽然集会人数没有预期多，但集会地点还是太小。另外，他们在没有获得许可的情况下，借用了圣道公会的中央教堂，此前不久教堂主日学校已经解散，这座可以轻松容纳 1000 人的建筑现在是空的。这里有许多演讲者，其中有一位年轻的演讲者尤其受到欢迎，他能够吸引那些具有好战情绪的听众。这位年轻的演讲者强调损坏日货最终只能伤害自己的国家，并告诫其他人不要视日本为仇敌，但同时要坚持废除"二十一条"（Twenty one Demands）。

　　温州学生会组织了搜查队，对来往温州的船只以及海关进行强行检验，这些学生会重点检查出入境旅客的行李。他们的这项措施，由于一些未经授权的社会闲杂人等的加入，很快就开始影响海关的正常工作，海关税务司不得不写信给温州外事交涉员，交涉员又将此事上报给道尹，道尹随后又向几所学校的校长发了一份盖有印章的公文，要求这些学校的学生避开海关与其他海事部门，但道尹既没有说明哪些地方可以搜查，也没有规劝学生停止搜查。

一些合理的建议

　　当学生代表们找到艺文学堂代理校长时，校长表示，无论学生们或校

长本人多么厌恶日本人的行径，但 1915 年的条约在事实上是存在的，以此为由没收日本货物或阻碍对日贸易的人就是不法分子，如果有任何学生因为参加抵制活动而遇到个人麻烦，校长将不会采取行动保护他。校长进一步表示，中国目前最需要的不是改变外交关系，而是商人、学生和百姓共同努力，建设一个官员廉洁、行政公正并且国家统一的中国。如果学生们将斗争的矛头指向腐败、无能的官员身上，将会取得更好的效果。同时只要中国内部的无能与纷争继续下去，阴谋家们就可以图谋私利。

校长规定 18 岁以下的学生不得成为搜查队的成员，住校学生不得参加任何夜间会议，或参加任何进行夜间抵制活动的组织，违者将被开除。住在城里自己家中的学生可以代表其他学生进行活动，并在第二日进行报告。当天学生们选出了 6 名代表担任某些职务，且这些职务是轮换的。
（温州，4 月 21 日）

《温州纪事：学校假日旅行与抵制日本》，《北华捷报及最高法庭与领事馆杂志》，1923 年 5 月 19 日

温州纪事：学校假日旅行与抵制日本

（本报记者报道）

温州的中学最近都在放期中假。艺文学堂的 70～80 名师生举着旗帜，敲着铜鼓列队出发。旅期共计一周，前往平阳的路程将花两三天时间，这两三天在以岩石风景闻名的山中穿行。目前已过去四天，天气非常适合郊游，让人想起了遥远的童年时代的典型的英国五月天——灿烂的阳光、蔚蓝的天空点缀着雪白的云彩、凉爽的微风，阳光和煦，无数的花在漂亮的假日盛装中微笑，虽然阳光有时刺眼，但新鲜的绿色嫩叶让人们的眼睛得以放松，雨点也格外体贴，仅在夜间挥洒。

对日货的抵制运动未被忽略，并且学生们已经制订了轮班宣传的规定。但抵制运动并不针对出口日本的中国货物，三艘日本轮船本周已经在温州装载了大量木炭，它们分别是"大新丸号"、"山城丸号"（Sanchoh Maru）以及"海鸟丸号"（Chokai Maru），其中第二艘船仍在港口忙碌地装货。

本报记者最近报道，大约 80 名在福建作战的士兵到达这个港口，这些逃兵现已被转运他处。现在有报道说，大约 2000 名驻温的北方士兵将被派往南方的福建参与战斗，另外将从北方调派其他军队以替其驻防。①

部队换防

新的军队已开来温州接替现已在福建的北方军队，这些军人是浙江

---

① 指的是 1923 年，在吴佩孚指挥下，直系孙传芳与周荫人军队入闽事件。参见徐天胎《福建民国史稿》，福建人民出版社，2009，第 52～53 页。

人，没有以前的北方军人孔武坚毅。在温州的山上有不少墓碑，墓中埋的都是山东与直隶士兵，对这些北方士兵来讲，想要适应温州的气候与生活条件十分困难。

城市周围的平原现在大部分被淹没了，"水龙"正忙着把运河里的水抽到田野里，农民们正辛勤地在田里插秧。与稻田插秧同时进行的是春小麦和油菜籽的收割和脱粒，其中大部分现在已经完工。目前城里的建筑工程进度都很慢，这是由于处于春季农忙时节，工人们需要优先回乡忙农活。

海关最近查获了一批非法商品，包括老式的长矛与大刀，早年间温州的勇士们常会肩上扛着它们。这些旧武器是从上海贩到温州来当废铁卖的。（温州，5月6日）

《温州喜迎降雨：对农民和庄稼的天赐甘霖，亚细亚石油公司的新项目》，《北华捷报及最高法庭与领事馆杂志》，1923 年 6 月 9 日

温州喜迎降雨：对农民和庄稼的天赐甘霖，亚细亚石油公司的新项目

（本报记者报道）

在帝国日（Empire Day）① 这天，外国社区在温州特有的闷热天气里感受到的只有酷暑与乏力。有几天曾下过雷阵雨，降雨有时也会持续很久，但只能暂时缓解酷热。阴凉处的气温只有 80 华氏度，但由于空气永远都是黏糊糊的，人们并不会比一天当中高温时舒服多少。同时气压似乎是正常水平的两倍，有些人甚至说气压可能更高。无论如何，人们的精神似乎都因为肉体的痛苦而受到影响。

通常情况下，火灾一般发生在下半年，但最近已经发生 4 到 5 起火灾。幸好被焚房屋并不多，一星期前在海关和邮局对面的北门有 4 家鱼铺起火，鱼铺与海关仅相隔一条道而已，居住在江心屿的港务长听说后立刻返回城里，他和其他同事不仅要确保文件安全，还要防止火势蔓延。幸运的是在凌晨两三点钟，大火终于被扑灭，海关完好无损。

人们对降雨感到特别欢喜，因为春季干旱，田地缺水，无法插秧，再加上去年收成不好，使得前景堪忧。在降雨后，农民们正忙着插秧，木柴的价格上涨了 20%。这是由于现在的船夫都在田里干活，运柴船闲置下来或转为运输其他货物所致。

自上次报道以来，英美烟草公司（B. A. T.）的施开士（Cance）夫

---

① 也被称为维多利亚日，是大英帝国为了纪念维多利亚女王所设节日，日期为 5 月 24 日前的第一个星期一。

妇①已经离开了温州，他们在温州居住了 7 年，目下将移居到杭州。施开士夫妇以热情好客而闻名，许多人会想念他们熟悉的施开士先生，因为他经常在温州府的不同地方旅行。亚细亚石油公司的霍普金斯（Hopkin）、里斯（Rees）与斯奎尔斯先生已经就公司业务调研了好几日，据说亚细亚石油公司正考虑在城北瓯江支流楠溪附近建立新厂房。② 他们为了避免在路上碰上匪徒，每天必须步行大约 40 英里，以在天黑前赶到目的地。

据报道，最近发生在上海的火灾摧毁了一幢建筑，导致一家船运公司的经理对保险很感兴趣，因为火灾发生在该地投保的当天晚上。

这里的一位中国官员，他的妻子住在上海，正在上海赫德路（Hart Road）为自己和家人建房子。总面积大概 4 亩，每亩地价 4000 两白银。

撞船事故

"广济号"和"永宁号"（Yungning）在海门发生了碰撞，"永宁号"轻微受损。这导致后面的船只不得不推迟离港，前几天（5 月 27 日）③，"永宁号"停泊在东门检查螺旋桨。这艘开往厦门的小轮，过去一直都是悬挂日本旗，最近悬挂葡萄牙旗驶入温州。

最近温州一所中学的老师在给两个班级的考试中，出了"讨论抵制日货的方法""抵制日本从何处入手"的文章题目。学生们抓住了一个卖日本胶靴的小贩，这名小贩被穿上红衣服，脖子上挂着日本靴，然后被学生牵着游街。（温州，5 月 24 日）

---

① 最早是五味和老板杨直钦向上海购买英美烟草公司产品在温州销售，后来由于销路渐有起色，上海方面总公司遂派外国人来温直接设立分公司，管辖温、台、处三地，负责人即施开士。参见陈守庸《英美烟草公司在温州的经营活动》，《温州文史资料·第六辑》，浙江省新闻出版局，1990，第 251～257 页。

② 美国美孚石油公司与英国亚细亚石油公司在温州展开激烈竞争，在 1920 年美国美孚石油公司新建厂房和扩大销售渠道后，1923 年英国亚细亚石油公司为了回应挑战，也在楠溪江清水埠建立新栈房，并扩大西门油栈，派"海光轮"按月送油来温，同时新建六处经销处。在此后的英美竞争中，英国石油公司逐渐占据上风。参见陈于滨、李渭钧《美英石油公司在温州争夺市场纪实》，《温州文史资料·第六辑》，浙江省新闻出版局，1990，第 123～129 页。

③ 原文如此，应是误记。

《温州台风：趋于向西北长江流域移动》，《北华捷报及最高法庭与领事馆杂志》，1923 年 8 月 11 日

温州台风：趋于向西北长江流域移动

（本报记者报道）

周二徐家汇天文台宣布，靠近海岸线的台风不会直接对上海造成威胁。

上午 10 点半，台风有向温州移动的迹象，但由于台风不足以威胁到长江口船只，因此天文台并没有发出预警，但据报道称，长江口一整日天气状况都很糟糕。

到下午 4 点半，徐家汇天文台的气压相较于周一相同时刻的 29.72 英寸下降了十分之一英寸，昨天上午 9 点的气压是 29.69 英寸，随后气压开始显著下降。到中午时，气压降到 29.63 英寸。下午 5 点，外滩上的黄包车被吹得东倒西歪，气压计度数此时已降到 29.62 英寸，并仍在下降。

江上悲剧

周二下午 3 点后不久，由于江上突然刮起横风，并伴随不利的潮水，因此中国船只想要装运煤炭十分困难，虽然船员们设法使船停靠在公园，但突然一阵狂风从侧面刮了过来，紧接着一阵大浪打来。原本船只就装着煤，再加上海浪打到船上，船身在浪中时隐时现，人们几乎已经看不到船，只能在浪退下去时看到船尾柱。碎木料、杂物很快都被大浪冲走。船员们很容易就脱身了，然后忙着用长杆和渔网将轮船残骸捞上浮桥，上游的舢板船则忙着捞起小一点的木块当柴火用。

在此危急时刻，看热闹的人迅速聚集，只见大副大声喊着命令并拼命在打手势。围观的人都知道大副想干什么，但他的船员完全无动于衷。几分钟后，汹涌的潮水甚至已经淹没了船尾柱。但船舵和船橹最后都保住

了。经过一个小时的奋力拼搏，他们决定将船拉回岸边，以免船被进一步冲进江心后将来打捞船只的麻烦。船员们在船尾锁上重链，在船头锁上轻链，同时钩上了滑车——苦力们半裸着身子在水里干活，以便把绳索系牢。随后又从公园召来十几个或更多的苦力，慢慢将船拉回岸边，我最后一次看的时候他们已经有了很大进展，但还没有完全出水。

如果发生最坏情况，漂艇总会（Foam）的船员会把船都移往更安全的锚地。法国码头只剩下几艘舢板，事实上到晚上时，所有小船都从平时的锚地消失了。

九江地区气压极低

预警是在周三上午 9 点 30 分发布的，台风在白天继续向上海以西数百英里地区移动，到晚上时，据说港口区域已脱离危险。

但在当地水面仍出现猛烈大风，甚至在黄埔地区出现了狂风（gale）。

气压计稳定保持在 29.73 英寸。这一天，台风中心一直向西移动。星期一晚上在温州附近登陆后，它转向西北或西北偏北方向，开始向长江流域移动。早前九江传来消息，气压下降到 29.55 英寸，当地的低气压同时还伴随着强劲的东北风。

周一晚上的大风没有造成人员伤亡或财产损失。

《温州的新事业：修建儿童公园，传教士休假，诸多人事调动》，
《北华捷报及最高法庭与领事馆杂志》，1923 年 9 月 1 日

温州的新事业：修建儿童公园，传教士休假，诸多人事调动

（本报记者报道）

这个港口一直面临传教士人手不足的情况，但施德福（Stedeford）①从来不会缺席，关于他在这个港口常年尽职尽责的工作事迹可以这样形容：

> 此间男女，南来北往。
>
> 唯有此人，终止于斯。

内地会的传教士，包括司先生（Schlichter）夫妇和汤普森（Thompson）先生，以及圣道公会的谢道培夫妇都将迁往其他教区，另外内地会的其他外国职员今年将会在圣道公会的别墅里度过最炎热的数周。

夏初，海关税务司在原来别墅的后面又盖了第二座，入夏以后，税务司及其家人得以入住其中。相对于城内，别墅的选址更为便利。别墅建在 1400 英尺的山上，每天可以乘抬椅上下山处理事务，传教士也可以很容易地与他们的中国工人保持联系。内地会的白德邻（F. S. Barling）夫妇在上个月已经离港回英格兰休假，圣道公会的孙光德小姐也离开温州，转到其他地方寻找工作。

---

① 施德福约于 1910 年从爱丁堡医学院毕业，来温从事医疗事业达 40 年之久，直到 1950 年才离开温州。他是白累德医院最后一任院长，也是任职时间最长的院长。参见徐章《回忆英籍医生施德福夫妇》，载温州文史资料委员会编《温州文史资料·第十七辑》，2003，第 270 ~ 272 页。

圣道公会的山尔曼牧师，在西溪（West Brook）地区做巡回布道时目睹了一起严重的宗族械斗，敌对双方都持有武器，并且有人在争斗中死亡。其中一人被敌对宗族俘获，他的尸体已被长矛刺穿，两个青壮年用肩膀将其扛走。

本地商人和教育家对社会改革表现出极大热情，他们成立了一个名为"社会改革协会"（The Association for the Reformation of Society）的机构。董先生（Tung）担任了主席职务，并在 7 月 19 日于三港庙（San Kan Temple）发表了演讲，当天听众极多。此外温州的小学教师组成了一个互助协会，协会规定除非校长死亡或成立新小学外，新入职教师不得掌管学校事务。

7 月 26 日，温州学生举行了一次会议，一些学生在小庙（Little Temple）讲述了学生程寿（Dzang So）的悲剧。

我得到消息，温州将会开办新的公益事业——第一个儿童公园。这个公园将由受过良好教育、具有热情和公共精神的绅士负责管理。（温州，8 月 18 日）

《温州被唤醒：夏季的沉闷已经过去，台风、学生热情与妖言惑众》，《北华捷报及最高法庭与领事馆杂志》，1923 年 9 月 29 日

温州被唤醒：夏季的沉闷已经过去，台风、学生热情与妖言惑众

（本报记者报道）

在某种程度上，温州人又可以舒适和宽慰地生活、运动和呼吸了。温州居民再也不需要，或者说已经很少有人再需要，在晚上躺平后背，蜷缩双膝，缩在宽 3 英寸、长 6 英尺的木板上露天入眠了。即便如此，在大白天仍能看到那些吃苦耐劳的苦力们在一条狭窄的木板上午睡，木板一头伸向臭气熏天的运河。许多人在炎热的夏夜在街上铺床，但现在夜晚的大街已不再喧闹。因为令人神清气爽的秋风已经来了，现在晚上多半要盖毯子，鉴于此种天气，人们选择回到屋里过夜。

风灾

最近仅隔数日，就接连发生了两次台风，造成了相当大的损失。圣道艺文学堂近 400 英尺的院墙再次被吹倒，去年 9 月也发生过类似事件，这堵墙在今年年初被重建，但在今年 9 月又倒下了。在温州很有必要记住这句歇后语——"九月，留神！"①

瓯江河口外 8 到 10 英里的洞头黑牛湾附近的群岛，在去年的风灾中损失严重，据说今年遭灾更重。这导致许多人陷入贫困，物价与工价都变得很高。岛上的人很依赖从大陆进口大米、木材、建筑材料以及许多生活必需品。温州周围的平原现在成了一个大湖，某些地方深达 5 英尺，或者正如某些人说的那样，城外已经形成了一条河流。

---

① 英文的"September"和"Remember"押韵。

那些选择到瓯江对岸山上别墅消夏的外国人，以及那些远至莫干山、烟台甚至上海消夏以享受舒适环境的人现在都回来了。内地会的慕传荣（Moler）小姐①也从美国度假归来，与她同来的还有内地会的潘美贞（Banks）女士。②

青年的想法

温州的青年们再次对进入学校学习知识充满热情。艺文学堂的招生名单很快将会超过 200 人，尽管采用了严格的录取标准，但目前已有 194 名学生入学，另外的学生则尚未入学。其中有 122 人选择住校，教会为此额外购买了 20 张床。每天早晨，学堂小教堂里都挤满了 15 到 25 岁的目光炯炯的年轻人，这真是一幅壮观的景象。代理校长每天早上都借此机会亲自在聚会上发言，并从基督教的立场宣讲应如何处理当前的问题，如"对日本的抵制及其错误""抵制中止""日本地震及其国内乱象""国际关系""错误的倡导"等等。

对付造谣者最好的办法

有一名四川人在温州妖言惑众，并印刷和散播谣言册子，据报道此人现在已被当局监禁。

最近温州发生大火，烧毁了南门主要街道两侧的 40 多家店铺，幸亏有城墙阻止火势蔓延到南郊。

我们的最后一条消息是，英美烟草公司的沃尔夫（Wolff）先生将离开我们前往上海，随后回国。我们中的一些人会怀念他曾带来的快乐时光，我们希望他能万事如意。（温州，9 月 22 日）

---

① 内地会女传教士，1910 年驻平阳传教。参见黄光域编《基督教传行纪念（1807—1949）》，广西师范大学出版社，2017，第 291 页。

② 内地会传教士，全名为 A. G. Bank，1905 年在安徽传教。参见黄光域编《基督教传行纪念（1807—1949）》，广西师范大学出版社，2017，第 236 页。

《浙江军队调动：上周军舰开到温州，未发生战斗》，《北华捷报及最高法庭与领事馆杂志》，1924 年 1 月 19 日

浙江军队调动：上周军舰开到温州，未发生战斗

（本报记者报道）

在温州的历史上，从来没有一周之内聚集过这么多轮船，数十年来也从未聚集过这么多军队。

昨天有 11 艘轮船停靠在港口，其中包括法国炮艇"爱格尔号"（Algola）和 4 艘日本大型轮船。这些日本轮船买下了所有能买到的木炭，因此木炭价格飙升，据说因此导致其中一艘日本船空船离开港口。

上周，一艘中国兵舰第二次访问了这个港口，并从杭州带来了另一队士兵。据报道，至少有 5000 名士兵已经抵达温州，数百艘江船已经投入使用，将士兵和物资运送到上游 90 英里的衢州府（Chichowfu），预计那里不久就会发生战斗。然而到目前为止，尽管有很多传言，但没有确切的消息表明已经爆发任何实际战斗。

温州有传言说，如果卢永祥将军自愿离开浙江，就不会爆发战争。这种说法与最近《北华捷报》的报道不同。另外有人说根本不会爆发战争，现在已经宣布和平。但南方的孙将军派遣了大概 1 万人从福建出兵，并拒绝撤退，当地居民①已经向孙将军的军队奉献了 5 万银圆。

城市大火导致 1500 人无家可归

隆冬时节，天燥多风，因此时常发生火灾。两周前，我在温州上游 40

---

① 指的是衢州、严州、金华等处商业团体。刘绍宽在日记中记述"地方招待军事多所需费"。参见温州市图书馆编《刘绍宽日记·第二册》，方浦仁、陈盛奖整理，中华书局，2018，第 763 页。

英里的小城青田，看到了一个月前火灾焚后的大片废墟，这场大火导致大约 500 户人无家可归。

这个美丽的小城，一侧有快速奔流的小河，群山耸立，山涧清澈，一系列狭长湖泊点缀其间。虽然山峦使得当地环境优美，但也经常导致天灾，一旦进入汛期，山中积聚的洪水就会喷涌而出，淹没整个城市。在 1912 年的大洪水中，虽然青田坚固和高耸的城墙被冲毁，但最后仍有 20 栋建筑不倒，许多百姓也得以幸存，其中一个 15 岁的女孩抱着杂物被洪水冲到 50 英里外大海中的一个岛上，这个岛离海岸也有数英里。1922 年的风灾中，青田又一次严重受灾。我在青田城墙边停船下锚时，下锚点的水深已经两倍于停泊大西洋客轮的要求。我看到人们撑着木筏在浅滩上航行，不断发生的洪水把无数的石头冲下山并填满河床，这座城市每年都会被数英尺深的水淹没。

在一个月前，温州南部的瑞安也发生了大火，据报道至少有 1000 户居民遭受严重损失。据说使用外国火油与油灯是导致火灾的主因。[1]

价值 1.2 万银圆的鸦片被销毁

数天前政府公开销毁价值 1.2 万银圆的鸦片，这些鸦片是最近收缴的。将来如有鸦片收缴，还会继续销毁。（温州，1 月 13 日）

---

[1] 许多人在火灾发生后用水扑灭火油油灯引起的大火是导致大火灾的主要原因，类似的火灾事件在许多城市发生过。

《宁波轮船失事：温州出发之平阳轮在海门触礁》，《北华捷报及最高法庭与领事馆杂志》，1924年3月22日

宁波轮船失事：温州出发之平阳轮在海门触礁

（本报记者报道）

自上次发送电报以后，这里最新的消息是有一艘中国轮船失事，这艘船一直来往于甬温之间，每周都有定期航班，且已行之数年。

"平阳号"据说是由一艘旧炮舰改造而成，是温甬航线三艘轮船中乘坐最舒适的一艘。大约一个月前，该轮像往常一样在星期五从温州出发，经由海门、舟山前往宁波。数日后，温州收到了该轮在海门附近失踪的电报。有消息称船上200人全部丧生，但也有消息称没有人丧生，但船只遭到了海盗洗劫。

一位中国青年告诉我，事故发生时，他的兄弟也在乘客中，目前已经回家。根据他的说法，船只在驶出海门4至5个小时后，因为遭遇大雾而撞上礁石，2小时后船只不幸沉没，所有货物与行李都沉入海底，所幸有许多小船前来救援，因此没有乘客和船员伤亡。这是宁波最近发生的第二起海难事故。

招商局温甬航线的"广济号"在过年之前就已经停班，现在传言说有一家公司将会租用该轮重开航线。但是在周五，并没有看到这艘船入港，据说这条航线去年亏损了大概2万银圆。如果宁波公司愿意补偿这笔亏损，那么这条航线就会继续开下去，永川公司和永宁公司都同意，但是宝华公司（Pao Hua Co.）拒绝了。还有传言说，招商局的竞争对手将开通一条沪温航线，但目前为止还没有看到轮船出现。

温州传教士的先行者

在过去的6个星期里一直停在上海检修的"飞鲸号"现已重新开航，

船上的乘客包括谢道培夫妇及其女儿，他们将经由加拿大返回英国。在海关税务司及其夫人的盛情邀请下，一大批外国居民于星期二晚上在其家中聚会，以正式向谢牧师道别。

山尔曼牧师将接替谢道培牧师担任温州圣道公会主席职务，除了监督1922年9月被台风摧毁的教堂重建工程外，他还要负责管理近170座教堂。

谢牧师是在27年前第一次抵达温州，谢夫人是在23年前第一次抵达温州。谢道培牧师目睹了圣道公会的教堂从90座发展到270座，以及教会医院与中学的兴建，这所中学在蔡博敏的带领下已经有242名学生。蔡博敏作为一名教育家的名声远超温州及附近地区，可以说在全中国都家喻户晓。25年前中学还处于起步阶段时，谢道培在家里办了一个英文学习班，其中有一个勤奋聪明的中国小男孩，他就是现在北京的李博士（Dr. Timothy Lear）①。

抚今追昔二十七载

温州今天的城区样貌与27年前相比已大不相同，城区范围明显扩大，并且多了许多洋房或半洋房风格建筑，这些建筑多为中国人所有。另外增加了许多销售洋货的店铺，这些店铺销售外国罐头、面粉、衣帽、鞋子、灯具、工具、钟表等，以及许多其他在27年前被中国人认为是被"诅咒"的洋货。狭窄的街道上奔行着数百辆黄包车，电灯使得中国学生们在晚上能更舒适地学习，电话线正在向四面八方伸展。我们目前有两条电报线与外面的世界连通。一位温州老居民曾向我描述刚到温州时所面临的困境："一入温州，如井底之蛙"，现在这种情况终于一去不复返。洋伞甚至洋手杖在温州也很畅销，卖遮阳棚同样是门好生意。一位每年销售3万顶遮阳棚的商人在昨天告诉我，温州大概每年要向美国出口30万顶遮阳棚。

最大的变化来自我所居住的街道，这种变化在25年前几乎是不可能，

---

① 从时间和姓氏上判断，可能是李宝昌。之所以取名Timothy Lear，可能是为了向曾经参加过艺文学堂开学典礼的李提摩太（Timothy Richard）致敬。参见郭绍震《解放前温州城区的几所教会学校》，《鹿城文史资料·第十七辑》，温州鹿城文史资料委员会，2004，第199~200页。

但现在已迅速发生。当人们知道这种可怕的梦魇、致命的诅咒有多么难以摆脱，又看到这种变化时，人们可以感觉到中国迟早可以，或许能够很快摆脱束缚她的障碍，然后自由地、坚强地、善良地、高贵地崛起，在通往注定要达到的世界高度的征程中，获得一个位置，成为自由、互助和正义的领袖。（温州，3月9日）

《艺文学堂遭窃：屡次得手后窃贼已被捕》，《北华捷报及最高法庭与领事馆杂志》，1924 年 5 月 17 日

艺文学堂遭窃：屡次得手后窃贼已被捕
（本报记者报道）

　　艺文学堂最近 6 个月内发生了一系列盗窃案，涉案金额近 500 银圆，数天前这名窃贼终于被逮捕。小偷频频得手的有利条件是他曾在学堂上过几个月学，在 4 年前被开除，此后又接连被两所学校开除，他对艺文学堂内部情况很熟悉。他作案的时间都选在下午的上课时间，这个时间点学生都不在宿舍。他在潜入学生房间后，会将偷来的衣服穿在里面，然后在外面罩上自己的外套，随后带着弄到的钱迅速逃走。

　　小偷被抓到的过程也极具戏剧性，一位正在搜寻丢失物品的老师提着灯笼走进大厅，小偷在听到动静后便躲到窗户外面，并把窗户给拉了下来。窗外其实非常危险，窗台仅宽数英寸，离地面则起码 20 英尺。尴尬的是，在灯光的映照下，窗外人影在大厅内看得一清二楚，小偷立刻无所遁形。共有 30 名学生遭窃，另外还有 200 名学生虽然没有遭窃，但也义愤填膺地加入抓捕小偷的行动中，小偷逃跑的机会极为渺茫。伴随而来的嘈杂声可能会使不知情者以为一群土匪正在攻城。学生们在寻找小偷可能的同伙的过程中玩得很开心，他们甚至提着灯笼到屋顶上去找。小偷最后全部招供，小偷的父亲境况也不太好，最终学生们同意从小偷父亲那获取一半的赔偿，小偷则在被警局关押三天后释放。

温州领事馆关闭

英国领事翰垒德（Handley Derry）① 在瓯海关税务司威立师（C. W. S. Williams）先生的邀请下做客温州。温州的领事馆即将要移交给瓯海关，海关已经租用这栋大楼好些年了。事实上自1900年起，英国就取消了驻温州领事。但许多人仍牢记着当年的惊险时刻，那一年人们被迫到江心屿上的英国领事馆避难，至今大家仍心存感激。②

电厂

本周传来温州将开设新电厂的消息，成千上万人为此欢欣鼓舞。1912年协利电灯公司（Andersen，Meyer & Co.）在温州开办了第一家电厂，虽然用户不多，但照明质量一直不错。然而经营这家电厂的中国公司多年来不断增加电灯，导致灯光不断变暗，以至于到了不可收拾的境地。新建电厂发电量达到4000千瓦，将足以满足未来数年温州的用电需求。电厂设备由德国制造，总计花费3万银圆。（温州，5月5日）

---

① 其父在印度公共部门任职，其本人在1901年20岁来华进入外交界，1924年担任驻宁波领事职务。参见 "From Day to Day," *The North - China News*，1924 - 4 - 1，No. 10；中国人民政治协商会议云南省昆明市委员会编《昆明文史资料集萃·第七卷》，云南科技出版社，2009，第5279页。

② 指的是1900年庚子事变外国人到江心屿避难事件。

《皇家"风铃草号"驶抵温州：1913 年以来第一艘抵达温州的英国军舰，保护盐税》，《北华捷报及最高法庭与领事馆杂志》，1924 年 7 月 5 日

皇家"风铃草号"驶抵温州：1913 年以来第一艘抵达温州的英国军舰，保护盐税

（本报记者报道）

上周，一艘英国炮艇在温州港口停泊了三天，这是自 1913 年以来的首次。我们之前好几次的期待都落空后，英国皇家海军"风铃草号"（H. M. S. Bluebell）终于在上周四抵达江面，并在城市对面下锚。江边的城墙上很快就有成群的中国人围观这不寻常的景象。炮舰停泊期间，天气一直都不好，有一天的降雨量超过 2 英寸，尽管如此，港口里还是有许多外国人接受舰长的邀请参观战舰。城里为船员们安排了一场足球比赛，尽管场地状况并不好，但比赛还是很精彩。

炮舰来此是与盐税有关。① 福建省已经截留了该省盐税，盐务局的两艘船有被南方革命党吞并的危险，因此"风铃草号"［舰长是史密斯维克（Smithwick）］奉命将船护送到安全区域。也许是由于温州邻近南

---

① 中国近代盐税已在历次借款中被抵押给外国，其中英国牵涉最深，主要涉及两笔借款，一笔是 1912 年的 500 万英镑克利斯浦借款，一笔是 1913 年 2500 万英镑的五国善后大借款，年利息都是五厘。1924 年中国每年盐税收入 9000 万英镑左右，但由于各省截留，中央每月仅能收到 300 万英镑左右。因为各省截留盐税的做法直接威胁到列强利益，英国因此派遣炮舰护盐。此外，也有向南方孙中山截留盐税、关税示威的意思。参见《中国盐务概况》，《银行月刊》1924 年第 12 期，第 1 ~ 3 页；布鲁奈尔《英帝国在华利益之基石：近代中国海关（1854—1949）》，中国海关出版社，2012，第 67 ~ 97 页。

方数省的缘故，杭州盐务总署已在温州设立分署，并由一名外国人莱斯（Reiss）负责，他目前正在走访边远县城，此项任命是临时任命或是实质任命还有待观察。（温州，6 月 22 日）

《浙江自治：宪法，女人没有选举权，男人凭借教育和金钱选举》，
《北华捷报及最高法庭与领事馆杂志》，1924 年 7 月 12 日

浙江自治：宪法，女人没有选举权，男人凭借教育和金钱选举

（本报记者报道）

《浙江自治宪法草案》① 在温州引起了商人和学生的极大兴趣，省长在温州任命了 3 人参加为期 5 个月的临时审查委员会。此外每县商会可以选举 2 名代表参加自治法会议，温州 6 县共拥有 12 名代表，永嘉商会会长唐伯寅已经当选。各县教育会与县农会也依样办理，许德民（Hsu Te - ming）和蔡经贤（Tsai Kuan - fu）也已当选，此二人曾担任过省议会咨议的职务。

新宪法在概念上似乎是完全民主的——所有官员，从省长到地方官员，都将由人民选出。

但女性不能享有选举权，这让很多女学生颇感失望。新宪法对于选举权资格的规定与之前的政体很类似——部分取决于一个人的受教育程度，部分取决于他的经济状况。

恶劣的学生

浙江第十中学的校长可耻地辞职了，居住在北京的温州籍学生不断给北京与上海的中文报纸投稿，指责该校长不称职。他们指责这名校长一身

---

① 浙江省自治运动中搞的所谓"九九宪法""三色宪法"实际都是议而未行，原因在于卢永祥只是想借自治运动抵抗直系压迫，并非真心想施行宪政。参见李剑农《中国近百年政治史》，上海人民出版社，2014，第 436 页。

都是毛病，唯一该做的就是辞职。这些学生对省教育厅形成了一定影响力，校长最后被迫辞职。① （温州，6 月 30 日）

---

① 1924 年温州中学校长邵聪被迫辞职，金嵘轩继任。据张棡记述，除了学生对邵聪不满外，邵是"被人挤走"，温州文人群体似乎相当轻视邵聪，如张棡就形容邵聪是"不学无术"。参见温州市图书馆编《张棡日记·第六册》，张钧孙点校，中华书局，2019，第 2794 ~ 2795 页。

《温州贸易受阻：海关为迫切的改造与资金问题提供建议》，《北华捷报及最高法庭与领事馆杂志》，1924 年 8 月 9 日

温州贸易受阻：海关为迫切的改造与资金问题提供建议

（本报记者报道）

　　海关所在北门的路况糟糕且不体面，无法与日益增长的温州贸易状况相匹配，从北门入城需要转五个弯，另外江边的不卫生状况也值得注意。北门入口，实际包括鱼市在内，有时会挤满货物，导致行人很难从城里抵达邮局、海关或客轮码头。

　　海关当局已向当地官员提出改造建议：（1）对北门码头进行改造；（2）码头与城内建一条宽阔的直道；（3）建设堤坝以改善河滨地区环境。永嘉县议会（District Council）对这些建议进行了讨论，并表现出相当大的兴趣。

　　主要的问题是如何筹集必要的资金，海关当局提出了若干建议，其中一条主要办法是对进出口货物税收以及手续费加征 5%。县议会专门成立了一个特别委员会，对此事进行审查和报告，该委员会对县议会做出如下建议。

　　（1）收用私有房产、码头建设和滨江改造工作应由执行委员会（Executive Committee）承担。执行委员会应提出建议，并须提交县议会批准。执行委员会应当与海关税务司就海关仓库和滨江岸堤建设事宜进行合作。

　　（2）在收用私人房产时，执行人员须根据《收用土地章程》估计物业的价值。

　　（3）应同时准备数份竞争性的建筑工程合同概算，提交县议会审议。

　　（4）一旦加征关税，相关工作应随之启动。

　　（5）应由海关代征 5% 的关税，以支付工资与相关费用。

（6）仅对进口货物收取费用。所有出口货物应予豁免。

（7）所筹集的资金不得用于城市改造以外的任何其他目的。

当海关在 1923 年报告中的提议被提上日程后，贸易受到了一定程度的影响。按照计划，五年之内起码可以筹集到 5 万海关两的资金，温州可以用这笔钱实施伟大的改造工程，当然，钱一定得花在城市改造上。（温州，8 月 2 日）

《浙南战争：面对闽军攻打，无意抵抗》，《北华捷报及最高法庭与领事馆杂志》，1924 年 9 月 27 日

浙南战争：面对闽军攻打，无意抵抗

（本报记者报道）

在孙传芳将军的带领下，[①] 福建军队占领了浙江边境上的一个战略据点。[②] 人们原本希望浙军能在此设立第一道防线，但闽军占据了先机。温州地区的浙军已设立三道防线。第一道防线在平阳县南的河岸，第二道防线在瑞安城南的飞云江，第三道防线设在温州的主运河上，距温州城约 33 里。三条防线上的士兵人数都很少，可能总共不超过 1500 人，而对方的部队也不会更多，到目前为止还没有爆发战斗。

闽军主力与赣军合力向西北方向进攻，分别从三处越过浙江边界，一路从泰顺向兴宁进发，一路从浦城向龙泉进发，一路沿江西边界向衢州进发。无论闽军的真正目标是哪里，闽军占领龙泉后即可进攻东北部的处州，然后进攻温州，或是折向北部与赣军合力，闽军会如何选择目前还不得而知，但一般认为闽军会选择第一条方案。

除了少量军队外，温州缺乏守城部队。如果闽军突破了三道防线，当地官员决定将欢迎新军阀入城。（9 月 18 日）

战争供款

10 天前温州已经向浙军供款 1.5 万银圆。昨天浙军又向政府官员提出

---

① 1924 年 3 月，孙传芳与周荫人在解决掉王永泉后彻底控制福建，当年 5 月直系任命孙传芳为闽粤边防督办，孙传芳假意宣称要协助陈炯明攻取广州，实则暗地里联系江苏齐燮元，实施所谓"四省攻浙"计划。卢永祥与齐燮元的江浙战争爆发后，不仅导致闽军入浙，也引发了广东孙中山与奉系向直系宣战。参见徐天胎《福建民国史稿》，福建人民出版社，2009，第 58 ~ 59 页。

② 应指闽浙之间的必经之路浦城，浦城当面正对浙军仙霞岭的炮兵阵地。

了大概 3 万银圆的要求。温州方面决定先行提供 1.5 万银圆，待一个月后再提供剩下的一半。

最新的消息是，闽军已经占领龙泉，但这条消息还需要进一步地确认。还有消息称赣军已经占领处州府，此消息同样需要进一步确认。浙军已经退往金华。

浙南地区对卢永祥颇生怨言，卢本非浙江人，但因为其一己之私而导致浙江陷入战火。守卫浙南的都是浙江省军，没有一支国军被派来抵抗闽军。温州官民认为如果加入直系的话则可以免于战火摧残。浙南与直系连成一气，似乎已为期不远。（9 月 19 日）

卢永祥已被驱逐，人民欢欣鼓舞

昨日温州人还惶惶不可终日，现在已欢欣鼓舞。人们已不再考虑避难和藏匿财物的事情，市面已恢复正常。根据电报消息，昨天下午 3 点半左右在杭州发生了政变，省长已经换人，卢永祥已经在内战中下野。至于卢永祥接下来是带着残军加入张作霖，或是与孙中山合力，抑或到某个无人知晓的地方隐退，对温州人来讲没有人会关心。（9 月 20 日）

《外埠消息：温州高兴得太早，闽军已攻入》，《北华捷报及最高法庭与领事馆杂志》，1924 年 10 月 11 日

外埠消息：温州高兴得太早，闽军已攻入

（本报记者报道）

闽军被命令向"独立的"台州、绍兴
和宁波进发　当地正强征劳役

温州人高兴得太早了，虽然浙军和闽军都收到退兵命令的消息是真的，但温州人很快就发现事情没那么简单。温州的司令①说没有接到上级命令，因此仍要坚持抵抗闽军。各种各样的谣言又在城市里传开了，更多的人开始出走，主要是妇女和儿童。据估计，整整 7/10 的人已经逃离。城市一片冷清，犹如死城。商店大多关门了，街上人很少。

22 日，司令发布了一个很长的公告。在公告中，他表示自己只是守土，绝非奸诈之徒。14 日至 15 日，他们在龙泉等地进行了激烈的战斗，他们的失败是由于各县人民的背叛，将军情通报给敌人。司令接着又提到了福建人的残忍和野蛮，以及他们残杀伤员的行为。（注意：所有媒体报道都高度赞扬了闽军对人民秋毫无犯。）

龙泉已被抢三日，吴凤炎（Wu Fung - yen）② 这个无耻之徒，已被任命为县知事。当地百姓每月要付给闽军 2 万银圆，这是对欢迎闽

---

① 浙军司令郝国玺，后被吕文起劝说回浙，免致地方糜烂。参见温州市图书馆编《刘绍宽日记·第二册》，方浦仁、陈盛奖整理，中华书局，2018，第 766 页。

② 龙泉被占领后，原知事彭周鼎已逃跑，代理知事为蔡岭，并非姓吴。龙泉当时社会秩序混乱，全靠一众乡绅维持地方秩序，这里可能指的是龙泉农会正会长吴仰贤。参见有为、斐然、太一、振才《军阀孙传芳军队践踏龙泉》，载龙泉政协编《龙泉文史资料·第六辑》，1987，第 123 ~ 125 页。

军之人的警告。我确实无能，且应受责备，但我必将为此次失败复仇。诸君也应当清楚知道孙传芳军队的残暴。

停战令

这份有趣的文告公布不久，郝司令（Ha Sz Ling）就接到停战的命令。但停战执行起来有一定困难，因为浙军每退一里，闽军就前进一里，使得浙军好像是战败一样。浙军士兵希望进行抵抗，却发现大势已去。浙军的机关枪无法使用，因为枪械缺少零部件。同时他们也害怕使用大炮，因为大炮在处州炸过膛，开炮的危险比面对敌人的危险还要大。郝司令正在征用所有能征集到的船只以便运走军队。目前已经驶离三艘轮船，分别开往海门、宁波和上海。浙军很可能在明天（9月30日）就会全部撤离城市，闽军将随之入城。平阳在两天前已被占领，瑞安今天也已被占领，从瑞安到平阳之间70里的道路在过去两天同样已经被闽军控制。

法国与日本炮舰

一艘法国炮艇"克劳娜号"（Craonne）于24日抵达温州，它的出现大大减轻了人们的恐惧。一艘日本炮艇也预计今天到达。"克劳娜号"的船长派了一支护卫队以保护法国人在城里的财产，并表示如果有必要，他将尽一切努力保护其他外国财产。

毫无疑问，一段时间以来这里的人们一直处于恐慌的边缘。他们害怕三件事：第一，浙军在撤退前会提出金钱要求，如果得不到满足，他们可能会进行公开掠夺；第二，闽军以胜利者的身份进城，按照旧时传统，他们将享有三天的"自由"特权，然后才会被军官收束纪律；第三，在浙军离开和闽军入城的这段空窗期，许多不法分子将会出来闹事。其中一个特别令人畏惧的黑帮团体叫青洪帮（Ching Ong Poa）①。根据报道，当地一名

---

① 温州青洪帮并没有严格组织，团体极为散漫，不过是每个师傅都有些徒弟而已。徒弟多为农民，因为受到压迫，为了免遭人欺负才加入帮派。徒弟拜师傅，须向师傅纳彩一圆，师傅需要用钱还会向徒弟要钱。参见《关于永嘉县的社会调查及农民协会组织情形》，载中央档案馆等编《上海革命历史文件汇集：杭州、绍兴、嘉兴、温州地区（1925—1927）》，上海群众印刷厂，1988，第263~264页。

铁匠卖出了 2000 多把匕首，乔装的警察当场仅发现了 40 把匕首，随后铁匠被捕，匕首也全部被没收。随后县知事发布命令通知所有铁匠，如果有人敢私自打造兵器，一律枪决。（9 月 27 日）

闽军到来

至 27 日晚，浙军所有部队，除去一些因为丢失武器被解散的部队以及逃兵外，大部分已转移至浙北港口。浙军征用了温州港口里所有轮船，随后静悄悄地离开了。温州于是开始为迎接闽军做准备，① 驻扎军队的兵营和庙宇全都插满了旗帜和灯笼。还为军官们准备了 24 桌宴席，并宰杀了大量的猪供士兵们食用。到昨天中午，闽军或乘船或步行，陆续抵达温州城。他们中的大多数似乎衣衫褴褛，疲倦困苦，一点也不像得胜之师。他们到达以后，这座城市又恢复了原来的面貌，店铺重新开张，在教堂和红十字会中心寻求庇护的人陆续回家。人们再次出现在街上，城市开始恢复欣欣向荣的景象。（9 月 20 日）

恐慌与报社再次停刊

英国皇家海军"荷里霍克号"（H. M. S. Hollyhock）昨天从汕头驶来温州。舰长皮斯（Peace）与瓯海关监督一同拜访了新的司令②，新司令向两人保证会尽一切努力保障外国人的生命财产，同时也不需要惊慌，城市正在恢复正常。然而事情还没有结束，一切远未恢复正常。有消息称，台州、宁波和绍兴已经宣布独立于杭州省政权，闽军因此要继续向台州进军。男人们被迫为军队充当役夫，街上的黄包车夫和轿夫已经完全消失。他们要么被军队强行带走，要么害怕地找地方躲藏起来。现在穿长袍也不能保证安全，军队拉夫时会把受害人的长袍下摆剪掉，这样就可以名正言顺地凑人数。毫无疑问，闽军许多士兵吸食鸦片，鸦片在福建更便宜，所以这些闽军士兵在温州很难搞到足够的毒品。因此只要支付一笔烟钱，穿

---

① 据《符璋日记》记载，浙军郝司令离去时，温州送 2 万元。闽军入城时，城上悬白旗，书"欢迎胜军"四字，供张费用 1 万元。参见符璋《符璋日记·下》，中华书局，2018，第 916 页。

② 指孙传芳的部属彭德铨，报纸一般称其为彭司令。

长袍的人就可以在街上自由通行。当天晚些时候，司令发布了一份公告，称报行工作没有得到其批准，所有报社应立即停刊。同时，温州地方当局已经向军队保证如有需要将会提供 500 名役夫。此外，闽军向台州进军的命令已被延后。（9 月 30 日）

《宁兴号在温州被劫：8万银锭与货物遭海盗劫去》，《北华捷报及最高法庭与领事馆杂志》，1924年10月11日

宁兴号在温州被劫：8万银锭与货物遭海盗劫去

（本报记者报道）

中国沿海相当长一段时间以来没有出现大规模海盗，但这并不意味着海盗已被肃清。周二，上海接到了一艘船只遭海盗袭击的消息，这次袭击与以往历次的海盗行动的结果一样，同样伴随着流血与死亡。

最新的受害者是三北公司（San Peh S. N. Co）的"宁兴号"（Ningshin），这艘船在上海很有名，经常往来于上海和福州以及其他沿海地区。

"宁兴号"在托格森（Torgersen）船长的指挥下，于星期四离开上海驶往福州，并载有大量旅客、货物和马蹄银。周五，当船驶近温州时，34名乔装的海盗突然发难控制了船，大部分船员以及乘客被俘虏，外国船长和大副也被控制住。

海盗完全控制船后，将船开到了大鹏湾，此地离香港不远，且为海盗所控制。大概有30箱马蹄银、邮件、大量布匹以及从绝望的乘客身上搜刮的钱财被劫去，随后海盗安全地将战利品带上了岸，并放"宁兴号"前往厦门。据报道，"宁兴号"在星期二抵达了厦门，预计将在周三抵达福州，如果不出意外，将在一两天内回到上海。

舵手被杀

目前我们还没有拿到一手资料，但毫无疑问，当海盗发动第一波袭击时，船员们进行了一定程度的抵抗，在抵抗行动中，一名中国舵手被杀，另有一名中国水手受伤，海盗通常会全副武装。

目前上海方面对海盗劫掠货物的总价值还无法给出准确估计。据了

解，仅银锭一项损失就高达 8 万银圆，幸好这笔钱已经投保。根据我个人收到的一份电报显示，海盗的赃物总值超过 15 万银圆。

目前有传言说"宁兴号"的一些船员与海盗勾结，但在该船返回上海之前，这些谣言不可能得到证实。

"宁兴号"是一艘典型的中国沿海船舶，吨位约为 2000 吨。它是专门为抵御中国沿海的恶劣天气而建造的，这艘船最初属于省港澳公司，6 年前三北公司为了满足上海与福州之间航线需要，买下此船并对其进行了改造。

《浙江禁烟运动：声势浩大的游行，是否厉行检查仍未可知》，《北华捷报及最高法庭与领事馆杂志》，1924 年 12 月 20 日

浙江禁烟运动：声势浩大的游行，是否厉行检查仍未可知

（本报记者报道）

一场伟大的反鸦片运动在温州已经进行了一段时间，自闽军到来后，吸鸦片的人越来越多。许多有责任心的人，无论是外国人还是当地人，都感到应该做些什么来遏制这种日益增长的邪恶。所有有志于此的人都被邀请到城西圣道公会教堂开会，以讨论如何解决鸦片问题。这次会议也标志着中华国民拒毒会温州分会（local branch of the Anti – Opium Society）① 的正式成立。目前该会已经召开数次会议，并制定了大量章程，其中最主要的目标是，禁止种植鸦片，禁止所有鸦片的进出口贸易，禁止吸食鸦片。

相关职责

1. 彻底调查所有与鸦片有关的情况。
2. 以演说、报章、公告、小册子等方式进行宣传。
3. 对地方当局施加一切可能的影响，禁止种植和吸食鸦片。
4. 与上海拒毒会总会进行合作。

协会成员誓词

协会成员承诺：

1. 不得以任何方式参与鸦片的种植、销售、出口、进口、制造或吸食

---

① 1924 年，由于日内瓦国际禁烟大会即将召开，而国内军阀混战，政府无暇顾及，故中华医学会、上海总商会等 40 个团体在当年 8 月 15 日成立了民间组织中华国民拒毒会。参见中华国民拒毒会编《民国十九年度拒毒运动指南》，1929，第 141 页。

活动。

2. 尽其所能说服他人断绝毒品。

3. 协助其他地区的反鸦片团体。

4. 协助相关情况的调查，并向本会报告。

资金

资金由职员和成员自愿提供。

12月7日星期日，拒毒会组织了一场规模庞大的游行。据估计，有超过3000人参加。人们举着数百面印有口号的小旗，临街散发传单，同时还有鼓手、笛子手以及喇叭手随队奏乐。无论从声势看，还是从组织看，这次游行都获得了巨大成功。

虽然人们发表了许多演说，写了许多字，用了许多纸，走了许多英里路，喝了许多茶，但人们又对最后的实际效果是否能与大家所耗费的时间与精力相称感到怀疑。（浙江，温州，12月11日）

《浙江不再种植罂粟：温州传来令人鼓舞的报告，贸易增长，土匪减少》，《北华捷报及最高法庭与领事馆杂志》，1925年3月28日

浙江不再种植罂粟：温州传来令人鼓舞的报告，贸易增长，土匪减少

（本报记者报道）

1915年之前，温州是一个大规模种植鸦片的地区。每年的这个时节，都可以在温州各县看到罂粟花。

但目前值得浓墨重彩指出的是，无论你是走水路，还是经过平原和山谷，抑或是前往浙江的荒僻之地，都再也无法发现鸦片种植的迹象。10年以来，温州一直遵守鸦片禁令，没有任何迹象表明农民会恢复鸦片种植。

现在农民种植的小麦的数量越来越多，今年春季作物丰收有望。

但在温州出现了鸦片走私猖獗的情况，福建被认为是走私鸦片的主要供给地。必须指出的事实是，有许多人在这种贩运中工作，而且有大量的人对毒品上瘾。温州市拒毒会已经证明了它不仅仅是个空名，事实上它还得到了所有官绅的支持。

在过去的两个月中，温州城内的每个衙门都任命了新官员。虽然这些任命都是代理，却具有重大意义。人们因为和平时期的到来而更具有发展的信心，商业已经显示出日益繁荣的迹象。最近江河区域没有出现海盗，山区强盗也已消失。

我们的港口仍居于贸易上的次要地位，实事求是地讲，温州港口发展得很慢。去年海关的贸易报告显示税收在增长，但我们正处于和平时期，贸易增长是理所应当的事情。

为了方便行政管理，盐务当局决定将台州与温州划分为独立的盐区。迄今为止，浙江省仅在杭州设立了一个行政中心，我的理解是温州将被设为另一个行政中心。

事隔 10 年之后，浙江基督教联合会（Chêkiang Federation Council）在温州召开了年会。目前已经准备在 4 月 24 日召开委员会会议，预计在 27 日闭会。（温州，3 月 20 日）

《温州受欢迎的官员：代理海关税务司已改任宁波》，《北华捷报及
最高法庭与领事馆杂志》，1925 年 4 月 25 日

温州受欢迎的官员：代理海关税务司已改任宁波

（本报记者报道）

　　威立师先生以海关税务司①的身份在温州待了三年，今天他将前往宁
波，以担任宁波海关首领。

　　在人员流动频繁的地方，一位官员能得到社会各阶层真诚地敬重，这
不是一件容易事。中外居民的遗憾之情溢于言表，很少有人见过类似的真
诚的告别场景。在过去的三年中，这个港口的贸易取得了稳步的增长，能
够遇到威立师这样的好官员真是我们的好运气。金陵关的裴纳玑（Bernad-
sky）将被任命为瓯海署税务司，预计将于本月上任。

　　其他的人事变动还包括卡米塞德（Camiade）请假返乡，另外卡瑟尔
（Coxall）被调到了岳州。（温州，4 月 14 日）

---

①　"Commissioner of Custom"是海关专有名词，翻译为"税务司"，为一地海关最
　　高长官。

《浙江教会工作：浙江基督教联合会在温州举办会议》，《北华捷报及最高法庭与领事馆杂志》，1925 年 5 月 16 日

浙江教会工作：浙江基督教联合会在温州举办会议

（本报记者报道）

需要指出的是，基督教联合会可能并不像 20 年前的基督教传行运动那样成功，但这并不意味着基督教联合会在宣教活动中毫无作用。

科克伦（Cochrane）博士的倡议已经取得许多成果，特别是 1907 年的上海会议以来。多年来各教会之间的友好合作已经成为一个明显的趋势，即效率更高、不进行重复工作，教会活动正在稳步扩展。

浙江省一直是基督教联合运动的忠实支持者，每年都会有代表聚集在各个城市举行会议。

11 年前，温州曾召开过基督教联合会议会，今年 4 月 24 日，这个古老的城市再次成为会场。25 名代表出席了会议，他们分别代表了以下团体：英国圣公会（C. M. S.）、北方长老会（Presbyterian North）、北方浸信会（Baptist North）、伦敦传教会（London Mission）、内地会和圣道公会。

三场紧张的会议

温州地方教会热情好客，接待了各地教会成员。4 月 23 日晚，在圣道公会教堂举办了盛大的欢迎会，来宾们都感到很自在。从第二天上午开始（星期五和星期六），会议将每天处理三项紧要事务，并于 4 月 27 日（星期一）召开闭幕会议。即将退休的主席倪良平（Nyi Liang－ping，英国圣公会）牧师做了鼓舞人心的讲话，随后选举了新一届主席团成员：圣道公会的海和德牧师担任主席，北方长老会的年希时（Nia Ts－shi）担任副主席，北方长老会的华人尹济生（Yin Ji－shung）担任秘书，圣道公会英籍柯

义培（A. A. Conibear）牧师担任秘书，北方浸信会的包齐清（Bau Tsih – chin）牧师担任司库。

司库的报告显示，联合会的财务状况良好。会议修改并制定了新章程，其中最重要的修改是将联合会的名称更改为"浙江基督教联合会"（The Chêkiang Christian Church Association）。新章程规定，联合会从原来的每年一会改为两年一会，并限制各教会代表人数。

另外会议还处理了诸如祖产与权利、鸦片、教堂、财务，以及各省非基督教运动等问题，对上述问题以和解的精神做了细致处理。

教会应更中国化

也许最有趣和争论最激烈的话题，是一名中国代表[①]提出的"中国教会应在教义与政治上更中国化"的提案。众人在讨论中认为，虽然教会在表面上可以有许多变化，并且也必然随时代而变化，但基督教的本质内核不应改变。中外代表对这个问题进行了公开公正的辩论，但该提案并未付诸表决。周日上午，代表们在内都会和圣道公会进行了讲演，下午有1000多名本地基督徒在圣道公会的教堂参与了联合大会，800多名师生在艺文学堂聆听了包齐清牧师富有文化气息的演讲。

会议也没有忽视社交方面，会议共举办了两次花园聚会和两次中式宴会，会议气氛融洽，受到各代表一致称赞。

这次温州会议在各方面都是成功的，这对于1927年召开的杭州会议来讲无疑是一种挑战。

---

① 温州圣道公会的尤树勋牧师鉴于外国教会在五卅惨案中偏袒英国，激愤之下脱离教会，并于1925年6月6日在温州仓河巷37号成立了"中华基督教会"，主张脱离外国控制，建立中国人自己的"本色教会"。支持尤树勋的还有彭文潽、李镜澜、陈静凡等人。参见《温州基督教会启事（浙江）》，《兴华》1925年第32期，第31页；《温州圣道公会改组》，《兴华》1925年第32期，第30~31页；《温州基督教会通启》，《兴华》1925年第41期，第30~31页。

《冷静的温州人：报纸与挑唆者煽动失败》，《北华捷报及最高法庭与领事馆杂志》，1926 年 6 月 12 日

冷静的温州人：报纸与挑唆者煽动失败

（本报记者报道）

对于这个通商口岸而言，今年的 5 月 30 日①是过去一年当中最平静的一天。近一个月以来，关于这一天将要出事的谣言满天飞，当地报刊和演讲日复一日地播下不信任与仇恨的种子，但不知何故，这些努力最后没有收到成效。

官方约束

此次煽动群众情绪的失败，可以归结为以下几个原因。首先，我们应该公正地承认，地方官员的态度是善意的，同时也是强调和平的。他们对学生进行了约束，虽然这种约束与管制总是错失时机。他们的政策一贯是允许释放一定的"民气"，这样可以保障安定。

没有出现重大排外事件的第二个原因是，在过去的 12 个月里，城内的店铺与生意日趋繁荣。

在城市的各个角落都可以看到繁荣的迹象。今年是雨伞行业最景气的一年，皮包行业也已成为一个庞大的产业。虽然生活成本日趋增长，但人们似乎没有感受到钱包紧缩的压力。良性的贸易无疑是维系中国城市安定的重要因素。

接下来，是由于温州人固有的冷静性格。40 多年来他们一直保持着良

---

① 即五卅惨案一周年，根据张棡记载，温州中学在 5 月 4 日为纪念五四运动放假，5 月 9 日为纪念"国耻日"设演讲会，5 月 30 日又是五卅惨案一周年。5 月多事，故社会气氛紧张。参见温州市图书馆编《张棡日记·第七册》，张钧孙点校，中华书局，2019，第 3045、3048 页。

好的记录，没有发生过排外骚乱。主要士绅和各行会领袖在平息骚动和追求安定方面对人民起到了很好的引导作用。

……

小麦已经顺利收获，品质相当不错。现在，稻田里绿油油地长着希望的幼苗，这表明这季水稻种植有个不错的开头。

皇家海军"皮特菲尔德号"（H. M. S. Petersfield）在 5 月 20 日抵达温州，并于 5 月 30 日中午开往宁波。（温州，6 月 2 日）

《外埠新闻：温州的南北之争》，《北华捷报及最高法庭与领事馆杂志》，1927 年 3 月 19 日

外埠新闻：温州的南北之争

（本报记者报道）

温州

这个条约口岸曾经既被北方统治过，也被南方统治过，现在它突然发现自己正承受着沉重的财政负担。这个城市及邻近地区缴纳的供费已近 100 万银圆。

花钱保平安被认为要比战乱导致地方糜烂更划算，人们多多少少会有抱怨，直到富人发现刺刀的寒光比银子的亮光更有说服力。

北方军队的善举

北军的到来，使得大量百姓出逃，宣传工作使得所有人都害怕并且不信任孙传芳。在 14 天的时间里，一共有 1.8 万人被安置在温州，[①] 除了让店铺承办伙食之外，这些外军并没有造成更多麻烦。[②] 他们像平民一样买东西付钱，同时也严格尊重所有外国人的生命财产，不干涉教会

[①] 1926 年 11 月 15 日，福建督军周荫人部因受到北伐军追逼退往温州，造成温州人心大乱，他们 11 月 29 日撤退。1927 年 2 月 12 日，国民革命军入城。2 月 17 日，北伐军到杭州，浙江全省光复。参见浙江省温州鹿城区委员会文史资料工作委员会编《鹿城文史资料·第五辑·温州城区近百年记事（1840—1949）》，1990，第 102 ~ 104 页。

[②] 需要指出的是，温州当地士绅的记载与《字林西报》记载不同，如《符璋日记》记述，闽军败退到温州后，不仅勒索地方、招募土匪，而且公开抢劫中国银行。参见符璋《符璋日记·下》，中华书局，2018，第 1032 ~ 1037 页。

活动。

在他们占领这座城市期间，当地的学生团体和国民党领导人停止了对所有英国人以及孙传芳的激烈抨击，这真是一段难得的清静时光。但这种安宁就像台风眼一样虚幻。

北方军队随后退往台州与宁波，中国难民也随之返回家园。

······

弥天大谎

当地的"赤色分子"们在这个短暂的平静期后又开始了他们的宣传，他们的谎言比之前的还要夸张！他们宣称随着南方军队的到来，将会开启新纪元，只需要30文钱就能买到1银圆的大米，再也没有人会缺钱。海关与常关的税收将供人民自由支配，再也没有富人与穷人之分，因为有钱大家使。充满激情的演讲者为了强调其所说的"真理性"，先是抬出孙传芳的画像，又抬出令人厌恶的外国人画像，并向其开枪。他们告诉人民，除掉这些敌人，所有上述承诺的美好景象都会得到实现。

为什么人们会渴望"南方"军队的到来？尽管他们相对于毗邻的福建而言，他们是改换阵营的"北方"叛徒。

第一支百人队伍终于到来，无数的旗帜欢迎国民革命军第十七军入城，他们随后通过水陆依次抵达。鼓动者与宣传者马上带着大量印刷品开始照例的宣传。每一堵空墙、每一份电报都充斥着他们肆无忌惮的言论以及充满煽动性的鼓动。在大街上，令人厌恶的海报随处可见，群众集会和街头的演讲变得更加排外和反基督教。

所谓的基督教传教士

人们永远都不会缺乏杀人的动机，据报道，令人感到耻辱的是一名自称是中华基督教会（N.C.C.）成员的著名演说家，呼吁他的听众，要对一位当地曾出任过浙江省议员的公民采取"用刀砍断其骨头"的行动。这位议员随后受到了恐吓，他决定暂时离家可能会更安全，详情下文将会讲到。

目前的结果是，尽管城里只有3000名士兵，圣道公会的学校、教堂和主日学校，以及内地会的教堂与女子学校都成了士兵的宿舍。而之前北军驻扎温州时，虽然北军人数超过 1 万人，但依旧能找到足够的中国人的建筑作为住所。

一些传教士逃离

已经有明确的警告指出，外国人已经难以维持其境遇，传教士社区的 10 名男女和儿童已离开港口。尽管第十七军军长曹万顺（Tsao Wan－shun）将军向海关税务司保证："所有在温州的外国居民都会受到他的充分保护，教会或外国人控制下的学校和私人住宅不会被士兵占领。"但对圣道公会和内地会的成员来说，暂时撤离是明智之举。温州的外国人中共有 23 名成人和 6 名儿童离开，除 4 名美国人外，其余皆为英国人。圣道公会的施德福医生与戴蒙德（Dymond）医生决定留下来，尽可能维持医院的运转。在过去的几年中，每年有超过 4 万人次患者接受治疗。此外，作为一名海关医官，施德福医生认为自己有责任支持海关的工作人员。

只要曹将军还待在温州……整个城市目前还算安定，2 月底时，曹将军去了台州和宁波，温州只剩下数百名士兵。

暴民法时刻

3 月 4 日，国民党举行了大规模的"反英"群众大会。推翻海关，抵制英国货，停止所有的传教工作，谴责省议员张焕燊（Tsie Hue－sang），这些都是他们煽动的主题。[①] 之后队伍在城市中游行，他们停在海关大楼外，打碎了几扇玻璃和大门，但他们的领导人阻止群众进一步破坏。在常关，他们又破坏了许多家具，并袭击了中国帮办。另一群主要由工人和苦力组成的队伍，跑到议员的家里乱砸，家具和衣服都被毁成碎片。门、窗和所有木制器具都被拆掉，甚至屋顶也被掀了。暴徒来得毫无预兆，这家人只能仓皇从后门逃走。

---

① 张棡对此事感慨颇多，他认为鲍鼎新、张焕燊遭此横逆，虽然是平时作恶咎由自取，但根源在当年北京学生火烧曹汝霖家宅，使得全国学生有样学样。张棡有感于世变，因此感慨说："涓涓不塞，将成江湖。今已江湖日下，狂澜不制，生此乱世，为恶固不可，为善亦未如之何也。"参见温州市图书馆编《张棡日记·第七册》，张钧孙点校，中华书局，2019，第 3156 页。

此外，整个城市张贴煽动"推翻"基督徒与"外国宗教"的海报。

从3月4日暴徒采取的行动来看，几乎可以肯定，更多麻烦正在酝酿。

仍住在温州的外国人有：2名医生、2名已婚和2名单身的海关工作人员、1名天主教修女（英国）、2名已婚的美国传教士及其3名子女、海关税务司裴纳玑夫妇及其6名子女以及2名俄国女佣，以及数名法国天主教传教士和修女。

《温州清共：政府积极铲除极端主义》，《北华捷报及最高法庭与领事馆杂志》，1927 年 4 月 23 日

温州清共：政府积极铲除极端主义

（本报记者报道）

根据今天上午在上海收到温州 4 月 17 日来电，中国政府正在努力清除城里的激进分子，并逮捕了几名国民党省党部和总工会里的共产党人。

电报补充说，目前有 24 名日本人，包括 10 名妇女和儿童，以及 30 名中国台湾人居住在该城。（上海，4 月 19 日）

《温州的布尔什维克化》，《北华捷报及最高法庭与领事馆杂志》，
1927 年 5 月 14 日

温州的布尔什维克化

大约在 6 年前，我被诚恳地邀请前往温州，调查该地是否受到了布尔什维主义的影响。必须要承认，此项委托令我感到惊讶，而且在一定程度上给我带来了乐趣。在与各阶层人民交往的 30 年间，我走访过温州旧府的各个城镇与村庄，但从来没有产生过做这种调查的想法。根据这项提议进行调查是有价值的，虽然我认为在这样一个给外国人留下和平、知足和勤劳印象的民族里，想要去传播那种理念只是徒劳。

当时在对 7 个县进行调查后，报告得出的结果是没有发现任何布尔什维主义或相关宣传的踪迹。这是 6 年前！当时的这个结论是多么盲目的自信啊，而现在个体的幸福，甚至是一个民族的生命，都在被某种巨变所影响。

……

俄国人暗中资助

鉴于浙东南温州共产主义运动的增长，正如一位观察家所言，此事不仅重要，同时也能让那些仍然拒绝承认莫斯科正在目前中国动荡局势中暗中操作的榆木脑袋开窍。1925 年 5 月 30 日之前，想要在温州找到布尔什维克宣传征兵的证据并不是难事。当地的一家报纸已经光明正大地改变了立场，它认为官方默许的态度不会带来危险，这家报纸已经逐渐成为俄国道路的拥护者……

到 1925 年 6 月中旬，人们开始更加公开大胆地鼓吹苏联政策。到目前为止，那些秘密的做法已经转变为在街角的报亭公开传发小册子。

"好心"的中华基督教会成员

正在此时，一名中华基督教会的成员以肯定的语气告诉我，所有外国

财产在不久之后都会被没收。此外他还好心地提醒我，与英国人以及英国教会将要遭受的苦难相比，义和团当年造成的恐怖都要相形见绌！他花费了很大力气去达到这一目标，他写了大量的宣传小册子，并在城镇乡村广泛传播，这一点毋庸置疑。不消说，他不得不辞去牧师职务，但具有讽刺意味的是，他仍然是中华基督教会里"可敬"的董事成员。

上文提到的人就是尤树勋（Yui Ji - sung），[①] 他是赤色分子中的赤色分子，顺便提一句，有趣的是，目前那些致力于肃清温州极端分子的人正悬赏 100 银圆捉拿他。

布尔什维克的策略

目前温州的布尔什维克分子可能会实施以下策略。

（1）学生会将被似是而非的许诺、狂热民族主义者的呼吁以及莫斯科乌托邦的诱惑所俘获。

（2）煽动年轻人反对他们的父母，告诉他们列宁主义远比孔子学说更为重要。

（3）广州成为这些学生的麦加。大量的人被诱导进入黄埔军校，不仅仅是为了军事训练，还是为了成为布尔什维克宣传专家。很多找不到出路的学生，被黄埔军校每月 10 元至 20 元工资的职位所吸引。同时相关宣传还向他们保证每年会发 13 个月工资，并承诺未来会把这些年轻人送回家乡当官，当官后工资从每月 50 元到 150 元不等。不久之前，当地还流行一句俗语叫"温州人不迁移"。但这句话现在已经不管用了，除了上述原因以外，还有其他原因使当地人陷入不理智的思考，可以归结为以下各条。

（4）在许多温州人向往的圣地中，莫斯科已经取代了广州的位置。有两件事可以证明此观点：首先，仅在青岛就有 1000 多人前往俄国，其中大部分是农民。温州一个村庄的 52 户人家里，有 48 户去了俄国。去年，一个年轻农民借了 300 银圆作为前往莫斯科的路费。不到 6 个月，此人不仅

---

① 组织基督教自立运动是温州中共支部在全国的一项独特举措，尤树勋在 1926 年 11 月 6 日加入了中国共产党，是温州共产党独立支部最早 12 名成员之一。参见支华欣、郑颉峰《教会自立的先驱尤树勋》，《温州文史资料·第九辑》，浙江人民出版社，1994，第 213~214 页。

还清借款，还往家里寄了 400 银圆，并承诺年底前还能再寄几百银圆。北京的当权者们，才刚刚意识到边界人员流动的重要性！

（5）还有一个关于布尔什维克在温州地区发展的迹象需要记录。在过去两年当中，有过一种 2 至 4 人的小组悄无声息地在农村中从事渗透活动，他们的任务是为组建农会（Peasants' Unions）奠定群众基础。

......

《温州"清共"：艺文学堂师生被逮捕，一人已被处决》，《北华捷报及最高法庭与领事馆杂志》，1927 年 6 月 11 日

温州"清共"：艺文学堂师生被逮捕，一人已被处决

（本报记者报道）

5 月 21 日，100 多名士兵被命令秘密突袭艺文学堂，目的是根除共产主义活动。

搜查从下午 4 点持续到晚上 11 点，结果逮捕了 5 名教师和学生。校长不在城里，所以逃过了逮捕。

第二天，这 5 个人被带上法庭接受审判。4 名囚犯被释放。但晚上 10 点，一个名叫蔡雄（Tsa Ning‑gyi）的年轻学生在当地一个小市镇上被枪决。

艺文学堂师生实际早已撤离，上述师生来自借校上课已 3 个月的瓯海公学（Ao Hoe School）。

值得注意的是，在某些情况下，占领教会学院和教堂并不像某些民族主义者所预期的那样"光荣"。

一旦被证明仇恨外国人就有可能被处以罚款或取缔组织，更不用说无论白天黑夜都要面对行刑队的危险，这一定很令人不安。对于一些年轻的革命者来讲，将教会学校充公可能是件小事情，但他们现在应该发现想要运转一所学校需要花费很多钱，所以他们在将教会学校充公后又不得不将其关闭，就像宁波的圣道公会学校那样。

温州最近在推行新的募兵办法，当局强制征召 15 至 16 岁的年轻人入伍。"海晏号"（Hoean）上一次离开温州时，船上载着 300 名着便装的新募士兵，他们将被带往上海金利来码头。（温州，6 月 1 日）

《7个月后的温州：不再有排外行动，明智的撤离》，《北华捷报及最高法庭与领事馆杂志》，1927年10月1日

7个月后的温州：不再有排外行动，明智的撤离

（本报记者报道）

以下是我们的记者在离开7个月后，最近访问温州的情况。

在过去7个月里，由于大多数外国居民撤离，从这个通商口岸得到的一手消息很少。这段很长的时间里，除了一些日本人外，几乎没有外国人在温州居住。传教士、商人和海关人员几乎都离开了港口。

离开温州一段时间毫无疑问是明智的，我们可以毫无痛苦地再返回温州，同时也不需要承受任何清算。尽管有"极端分子"进行宣传鼓动，但温州居民并没有狂热排外，可以说温州人维持着多年以来的好名声。

至暗时刻

1927年的3月和4月是黑色的月份，官方权力被各种委员会和协会篡夺。接下来政府对"极端分子"进行了镇压，一些人被枪决，一些人被监禁，还有很多人逃到宁波与上海藏身。那些曾被各协会查封的教堂现在又被归还给了教会，并恢复了正常服务活动。

然而圣道公会下属艺文学堂的校舍依旧被另外一所竞争性学校占据，理由是如果他们不占校舍，其他学校也会占据。6月时，为了寻找布尔什维克宣传的证据，军队曾突袭了这所学校。几名教师和学生被捕，经过调查，一名学生被处决。尽管如此，学校大楼和校长住所仍被这群人占领着，事实上校长住所已经被这群所谓的教育家们洗劫了。中国人里许多非基督徒也厌恶这次暴乱，他们认为会导致这座城市的好名声被玷污，在整个运动当中温州没有一处传教场所或教会房产被洗劫。

表面上的和平

从表面上看，城市已经恢复了平静。农民可以自由地带着他们的货物进城，商店都在开门做生意，并且看起来都是公平买卖。有报道称今年水稻收成不太好，秋收不太可能达到往年水平。所以已经不得不进口大米，大米价格也应声上涨。

当地正在闹匪患，几乎每个县都有土匪。山区遭抢的人说土匪都是当地人，不是溃军。

目前驻扎在温州的军队人数很少，有三个组织被承认在当地拥有合法权力，分别是地方党部、地方农会以及地方工会。

如果条件允许的话，希望领事能够允许外国居民重新回到温州港居住。（上海，9 月 23 日）

《温州和平近况：军队来去匆匆》，《北华捷报及最高法庭与领事馆杂志》，1927 年 10 月 15 日

温州和平近况：军队来去匆匆

（本报记者报道）

两三个星期以前，我们可以报告说，在温州及其附近地区驻扎的部队很少。然而，上个星期三和星期四，3000 名士兵来到这里，他们大部分是浙江处州选拔出来后，从瓯江上游赶来的。这些军队抵达温州时，显得十分匆忙和疲惫。随后军方征用了招商局的"海晏号"，以及两艘宁波船"平阳号"与"永宁号"。据说这些军队将被派往福州，但也有很多人偷偷讲这支部队的真正目的地是宁波。

1700 人挤在"海晏号"上，其余的人挤在剩下的两只小船上。他们于周五上午离开温州，周六抵达宁波并在那里下船。

似乎完全没有派遣这些军队前往宁波的必要，因为宁波地方上相当安定，从前的居民可以毫无阻碍地返回家乡。因此有人确信这支军队最终目的地应是杭州。

招商局定期开往温州的两艘船由于货仓苦力罢工，暂时停滞在上海。

温州目前相当安定，几天前，该城一位著名学者宣称，当地居民驱逐外国居民是"丢脸"的行为，他们希望外国人重新回来。（温州，10 月 4 日）

《温州近况》，《北华捷报及最高法庭与领事馆杂志》，1927 年 10 月 22 日

温州近况

（本报记者报道）

致《北华捷报》编辑：

先生，在贵报最近的报道中（9 月 22 日、23 日或 24 日），我很高兴读到几行有关温州的消息。据说在所有欧洲人离开后，这座港口已经维持了 7 个月的和平。从复活节到 5 月中旬，除了一些日本人外，其余驻温外国人都前往了上海，这确实是事实。但令我惊讶的是，你们的记者（我猜想他一定是一名老温州居民）没有注意到，天主教会的三位欧洲神父已经回到了温州。不久之后，6 名仁爱会（Charity Mission）的欧洲修女也将随之返回，并立即开始在董若望济病院（Jean – Gabriel Hospital）和永嘉育婴堂（Municipal Orphanage）开始她们的工作。① 不用说，温州人民同情外国人的遭遇，自我们回来以后，从来没有听到过一句敌意的话。

在温州的内陆地区（处州区域），我遇到了内地会的德国与瑞士传教士仍在坚守岗位。一名从属于加拿大天主教会（Catholic Canadian Mission）的西班牙牧师拒绝离开。另外还有 4 名神父在离开一个半月后又回到处州。

您那位可敬的记者还肯定说有教堂被占用。的确，有些教堂曾在一段时间内被用作工会俱乐部等，但到目前为止，天主教会、学校及其处所未被骚扰，我们相信和平状况将会延续下去。

我是您诚挚的仆人，

普罗斯特（J. Prost）

温州，1927 年 10 月 6 日

---

① 法国仁爱会，也被称为修女仁爱会，创立于 1633 年。董若望济病院和永嘉育婴堂分别创立于 1913 年和 1919 年。参见雷立柏《我的灵都：一位奥地利学者的北京随笔》，新星出版社，2017，第 146 ~ 147 页。

《温州当局藐视命令：知事拒绝交还教会房产，共产主义学校的大本营》，《北华捷报及最高法庭与领事馆杂志》，1928 年 9 月 15 日

温州当局藐视命令：知事拒绝交还教会房产，共产主义学校的大本营

温州艺文学堂，这座精美的建筑被一所中国学校非法占据了一年半，尽管南京和杭州下达严令，但温州城知事拒绝协助归还。

尽管地方当局与南京方面一再向圣道公会保证，将会从那所当地学校的手里把学校大楼和校长住所归还给教会，但已经时隔一年半，这些房产仍被中国人占据，同时该本地学校还有很强的通共嫌疑。显然在当地官员的纵容下，非法占有者要么无视命令，要么继续编造占有房产的借口。最近的报道显示，索还教会房产的时间表仍遥遥无期。

一年半前，温州市瓯海公学的校长及其职员，在未经许可的情况下接管了艺文学堂校舍，该校一直被怀疑从事共产主义活动。1927 年 5 月底，军方突袭了该校，6 名教师和学生因为被怀疑是共产主义者而被捕。第二

天，其中一人被当局处决，学校被解散。

"共党"分子再次占据学校

1927 年初秋，瓯海公学恢复办学，再次占用了教会大楼，从那时起，所有驱逐他们的努力都付之东流。由于县知事的阻挠与国民党当局的无能，相关命令无法被执行。

此外，这所学校仍被怀疑是共产主义的温床，一位温州商人宣称有 60 多名学生和教师是这个颠覆性政党的党员。据报道，该校教师宣称："如果再向他们施压、要求他们离开学校的话，他们就会重新挑起事端，驱逐所有外国人。"这种威胁表明该校确实倾向于采取违抗法律和秩序的办法解决问题，尽管共产主义在温州已经根深蒂固，但外国人不会将此威胁放在心上。

藐视政府命令

5 月初，国民政府已下令将该处房产归还给教会，但尚未采取任何行动。所有地方官员除一人外都愿意执行政府命令，但就是这一个人——温州知事似乎有能力阻止这一行动。

最近有人建议教会去收回房产，赶走鸠占鹊巢的瓯海公学。但这不是一个教会该干的事，而县知事拒绝在此事上提供任何帮助。相反我们得知，他写信给上级要求允许瓯海公学占据教会校产直到 1929 年 2 月底。温州的交涉员建议教会去拜访一下这位县知事，亲自与他讨论学校将如何以及何时归还。

这是显然在罔顾杭州省政府和南京中央政府立即归还校产的命令！

圣道公会主席海和德先生拜访了县知事并请他采取行动，但没有得到任何回应。在谈判的一个多小时里，知事始终忽视归还住所的主要症结问题，并企图迫使教会默认现状。这种企图当然不可能得逞，一切又恢复到原状。

更多诡计

在此之后这位顽固的知事似乎受到了一定压力，因为教会随后收到了他的请求，要求教会允许瓯海公学一直待到 10 月 25 日。根据来函所示，瓯海公学校长已经租了一幢有 40 个房间的楼房，但相关维修改建工程需要两个月的时间。

经过调查我们发现这只不过是个借口，瓯海公学租用的房子的状况根本没有那么糟糕，四五天的清扫足以使它适合入住。我们没有看到工人维修的迹象，而且大楼业主否认他们正准备将房子的一半租给任何人。看起来信函所说纯系谎言。

我们再次向知事发起的申请目前还没有得到回应，同时瓯海公学已开始重组工作，根据最新消息，该校仍在进行会议商讨。

《温州太平年：五谷丰登，浙东繁荣》，《北华捷报及最高法庭与领事馆杂志》，1928 年 9 月 29 日

温州太平年：五谷丰登，浙东繁荣

（本报记者报道）

　　温州正逐渐但确定地恢复往日的平静与安宁。由于温州所处地理位置，再加上远离军事要冲，我们在过去 6 个月里躲过了许多其他城市不幸的遭遇。今年在温州很少会看到军人，即便有也多半举止得体。因此这座城市显示出了商业繁荣的迹象，对老百姓来说，去年的乌云已差不多散去。

　　温州恢复安定的另一个重要条件是第一季水稻获得了大丰收，据说已经有 20 年没有这样的好收成了。1927 年当地人 1 银圆只能买到 9 斤至 12 斤大米，今年则可以买到 20 斤以上。土豆收成也很好，此外第二季水稻也有望获得丰收，当地报纸预测粮价将会下跌。尽管前景乐观，当地官员仍禁止粮食出口，并对违反出口禁令的人提出严厉警告。保证大家的饭碗都能装满的政策，在当地创造了一种安定愉快的气氛。

新的公园

　　其他许多城市在进行革新，温州为了不落人后，决定拆除一部分城墙。拆除的部分位于外国人俗称的邦妮角（Bonnie Corner）与北亭之间。[1] 政府计划将城墙外宽阔运河范围的大片土地，以及城墙内的一大片菜地全部规划成一个公共公园。待其建成之后，必将吸引无数游人。

---

① 北伐成功后，为了纪念孙中山，温州在 1928 年开始拆毁华盖山至积谷山城墙，并建设中山公园，该公园至 1930 年完工。《完成于民国二十年之温州中山公园》，《浙瓯日报廿四年元旦特刊》1935 年 1 月，第 15 页。

像其他地方一样，温州也存在抵制日本的活动。抵制形式与其他地方大同小异，目前没有发生不愉快的事件。在一名日本籍税务司、美籍港务长和俄籍引水人的领导下，海关职员一直稳定而高效地工作着。

肃清"共党"

最近常有温州附近山区盗匪出没的报道，地方官员和各县知事都采取了协调措施来控制和镇压盗匪。最近各县知事集中在温州城开了一次会，讨论如何解决远离城市的市镇乡村的防卫问题。

这个地区还有"共党"分子进行活动，这是不能轻忽的，就在数星期前，"共党"5名领导人被肃清。自此之后，"共党"的许多领导认为退到温州海湾附近的岛屿可能是更明智的选择。温州地方官员对此极为警惕，值得称赞的是，他们在尽可能地采取预防措施，防止城镇和乡村落入"共党"手中。

让人愈发困惑的是，归还圣道公会校产的命令仍未得到执行。如果南京和杭州的命令不被执行，那么不仅外国人会怀疑中国法律与秩序的稳定性，连受人尊敬的守法公民恐怕也会心生疑窦。希望这个错误很快能得到纠正。

躲过台风

温州很幸运地躲过了最近一次的台风，上周四晚上是最危险的时候，一股强烈的西北偏北风肆虐而来，气压瞬时下降到 29.23 英寸。暴雨过后，河水泛滥，第二季水稻收获要到 10 月底，希望农作物不会遭受太大损失。

《温州恐怖的大火：消防队不堪其用，损失估计50万银圆》，《北华捷报及最高法庭与领事馆杂志》，1928年11月3日

温州恐怖的大火：消防队不堪其用，损失估计50万银圆

（本报记者报道）

上周日晚上，一场多年来最具破坏性的火灾肆虐了温州市的重要街区。火势最早起于一家纸铺，这家店铺位于著名的东门街康乐坊（K'oa - loh - foa），随后火势蔓延至城市主要街道。这些街道两旁的店铺全都燃烧起来，一时之间这个商业区看上去全都要被焚毁。火舌越过街道和运河，一家又一家商店，一座又一座房子，壮观的火柱冲天而起，照亮了整座城市。大火持续了两个半小时，不幸的是由于官员们的命令，许多机器在维修，消防队只能调用一半的力量，无法全力灭火。

中国人估计这场火灾造成的损失为50万银圆，而且只有五六家商铺和房子上了保险。（温州，10月23日）

《"开塞姆号"遇险：大浪中几乎倾覆，温州避难》，《北华捷报及最高法庭与领事馆杂志》，1928 年 11 月 24 日

"开塞姆号"遇险：大浪中几乎倾覆，温州避难

"开塞姆号"（Cassum），也就是前皇家海军"胡特拉克号"（H. M. S. Woodlark），在从上海驶往香港过程中遇险的事情，我们已经通过"新疆号"（Sinkiang）船长马瑟（Mather）了解到相关简要情况，该船曾在温州以北 70 里处遇到过"开塞姆号"。

马瑟船长接受《北华捷报》采访，向我们讲述了周六上午，也就是 10 日发生的事情。当时他看到不远处有一艘船在他的左舷船头"全速前进"。当他靠近那艘船时，他看到那艘船正在挥舞旗子发出信号。可以知晓两条旗语，一条旗语是"你能给我们煤吗"，另一条旗语是"向上海报告"。马瑟船长回答说："跟我去一个锚地。"然后他向牛山岛（Shetung Island）背面驶去，并在那里下了锚。

速度降至 3 海里

"开塞姆号"随后停靠在了锚地——美孚石油公司某轮船旁边，"开塞姆号"船长耐特（Knight）解释了他当时的困境。尽管他知道船最高可以 13 海里的速度航行，但当时他最多只能用 6 海里前进，很多时候他的航速只有 3 海里多一点。耐特认为这是上海装运的煤质量差造成的，两名船长就其处境开了一个短会。这次会谈的结果是，两位船长认为最好的办法是"开塞姆号"开到温州装煤，虽然"新疆号"能够给"开塞姆号"一些煤，但船离温州已经很近，没必要这样做。再者海上移送，必定很慢，这意味着"开塞姆号"必须要在这个并不合适的锚地停一夜。随后两船分手，马瑟船长则立即向英国驻上海领事发送电报，按照耐特船长的要

求报告了"开塞姆号"的位置。

"开塞姆号"是在东矶岛（Bella Vista）背面的黑石湾（Barren Bay）陷入绝境，随后该船在牛山岛北面与"新疆号"交换旗语，并在牛山岛北面下锚进行了短暂会谈。

未遭倾覆的好运

在谈话的过程中，耐特船长说，由于煤的质量，他的工程师们一直无法保持蒸汽机的运转，结果是航行中出现了很多困境。"开塞姆号"必须贴着海岸行驶，这样才能保证随时能控制住船，但鉴于目前的大浪和强风，这艘小船必须要有足够的动力才能应付接下来的旅程。

耐特说："我们差点被海浪掀翻，然后风把我们吹向礁石，幸好我们没撞到。"

马瑟认为"开塞姆号"从温州到香港的航程，只能在白天行驶，夜间必须选择合适的锚地停泊。据目前消息，该船在温州停留了5天，这无疑是因为耐特船长无法获得合适的煤，并且没有掌握天气报告。

离开温州

"开塞姆号"船长的妻子已于11月18日通知本报说，她已经收到丈夫的电报，该船已于11月15日离开温州。

《中国造纸计划：准备在浙江温州建厂》，《北华捷报及最高法庭与
领事馆杂志》，1928年12月22日

中国造纸计划：准备在浙江温州建厂

　　为了把日本新闻纸业挤出市场，同时满足中国各大报纸的需求，当
地的许多商人，包括虞洽卿（Yu Yaching）、王一亭（Wang Yi-ting）、
许世英（Hsu Shib-ching）、方椒伯（Fong Chu-pa）、冯少山（S. S.
Fung）等人，制订了一个雄心勃勃的计划，决定建立中国第一家新闻纸
造纸工厂。①

　　他们提议厂址选在浙江温州，因为此地有大量木材作为原材料，同时
交通也相当便利。②

　　发起人和浙江省政府签订了一项协议，该协议规定该工厂可以垄断新
闻纸造纸产业30年，作为回报，6%的利润将归省政府所有。此外，该公
司在10年之内将享有免税特权。

---

① 以上所列发起人，都是上海总商会的重要人物。

② 中国近代历来所用新闻纸都是从外国进口，至1928年每年进口费用不下3000万
　元，故亟须自造新闻纸。而新闻纸最重要的原材料是杉木，杉木出产最多的地方
　是东北，但东北杉木位于内陆，运输不便。浙江温州同样盛产杉木，再加上水运
　便利的区位优势，所以温州是浙江新闻纸造纸厂最佳选址地。这就是著名的"温
　溪造纸厂"计划，虽然后来又得到中央政治会议批准，但由于时局变化，再加上
　财力不济，造纸厂迟迟难以动工。一直到1936年4月，该计划才得以启动，预计
　一年时间完工，后因抗战爆发而中辍。参见《温州将有国产新闻纸》，《东省经济
　月刊》1929年第4期，第5~6页；温溪纸厂筹备委员会编《中国造纸股份有限
　公司计划书》，温溪纸厂筹备委员会编印，1935，第11页；张忠民、朱婷《南京
　国民政府时期的国有企业（1927—1949）》，上海财经大学出版社，2007，第
　307~308页。

　　一个专门董事会已经成立，由专门在海外学习造纸技术的留学生金翰
（King Han）① 先生担任公司主管。

---

① 由于温溪造纸厂计划不断被推迟，金瀚后在实业部工业研究所一方面继续筹划造纸
　厂建设，另一方面研究亚硫酸纸浆法。参见范敬平《难忘的两位老师》，《浙江文
　史资料选辑·第三十四辑》，浙江人民出版社，1987，第231页。

《温州艺文学堂终于被归还：时隔两年所有值钱物件都被偷走》，
《北华捷报及最高法庭与领事馆杂志》，1929 年 1 月 19 日

温州艺文学堂终于被归还：时隔两年所有值钱物件都被偷走

（本报记者报道）

在被占据两年后，艺文学堂终于重新回到教会手中。

署理县知事有一句话很重要，可以作为官方意见，他说："艺文学堂是借出去的。"那么这些借用教会优质房产的人又是如何看待他们物归原主的责任呢？我们可以用以下事实来进行判断。

（1）学校和校长住所几乎被洗劫一空，房间里的家具与设施一干二净。

（2）他们连一个小瓶子都没有留下，更不用说科学实验室里的一个有价值的仪器了。

（3）所有电气配件都被无情地切断，并被席卷一空。

（4）整个学校处于难以形容的肮脏污秽状态。

（5）在学生们离校之前，许多窗户被故意打碎了。

我很遗憾将这些事情公之于众，但隐瞒事实对这个国家没有好处。这群男人和青年以"爱国者"自居，但他们其实是披着教师与学生伪装的（国家）公敌。

1 月 11 日，学校终于又回到教会手中。

注释：在过去的几个月里，南京政府一直试图将学校还给圣道公会，并多次向温州当局下达命令，但直到目前为止，地方的顽固力量依旧很强大。（温州，1 月 12 日）

《温州教会财产：彻底洗劫后才被归还》，《北华捷报及最高法庭与领事馆杂志》，1929 年 4 月 20 日

温州教会财产：彻底洗劫后才被归还

（本报记者报道）

　　经过 12 个多月的谈判，温州圣道公会的财产终于归还给了它的合法主人。几个月来，地方当局不顾南京外交部的命令，允许瓯海公学的校长侵占教会校产，事实上瓯海公学早在 1927 年就"吞并"了教会学校。但经过长久努力，当教会显然决心千方百计要得到他们自己的房产时，温州交涉员与瓯海公学终于同意在 2 月归还学校。

　　房产虽然被归还了，但家具和设备在很大程度上都被掠夺了。

　　这些建筑虽然被归还了，但是其中的家具和设备大都被抢光。课桌、表格、餐桌、书籍、登记簿、床、锁、电灯设备，几乎都不见了。价值 3000 银圆的化学和物理仪器甚至都没有留下一个 2 盎司的烧杯。校长住所内的画作、椅子、地毯、亚麻布、瓷器等——这些物品大多被锁在箱子里——现在也不翼而飞。据保守估计，总的损失高达 1 万银圆，这些损失目前还无人赔偿。

　　希望学校能在秋季重新开学，维修工作正在进行中，同时新家具也在赶制。开学招生人数被限定在 100 人至 150 人，这样做是必要的，虽然自 1924 年学校扩建以后，学校正常应可容纳 300 人左右。

　　艺文学堂既要与教会目标相一致，也要努力满足政府对私立学校的所有要求——其中也包括教会学校。如果学校最终发现自己受到过度限制，乃至于与教会存在目的相背离，那么整个教会教育工作的价值就需要重新予以考虑。（温州，4 月 9 日）

《温州繁荣时代的到来：前所未有的境况，随之而来的变革》，《北华捷报及最高法庭与领事馆杂志》，1929 年 5 月 4 日

温州繁荣时代的到来：前所未有的境况，随之而来的变革

（本报记者报道）

温州似乎已经进入了一个空前繁荣的时代。在过去的 25 年间，贸易从未如此繁荣过。温州在过去已经发生过许多次火灾，每次火灾过后都能看到更现代、更宏伟的建筑在旧商店、旧房屋的废墟上拔地而起。街道逐渐拓宽，装设了现代平板玻璃的店铺将更具竞争优势。20 年前，每 10 天才有一艘小轮船到达温州，现在，温州每周有 5 艘定期轮船抵达，此外还有许多其他船只不定期到达。鉴于以上种种，温州要建公园也就不足为奇。就像世界上另外一座著名城市一样，① 温州同样建在七丘之巅，城东两山之间的土地已被利用建设新公园。部分城墙已被拆毁，坟场被填平为缓坡地，同时兴建了花丛灌木、亭台楼阁、湖泊桥梁供人休憩。

当地政府随后应考虑改善这座城市的卫生状况。许多运河已经淤塞多年，其中的积水和腐烂的垃圾，以及在城市各处都能遇到的露天化粪池是各种疾病的滋生地。温州几乎每年都有霍乱疫情暴发，有时会造成可怕的后果。

现代戏剧

最近一两个星期，上海的一个剧团来温州表演。花钱看戏剧表演是一种新鲜事。通常人们会去寺庙，坐在很高的位置上看戏，高椅会将人抬到离地 3 英尺的高度，让人在闲暇享受的同时完全不用花钱。这家上海公司

---

① 指罗马，罗马也被称为"七丘之城"，或"七山之上永恒之城"。

带来了一种新的戏剧模式，他们搭建了舞台和场景，并围绕一系列时事进行表演。

人们可以看到蒋介石坐在一间装有现代办公家具的房间里，处理国家事务。有一出关于济南事变的戏，通过一位中国目击者的视角，以非常现实的方式展示了日本人的种种暴行，充分调动了观众的热情，并得到他们的赞许。票价是 1 角或 2 角，公司每个月的日常开支是 1500 银圆。

一场抢劫

最近某晚，某富商在寓所遭匪徒劫持，并被勒索 2 万银圆，否则将遭不测。该富商上楼取钱时，乘歹徒不备跳窗逃走。随后该富商找到警察报案，待警察赶到时，歹徒已得手并溜之大吉。

海盗活动

瓯江与瓯江口的海盗活动最近相当猖獗，在某些情况下，我们的船只不得不配备老式加农炮，以及多达 100 名的船员。轮船一般较为安全，不会被海盗抢劫，但帆船常遭不测。最近被捕获的几名海盗已被处死。（温州，4 月 23 日）

《浙江捕获盗匪：岛屿上捕获了可怕的匪帮》，《北华捷报及最高法庭与领事馆杂志》，1929 年 7 月 13 日

浙江捕获盗匪：岛屿上捕获了可怕的匪帮

（本报记者报道）

位于瓯江口外的披山岛（Pien San）约有 160 名匪徒被捕或被击毙。[①] 披山岛是一座长约 8 英里、宽约 1 英里的海岛，岛上岩石密布，仅有两个狭窄入口可供通行，易守难攻。据说这支匪帮的人数为 268 人，全都配备了非常现代的步枪与自动武器。

这伙人利用"借来的"帆船进行抢劫，但他们不会使用同一艘帆船超过两天，当局很难在海上抓捕他们。在进行抢劫之前，这伙匪帮会先向神明请示，询问在哪个方向抢劫比较吉利。但这一次，神谕误导了他们，匪徒们刚出披山岛就遇到了政府的军舰。交战结果是匪徒有 160 人被捕或被杀。残党撤退之后已经恢复了其旧时巢穴，说明战斗中有相当多匪徒逃走。但他们全部被捕只是时间问题，饥饿会将他们赶出来。（温州，7 月 4 日）

---

① 台州北盐场张云卿、张云宗、陈云龙等，领匪徒两三百人，啸聚披山，抢劫过往船只。此次剿匪水陆并进，且调动了正规军，使用了军舰，规模之大相当罕见。尹小眼后继续占据披山岛，国民党当局对其毫无办法。温州、台州帆船从此地经过，必须向披山岛海盗购买"片子儿"（保护费），一时成为惯例。参见《水陆军警围攻海盗之经过》，《申报》1929 年 7 月 4 日，第 10 版；《披山又有大批匪徒啸取》，《申报》1929 年 9 月 9 日，第 11 版；叶汉龙、徐咏衡《瓯江流域的木材业》，《温州文史资料·第六辑》，浙江省新闻出版局，1990，第 92 页。

《痛苦围绕着温州：粮食歉收与三次风灾》，《北华捷报及最高法庭与领事馆杂志》，1929 年 8 月 24 日

痛苦围绕着温州：粮食歉收与三次风灾
（本报记者报道）

温州今年早稻几乎全部歉收，在许多地区已引发严重灾难。即便对温州来讲，这个夏季的降雨也实在太多，稻米由于缺乏光照严重影响了收成，粮价已经猛涨。在短时间内，粮价从 1 银圆买 11 品脱稻米，涨到 1 银圆只能买 8 品脱稻米，并且价格还在持续上涨。

我们已经历三次风灾，虽然还没有达到 7 级狂风等级，但降雨实在太多。最近的一次降雨中，雨天从 8 月 7 日一直持续到 14 日，温州附近平原内涝成湖，房屋与堤岸出没于波涛之中。城里所有运河都被淹没，街道皆积水。想要通过任何一道城门都要涉过深水。即使未来放晴，想要水退也得不少日子。在一些农村，由于粮食歉收，穷人几乎陷入绝境。为了得到粮食，当地出现了抢富户粮食的局面。

除非天气大大改善，否则第二季水稻作物也将面临歉收的危险。温州的粮食需要一个月的充足光照。（温州，8 月 15 日）

《温州一起纵火案：电话交换机被毁，可能为"共党"所为》，《北华捷报及最高法庭与领事馆杂志》，1929 年 9 月 14 日

温州一起纵火案：电话交换机被毁，可能为"共党"所为

（本报记者报道）

上周日晚上在温州发生了一场严重的火灾，电话交换机被完全烧毁。整个事件都笼罩在神秘之中，所有证据都表明这是一起蓄意的恶性案件，目的是妨碍官员们履行职责。当时大楼里有三人，但他们成功逃脱，无人受伤，目前还没有具体解释。

此次事件给人的总体印象是，可能为"共党"所为，但事实是否果真如此，恐怕也难以确定。由于担心这只是公共服务设施破坏行动的开始，电灯公司已经设立警卫来保护其产业。电话公司目前已经接到命令，必须要在三周内恢复正常工作，此项命令是否能够得到执行，值得怀疑。（温州，9 月 7 日）

《温州暴发霍乱疫情：疫情已趋缓，艺文学堂已重新开放》，《北华捷报及最高法庭与领事馆杂志》，1929 年 9 月 14 日

温州暴发霍乱疫情：疫情已趋缓，艺文学堂已重新开放

（本报记者报道）

温州再次出现霍乱流行，可以确定的是，这场疫情可能是从遥远的南方传来的。据报道，在平阳县以南 30 英里的地方，霍乱传播范围极广，且平阳每天都有轮船往来于温州城与瑞安之间，这加速了霍乱的传播。大约一周前，温州南门附近出现首个病例，此后疫情迅速蔓延。20 名患者已被送往圣道公会的白累德医院接受治疗，据医生报告，此次霍乱毒性极强。其中有 3 人已死亡，其余患者在接受生理盐水注射治疗后反应良好。不幸的是，许多病人只会将"外国"医院作为最后的医治手段，因此许多霍乱患者被送入医院时，为时已晚。

幸运的是，天气的变化遏制了疫情的进一步传播，气温已经转凉，最近三天偶尔还会下雨。

艺文学堂重开

艺文学堂在关闭两年半后今天终于重新开放。虽然学校还没有注册，但在符合教会原则的情况下，学校将按政府中学法规相关规定办理。学校已经组成了华籍董事会，并任命了一名中国籍校长，前任校长将担任顾问职务。共有 200 名学生收到了入学通知书，占总申请人数的一半左右。所有的建筑都已翻修，并制造或购买了新家具。一群学生在当局默许下曾占据这些建筑，而现在当局命令他们赔偿曾经因为破坏与侵占所产生的部分巨额费用，也许我们不应对此抱有希望？（温州，9 月 4 日）

《温州饥荒：农作物被某种未知生物破坏》，《北华捷报及最高法庭
与领事馆杂志》，1929年10月12日

温州饥荒：农作物被某种未知生物破坏

（本报记者报道）

由于温州稻谷几乎绝收，上千家庭要面临断粮的绝境。乐清与玉环遭灾最重，民众甚至开始吃草或任何能得到的植物。成百上千的家庭来到温州城，沦为街头乞丐。一些人为了防止灾民卖儿卖女，正在努力照看孩子们。数天前，有一位父亲以14元将儿子卖掉，孩子母亲随即投河自尽。

农作物歉收是由于某种昆虫从根部啃食作物。虽然近年来不断发生洪水，但人们好像不记得以前曾发生过这样严重的饥荒。出现虫灾的原因，目前有各种各样的谣言，有最荒诞的迷信说法，也有存在一定道理的说法。比较可靠的说法认为，这是某种蛾的幼虫所致。[①] 除非找到真正原因并采取预防措施，否则明年还会发生类似灾难，这当然是省立大学农学专业接下来需要去调查的。

霍乱流行

温州霍乱疫情日趋严峻，圣道公会白累德医院已接收400名患者，死亡人数接近20%，除一名不听劝阻强行离院随后又回来的患者死亡外，死者多为幼童与老人。

百姓极为不安，这样动荡的局势很容易引发事端。官员似乎已经有所警觉，自上个月电话交换机被焚毁后，电厂与电话局都加强了守卫，目前还没有异常事件发生。（温州，10月5日）

---

① 据相关报道，这次虫灾是由于三化螟蛾二次孵化，白蛹盈田，螟虫遍野。参见《浙省温属各县灾情奇重》，《申报》1929年8月24日，第13版。

《盗匪入寇龙泉：对教会善良的回报》，《北华捷报及最高法庭与领事馆杂志》，1929 年 11 月 16 日

盗匪入寇龙泉：对教会善良的回报

（本报记者报道）

从温州调集的 150 人，从处州调集的 200 人，已经赶往龙泉增强防务，并未遇上那伙 500 人的匪帮，这伙匪帮对龙泉地区的生命财产造成了极大伤害。不久前，匪徒们抵达龙泉后，打开监狱大门释放了所有犯人。同时还劫持了县长、警察局局长以及城内 20 余名富人，以勒索赎金。一名囚犯带着匪徒在城内抢劫，当他们闯入城内唯一的外国传教士奔德（Bender）夫妇家里后，囚犯告诉匪徒："别抢这个房子，这里的主人很好，对富人与穷人一视同仁。"土匪进屋看了看后就秋毫不犯地离开了。据报道，大约有 20 名无辜的人丧命。县长后来想办法逃离魔掌，但其他人仍在土匪手中。

被绑架的孩子

温州附近许多地方发生了饥荒的悲惨故事和一些无法无天的事情。自杀尤其是女性自杀现象相当普遍。温州城北 30 英里的皮里村（Pieh–Li）有 4 名儿童被绑票，绑匪要求每人 1000 银圆赎金。其中 3 个家庭最多只能凑到 20 银圆，而第四个家庭即便将所有家产全部卖光也凑不够 10 银圆。（温州，11 月 9 日）

《上海轮船被劫：海盗假扮乘客劫掠"广济号"》，《北华捷报及最高法庭与领事馆杂志》，1929 年 11 月 16 日

上海轮船被劫：海盗假扮乘客劫掠"广济号"

招商局又一艘船遭到洗劫。[①] 这次轮到了老旧的"广济号"，此船 1000 吨左右，已经在中国沿海航行多年。"广济号"原本在沪瓯航线上行驶，这起暴行发生在一个名叫海门的港口附近，这是浙江海岸的一个小港口。

假扮为乘客的海盗们在控制船只后，将船开到了一个叫石浦（Shipu）的小港口，随后登陆突入该地警察局，抢走局内所有枪械弹药。海盗得手后随即弃船，这艘船目前在石浦港当局控制下。该船现在已经得到驶返上海的命令。

根据海门发来的无线电信息，虽然海盗在上岸前抢走了衣服与贵重财物，但船上所有人都平安无事。另有报道说，有一名乘客遭到殴打，另有一名乘客被掳走。

"永泰号"的目击报告

"广济号"在 11 月 5 日满载货物与乘客离开温州，海上行驶 20 小时后，船只被海盗控制，船员被迫将船开往石浦。另一艘船"永泰号"（Wing Tai）发现"广济号"航行的方向与其固定航线不相符，于是向宁波招商局分局报告了此事。

据一些当事人的讲述，船离开温州一天后，海盗劫持了船长、船员和轮机长，并下令将航线转向石浦。海盗们一接近港口就分成两队，一队留

---

① 据相关报道，匪首名叫冯虞亭，在劫船抢夺石浦军械后，又抢占冯家炮台，后被水警局督察长唐仑、陆防队长邢国鸾等击毙。参见《水警击毙海盗》，《申报》1929年 11 月 17 日，第 11 版。

在船上，另一队上岸。

当船驶进石浦港时，船长和船员们被用绳子捆了起来。海盗登陆队闯入石浦警察局，获得了大量武器弹药。随后留在船上的第一队海盗和返回的第二队海盗开始搜索乘客财物，同时命令中国籍船长驾船离港。待船驶进浙江沿海一小港后，海盗们分乘小船逃走，同时还带走了一名乘客以勒索赎金。这艘船上载有 2.7 万银圆，是中国银行（Bank of China）从温州运往上海的现银，这么一大笔财富却完全被海盗们给忽视了。

乘客的悲惨故事

招商总局上海分局收到以下电报内容："'广济号'于今天（星期一）下午 6 点 30 分抵达海门，并等待下一步命令，另水警将使用该船追击海盗。船长汤（Tong）①。"

招商局随后同意了上述请求。被劫船只现正在水警的带领下追捕海盗，因此也暂停了浙江港口至上海之间的货物运输。

该船的一些乘客已返回上海，他们讲述了所遭遇到的悲惨故事。

似乎有 8 名海盗在温州上船，船离开港后不久，他们控制了船长和高阶船员。海盗们将船员捆绑起来，并告知他们的意图并不是劫船，而是抢水警的武器弹药。在海盗的威胁下，汤船长被迫驾船行驶，并驶近一个小岛。海盗头子向天空开了三枪，随后 100 多名海盗现身海岸，并乘着小船上了"广济号"。海盗命令船长继续行驶，该船于 11 月 7 日晚 7 点抵达石浦。海盗在船上留了一队守卫开始下船登陆，虽然港口里停着 3 艘小巡船和 1 艘炮舰，但海盗们还是轻而易举地制服了水警和军舰船员，并俘获了 2 艘巡船。共有 7 名水警被杀，2 名被俘虏。炮舰开火后，海盗们退回到"广济号"上。在整个交战过程中，"广济号"上乘客有 1 人死亡，数人受伤。

水警征用两艘轮船追击

海盗团伙离开石浦三小时后，恰逢"大华号"与"舟山号"抵达港口，水警随即征用了这两艘船，并驾驶"大华号"追击海盗。终于两船在

---

① "广济号"船长汤和生。

一个名叫金清港的小港口相遇并交火。海盗意识到是时候撤离了，于是用轮船上的小船载着赃物逃离到岸上。在此之前，他们还系统地搜查了所有乘客，掳掠了价值数千银圆的珠宝与其他贵重物品。他们还从保险柜里抢走了近 3000 银圆的现金。乘客们说，海盗离船登岸时水警没有开火，但后来又打了两发炮弹，所幸没有击中"广济号"。他们将这种情况归结于后来所听到的说法，即水警害怕会误伤乘客与船员。一位刘姓乘客遭到绑架，"广济号"被解救后驶向石门，后被水警征用继续追捕海盗。一些乘客设法搭上其他开往上海的船，于昨日到达上海。

海盗欲顽抗

听闻金清港这个小港口现在全是军人，他们是浙江省政府派过去剿匪的。海军部的两艘军舰预计也会抵达，以协助水警剿灭海盗。海盗目前已在鸡蛋山（Chih Tah Hill）部署三尊大炮，这里是他们的老巢，显然这群海盗已准备负隅顽抗。

《温州忧虑的时日：乡村盗匪横行，缺乏自卫手段》，《北华捷报及最高法庭与领事馆杂志》，1929 年 12 月 7 日

温州忧虑的时日：乡村盗匪横行，缺乏自卫手段

（本报记者报道）

我们刚在温州度过了一段非常焦虑的时期，那是由于附近土匪遍地，而我们又缺乏自卫的手段。边远地区无法无天的故事每天都在上演，从乐清到台州，全副武装的土匪到处横行。[①] 在温州以西的处州地区传教时，如在龙泉、云和、松阳等地，传教士们发现由于农村的动荡局面根本无法开展任何活动，只能暂时撤离。温州官员为了防止土匪偷袭，采取了种种措施，但他们所能依靠的只是一支 400 人的警察队伍，人们为此深感焦虑。几天前温州召开了一次政府与商界的联合会议，决议招募一支保卫团，[②]但目前还没有达成一致意见。三天前，1500 名士兵从杭州出发经宁波抵达温州，人们悬着的心终于放了下来。同日，一艘法国炮舰抵达温州，目前仍停留在港内，据报将会于明天离港。

霍乱疫情

经过三个多月治疗霍乱病人的艰苦努力后，白累德医院职员正在恢复

---

① 当年 11 月，在楠溪甚至发生了警察局被土匪缴械的恶性事件，此后警察被缴械、土匪攻打县城事件频发，地方秩序近于崩溃。参见温州市图书馆编《刘绍宽日记·第三册》，方浦仁、陈盛奖整理，中华书局，2018，第 989 页。

② 根据刘绍宽记述，保卫团的经费来自 1930 年的"带征"，所谓带征，也就是田赋加征。田赋带征是近代温州地区办理各项事务获取经费的常见办法。参见温州市图书馆编《刘绍宽日记·第三册》，方浦仁、陈盛奖整理，中华书局，2018，第 988 页。

常规工作。城市里的疫情已逐步趋缓，但大多数患者还是会被送来医院，因此医生与护士仍在没日没夜地工作。医院共治疗霍乱患者 998 例，除未经允许私自离院者外，死亡率仅 10%。在这 10% 中，绝大多数是幼儿或高龄老人。不幸的是，尤其是在疫情起始阶段，有些患者在病情刚好转就急切出院，但这些病人往往仍具有传染力，导致许多这类患者的家属被传染。医生认为，这种私自出院所导致的死亡人数占死亡总人数的 20%。由于采取了所有必要的预防措施，无论是外籍员工还是中国员工都没有染上霍乱。在温州历史上，从来没有像近几个月这样有如此多人接种霍乱疫苗。

（温州，11 月 25 日）

《浙江沿海盗匪：温州周边剿匪，农村艰困》，《北华捷报及最高法庭与领事馆杂志》，1929 年 12 月 31 日

浙江沿海盗匪：温州周边剿匪，农村艰困

（本报记者报道）

温州方圆 50 里内的土匪已被全部清除，有些被士兵俘虏的土匪被带到城里受审，可能将被处决。还有一些土匪在逃跑时被击毙，但也有许多土匪逃脱了。士兵在当地执行剿匪任务十分困难，因为附近都是山区，而土匪熟悉每一条小路和每一个洞穴，士兵却对地形很陌生。出于对土匪的恐惧，村民即便不参与匪帮，也不会为军队提供情报。

温州北部的许多地区仍有许多土匪，例如这些土匪曾策划在白天进入学校然后恐吓孩子们说出自己的家庭背景，然后绑走他们认为"最有价值的人"，并索要赎金。在最近皮里村的一个案子中，一位父亲为此支付了200 银圆赎金。不幸的是，赎金还未交付成功，这名传话的中间人就被士兵捕获并被关进牢房。这位父亲不得不多交数百银圆将中间人保出来，然后又全额支付了儿子的赎金，否则他的儿子无法活命。据说这位父亲一共支付了超过 2000 银圆。

温州附近一名农会领袖被怀疑不仅拥有有关共产主义的知识，而且积极散播共产主义书籍。他被逮捕后，在审讯中，他承认自己每月从外界获取 40 银圆的报酬。数天前，他被判有罪并枪决。[①]

数千人沦为乞丐

令乐清县长感到苦恼的是，城内数千户，有的甚至是全家老小，皆流

---

① 何中，化名何农，在永嘉会昌（今三溪）组织农会运动，被捕后于 1929 年 12 月 10 日下午 2 时，在温州城内资福山麓（今华盖山）刑场被处决。参见《温州枪决一共匪》，《民国日报》1929 年 12 月 17 日，第 6 版。

向农村乞讨红薯活命。虽然周边山区因为缺少水源不能种植大米，但在今年稻米歉收的情况下，山区许多地方的红薯与土豆收成还不算那么糟。但由于缺水，山民今年的收成也只有往年的一半。土豆突然变得金贵了，想要乞讨到土豆也很困难。经常可以看到3～5人的家庭，带着全部家当沿路乞讨，他们的脸上和身上都透露出生活的艰难，他们的灵魂早已离开了躯体。（温州，12月20日）

《寒潮已到浙江：三十年所未有，市场价格飙升》，《北华捷报及最高法庭与领事馆杂志》，1930 年 1 月 21 日

寒潮已到浙江：三十年所未有，市场价格飙升
（本报记者报道）

筹集赈济金

上周温州遭遇了 25 年来的最低气温，每天晚上都是 5～7 度的霜冻天气，白天气温仅略高而已。不幸的是，在低温天气到来的同时，温州正遭遇极大痛苦与贫困。目前政府已筹集到 10 万银圆以缓解百姓痛苦，这些人因为饥荒从农村蜂拥入城。温州的各座庙观里有 1.5 万人完全依靠慈善事业维持生计。当局正在试图赈济灾民，并设立了一系列粥厂。凭义赈会发给的粮票可以领取到粮食，在寺庙的庭院以及角落正燃烧着数百堆小篝火，人们在这些地方煮米饭。仍有许多人被拒之门外，践踏事件时有发生，甚至有婴儿被踩死。据报道有许多人被冻死，主要是幼儿。

有三名商人各捐了 1000 银圆为大约 900 名灾民购买保暖衣物。另一名商人则为 300 名妇女与儿童提供住处与食物，尽管已经做了这些努力，但灾民们仍旧感到痛苦和饥饿。10 万银圆的赈济金就快用完了，到今年 4 月，第一季小麦才能收获。（温州，1 月 14 日）

《浙江脑膜炎流行：沿海疫情严重，丰收在望》，《北华捷报及最高
法庭与领事馆杂志》，1930 年 4 月 1 日

浙江脑膜炎流行：沿海疫情严重，丰收在望

（本报记者报道）

哎，流行病与绑架，已经在共和国的这个地区流行了很长时日。霍乱疫情刚过，现在脑膜炎疫情又来了，突然出现了许多病例，且患者症状往往十分严重。城里的马罗（Marrow）医生告诉我，目前已经收治了 20 ~ 30 名患者，平均每天接收 3 ~ 4 名患者。上周一位中国牧师从 10 ~ 12 英里外的乡村赶来购买疫苗，以便进行接种，据他说感染的家庭非常多。目前上海的疫苗已经告罄，不得不派遣医生前往北平购买。

盗匪依旧猖獗

这名牧师告诉我，在这座城市以北或西北约 20 英里的山区中有一个小村落，这个村落有一个风景如画的名字——梅溪。梅溪已有 24 个孩子被脑膜炎夺走生命，附近一个更大的村子也染上了这种病，情况非常糟糕，有的家庭有三至四口人被夺走生命。

这个较大的村庄还生活在对强盗的恐惧之中，温州周边强盗相当猖獗。有传言说，我所熟悉的一个村庄最近遭到袭击，有两名警察被土匪拷打致死。随后 200 名士兵被派往该地驻屯，仅待了一晚就赶往另一处被土匪抢劫的地点。今天得到的消息是，青田县监狱的犯人全部越狱，由于担心生命受到威胁，青田县县长已经逃入温州城内。

丰收在望

这是一件令人高兴的好事，必须要将其记述下来，温州附近的平原现在一片金黄，触目所及，直至群山山麓尽是芝麻花，空气中全是花香。粮

食长势很好，大豆也不错，如果天气温暖，光照充足，6~8个星期后，小麦就会有好收成。有些地方的小麦已经出穗一周了，有些地方则已经出穗两到三英尺高了。此次丰收将给这个遭受饥荒地区的许多人，带来新的生命和希望。

海关人员最近在一艘本地船只上稽查出走私丝绸和布匹，估计价值为1600~1800海关两。我们现在有一位海关税务司，他给这个小外国社区带来了一些变化。

从前上海轮船只要抵达港口，邮局的雇员就会派送一份书面通知，告知上海和宁波邮件揽收的日期与时间。这个便民的习惯做法，现在已经被废除了。

一座孤岛的苦难

内地会又收到了一笔慷慨的捐款，以帮助在饥荒地区受苦的中国教徒。圣道公会也不时得到这样的帮助，并在数月以来一直为同样困难的中国教徒提供经济援助。牧师欧文·孙光德本周将带着第二批物资前往最需要帮助的地区玉环岛，此地离海岸30~40英里，并位于瓯沪航线上。圣道公会在这座岛上建立了大约6个教团，孙光德先生的援助对那里许多处境危急的基督徒意义重大。我在4个月前受到玉环县县长的邀请前往探访当地人民的困苦情况，县长希望我能与上海的华洋义赈会取得联系。官方随后将发布一份详尽的报告，今年玉环在风灾中有超过200艘船沉没，无数路段被毁，大量房屋倒塌，庄稼因为洪灾、虫灾、旱灾和风灾而绝收。不幸的是，这个地方太偏僻了，除了圣道公会给其成员提供的帮助外，没有任何救济物资送达那里。（温州，3月20日）

《温州无法无天：绑匪与劫匪，艺文中学被迫关闭》，《北华捷报及
最高法庭与领事馆杂志》，1930 年 4 月 15 日

温州无法无天：绑匪与劫匪，艺文中学被迫关闭

（本报记者报道）

　　温州常态性的麻烦在最近显著增加——无法无天的强盗与海盗，隔三岔五地绑票。最近在青田县的西山又发生了一起绑票大案。

　　一名圣道公会的中国教徒在城里买下一幢房子，并将其家人从松溪山区接到城里避难。在松溪，土匪活动异常剧烈。他收到强盗的消息，威胁说如果不给他们 1000 银圆，就烧了他的房子。他赶紧赶到建有城墙的枫林，并在那里与强盗谈判，表示只愿意出 200 银圆。目前我还不知道谈判结果。大约一个月前，我遇到一个住在农村的基督徒，他告诉我自己的家①遭到歹徒袭击，并被抢走了 250 银圆。还有更可怕的传说，我希望这些故事没有一个是真的。有一名妇女在温州的乡村同样遭到匪徒入室抢劫，因为开门太慢，被匪徒砍掉了手。这并非不可能，在去年年末，曾有一个受伤的病人被送到白累德医院，因为伤势太重而死。死者生前曾与其他几人乘坐小船逆江前往温州城，结果小船在航行过程中被打劫。匪徒发现他们身上没带钱，就朝此人开枪并击中其腹部，最终使他丧命。

　　温州艺文中学已经被迫关闭，学校关闭并不是因为缺少学生，而是由于政府在今年采取了实验性的新政策所致，在此情形下，校长蔡博敏认为学校已不能充分发挥其功能。蔡博敏校长具有卓越的社交能力与友善的品质，他常令人感到愉快又幽默，待人热情好客，对于他所遭遇到的挫折，我们的小社区都感到难受。他投入这项无与伦比的教育事业中已经 28 个年

---

① 原文是 horse，应是 house 的误写。

头，从 1902 年建校到 1930 年年初，他一直担任校长的职务。现在这所学校已经附属于白累德医院，并住着一名外国护士雷妮（Raine）小姐，她不久将会前往日本结婚。此外还有一些中国护士，这是史密斯（Smith）护士和雷妮护士开启的新事业，这些中国护士在接受完培训后，就可以在上海注册拿到执照。将来她们准备以此为基础，再开办专门的妇幼医院。蔡博敏校长上个月离开温州，前往中国北部的唐山担任该地中学校长。这里的许多中国人——他以前的学生以及其他许多人对此感到遗憾。蔡博敏是许多中国穷学生的老大哥，他会用自己的钱帮学生付学费，并提供各种帮助。教会的穷人也发现他是一个慷慨和乐于助人的人。人们可以在社会各阶层中找到他的学生，著名者如李博士（Timothy Lee），另外在医界、商界、政界与教会都有他的学生，既有从事传教工作者，也有从事教会教育工作者。

星期六，这里的警察局局长来拜访我，要求使用学校的学生床位。因为本周末将有大批士兵被派驻此地，部分士兵将会被调往瓯北剿匪，部分士兵则留在此地守城。七圣庙也被安排了接待任务，但士兵目前尚未抵达。（温州，3 月 3 日）

《温州河道危险：大型船舶进港须冒风险》，《北华捷报及最高法庭与领事馆杂志》，1930年4月15日

温州河道危险：大型船舶进港须冒风险

（本报记者报道）

自上次发出稿件以来，我们又有了一艘招商局的新船"嘉禾号"（Ka-ho）从事货运工作，此船在开往福州之后再返回上海。招商局的"新昌号"（Hsinchang）也曾到港运货，此外招商局在温州还有固定航班"海晏号"与"广济号"。有一艘船在江中搁浅，另一艘船准备救援时不小心碰到了水道中的岩石，所幸没有造成大碍。另有一艘轮船想要去把它拖出来，但马力不足，第二天早上，此船靠自己的蒸汽机摆脱了困境。

在过去的两周内，一艘400到500吨的木船体轮船在此下水，据我所知，这是温州港有史以来建造的规模最大的船只。

共产主义"暴行"

从浙西边境线上传来了共产主义活动频繁的消息。据报道，前些时候派到那里的一个营已被击败，营长被击毙，2名士兵被俘。据说居住在该地区内地会的一名女士已遭围困，人们原以为她会来温州避难，当地的4名中国官员已经逃走。我了解到松溪县的反抗活动依旧猖獗，这批队伍的领袖在报纸上并不出名，但他曾是杭州和南京官场的重要人物，后来因其对共产主义的同情而被革职。如果此事是真的话，那么以下谣言可能也是真的，据说这伙人的衣服上绣着"共产"两个字。

据说乞丐最近在温州一条大街上引发了一场火灾，大火烧毁了大约两个广场大小的商店和房屋，近100户人家被夷为平地。

脑膜炎传染的危险

圣道公会的女执事辛普森小姐在其工人的帮助下，刚刚在城里办了一

个妇女圣经阅读班。两周内有超过 50 人参加，值此危险时期，仍有许多妇女从农村远道而来。在撰写这篇新闻稿时，该班正在上第二次课，来自温州邻近农村地区的 30 多名妇女与女孩，全都被安排在教会住宿。

本来会有更多的人参加的，但由于担心城里脑膜炎仍在流行，几名妇女不敢从 9 英里外江边的一个小岛来到这里。那座小岛最近出现了 4~5 个脑膜炎病例。血清供应已再次耗尽，脑膜炎病人不得不从白累德医院返回家中。医院马罗医生报告说，上周有更多的人因脑膜炎住院。在英国领事馆所在的江心屿，虽然居民人数不多，但也出现了 2 个病例。

土匪的流弹

上周有人因为枪伤住院，但由于路上耽搁太久，最终还是不幸丧命。这名受伤的妇女来自浙西，是罗马天主教会医院送来的。这名患者原本在上述医院接受了 6 天的治疗，又带着严重的枪伤经过 2 天送抵温州。我在白累德医院看望了她，这时她已气若游丝。当有人问她遭遇了什么不幸时，她用一种几乎听不见的耳语回答说，她刚起身就被土匪流弹击中。医生发现病人的盆骨已经骨折，膈肌似乎也被穿透。（温州，4 月 4 日）

《士兵搜查鸦片："泰顺号"上发生不愉快事件》，《北华捷报及最高法庭与领事馆杂志》，1930年5月6日

士兵搜查鸦片："泰顺号"上发生不愉快事件

（本报记者报道）

上周，招商局的"泰顺号"在士兵搜查鸦片的过程中，其买办遭到粗暴对待。船员告诉我们，士兵在未经授权的情况下搜查船只，并不断攻击试图与他们讲道理的人。

"泰顺号"在事发当天已经接受了海关人员的检查，没有发现鸦片。随后来了一队士兵，在一名下级军官的带领下登船，并宣称是来搜查鸦片的。① 船上买办的一名职员要求士兵出示证件，但这些士兵没有出示证件，并将这名职员抓住狠狠打了一顿。

士兵将船从头到尾搜查了一遍，发现有一名旅客在吸鸦片。此人随即被拘捕，顺带地，财物在此过程中也被抢，包括一对戒指。士兵又冲进买办船舱，要求买办对此事负责。买办的会计和仓库保管员试图进行解释，但这些士兵拒绝听，并称在买办缴纳罚款之前，买办的两名下属都要被关起来。这些不幸的人都被带走了，在"泰顺号"起航时，他们仍然遭到拘押。

---

① 这支军队应为永嘉军警稽查处的队伍，属税警组织，严格上讲不属于军队。但此时正值红十三军攻打浙南，温州城周边风声鹤唳，故税警敢乘乱勒索。

《温州码头工人骚乱：因轮船卸货产生帮派争斗》，《北华捷报及最高法庭与领事馆杂志》，1930 年 5 月 6 日

温州码头工人骚乱：因轮船卸货产生帮派争斗

温州码头两帮苦力 25 日在码头发生严重纠纷后，宣布对招商局进行集体抵制，拒绝卸货。因此，"泰顺号"和"广济号"等船不能按时到达上海。

当冲突爆发时，一位绅士正在"泰顺号"船上，他在接受本报采访时说："事实与中国报纸报道相反，并没有 6 人被杀，而仅两三个人受轻伤。"

我们的这位报料者说，"泰顺号"一抵达温州，就雇了海员帮（Seamen's Union）负责将大米卸下船，然后运到码头另一边的货栈。正当卸货时，海员帮的敌对势力柴爿帮（Firewood Labourers Union）过来要求揽活。海员帮予以拒绝，并使用棍子、铁棒、钩子以及其他工具攻击柴爿帮，后者进行了抵抗。买办的一名职员进行调解时，遭到柴爿帮苦力的捆绑与殴打，他随后逃到招商局办公室才躲过一劫。

警方介入并逮捕了帮派的几个头目，这似乎激怒了两个帮派的成员，他们随后联手冲进警察局去营救他们的头目，结果导致了一场混战，警察不得不向空中开枪以震慑人群。这两个帮派占领警察局不成，随后又将注意力转到"泰顺号"身上，试图强行登船，但遭到警察和船员阻止。

在骚乱中，有数百包大米被偷，买办现在已经被要求为此负责，但我们的报料人说此事与他无关。

码头的苦力们随后宣布要举行大罢工，他们在"泰顺号"的船舷上贴了一张巨大的红纸，宣布全体抵制招商局，并宣布他们将拒绝从招商局船上卸下货物。

调解人随后从中斡旋，货物被转移到招商局仓库，但问题仍未解决。与此同时，"泰顺号"与"广济号"返回上海的时间已经被耽误。

《小麦缓解饥荒：勇敢抵御土匪：团伙中三人被击毙》，《北华捷报及最高法庭与领事馆杂志》，1930 年 5 月 13 日

小麦缓解饥荒：勇敢抵御土匪：团伙中三人被击毙

（本报记者报道）

在这样艰难的时期，我听到一位爱发牢骚的农民说温州今年的小麦收成很好，这实在令人宽慰。尽管天气潮湿，大人和孩子们正忙着收割和打谷。虽然当地人几乎不会将小麦作为口粮，它在很大程度上还是挽救了局势，至少暂时挽救了许多长期处于饥饿边缘的家庭。

数星期以来，除固定航班以外，来往于这个港口的中国与日本轮船明显增加，贸易与 20 年前甚至 10 年前相比正显著增长。在城区与郊区，越来越多的大型洋房与商业场所拔地而起，也证实了贸易的繁荣。有轮船将大米运到该港口销售，居民以 1 银圆 6～7 品脱的价格购买。由于本地出口繁荣，需要有更多的船运量。瓯江上日本汽船的白色条纹烟囱在之前并不常见，这些船主要从事木炭运输贸易。

但可怕的故事仍层出不穷。一个以前受雇于我的苦力，上个月到山里他已经结婚的女儿那里去买大米，那里去年的收成比大多数沿海地区好，但只能买到 3 银圆的粮食。他告诉我，30 多名土匪袭击了一户人家，幸运的是这户人家有武器，劫掠者中三人被击毙，其余星散。据报道，大约一周前的一个晚上，温州 10 名士兵坐舢板过河。行船过程中起了争执，士兵们打了船夫，将其胳膊打成重伤。船夫将士兵带到一个沙洲，告诉士兵已经到岸，由于临近黄昏，士兵未能发觉。船夫随后离开，将士兵留在沙洲上。涨潮的时候，这群士兵中有 8 人被淹死。

圣道公会的孙光德（Irving Scoot）牧师正在沿海城市乐清（中文是悠扬音乐的意思）进行巡回传教，遇到一群匪徒入侵城市，为数不多的警察全部逃走，匪徒释放了监狱里的 20 多名囚犯，其中 2 人随后再次被抓获。

前几天有个士兵，是个很穷的温州本地人，受诱骗而加入军队，因为没有薪水同时又遭军官虐待而逃走，躲在新河街（今信河街）。伴随着惨叫声，这名开小差的士兵被抓了回去，不仅被打得半死，还被切掉一只耳朵。

碧莲镇前是干净的鹅卵石，城对面是陡峭湍急的悬崖，瀑布垂落在山脚下。4月底时，这座筑有围墙、让人微笑的水晶洁白之城的居民因为村长遭到杀害被吓坏了。这名村长在执行公务时指认了几个土匪，这些土匪恰好是其同族且居住本城的人。另外两个强盗闯进他家，一枪打穿了他的脑袋，村长的儿媳目前正在温州上告。

最近附近有大量土匪，同时据说在新桥（New Bridge）有大批共产党，据报告有300人左右，新桥村距温州城大概3英里。4月30日新桥有一名警察，以及三四名当地居民被杀害。温州目前已实施军事戒严，店铺必须在黄昏关门，士兵在街上巡逻并盘查可疑人士。城门守卫全副武装，据说指挥官官邸有大炮守卫，同时还采取了宵禁措施。数周前据说将调北方军队来温州驻扎，但中途又终止了计划，因为这些军队来自冯玉祥，听说冯玉祥是个很坏的人，一旦冯系部队与蒋介石部队反目成仇，温州恐遭蹂躏。

有报道说活跃于温州北部楠溪的土匪，据信全是共产党，准备汇合其他队伍攻打并占领平阳城。距前文提到的新桥大概6英里，在一个八九英里长的谷地入口处有个大村庄名叫大青（Djuchi），有名前军官，同时也是当地拥有1000亩土地的大财主，在村里盖了豪宅。据说他自己组建了一支有40名青壮年的民团，但邻近地区的土匪头目施史（Zie-Shi）给他写了一封信，要求他备好80桌酒席等土匪上门。这名财主没有儿子，只有一个侄子。考虑到目前的危险，这名财主带着小妾前往上海避难，仅留侄子和大老婆在家。

昨晚，5月2日，我们在房子里可以听到巡逻士兵与路人争吵的声音。一名海关职员报告说，在东门外士兵与共产党发生了冲突，并且看到双方交火。到今天晚上为止，这个谣言还没有得到证实。今天晚上我在城墙上散步时，看到了招商局的轮船"广利号"（Kang-lee）停泊在江中，且有穿制服者站岗，码头上停泊的"遇顺号"（Sai Shun）也有人保卫，同属招商局的"广济号"在数天前已离港前往上海。

下午6点，原本热闹的北门商店全部关闭，这样的场面很不寻常。前文提到的 10 个士兵，有 8 人被淹死，现在据说他们原本是想要带着武器，偷偷过河参加北方的土匪队伍，最后因为殴打船夫而被带到沙洲。从军队这几天几夜在城里的活动来看，似乎有充分的理由相信当局感到了一种迫在眉睫的危险。（温州，5 月 3 日）

《温州戒严令：抵御土匪的非常举措》，《北华捷报及最高法庭与领事馆杂志》，1930 年 5 月 20 日

温州戒严令：抵御土匪的非常举措

由于土匪和海盗的活动，温州当局实行了非常严格的戒严。日落到第二日黎明之间施行宵禁，行人在白天有时也会受到盘查。下午 6 点以后，一切交通都被切断，没有特别许可，任何人都不允许上街。

所有码头和重要地点都有守卫保护，日落后任何船只都不允许进出港口。

由于采取了以上措施，瓯沪之间已无船只来往，据报道，至少有 2000 名原本打算去南方港口的人滞留在温州，据说其中还有许多外国人被迫取消行程。

《浙江东南盗匪：一系列城镇被洗劫》，《北华捷报及最高法庭与领事馆杂志》，1930 年 6 月 3 日

浙江东南盗匪：一系列城镇被洗劫

（本报记者报道）

本月的第二周，温州楠溪的枫林镇遭到 1000 多名土匪袭击，据报道，有 20～30 人在战斗中丧生。枫林镇是一个有几千居民的小镇，周围有坚固的城墙。这里的居民是吃苦耐劳的山民，也是粗犷的基督徒。我了解到的袭击有两次，第一次是在上午 9 点，好像被挫败。当天晚些时候，据说约 20 名当地人与土匪勾结进行了第二次袭击，导致土匪在下午 4 点左右进入城镇。

枫林镇有一些居民被杀害，13 座房屋和 5 座寺庙被焚毁，此外还有其他的毁损。一名男子冲进圣道公会教堂，显然是为了进行躲藏。后来此人以为土匪已经离开，便手持菜刀来到教堂门口查看，结果被强盗击中。数天之后大量驻守北城的士兵被派去剿匪，这伙强盗绕道向西，从处州的乡村逃跑，逃到温州南面 34 英里的、有城墙的平阳。

军队似乎在楠溪地区与土匪发生过交战，因为上周城里处决了几名土匪，人头被挂在城门口示众。军方还摧毁了楠溪的五尺村（Ng‐ts'i），此地是臭名昭著的土匪的老家，这些土匪长期以来一直在该地进行劫掠。

这些楠溪的匪帮在抵达平阳后，于 5 月 24 日（周六）袭击了该城镇，其总人数超过 1000 人。平阳内地会的伊宝珍小姐给温州负责人王廉牧师写了封信，这封信提供了一些此次事件的细节。尽管经历了一段担惊受怕的时期，但内地会所有成员［包括白德邻牧师夫妇与他们的孩子、伊宝珍小姐、兰格小姐（Lange）］都很安全。袭击发生在西门，星期六那里爆发了激烈战斗。虽然这两位女士居住在城墙外，但她们没有受到任何骚扰。星期天，白德邻先生出门寄了一封报平安的信件。他们说共计超过 200 名匪

徒被击毙，并且城内正在对残党进行严厉搜索。当笔者星期天写这份新闻稿时，局势还算平静。笔者的秘书与衙门有不少联系，今天他为笔者提供了此次事件的其他细节，大意是超过100名土匪被击毙，军方缴获了100支步枪，军方仅1名士兵死亡，6人受伤。这伙袭击者已经向南撤退。

上个星期，整个城市都震惊于灵溪（Lich'i）大峇嘉村（Djiae－o－Ka）遭到大伙匪徒袭击，匪徒带走了2名妇女，焚毁2艘小轮，并试图抢夺"青田轮"并将其焚毁，但"青田轮"成功切断连接其他客轮的拖绳。当"青田轮"来到温州时，船身有一个赤红色的大洞。传言说在瓯江北岸还潜藏着大量匪徒，他们准备藏在船里，在上个星期天袭击温州。然而，目前温州还没有发生这样的事件。在撰写此稿件时，城里的气氛较之数月前更为平静。

但到处都有抢劫、纵火和流血事件发生。接受一位同事的采访之后，我提起钢笔继续写作。这位同事正接受一位来自上游12英里的人口众多的山谷地区的牧师的采访。这位牧师带来消息，他巡回布道的村庄同样遭到袭击，许多人失去了一切。他现在要去寻找军队长官寻求保护，因为另一个村庄很有可能不久也会遭到攻击。他告诉我，该地区的5名圣道公会教徒被抢劫，并失去了所有财产。（温州，5月27日）

《温州可怕的场面：公开处决的恐怖故事》，《北华捷报及最高法庭与领事馆杂志》，1930 年 7 月 8 日

温州可怕的场面：公开处决的恐怖故事

（本报记者报道）

在写作中，你会感到在被不间断地掠夺，以致于不仅对编辑来说，而且对作者自己来说，都必须产生一种满足感，才能让继续接纳和写作这些暴力事件坚持下去。温州就像其他地方一样，大众的日常生活每天都在被暴力所侵犯，大众正痛苦地经历着这种影响的后果。

无数的强盗团伙使用"疯狂的办法"将待宰的受害者进行标价，50 银圆、60 银圆或 100 银圆，他们会根据一个人在村子里的名望与财产进行标价，抢劫勒索所造成的损失使得本地商业遭到重创。

山村的一名乡下店主，在 4 天前下山来到温州城，告诉我他刚刚因为土匪抢劫损失了 300 银圆。因此他正在城里为 4 箱货物与财产寻找安全的存放地点。有 4 名女孩参加了圣道公会汤小姐（Simpson）举办的夏季学校（Summer School），这所学校共有 50 名学生。这 4 名女孩准备在周末回到12 至 15 里外的家中，因为有消息说她们的家被强盗洗劫了，这户人家并不算小康之家，而是普通的、辛勤劳作的小农户。

由于许多男孩被绑票，乡村学校的教育事业遇到了挫折。农业也在遭受重创，现在农民经常会问种田有什么用，既然种田会被那些不播种的人掠夺，即便收获又有什么用呢？社会进步也遭到打击，中国文明在全国范围内遭受了难以形容、无法估量、不可补救的损失，到处充斥着谋杀、鲜血、掠夺和复仇的怒火。

文雅的处决艺术

上周有两位先生找到我，其中一位刚看到可怕的场景，他描述的场景

与中世纪令人作呕的无情场景一模一样。两名强盗被抓获，一人被砍头后，头吊在另一个人的脖子上。另一个强盗随后被处死，两颗头颅就这样被悬在城门口。

在这个城市里，我的房子外 300~400 码距离处，有一座风景如画的小山丘，我们将其称为亭山（Pavilion Hill）①。城墙从东一直延伸过去，山有 150~200 英尺高，山顶有一座整洁的小亭，石柱与石座相连接，支撑着六角形的弯曲屋顶与瓦片。

这座美丽的小亭迎风敞开，在这里可以看到大海和岛屿、河流和平原、城市和山脉、稻田和微笑的村民。正在拔高的不安分的竹子，拥抱着一座三进的佛教寺庙，寺庙向西可以俯瞰整座城市，似乎在无休止地沉思，耐心而又焦虑地沉思着城市的命运。山下和亭子周遭是绿树覆盖的山坡以及许多空地，其中一处空地就在寺庙下方，最近无数土匪在此地被枪决。②

周三，6 月 4 日，我正在楼上阳台写作，突然听到短暂而尖锐的子弹声，抬头看见一队士兵站在寺庙下方的绿地上，在士兵前方几步远处，有蜷缩成一堆的蓝色。我推了推眼镜，看清是死者穿着的乡下人常穿的蓝棉布衣服，样式极为普通。很快人群聚拢到山上，各色人等都有，有穿戴华丽的妇女，有领着年仅六七岁、穿戴整洁的女儿来看热闹的父亲。旁观者用脚踢开死者的衣服，想看看他的伤口。这样持续了数小时后，两个苦力抬来一口不起眼的棺材，把尸体塞进去抬走了。

几天后传来的两声枪响，使我再次望向山丘。从群众五颜六色的衣服看，就好像在举办夏季节日，而他们刚刚观看了两名土匪被枪决。随后我看到一名士兵手持两英尺的阔剑跪在草地上，我在屋里看不真切，但可以看到他正朝向某个物体不停地挥舞武器，一下！两下！三下！他停顿了几秒钟，然后换了个姿势，以便再次举剑。四下！五下！他站起身来，走了几步，拎着一颗留着短发的人头。士兵将人头放下，用草擦了擦武器，这时另一名士兵大步上前捡起地上人头，然后离去，可能要把它挂在某一座城门上示众了。（温州，6 月 25 日）

---

① 外国人所谓的亭山，也就是今天的华盖山。

② 此地即温州民国时期资福山麓刑场。

《温州的进步：浙江政府计划扩展贸易》，《北华捷报及最高法庭与
领事馆杂志》，1930年8月12日

温州的进步：浙江政府计划扩展贸易

为了改善浙东南的商业并增加浙江外贸出口，同时也是为了扩大瓯江（Wu River）① 区域的航运贸易，浙江省政府建设厅决定疏浚瓯江，同时建设温州至兰溪（Lanchi）之间的铁路。②

8月5日已派数名工程师与专家前往温州查勘，并希望在一个月内开始工作。

温州是浙江大港，目前有7趟固定航班来往于瓯沪之间。但温州并没有像所期待的那样繁荣，因为本地产品无法从浙南快速运输到其他地方，反之亦然。根据《申报》的说法，有鉴于此，浙江省政府建设厅决议建设温州港。

初步开发工作将由省建设厅官员负责，包括疏浚瓯江，使大型船舶可以直接驶往温州内地，而非停泊永嘉。永嘉之于温州，正如吴淞之于上海。

浙江建设厅官员还建议在浙江南部的兰溪修建一条铁路直达温州，以方便浙江内陆到沿海的产品运输。这些产品包括木材、木炭、火腿、桐油、纸等，这些产品在浙江都很有名气，如果能够出口，必将大大提振本地贸易与商业。

---

① 外国人常将瓯江称为温江（Wu River）。

② 此事由浙江省政府建设厅秘书长林士模提议，林原为北京大学留美同学会会长。参见《温州开埠之计划》，《工商半月刊》1930年第17期，第12页。

《外埠新闻：温州更多死刑案：16 人被同批处决》，《北华捷报及最
高法庭与领事馆杂志》，1930 年 8 月 19 日

外埠新闻：温州更多死刑案：16 人被同批处决

（本报记者报道）

　　自从上次——6 月 25 日写作以来，在亭山又杀死了很多土匪和共产党人。到目前为止，一共有 70 多人被处决。最近一批发生在 7 月 31 日，枪决了 12 人。在这批犯人中，有一名据说是宣传员的妇女以及她 19 岁的儿子。数天前，还有一批，共 16 人被枪杀，这些人跪在草地上，士兵依次走到他们身后，然后开枪。大多数时候，士兵会朝受害者补枪。这样的场景相当残酷，最后的俘虏不得不跪在地上，等着前面的人依次被杀，然后轮到自己。至于最近一次的处决，在外国人看来稍有一些文明精神，也许是他们想要故意表现出一点这种精神，尸体被裹上草席后才运走。

　　政府军队仍在山区作战，但似乎成效不彰。据说这些士兵与北方军队（其中一些是冯玉祥的军队）相比，战斗力要差很多，冯玉祥的军队在两个月前已经撤走。……尽管寡不敌众，政府军仍在勇敢作战，大约一个月前，他们捕获了一个非常重要的猎物，我今天从一个线人那里听到相关细节，据说他认识一些有关的人。

　　该地区共产党的领导人①已经被抓获，他是来自山区的年轻人，家住温州以北 30 多英里的一个大村庄②。在 30 多年的时间里，我曾在这个村子度过许多日夜，当地村民长期以好勇与宗族械斗而闻名。但他们战胜之后，立马又会变为坚定的基督徒。这里提到的共产党领袖是一名有才华的年轻人，毕业于当地的师范学校。

---

① 指金贯真。
② 永嘉县楠溪岩头。

他的家庭很穷，其父有10亩地，卖了5亩地，以便让儿子前往俄国。据说他在俄国学习并毕业，在那里似乎接受了更为严格的共产主义教育。报道说，他从来没有帮助过为他做出这样牺牲的父母，当他回到家乡温州后，就开始用俄国提供的经费在当地从事共产主义宣传工作。

几个星期前，这名叫金家济（Chin Chia-Chu）① 的年轻人来到温州，住在一个亲戚家里，他的亲戚在南门附近开了一家米铺。据说一名女学生向当局报告了他的临时住所，士兵被派去逮捕他。他试图用左轮手枪进行防卫，可惜手枪哑火，士兵们随即将其包围并俘获。金家济质问士兵们为什么要这样做，共产主义对士兵有利。但没有用，金家济告诉士兵们可以开枪打死他。

按照以往惯例，金家济在这座城市的小山上被处死。据说他被捕的重要性在于，由于之前本报曾报道的共产党的军事失利，金家济正在与其副手胡公冕（Ho Kung-mien）谋划先攻打并占领温州，然后溯江而上攻取处州，最后穿越农村地区抵达杭州。由于最能干的领导人被处死，现在看来这个计划实现的可能性已不大。

今天我看到的一则报道是，在温州以北20~30英里楠溪地区的筑有城墙的碧莲镇（Piehlien）驻扎的士兵，最近受到土匪猛烈攻击，有数名士兵被杀。不仅镇内兵舍被毁，武器也遭到抢夺，此外从城里征调帮助运输的苦力也被土匪带走。这些士兵的兵舍原本是借用的圣道公会的教堂与房屋，但我们没有收到那里牧师关于房屋受损的任何消息。这很可能是个假消息，但一切还无法确认。

最近得到的另一个消息是，在其他乡村地区有几个裁缝被土匪掳走，这些裁缝被命令为他们制作2000件军装。

圣道公会的一位女教工十分希望能恢复针对监狱女犯人的布道工作，②于是她给城内教会的中国秘书写了一封信，希望政府能够批准。这位秘书亲自阅读后，增添了一些内容，他强调针对犯人的传教是要提升人的良好

---

① 金贯真原名叫家济。

② 1919年，黄庆澜在温州任瓯海道尹。在夏时若牧师的交涉下，温州当局曾允许教会在监狱传教。参见《破天荒之监狱布道》，《通问报：耶稣教家庭新闻》1919年第859期，第7页。

品质，阻止他们堕落，并帮助他们成为有价值的国家公民，政府应该乐于同意这样的工作目标，并给予帮助。秘书在回复中也承认，地方党部（Local Tang pu）是反对基督教的，极有可能会反对监狱布道工作。至于他自己对基督教的态度和感受，他表示自己对基督教并不怀有敌意，但他不能无视党部的态度。不过他会写信给杭州方面，如果杭州同意，那么就可以在温州开展这项工作。当被问及罗马天主教会的姐妹为什么被允许做这样的工作时，他的回答是，罗马天主教会并不宣传宗教，而仅仅是劝导犯人向善，并为病人治病。当被告知圣道公会也会按这种方法行事，不仅会给病人发药，还会给病人带来食物时，他唯一的答复是"会给杭州写信"。（温州，8月6日）

《温州附近动荡不安》，《北华捷报及最高法庭与领事馆杂志》，1930
年9月23日

温州附近动荡不安
（本报记者报道）

　　圣道公会的孙光德夫人在回英格兰度假六个月后，于上周抵达温州。
此前，她的丈夫在香港迎接她。

　　由于教会新成员的加入和一些休假人员返回，我们的小外国社区人数
很快就会增加。我们的医院很快将会拥有另一名接受过全英式培训的护
士，另有一名刚大学毕业的年轻人，将会来到温州从事总务工作，狄奇
（Dcidge）小姐也将回来从事教育与其他工作。施德福夫妇也将在今年年底
返回，并且带着他们在休假期间出生的幼子。听说还会有一名年轻的医生
跟着一起来，他将参与温州的医务工作，但这条消息目前还没有得到
确认。

　　下面我的叙述，相较于长期以来温州本地报纸的报道，可能读起来会
让人更舒心一点。

　　周日，我和一个多年的中国朋友聊天，他是一位生活在农村的富裕农
民。僻静的小村庄在西溪山谷的一侧，周围是美丽树木覆盖的群山。他居
住的地方被称作梅岙（Plum Torrent），有些外国人可能知道这个响亮的名
字。他的房子建的堂皇而舒适，位于村子里大多数房屋的高处，能够俯瞰
整个村庄与山谷，我们曾在那难忘的岁月里一起在山头奔跑。当时他向我
展示了太平天国叛乱时期，因为传言敌人将会进攻而修造的圆形城墙遗
迹，他告诉我当地人已不再需要上城御敌。

　　多年以来，我这位朋友一直担任着当地圣道公会巡回传教士的职务，
同时还担任当地教堂牧师。这个村庄位于匪徒聚居区的中心地带，由于他
的社会地位，特别容易受到匪徒的注意，他认为当下最好的选择是在城里

住上几个月，他的儿子正在城里医院当助手。他经常参加温州城里教堂的周日礼拜，但最近几个星期我都没看到他，据说大约两个星期前他已经返回家中。

我后来问他为什么没来做礼拜，他说确实是回了一趟家。也许是粮食将要收获，因此他才要冒这样的风险。他说老家现在很平静，但附近地区动荡危险，他在路上不幸落入一伙强盗手中。匪徒在搜身过程中拿走了他的钱和手表，在搜查他的包裹时，发现里面有一本书，那是他的中文版《每日读经》（*Bible Daily Readings*）。土匪们看后说："哦，你是基督徒，好吧，基督徒没有害过我们。"于是匪徒归还了财物并放他走了。

几个月前，一名基督复临安息日会（Adventist）的牧师也有类似经历，一群强盗先是抢走了他的鞋子，然后在继续搜身时发现了他佩戴的教士徽章。强盗头目在得知他是基督复临安息日会牧师后，还给了他一双更好的鞋，然后放他走了。人们徒劳地叹息，希望能够用更轻松的方式来描述最近的时局，但现实往往阴暗。

虽然温州改变了刑场地点，但处决仍在继续。昨天处决了8名土匪，上周有一天处决了7人，另一天处决了3人，还有一天处决了2人。浙江四属（温台宁绍）① 剿共总指挥王文瀚（Wang Wen - han）已抵达温州，因此军队不会按照官方的命令将犯人送到杭州处决，王文瀚现在说的话就代表官方。

在本月9日，距离温州20英里的西溪河口最大村庄遭到大批匪徒袭击。根据当地媒体提供的数字，共有60至70座房屋被毁，四五个人遭到杀害。我的一名线人说匪徒使用了手榴弹——可能是燃烧弹，当时该地仅有40名驻军。另一份报道指出，在距离温州西部10英里的缙云（Chin - Yun）县，10天前遭到土匪大规模袭击，县长征收的17000银圆税款也被抢去。（温州，9月16日）

---

① 原文写的是五属，但实际上应为四属（温台宁绍），原文可能是对王文瀚的另外一个职务"外海水警局局长"有所误读。参见《浙水警与海盗激战》，《申报》1930年7月15日，第8版。

《温州商人罢工：反对提高商品税》，《北华捷报及最高法庭与领事
馆杂志》，1930 年 11 月 25 日

温州商人罢工：反对提高商品税

　　温州当局决定将进出温州的商品的税率从 20% 提高到 30%，导致温州
当地商人罢市，并鼓动码头工人参加。① 结果是，目前温州所有停靠码头
的船只都无法装卸货物。

　　11 月 17 日，温州当局决定提高税率，但遭到温州商人拒绝，并表示
只会按照旧税率纳税。商人同时在 11 月 17 日宣布，将会停止将所有受到
新税率影响的商品运往其他地方。商人代表呼吁当局取消增税，但当局态
度强硬，拒绝了该提议。

　　由于某些商人暗中缴税，并偷偷将货物运出，当地商人团体为了防止
这样的事情再发生，鼓动码头苦力参与罢工，结果导致所有在此停靠的船
只都无法装卸货物。

　　许多与温州有商务来往的当地公司受到影响。由于码头苦力罢工，从
温州订购的大量货物目前仍滞留在港口。

---

① 当地商人原本缴纳的是温州洋广货局 20% 的洋广货税，但由于当年洋广货局撤销，
　其业务被并入统销局，导致商人改为缴纳 30% 统销税，因而导致商人不满。但无论
　是洋广货税还是统捐税，实际都是海关正税之外的非法杂税。参见《温州闹捐风潮
　影响上海航业货运》，《申报》1930 年 11 月 22 日，第 12 版。

《浙江丰收：饥荒时期许多失踪人口被贩卖》，《北华捷报及最高法庭与领事馆杂志》，1930 年 12 月 2 日

浙江丰收：饥荒时期许多失踪人口被贩卖

（本报记者报道）

笔者自上次（9 月 16 日）发出关于本港口和本地区的新闻稿后，已经很长一段时间没有再写过稿件。但笔者高兴地发现，土匪活动虽未停止，但已大为减弱，据说在一些仍有匪迹的地区，土匪主要以小股行动为主，目标多为零散户。温州仍在处决犯人，但刑场已经迁移到城西南三角门内的山上。一名英国妇女最近来到温州，她是一名中国温州人的妻子，他们在 10 年前于伦敦相遇并结合，丈夫曾在伦敦销售青田石与其他中国古玩，现在他们已经对这个国家现阶段的可怕生活有了一定了解。他们的房子就在城里处决土匪和枪杀共产党的地方，离刑场很近，在那里正好能够看到悲剧的上演。就在几个星期前，他们全程观看了不少于 27 人次的处决。至于为什么要改变行刑地点，是由于山脚处有一口井，距离刑场有 40 码远，使用这口井的人抱怨说人犯被处决后鲜血会渗入井中，从而污染这口井。如今人们还在用这口井来打水。

有新人到来

两星期前，爱乐德（W. Roy Aylott）牧师从英国韦斯特克利夫来到温州，增加了我们外国社区的人数。他刚从大学毕业，并成为圣道公会的一分子，目前正在学习中文。他对于温州周边美景十分陶醉，喜欢温州的普通人，他们曾欢迎他的到来，温州男孩与女孩开朗的性格也使他开心。白累德医院的护士皮特里·史密斯（Petrie Smith）在经历了两个夏季的艰难工作后，决定前往上海换一份工资更高的工作。莫罗（W. A. N. Morrow）医生的报告节录，可以证明其工作的艰辛："1929 年 9 月至 11 月，因为接

收了大量霍乱患者，工作变得非常紧张……患者数量是往年的 4 倍，值得一提的是，城里虽然有中国人经营的医院，但他们总共只接收了不到 100 名患者。这一切要归功于本院在 1926 年霍乱流行期间所取得的优异成绩。在施德福医生接手后，医院总共接收了 971 名霍乱患者，治愈率近 80%。而这样的数据，还是在死亡率中有 9% 重复入院的情况下达成的……医护人员中无一人感染霍乱。"

史密斯护士有一名同事雷妮，目前已经结婚，现居住在横滨。在今年痢疾流行期间，史密斯护士身边没有任何一位受过训练的护士帮她。下面的数据，可以反映出她担负的责任有多么沉重。

门诊病人：37920 人次

住院病人：（男性）2610 人次；（女性）1263 人次

大手术：239 人次；小手术：529 人次

其中 1/3 的患者患的都是内科病，包括……详见下：肺结核、疟疾、脚气、伤寒、痢疾（包含阿米巴型与杆状型）、脑膜炎、喉炎、糖尿病、心、肺、肾、肝疾病。（温州，11 月 10 日）

《温州教师罢工：商人拒绝多付税金来支付薪水》，《北华捷报及最高法庭与领事馆杂志》，1930 年 12 月 16 日

温州教师罢工：商人拒绝多付税金来支付薪水

（本报记者报道）

我今天早上听一位校长说，永嘉乃至于全温州，除了教会学校之外，所有学校都关闭了。这种局面与三四年前的动荡时期有关，当时南方与北方在打仗，福建的一位将军和他的军队经过城市时向当地居民勒索了一大笔钱，商人们只能被迫满足其要求。在最近的饥荒中，永嘉商会让我也参加了华洋义赈会，我知道这些商人又捐献了数万银圆，由于诸如此类的事件不断发生，民间财富被不断攫取。

由于教育当局无法支付工资，当地教师已经开始罢工，他们关闭了所有学校并拒绝复学。当地教育局已经向省教育厅建议，通过向商人征税来支付教师工资。被这些持续不断的征税和苛求逼得绝望的商人答复说，他们宁愿罢市也绝不缴税，所以省当局建议不要征税。

当地教师指责教育局背信弃义，而这些"人民的公仆"则回应教师代表他们也是自身难保，只能按省教育厅命令行事，教师团体的答复则是罢课。我问线人如果私下以个人名义为孩子请老师上课，会出现什么样的状况，线人告诉我教师们不会允许这样的事情发生。

一个青年的复仇

在过去的几周里，当地的中国媒体一直在发表批评基督复临安息日会学校的信件和文章。我在那些报纸上读到了其中一些信件，据说为了让教会学校能继续开下去，许多教会学校已经更名为"神学院"。

另一篇报道说，一名男学生与教会学校校长发生争执，起因是这名男学生与一名女学生通信，并最终导致其被开除，这名男青年试图通过当地

中国媒体，"拿回属于自己的东西"。另有一名记者拜访了这所教会学校并提出了许多问题，诸如学校没有悬挂孙中山画像，学校里到处都是宗教画像与文献，学校花费很多时间教授圣歌与经文等。他们认为教会学校是非法的，同时对教会学校怀有敌意。

我得到的最新消息是，这所学校几乎所有学生——超过100名男孩与女孩都离开了学校。此外还有一名学生拒绝离校，他是牧师的儿子，他认为作为教会成员，他们应该出面管理学校。

悔改的"土匪"

令人高兴的是，最近几乎没有听到或很少听到土匪的消息，据报道，这可能是由于最近有一伙数百人的"土匪"及其"头目"向官军投诚的缘故。在楠溪第一个投降的"土匪头子"是胡协和（Hu Hsieh - Wei），[①] 他手下有84人以及40条枪。今年早些时候，他从俄国留学回来的兄弟已经被处决，胡协和在一段时间里担任了领导职务，他的老家也因此被官军摧毁。另一个投降的是活动于楠溪潘坑（P'an - K'eng）的谢文侯（Hsieh Wen - hou），他有25人和十几条枪。最后，是最近投降的董佐光（Tong Tsoh - kuang），他主要活动于西楠溪地区，手下有超过400人。董佐光在12月13日投降，并被授予上尉军衔。当地有希望恢复平静的一个证据是，内地会的女士们已经回到了与福建接壤的平阳传教站。

多里奇小姐归来

圣道公会的多里奇（D. Doridge）小姐已经从英格兰休假返回温州，她目前已经恢复了在学校的工作，顺便说一句，教会学校并没有受到最近教育风潮的影响。多里奇小姐受到了学生们热烈欢迎，学生们在入口处排成两列，当老师从他们中间经过时，学生们同时以中国式礼仪向老师鞠躬。

---

① 由于军事不利，胡公冕指示胡协和等名气大的人假招安，待机前往上海。1931年胡协和以在东门开办赌场为掩护，继续从事地下工作。1932年胡公冕潜回温州领导兵运，由于暴露，胡协和身份也遭暴露，在准备过程中自杀牺牲。参见蒋寿平《红军团长胡协和》，载永嘉政协文史委员会编《永嘉文史资料·第四辑》，第106~111页。

墙上贴满了条幅，条幅上写满了多里奇小姐的功绩与美德。大厅里挂满了彩带，孩子们举办了一场音乐会，并朗诵了欢迎词。孩子中的小姑娘们表演了一段迷人的舞蹈，并进行了优雅的朗诵。这些还缺乏完全自主意识的小姑娘们是多么迷人，我不得不说，如果真有仙女这种东西，那一定是中国小女孩。多里奇小姐对欢迎仪式以及其他客人的演讲表示感谢，随后全校职员与来客共同合照留念。

多里奇小姐将把她的一部分时间用于基督教勉励协会和城市邻近地区的主日学校工作，并希望找到机会接触一些其他城市学校的大龄女学生。护士菲森德（Fieldsend）小姐与多里奇小姐一同从英格兰来到温州，她目前已经熟悉了未来在两所教会医院的工作。此外为了适应其他职责，菲森德小姐还将跟随一位中国教师学习中文，以帮助培训中国女护士。（温州，12月3日）

《温州附近土匪》，《北华捷报及最高法庭与领事馆杂志》，1931 年 1
月 6 日

温州附近土匪

（本报记者报道）

星期六（12 月 6 日），我与一群英国女士以及绅士步行游览了瓯江北岸的群山，山高 1300 英尺，并修建有圣道公会的休假别墅。这些别墅已经闲置将近一年。数月之前，土匪曾"光临"过别墅，他们损坏了几扇窗户，带走了一些物件，剩下的家具对他们来讲不值钱也不好搬运。一名住在附近的中国看守告诉我，上周六土匪曾经出现过，并从附近的两个村庄绑架了六七人，要求家属交付数千银圆的赎金。附近几乎所有山民，包括周边村庄的人家，在土匪的侵扰下都逃走了。

与教师尖锐的谈话

我很高兴地告诉大家，我上次报道的教师罢工事件，将会很快结束。如果传言是真的，那对教师来讲是一种耻辱。据说省教育厅派了一名代表到温州进行调查，这名官员在与教师代表的谈话过程中语气强硬，他一边用手拍着桌子，一边指责罢工教师缺乏爱国心，要求教师们考虑一下国家的艰难处境。官员告诉教师们，他们自私自利，良心已经被金钱所蒙蔽。最后官员要求那些不愿意教书的人写下自己的名字，他们将被解雇，其他人将继续留任。然而没有一个老师敢于挺身而出——他们被吓到了，短暂的罢工就此结束。当人们走在大街上，已经能够再次听到课堂里传出的音乐声或朗读声。有人对我说，如果全国的学生团体都能拥有这样坚定的纪律精神，那么中国人民所遭受的痛苦与损失即便不能完全消除，也会大为缓解。

休假归来

星期四（12月11日），施福德和他的妻子从英国休假归来，受到了教会团体全体职员的热烈欢迎。当地的男女老少也欢天喜地地来到码头，欢迎施福德的到来。这足以证明施福德医生获得了包括中国人在内的许多人的尊敬。休假对于医生来说是一段悲喜交集的经历，虽然在这期间他们的儿子出生了，但同时他也经受了父亲、母亲先后去世的双重打击。施福德是一位在圣道公会任职多年的牧师，他担任过不止一个任期的主席职务，他的忠诚服务、杰出的传教与学术成就，受到了人们的尊敬。

花招

12月13日，一支约120人的小分队被派往温州南面20多英里的瑞安县剿匪。土匪已经逃窜，士兵们并没有追击土匪，而是返回了温州城。我将此事告诉了一位中国人，他回答说，士兵们在这种情况下就是这么干的。官军不会急于前往剿匪地点，等到他们赶到时土匪已经逃走，士兵回来就可以告诉他们的上级长官他们去了那个地方，但土匪已经逃走，所以他们自行回来，完成了他们的任务。

毒品药丸贸易

根据线人提供给我的消息，依据中华国民拒毒会对毒品情况的调查，本地存在数量相当可观的毒品贸易，包括鸦片、吗啡、红药丸、金药丸、白药丸。本地鸦片贸易始于90年前，其他种类毒品贸易始于20年前，温州鸦片来自福建，而其他种类毒品来自上海。温州每年输入将近4000斤、价值64万银圆的鸦片。温州有将近1000名零售小贩，其中绝大多数集中在东门。毒品吸食人数约8000人，其中大部分属于富裕阶层，大约有1/10是因为生病才吸毒，其余是为了追求生理快乐。在这些毒品中，药丸与吗啡的危害性最大。

弹性罚款

我的一名线人，以个人名义对一家反毒机构进行了调查。他告诉我，城里有好几个戒毒机构，戒毒人员在治愈后就能得到一张治愈证书。有些官员会根据瘾君子的经济状况，对他们处以 30 ~ 1000 银圆不等的罚款，另一些官员则会对吸毒者处以 30 天到 3 年不等的监禁。据说一些官员和一些有影响力的人自己就是瘾君子，有人建议如果这些人受到公开惩罚，就可以震慑以权谋私者。据报道，温州北部的楠溪地区广泛种植鸦片，而楠溪地区土匪首领最近带着手下与武器投靠了军方，现在楠溪的鸦片种植者都需要向他交钱以换取保护。

白累德医院的莫罗医生又收治了许多受枪伤的病人，数天前我去医院时曾看到其中几个病例。（温州，12 月 8 日）

> *《温州有新人到来：戴蒙德医生将接替其兄弟职务》，《北华捷报及最高法庭与领事馆杂志》，1931 年 1 月 27 日*

温州有新人到来：戴蒙德医生将接替其兄弟职务

（本报记者报道）

自从上次发出新闻稿后，白累德医院的医务职员人数又增加了。戴蒙德医生与他的妻子在 1 月 2 日从英格兰返回温州。戴蒙德医生具有高尚的品德，他接替了他兄弟哈登（R. P. Hadden）的职位，哈登也是一名医疗传教士，他曾在温州短暂工作随后被派往云南，最后死在了工作岗位上。哈登是由于感染疾病而死，而他的年轻的继任者同样也成为该病的牺牲品。

戴蒙德医生及其夫人受到了教会工作人员最衷心的欢迎，两家医院的工作经历，将更加充分地使其发挥专业才能。

这两兄弟的先祖很了不起，他们的父亲是邰慕廉（Rev. F. J. Dymond）牧师，也曾在云南传教，并且是已故的柏格理（Sam Pollard）牧师的终身战友。柏格理牧师曾发明苗族文字，并使用苗族文字翻译了《新约》的部分内容。邰慕廉在中国生活了 45 年，其中绝大多数时间在云南，他已于今年春季回到英国家乡。戴蒙德医生的一个妹妹在云南宣教过一段时间，现在与一名内地会成员结了婚。

土匪不抓老人

今天下午我与一名 70 多岁的老牧师谈话，他曾经不顾山区匪徒横行，坚持传教。他在执行传教任务时曾遇到土匪，但土匪没有伤害他。他的答案是自己已经太老，匪徒不会绑架他。他告诉我，在他做巡回布道的地方强盗活动依旧猖獗。有一日在村里教堂早祷时，他听说土匪要来了。但他拒绝离开，并像往常一样做了下午的礼拜。

星期五（1月2日），瓯江对岸的一个村庄被40名土匪袭击，有11人被绑架。有几个人从邻近的村庄来到城里，以躲避土匪。前几天，一位牧师告诉我，在他所在的地区，有700名士兵正在抓捕土匪，据说军队共抓获17名俘虏，但我没有听到进一步的消息。

缉私

来往于瓯沪之间的一艘轮船的船员告诉我，轮船在瓯江航行时，被中国巡逻舰"超华号"（Chao Hua）拦截并被搜查违禁品，此舰在该地区已巡弋一段时间。一位海关官员最近告诉我，当他登船搜查违禁品时，竟然遭到军队拿手枪威胁，军队似乎是在庇护货物走私。当地的中国报纸最近报道，厘金已经停止征收，两个机构——统征处（T'ung Chuen Chu）与洋广处（Yang Kwang Chu）① 也已经关闭。县长已发布告示，表示货商再也不必缴纳厘金，而被封闭的相关机构的财产将由县长处理。瓯海关的一名外国职员已经向我证明，相关厘金征收机构确实已经关闭。

天冷的感觉

温州已出现好几天的霜冻天气，运河冰块厚达半英寸。一天，一个回家的乡下普通农民讲，蔬菜全都被冻坏了。放眼所及，温州附近的平原全都种植着繁茂的阔叶蔬菜，现在这些蔬菜叶子全都蜷曲低垂，显得无精打采，人们担心这会给农民带来巨大的损失。（温州，1月13日）

---

① 正式名称分别为"统捐局"与"洋广局"。

《温州天气：一个中国皈依者的问题》，《北华捷报及最高法庭与领事馆杂志》，1931年2月9日

温州天气：一个中国皈依者的问题

（本报记者报道）

温州正在经历剧烈的气候变化。1月强烈的霜冻使得田野的植物大量蜷缩枯萎，但现在这些植物在阳光下，又重新焕发了生机。今天，田野呈现出一派令人满意的丰饶景象。

2月的天气其实也还是很冷，屋子里生火是第一要事，即便是骄傲的年轻人也穿起了保暖裤，在骄傲与冰冷的双脚之间，他们宁愿让自己在晚上能过得舒服点。

接下来是一个暖和的星期天，人们丢掉了冬衣，换上了轻薄的秋装，在平坦的路上缓步行走不到一英里就会汗流浃背。昨天我在山上看到过一场小雪，今天的情形是如此不同，稍微进行一点体育锻炼就要汗湿衣服。经过一个寒冷潮湿的夜晚后，紧接着是温暖和阳光明媚的一天，到了下午，网球比赛开打，即便是富有生活阅历的老人也穿上了短裤参与进来。

一名皈依者的困惑

无论是在物理学领域，还是在形而上学领域，崇高与荒谬总是处于交替变化之中。一天早晨，一个最近刚刚受洗的中国中年皈依者从教堂回家，在我经过时非常谦逊地叫住我。他说："先生，先生，有件事我想问您。我把《圣经》通读了一遍，但有一个问题始终困扰着我。我们人类，比如你和我都有姓，但是我找不到上帝的姓。您能告诉我上帝姓什么吗？"

我的回答是："我们的姓氏来自祖先，我们需要用姓氏来相互区分。但是我们被教导，上帝是自在自存、全能、无所不见、无所不知的，是与我们不同的永恒存在。上帝没有祖先，他不需要姓来与他人相区分。他没

有子嗣，但我们称他为耶稣。我们称他为——我们在天上的父！"

一两个星期前，圣道公会医院的一位孕妇生下了三胞胎，这对当地的中国人来说是一个巨大的奇迹，这个消息传开后，数以百计的中国人前来看望三胞胎。

圣道公会小学将在本周最后一次招生，从招生的热烈程度看，许多中国家长，甚至许多非基督教家庭，不仅看重孩子智力和纪律的培养，同时也看重孩子的道德修养。

这所学校共有几十个空缺名额，这是低年级学生已经升入高年级所致。申请人数是名额数的三倍多，学校已经爆满。父母们坦率地承认，他们已经让孩子从其他学校转学，因为其他学校没有教会学校的好氛围，他们更愿意让孩子接受基督教的教育，而不是让他们的孩子脱离道德和纪律文化。人们不得不相信，在这个幅员辽阔的国家里，有许多非基督徒的父母会很高兴看到教会学校恢复它们曾经享有的宗教自由。

土匪与海盗

在乡村许多地方，盗匪活动远未终止。我在 2 月 2 日的日记中写道："有人告诉我，玉环岛的土匪情况仍然非常严重，那里的一个村庄最近有 10 所房屋被烧毁，数人被土匪掳走。四天前温州城的一个旅店老板在西溪被土匪杀害，在早些时候，这位老板似乎为军队剿匪当过向导。最近这位老板做笔生意，居住地被土匪探知，土匪随后聚集 100 人，将其包围，老板被抓后不幸殒命。"

海盗状况同样如此——依旧在肆虐。昨天（2 月 8 日）上午，招商局的"广济号"离港前往上海，结果下午很早又开了回来，我前往招商局办公室探听情况，得知船刚驶出瓯江口外，船上 12 名护卫士兵就在乘客里发现了 12 名假扮的海盗，船只立刻返航并将海盗移交当局。今天"广济号"已抵达上海。（温州，2 月 9 日）

《圣道公会集会：青年代表齐聚温州》，《北华捷报及最高法庭与领事馆杂志》，1931 年 3 月 31 日

圣道公会集会：青年代表齐聚温州

（本报记者报道）

圣道公会刚刚在温州举行了年度会议，有近 200 名代表参加，其中一些代表来自距此地 2 至 3 天路程之外的教堂。此次聚会，城镇和乡村的青年代表人数很多，令人高兴和鼓舞。在我 34 年的回忆中，好像没有哪一次集会有如此多的年轻人。虽然雨下了一个星期，但大家脸上的微笑说明了"灵魂深处有阳光"。尽管在过去的一年里有饥荒与瘟疫，到处有抢劫放火和谋杀等威胁，教会仍然有强大的生命力。尽管有人放弃信仰，同时有将近 100 名教会成员死亡，但教会成员总数仅比前一年少 80 人。对于传教士来说，当听到一些地区（虽然不是所有地区）没有强盗出没时，他们感到相当振奋，因为外国传教士被建议可以再去那里传教。今年，一个大村庄由于所有房屋都被土匪烧毁，导致其基督团体缺乏礼拜场所。今天是温州连续第三天的春日晴天，当地一片欢腾祥和。

汤小姐脱险

教会最近的一个巨大变化是，教会的一些成员目前在内地农村地区传教。上海的周先生（Mr. Chow）① 作为中华基督教勉励协会的代表来到温州停留了数星期，并进行了宣讲。在圣道公会教堂内，以及前文所述的年会会议上，有许多观众听了他的演讲，他现在正在南部地区做类似工作。汤小姐以及多里奇小姐正在举办温州妇女圣经阅读班，我们刚刚得知汤小

---

① 指的是中华基督教勉励协会总干事周志禹。参见《中华基督教勉励协会第十九次董事会议记录》，《奋进报》1931 年第 8 期，第 4 页。

姐险些遭险，所幸最终得以逃脱。汤小姐乘坐汽船抵达目的地后，坐上了一辆黄包车。途中黄包车苦力与他人发生争吵，愤怒的苦力突然撒手，导致车辆翻倒在运河沿上，汤小姐抓住了运河边沿的一根柱子，悬在运河沿上，但仍无法脱身。所幸一名中国人看到汤小姐的窘境后，将其解救。

（温州，3 月 13 日）

《海军遭遇海盗：海盗袭击已被击退》，《北华捷报及最高法庭与领事馆杂志》，1931 年 4 月 7 日

海军遭遇海盗：海盗袭击已被击退

据海军部收到的消息，昨天在浙江温州附近，"楚观号"（ChuKuan）炮舰与一帮海盗爆发了一次小规模战斗。

炮舰原本是在旁保护一艘失事的挪威船只的打捞工作的。下午 3 点左右它突然遭遇一群超过百人的海盗，这群海盗驾驶帆船，接近失事船只并准备实施抢劫。

海军立刻用机关枪向海盗开火，海盗用步枪还击。战斗持续数小时，直到海盗们最终被海军火力击退。（南京，4 月 1 日）

《"威升号"自温州附近失事》，《北华捷报及最高法庭与领事馆杂志》，1931年8月18日

"威升号"自温州附近失事

经过海上风浪摧残与海盗劫掠后，怡和"威升号"（Waishing）疲惫不堪的43名幸存者已于昨日上午乘"广东号"抵达上海。幸存者向我们讲述了昨晚与台风搏斗的悲惨故事，上周一早晨他们的船只因避风而在南关湾（Namkwan）触礁。

这艘命运多舛的船的乘客与船员搭乘"广东号"来到上海，"广东号"是在温州附近接到求救信号后赶到南关湾船难现场的第一艘船。"广东号"在给予一切可能的救助后离开现场，而"威升号"则继续搁浅在礁石上。船长霍希氏（T. Hughes）和一些骨干船员仍待在船上等待"尤松丸号"（Yusto Maru）的救援，它原定于昨天中午到达。"印度战士号"（H. M. S. Sepoy）也从香港驶出，全速前往救援，以保护遇难船只免遭海盗进一步劫掠。

由于船长霍希氏与其船员们所展现出的高超航海技巧与冷静的态度，这场船难仅造成一人死亡，同时也避免了海盗们抢夺幸存者的财物并彻底洗劫这船船。事实上，"威升号"三等工程师赛明顿（R. B. Symington）先生曾竭力去救那名遇难船员，这名遇难者是买办的一名中国助手。当时转移的小艇上坐满了人，结果小艇被撞到悬崖上，在汹涌的大海中被撞得粉碎，这名中国人也落水了。虽然已经安全，但赛明顿先生还是毫不犹豫地潜了回去，想要救回这名落水者。当中国船员已经失去营救希望时，其他船员费了很大劲才把工程师成功拖上岸。

根据幸存者的讲述，当船长霍希氏得知台风将要来到的消息后，立刻决定将船开到南关湾暂时躲避，这是海关当局推荐的一个瓶颈状避风港湾。一切都固定好，并下了两根锚。黄昏时分风暴侵袭了"威升号"，它

在台风中度过了整个周日晚上。

在天亮前不久，人们看到锚的最后一节链条都已经绷紧，虽然船顶着狂风全力发动以减小链条的压力，但无济于事。由于船上货物很少，“威升号”离水很高，在巨大风力吹动下，直接撞在了礁石上。

霍希氏船长注意到礁石周围有一片沙滩，于是决定暂时将船移到沙滩上，以方便后续救援。但“威升号”此时缺乏足够动力对抗风力，周一上午8点该船遇到强风。由于船长担心台风继续下去会摧毁船只，于是命令放下救生舢板，但小舢板不幸被风猛吹，撞到了礁石。

船员们于是用马裤临时制做了救生圈，通过这种方法，除了自愿留在船上的人以外，其余的乘客和船员都被安全送上岸。

船刚遭撞击，附近的海盗就向船只与幸存者们蜂拥而来，并抢走了一切能找到的东西。当这些海盗变得更具威胁性时，霍希氏船长在海岸建立了一个营地，并召集手下，用剩余的一只手枪设置岗哨进行护卫。

与此同时，当船遭第一次撞击时，船上的主要无线电设备已经损坏，只能在备用电池支持下发出求救信号。台湾基隆电台收到这个信号，随后又转报给香港与海上其他船只。距离100英里的“广东号”船长霍奇基斯（Hodgekiss）在收到信号后，立刻全速赶往南关湾。“广东号”在周一晚上抵达海湾入口，但一直到周二早晨才驶入海湾。

这艘新抵达的船只随后将主要幸存者送到上海，同时还留下更多武器来保护留在船上的人。

（温州，8月16日）

昨天在上海收到报道说，这艘轮船正在倾斜，有毁坏的风险。

这艘船搁浅时留下了一批骨干船员，昨天“恒生号”向他们运送了额外的补给品。英舰和一艘日本打捞船已经待命。（温州，8月14日）

《空军剿共：温州居民情绪复杂》，《北华捷报及最高法庭与领事馆杂志》，1931 年 9 月 1 日

空军剿共：温州居民情绪复杂

（本报记者报道）

一个星期以来，温州的天气令人感到压抑，多云、暴雨、阵风，偶尔有点阳光。这种天气由从香港方面过来的台风引起，一两天以来附近农民们担心风灾可能会威胁到粮食收成，幸运的是台风已经减弱，我听说当地并没有因为风灾或洪水而受损。"嘉禾号"从上海出发开始了每周一次的旅行，它满载着乘客，此外船上还有两位外国女士。它被迫在瓯江口外的一座小岛上避难，导致航班延误了近 30 个小时，迟至周二夜晚才抵达温州。

天气有保持凉爽的迹象，人们都说今年夏天气温异常的低。在经历过 7 月初一个星期的闷热后，我的室内的温度计很少会超过 85 华氏度，最近气温又下降了一些。

南京当局已下令在温州附近建设机场，虽然规定的一个月工期已到，但工程仍在继续。西门外的一大片土地已被征用，前地主拒绝了政府的将土地作为礼物无偿赠送给国家的要求，接受了少量补偿。该机场作为宁波机场的姊妹站，将成为南方的重要航空基地。机场将纯粹用于军事目的，据报道，它的直接目的是用于剿共。并不是所有的市民都认为这个项目是个好消息。尽管他们意识到军用机场的存在可以作为防御敌军的有效工具，红军目前也正在蒋介石将军的进攻下撤退，但当地人认为机场的存在可能会将温州变为军事前线，我们将因此失去长久以来躲避战祸的好运气。

温州的行人最近在街道上突然发现有一队骑兵在号兵的引领下，押送一名女犯人，她被绑在一辆黄包车上，按照惯例，她的罪名被贴在身上。

她就这样被押着在城内大道上游街，随后被送往城外刑场处死。这个可怜的女人多年来一直是一个中国家庭的忠实仆人，这户人家有一个小男孩。一天早晨，激动不安的父母发现孩子神秘失踪，原来是强盗溜了进来，绑架了孩子并勒索赎金。通过侦查，受害者与绑架者最后都被找到。不幸的是，这个女人被其中一名强盗，同时也是她的亲戚所出卖。原来是这名女人偷偷打开院门，放强盗进来。不久，男孩在偏远的村子里被找到，这名仆人和同谋也被逮捕。（温州，8月18日）

《发生在温州的暴行：日本仓库遭洗劫与放火》，《北华捷报及最高法庭与领事馆杂志》，1931 年 11 月 17 日

发生在温州的暴行：日本仓库遭洗劫与放火

（本报记者报道）

浙江永嘉抗日救国会（Anti－Japanese Association at Wenchou）于周日下午洗劫了岩井洋行（Iwai Yoko Company，Ltd.），一群中国暴民在纠察队的带领下破门而入，洋行的商店、货仓、办公室全都被洗劫，员工也被抢劫。建筑被一把火夷为平地，造成的总损失估计超过 10 万银圆。

上海汉口路九号 A 岩井洋行办公室在昨天收到这一暴行的消息，这家洋行也是日本在中国的最大进出口公司之一，该洋行随后立即向日本驻上海总领事馆报告。驻上海总领事村井仓松（K. Murai）先生立即与日本驻杭州（浙江省政府所在地）领事进行了沟通，并下达指示，责成他向中国当局提出严正抗议，并要求中国当局为此事负直接责任。

由于中国民众的仇日情绪，事实上温州的日侨早在 11 月 9 日就已经撤离到上海，岩井洋行以及另外一家日本大企业铃木洋行（Suzuki Yoko Company）的产业，都已处在浙江省政府的监管之下。中国当局在回复的信件中，已经承认了相关责任。

据日本媒体报道，长期以来温州一直是反日宣传的大本营，为了避免两国人民爆发冲突，暂时的撤离是必要的。几天前，铃木洋行的上海办事处接到通知，由于抗日救国会纠察队逮捕了洋行留下来守卫的人员，该洋行在温州的办公场所以及大量商品与财产正处于无人看守的状态。中国当局已经接到了上海总领馆关于这一事件的通知，但在日方收到回复之前，周日的消息就已经传来。

根据电报的简要说明，在岩井洋行遭袭之前，温州举行了一场规模庞大的抗日集会。纠察队向超过 5000 名的群众发表了慷慨激昂的演讲，鼓吹

要"从地球上抹去所有日本的痕迹"，随后率领群众冲向洋行铁栅栏大门。在没有遇到任何阻拦的情况下，岩井洋行的所有财产被洗劫一空，末了他们还放了一把火。

据报道，中国士兵与警察全程无动于衷，消防队接警后，据称也仅在火起之后为防止火势蔓延到周边的中国建筑才有所行动。人们担心至今尚未受到破坏的铃木洋行，可能会是反日暴力的下一个目标。

《学生热衷反日：相对平和但更加活跃》，《北华捷报及最高法庭与领事馆杂志》，1932 年 1 月 19 日

学生热衷反日：相对平和但更加活跃

（本报记者报道）

在过去的几个月里，其他地方发生了激烈的反日学生运动，相比之下，温州享受着安全和宁静。这并不是说当地的学生组织不同情全国学联，只是说他们民族主义热情和反日情绪，还没有超出地方当局允许的范围。

温州的学生也没有闲着，他们一直在与全国救国会密切合作，组织抵制活动，同时还在学校当中进行军事训练，引人关注。现在温州每所学校都以军队编制"营"为单位进行组织，男学生们成为志愿兵，用假步枪进行训练，上下课的铃声也由号手吹号取代。

在学校图书馆显眼的桌子以及墙壁上，挂满了有关东北局势的地图与书籍，这些对日本相当不利。大街上许多海报的图画，配以深红色和图书馆中的一些文字内容。目前温州学校的高年级学生经常会有短假，使得学生与教职员工有能力就当前局势对文盲进行宣传和公开集会，他们还会前往日货店铺门口游行，甚至查封日货。小学生也在尽自己的一份力，这些可能还没有到三年级的孩子们，在街角进行演讲并喊着口号，敦促不爱国的成年人赶紧去参加抗日战争，这场景实在令人哭笑不得。这些孩子都戴着象征国耻的臂章，最后也是最有趣的是，所有人现在都穿着卡其色的制服。①

---

① 对于学生的爱国运动，张棡在日记中表现得比较悲观，他的看法是："各大学校学生均积忿求战，足见中国虽亡，人心尚未亡也。然热度虽高，无实力为后盾，恐已去亡不远矣，哀哉。"参见温州市图书馆编《张棡日记·第八册》，张钧孙点校，中华书局，2019，第 3633 页。

抵制的一个结果是银根短缺。店主们的钱全都被无法销售的日货套牢，他们只能向钱庄以高额利息借贷，而这些钱庄也陷入困境。如果这样的局势持续下去，他们将难以为继。即便银行介入，进行小额贷款，市面上银根依旧短缺，造成对贸易的干扰，给商业带来灾难。

在这次抵制日货运动当中，发生了荒谬而又严肃的事件。

最近就发生了一起这样好笑的事件，在这起事件中还让我们见识了英国老式木枷的刑具。一名温州人用诡计发现某商店正在卖日货，于是威胁店主将要揭发真相。随后此人同意如果店主拿出 60 银圆，他将保持沉默。这一切不知怎么被警察发现了，结果店铺不仅损失了所有日本货物，还被敲诈了 60 银圆。这名敲诈者不仅被罚款，而且每天下午都会被惩罚站在桶里，示众半小时。到了每日的固定时间，这个桶就会被摆在广场上，犯人站在桶里，桶高直到他的腋窝，这样他就充分"享受"他那引发轰动的恶名。（温州，1931 年 12 月 26 日）

《温州电影院：寺庙寒酸影片的竞争者》，《北华捷报及最高法庭与领事馆杂志》，1932年3月22日

温州电影院：寺庙寒酸影片的竞争者
（本报记者报道）

3月11日，一群外国传教士和华人基督徒聚集在温州码头的"海晏号"，向韦更生（G. L. Wilkinson）夫妇道别，他们将带着两个儿子第二次回美国休假。韦更生夫妇来自美国的加利福尼亚，已在温州的基督复临安息日会工作了14年，待休假一年以后，韦更生将继续负责该教会传道工作。这家人将于3月18日从上海直航美国。

当地的热门话题（至少在年轻人中是如此）是温州第一家真正的电影院的开业。电影院的开业时间本来安排在新年那一周，但由于上海的胶片没有到，所以不得不推迟。目前上海已经恢复和平，温州新电影院已经开张，每周将播放一次电影，电影内容包括惊险新奇的西方影片。新电影院比较逼仄，设有硬座，楼上的座位几乎贴着天花板，上海人可能会对此嗤之以鼻。但对于包容的温州人来讲，这样的环境已经足够奢华。过去温州人都是在晚上，前往两座寺庙中的一座去观看电影，寺庙里的两台古老机器缓慢地播放着暗淡的中国影片。

相较于上海的战乱，温州虽然也存在焦虑气氛，但相对平静。谣言四起，内容离奇。每天都会有消息说日本战舰正在寻找引水员，以便通过艰险水道占领城市。还有人信誓旦旦地说听到了敌人的轰炸机正在赶来轰炸我们的消息。

温州每天会有两次新闻快报发布，包括无线电新闻与电话新闻，但谣言仍旧很多，我们在很长一段时间无法获取上海报纸。自从海路成为温州唯一的贸易通道以后，到上海的轮船航线延误或断绝，导致温州商人极为焦虑。

另一个阻碍当地贸易的因素是银根短缺。当瓯沪之间的航班变少时，上海与温州往来运送银圆或钞票就变得极为冒险。银圆短缺曾一度引起骚动，当银行缺乏现银被报纸披露后，人们争相前往银行挤兑，换成美元或硬币。银行的回应是保证钞票并未贬值，如果人们继续进行挤兑银圆，他们将被迫关门停止业务。随着轮船航运的逐渐恢复，人们对银圆短缺的恐惧以及其他烦恼也已减少。①（温州，3月11日）

① 根据瓯海关贸易统计，1931年银圆一项，上海输往温州35万枚，温州输往上海185.1万枚。从这个数据看，瓯沪之间的银圆逆差是温州银根吃紧的根本原因。参见《瓯海关民国二十年海关进出国币枚数》，《通商各关华洋贸易全年清册》1932年第28期，第7页。

《温州附近土匪：传教士幸运逃脱，商人土匪》，《北华捷报及最高法庭与领事馆杂志》，1932 年 5 月 17 日

温州附近土匪：传教士幸运逃脱，商人土匪
（本报记者报道）

　　温州的内地会将因为某些外国职员休假而面临人手短缺。白德邻夫妇已经前往英国，他们将回到白德邻先生的家乡多佛。他们在 1915 年来到中国，白德邻先生一直负责平阳县的传教工作，而他的妻子则负责管理社区诊所。戴贵珍（G. I. F. Taylor）小姐也将在两周内动身前往英格兰，她曾在温州从事了 7 年的艰苦的妇女工作。

　　上周发生了一起令人不快的事件，内地会险些失去了他们的外国督学王廉，他险些被强盗抓去。他当时正与一名中国牧师顺着金安河走水路前往瑞安，由于恰逢涨潮，被迫上岸安顿一宿。夜幕降临后，一艘舢板船驶来，就在他们上游不远处停泊。王廉觉得这艘船很可疑，于是让船夫将船划得远一点，怎料那艘舢板船立刻尾随而至。同时在夜色中他们还看到岸边有一个人影闪动，并且很快追上了他们的船。

　　船夫试图把船划得快一些，但由于是逆流无法加速。突然他们与另一艘船相撞，王廉吃惊地发现他们遭遇了一支小型的舢板船队，船上站的全是人。而在天黑之前，这条河上明明还没有一条船。当他们相撞时，强盗们没有立刻动手，因为不确定他们是否就是选中的目标。强盗的犹豫给了他们时间，他们立刻将船驶入河中间。与此同时岸上的强盗向舢板船发出信号，这些舢板船立刻追赶过来，有的向上游划，有的向下游划，试图切断王廉等人的退路。然而王廉等人驾着船直接驶向对岸，船抵岸后，他们立刻跳上岸遁去。

　　敌人没有料到这一手，所以他们没有预先在对岸设防。两名传教士在皎白的月光下探寻良久，始终没有摸到前往瑞安的路。他们发现几乎每条

路都通向河边，最后他们躲在一座小岛的麦田里，两人在地上躺了一夜，既不敢动弹，也不敢出声。黎明时分，他们听到附近有土匪经过，这些土匪在抱怨到处也找不到逃脱的肉票。

这两个逃亡的人在天亮后，从不寻常的"床"上起来，浑身僵硬但没有受伤，重新寻找回城的路。幸运的是他们遇到了一位老村民，看起来也不可疑，两人向老人询问了当前位置。老人解释说，这里并不是一个岛，而是一个由河湾形成的半岛。他还向两人保证，此地并无土匪活动，可以安全通行。我能理解王廉先生和他的同伴听到这个消息时，感到十分吃惊。最终他们毫发未损，安全回家。

这次令人不快的事件给其他外国人提供了有力证据，证明当地土匪活动非但没有减少，反而似乎变得更具组织性。如果对本次事件进行分析，可以发现当地土匪组织已设置有领导、规则、信号、口令，同时还训练有素。当地有一些关于这些土匪的传闻有趣，但无法查证。当地人没有真凭实据，只是不断重复这些谣言。

根据流行的说法，这伙人都是秘密帮会的成员，白天是合法公民，晚上就出来做强盗，帮会头领保护每一个会众，并对会众敌人展开疯狂报复。这种帮会由于其秘密性质，因此比普通山区匪徒更具威胁性。我们无法确定自己身边的人是否就是这样的恶棍。即便有村民告诉你当地没有土匪，你也不能完全相信他的话。因为这些村民并不清楚自己的邻居是否是强盗。

显然，政府士兵是不可能缉拿这种类型强盗的，除非士兵们在夜间行动，但这是不可能的。因此官军会雇佣间谍与线民。由于一些间谍为官军与土匪双方服务，乡下因此弥漫着疑惧的气氛。即使在城市里，人们互相指责对方属于秘密联盟也是一件很平常的事。这座城市最近发生的许多灾难性火灾都归咎于一个被称为"黑社会"（The Black Society）的邪恶组织的行动，这种说法可能也不无道理。

最近一些在厦门被共产党军队打败的厦门官军，已经北逃至温州，并准备在此停留一段时间。（温州，5 月 1 日）

《雷高升被捕后遭处决》，《北华捷报及最高法庭与领事馆杂志》，
1932 年 7 月 13 日

雷高升被捕后遭处决

（本报记者报道）

在长时间的多雨天气后，地面已经潮湿积水，人们担心会影响到这个
季节的收成。雨季已经持续两月有余，几乎从未停歇，仅偶有几天放晴。
农民们希望能够看到阳光，以避免巨大的损失。由于降雨，今年气温低得
出奇，今天是 6 月的最后一天，人们才开始穿上夏装，即便如此，天气仍
很凉爽。

以前我曾报道过土匪在农村所造成的特殊问题，他们在山中活动，数
量仍然很多。我最近注意到，尽管必须承认士兵在某些地区起到了遏制地
方失序的作用，但士兵无法根除农村的土匪问题。但最近军方应用策略取
得了意想不到的胜利，整个事件几乎可以在杂志上当故事发表。

雷高升[①]是一名红军首领名字。某日有人跟他联系，表示如果他向官
军投降，政府不仅会赦免他，还会把他招进正规军，让他继续当指挥官。
事实上像这样的招降已有先例，雷高升表面上同意了，并选择孤身入城。
官员们表面上很尊敬地接待了他，让他带着军官与士兵制服回到山里，同
时还给他的手下发饷。

驻扎楠溪的政府军随后建议在一个寺庙中组织庆祝宴会，当宴会临近
结束时，他们叫来了摄影师，并礼貌地请红军士兵摆好照相姿势。红军士

---

① 攻打平阳失败后，红十三军遭挫折，中共中央决定撤销浙南特委，设立温州中心县
委，由王国桢任书记，雷高升任军事委员。1932 年后斗争形势继续恶化，雷高升原
本准备假意投降，但在"岩头事件"中被诱捕，据说在临刑前仍呼口号不绝。参见
上海市新四军历史研究会编《留住光辉照后人 浙南英烈事迹选编》，上海人民出版
社，2012，第 64~70 页。

兵们毫无防备地同意了，他们依次将步枪堆放在墙角，然后在照相机前集合。随后政府军突然翻脸，上前抓捕红军。碰巧红军首领的一名警卫人员没有照相，他立刻拿起枪并开火，向在另一处的红军士兵们示警，剩余红军得到报警后连夜撤退。士兵在追击过程中大概杀死了 25 人，红军首领被带到温州审判并定罪。雷高升是第一个被处决的，此人年过三十，据说此人之前原在政府工作。现在他被勒令坐上黄包车，作为坏人的榜样在城市里游街示众，也许还可以借此为军方做宣传。在这段残酷的游街过程中，这名红军首领不断向围观群众大喊：“我是一名共产党员，我是一名共产党员。”

《禁止宗教电影：温州不允许公开放映》，《北华捷报及最高法庭与
领事馆杂志》，1932 年 11 月 3 日

禁止宗教电影：温州不允许公开放映

（本报记者报道）

鉴于温州禁止在公共剧场放映宗教电影，当地的基督复临安息日会引入了一部讲述耶稣基督生平的电影《万王之王》（*The King of Kings*）[1] 以及其他短片，并在他们宽敞、现代化的教堂里放映。人们为了获得免费门票，每夜都在教堂门口吵吵嚷嚷。三周以来，每晚教堂挤满了观影的群众，简直令人窒息。牧师通过一个巨大的扩音器嘶喊，但在群众的喧嚣声中，人们很难听清他对影片的讲解。

温州的世俗电影院正在迅速增多，一年前温州除了当地寺庙通过便携式机器播放影片外，并不存在任何电影院。现在温州已经有了两家相当不错的电影院，并且每天都在放映中国影片。此外温州已建设完一座更大的建筑——这座建筑将表演舞台剧，包括中国传统戏剧、舞蹈，偶尔也会播放电影。我听说老板已经从上海请来一个女子剧团。由于现代城市生活的喧嚣已在市民中找到市场，温州将很快失去其迷人的乡村氛围。

在风和日丽的秋季，温州举办了城市运动会，与往年一样，赛事相当成功。中学的孩子们在三天的时间里奋力比赛。第三天的选手主要是市民，包括学校教师和学者，游泳、跑步、撑竿跳是他们最喜欢的项目，公园里一派假日的热闹景象。

最近，一群丝绸商人到温州寻找新客户时，公园又呈现出另一种景

---

[1] 1927 年的《万王之王》是第一部讲述耶稣生平的无声电影，20 世纪 30 年代配音后再次发行，在全世界广泛放映。参见许正林《基督教传播与大众媒介》，上海人民出版社，2015，第 538 页。

象。公园里首先举办了一场盛大的洋式宴会，主办方把所有懂得做洋菜的厨师都搜罗出来，随后宴请了将近70位客人，其中包括县长。随后的一两天里，各种颜色、样式的丝绸被展示，陈列得十分华丽，供店主、售货员和任何感兴趣的人欣赏。我不知道这种广告方式是否新颖和得体。

温州的中学正在饱受省拨款断绝之苦，自从日本在上海发动事变以后，温州所有教师被拖欠了将近三个月工资。目前已出现一些抗议活动，但还没有到罢工的程度。

9月，一名红军首领在楠溪被政府军捕获，几个月前雷高升也是在此地被捕。所有人都知道红军首领楼其团就在温州，大家也都认为军队其实也知道他的下落，却按兵不动。这些士兵在浙江几乎成功引发一场严重事变，在未被察觉的情况下，这支军队被策反。据我所知，这几千名南方士兵在夏天驻扎城里，他们中间有一种强烈的支持共产主义的情绪。这种同情无疑会因他们数月未能领到微薄的薪俸而更加强烈。楠溪的共产党人听闻此事后，立刻调集了一大笔银圆，派遣代表前往温州，不仅承诺提高常规薪俸，而且还会一次发给大笔现钱。共产党密使大胆地收买当地军队，如果不是国民党当局补发工资并及时调换其他地区可靠军队的话，共产党的这一策略很有可能会成功。

与此同时红军首领楼其团已经逃走，官军不得不翻山越岭地追击。新来的军队尾随着目标，但每次跟踪到红军首领的藏身地，都会被他脱身。这最终给一个村庄带来厄运。士兵们严密地包围了村子，结果进村后仍一无所得。200多名村民被扣押并经受甄别，其中有数人遭到极为恶劣的对待，只有几个老人被允许回家。我不知道这些村民被关了多久，直到他们被释放后，过了一段时间，楼其团才被追查到踪迹，随后被捕。（温州，10月19日）

《温州》，《北华捷报及最高法庭与领事馆杂志》，1932 年 11 月 9 日

温州

　　温州的情况在过去的两年中变化不大，现代化的进展很小。每年都有几家装有新玻璃的店铺开张，但成千上万古老的旧房仍然存在，并且将继续存在，直到它们被烧毁，我表达的就是字面意思。按照政府规定，商店在被烧毁后重建时，必须后撤 13 英尺。因此在城市主要街道上，有的地方窄得只能并排跑两辆黄包车，有的地方又宽得能跑汽车。这是目前温州引入机械化交通的状况，房屋重建的规定也是温州目前为不可避免的未来交通现代化所制定的唯一"规划"。两年多以前，当局建了一个公园。现在还有一所免费的市霍乱流行病医院。在这里每年会举办一星期的体育运动会，这对人民健康来讲是好事。电影院和剧院终于在这里落地生根，以上是我能想到的温州现代化的最新状况。

　　至于此地的土匪与一般安全状况，我们被群山包围，因此匪徒随时都有可能出现。为了保障安全，外国人去任何地方之前都必须先拿到该地区的调查报告。但温州长久以来的状况就是，如果发生了耸人听闻的绑票事件，人们就会说现在的温州比以前不安全了。但是，不能以发生暴行的数量来估计安全，而要以存在暴行的可能性来估计安全。对前者，目前还没有发生过针对外国人的暴行，而对后者，我又很难去估计。我所了解到的情况是，如果抛开土匪活动的时起时落不谈，总体上来讲安全状况并没有好转。

《温州的医疗服务：外国人员调动》，《北华捷报及最高法庭与领事馆杂志》，1933 年 5 月 31 日

温州的医疗服务：外国人员调动

（本报记者报道）

温州的各种医疗服务，有时也会显露出进步的迹象，有些是显著的改革，而不是渐进的改善。去年温州建立了一所市霍乱流行病医院，并且免费向公众开放，不仅缓解了一般医院的负荷问题，还能将霍乱患者与其他疾病患者隔离开。此外，一些免费诊所也在不断向穷人开放。我现在描述的这些医学事件，可能是温州这座古老城市从未有过的，也标志着进入了新的阶段。上周圣道公会医院举行了一场公开的毕业典礼，第一批毕业生被授予了中国护士协会的证书。医院院长施德福做了讲话，另外医学界的同人也宣读了贺词。这些护士的训练工作都是在皮特里·史密斯和菲利斯·菲森德的指导下完成的。

在温州，外国人离开或到来是罕见的大事，因此，很重要。最近瓯海关部门发生了一次人员变动，塔彭登（W. H. Tappenden）夫妇现在已经取代了狄普顿（W. H. Tipton）夫妇的位置，后者目前正在英国度假。塔彭登夫妇发现温州很安静，风景要比天津好很多，他们的三个孩子看到坐落在江心屿的新家，不仅有鸥、鹭筑巢的宝塔，还有绿树荫蔽的青山，认为这里是令人愉快的居住地。

电影院

大约在一年前，温州建立了第一家电影院。一两个月后，温州就建起了第二家。到目前为止，温州至少有四家电影院。温州目前最大的一家电影院刚刚安装了声画同步设备，为了看看其质量到底如何，我不久去观看了一部描述自然风光的影片。无论是画面还是声音都不是很清晰，但这部

电影没有吸引观众的热情还是另有原因。一位中国绅士后来对我解释说："我们更喜欢爱情和冒险故事，而且我们听不懂英语对话。"但是我认为，你只花不到3角钱就能坐到最好的座位，还能指望看到多好的片子呢！

第十中学是城市中规模最大、硬件最好的学校，最近该校向公众开放三天，并举办了一次展览。展品包括书法、绘画、雕刻、木工，以及植物学、昆虫学、生物学、物理学和化学学科的相关内容。小学生也参与了展览。校运动会也在同一周举行，学生们热情参与。

各校联合会举办了年度卫生大会，这是一个值得赞许的活动，但今年的活动主要是从事演讲和发传单，无论如何，这都是努力的一部分。我听说童子军们拿着簸箕和扫帚清扫了街道与人们的房屋，这做起来当然会更难，但更容易被人记住并效法。（温州，5月19日）

《新人来到温州：飞机与轮船交通》，《北华捷报及最高法庭与领事馆杂志》，1933 年 11 月 22 日

新人来到温州：飞机与轮船交通

（本报记者报道）

温州的外国社区最近增加了一名英国圣道公会的传道人员。胡宝华（Rev. Jenkins Hooper）牧师原本也是一名圣道公会牧师之子，他在曼彻斯特大学接受高等教育，并在维多利亚学院居住多年，毕业后直接来到中国。胡宝华在英国的许多地方，包括维冈、布里斯托尔和康沃尔都相当出名，但他为了牧师生涯而告别亲朋来到温州。胡宝华来到温州后陶醉于当地美景，又忙于学习独特的温州方言，因此他并没有因为与西方世界的生活分离而忧愁。

外国人员的流动在温州是一件大事，因为温州的外国人全部加起来也只有 30 多人，其中非传教士仅有 4 人。今年早些时候，罗马天主教会又增加了一些成员，包括 2 名来自波兰的牧师，圣道公会则将在 1934 年迎来 2 名新女职员加入。

上海是我们与外部世界沟通的唯一门户，最近温州刚刚开通了航空服务，每周都有飞机航班连通上海、福州与香港。以前我们只有通过水路才能抵达上海，货运则只能依靠中国货轮，这些船只运行很不稳定，且经常大修。飞机单程票的价格是 70 银圆，这样的价格很难与轮船竞争。但飞机象征的是对未来旅行方式的一种新期望。在这座安宁的中世纪城市上空听到飞机轰鸣声是一件怪异的事情，当看到民众因为看到火车、汽车以及最近出现的飞机而欢呼雀跃，也会让我感到相当怪异。

未完成的道路

我将再次报道温州第一条汽车公路建设的可能性。这条经过处州的公

路，将连接温州与杭州，这也将是第一条连接温州与外部世界的高速路。但之前我已经就此事报道过两次，但每次报道完后都毫无结果。虽然工程已经开始，现在我也不敢保证这条路是否能够建成。

10年前我听说为了建设道路而征收了新的烟草税，政府虽然把钱收了上来，但由于内战迭兴，又转而用这笔钱购买武器和弹药以对付福建军队，因此这条道路也就从来没有真正修建过。为配合修路计划，政府已在今年年初对普通民众增税，对地主每亩地将多征几角钱，对商人的每1000银圆资本征收25银圆，此外还对富人开征特别税。同时政府还发动群众购买低利率的投资债券，但人民反应并不热烈，部分原因是缺乏信心，因为人们记得政府从来就没还过钱。一个充满希望的信号是，政府本周宣布将在城外动工建设汽车道路，同时政府还希望扩建城市内道路，以满足更大的交通需求。目前温州的道路上唯一用轮子跑的车辆除了黄包车外，就只剩下自行车。

贸易状况一如既往的糟糕，而且很可能会持续下去，直到上海贸易状况有所好转。目前我没有听到太多抵制日货的消息，而且自从在北边签订和平条约以来，我已经看到一些大商店开始公开售卖日货。但学生们仍封存着之前抄没的日货，同时我也不认为不通过伪装手段日货可以自由地进入温州。随着另一个丰收的到来，村民比市民生活得更加如意，村民的顺遂也使得乡村盗匪活动普遍平静下来。（温州，10月27日）

《保守的温州：人们热衷于老派，通向风景胜地的公路》，《北华捷报及最高法庭与领事馆杂志》，1934年3月14日

保守的温州：人们热衷于老派，通向风景胜地的公路

（本报记者报道）

这是中国的新年，传统的庆祝活动和以前一样热闹，到处都是爆竹的噼啪声和锣鼓声，寺庙里也满是香火。昨天晚上，当每家门口都点上红色的小蜡烛，每家门前都点起火堆时，街道被照亮了。这些火堆比平时的大，再加上最近干旱的天气，很容易造成火灾。如果西历最终能在中国被采用，温州也一定不会最早使用。到目前为止，只有邮局这样的政府单位才会使用西历。

通常在这个时候，医院里只有很少的病人，病房完全空了。中国人会在新年期间用尽一切办法回家，不会在这期间离开家庭。温州一所医院一直饱受缺乏病人之苦，在新年前夕医院空荡荡的情景，使得医院管理层最终下定决心关闭医院。这是一所中国医院，也是该地区医疗方面的重要机构，拥有浙江最好的手术室之一。

公路的确切消息

终于有了一些关于修路的确切消息可以报道了。在过去的25年里出现过无数规划，始终无法建成一条公路，无论是在市内还是市外，但今年相关工程已经开始。温州向西延伸至处州的公路建成后将成为中国最好的汽车公路，这条公路将具有绝佳的风景，它蜿蜒绕过陡峭的群山的山脚，山下就是蜿蜒的河流，它从坚硬的花岗岩中开辟出一条通道。瓯江上游在温州附近有个入口，水逐渐清澈，木排从上游的森林顺着激流漂到下游。

从古代至今，通过划船或人力拖拽，人们从温州到处州大概需要三天

时间。如果公路修通，汽车可以轻松地把时间缩短两天。我最近去了施工现场，对工程过程中的爆破作业很感兴趣。工人们在爆破时使用的都是粗糙工具，因此过程相当危险，许多伤者被送往温州圣道公会医院治疗。安置炸药的孔是用普通凿和锤子凿出的，人们仅仅依靠绳索与撬棍把爆破后的碎石块从悬崖推落到河里。每一次爆破的声音都在群山里回响，声音往往回荡数秒。除爆破外，还有其他巨大的困难需要汗水和坚持不懈的体力劳动来克服。大量的砖石和泥土必须由人来背负搬运。铺设公路的小石子，全都是工人们用小锤子日复一日坐在那里砸出来的。此外每条溪流上都必须架起一座混凝土的桥梁，每隔几码就有一条河流。

山东获益

承办工程的企业的大量劳力来自山东，目前为止已经雇了大约5000名山东人，我在上周前往中国银行办事时碰到了他们其中的一些人，这些山东人在回乡过年之前会选择将工资兑换成银圆。山东人与温州人很好区分，最显著的区别是山东人穿着厚厚的北方衣服，他们身材更为高大，外貌更为粗犷。

在这个贸易萧条的时期，如何筹集公路资金是一个问题。除了进行风险评估外，工程还寻求公共投资，尽管不是很成功。我知道的情况是，政府已向私人资本征税，每1000银圆就要缴纳12银圆，1万银圆要缴纳150银圆，对非常富有的人还要征收特别税。道路计划完全是按照省里的命令进行，目前城市街道除了人力车和自行车外没有其他轮式交通存在。在旧而肮脏的"乞丐巷"的原址上，现在已经修了一条较短的汽车马路，大概是为了做样板以宽慰缴纳税金和无偿捐献的市民。有命令称要拆除成千上万的房屋，店铺也要为新的城市街道让路。

废弃的机场

去年秋季福建的起义威胁到浙江，蒋介石决定利用空军基地来武装温州，以抵御进攻。当局在城南平原选了一块地，这块地足以让飞机起降，在建设机场过程中许多农民的瓯柑树被砍伐，一些瓯柑还是未长成的青色。农民们得到了一些微薄的补偿，当局保证他们的爱国主义（虽然是强制性的）使他们免遭福建共产主义的强制没收。

很长一段时间，直到起义被镇压前，一支轰炸机和战斗机编队让温州人每天都生活在惊异与恐慌之中。与中国其他许多地方不同，战争行动对温州人来说基本上是陌生的。令人高兴的是军机已经离开，但机场土地似乎不会归还原主。

孙光德牧师离去

孙光德牧师夫妇已经带着他们的两个孩子，在上个月启程前往英国布里斯托的家。孙光德先生是温州圣道公会的主席，在过去两年多时间里，他一直在缺乏帮助的情况下进行管理工作。尽管人手不足，教会现在已成功地进入十年自给计划的第四年，这是值得赞扬的，孙光德先生带头发起了这项计划。孙光德一家希望1935年春天返回中国。

现金短缺

我先前已经提到过贸易存在危机，现在地方银行证实了这一点，因为这些银行普遍缺乏现金。有些银行的资本据说减少了一半，有的甚至超过一半，一些消极的造谣者已经在预言一系列的失败。

鞭刑

温州正在执行一种粗暴但有效的纪律管理方法。地方军政长官相信对做错事的人实行体罚是有效的，因此他不加限制且毫不留情地执行体罚，同时他还令人钦佩地主张无论何种阶级都应该接受体罚。他认为罚款对穷人不公平，对富人有利，而监狱的囚刑对人来讲是一种人格上的侮辱。我已经两次在大街上看到囚犯被士兵押着游街，囚犯头上戴着纸帽子，上面写着他的种种恶行，他的手被铁链锁在一起，一个士兵拿着皮鞭跟在他身后，折磨着他已经伤痕累累、鲜血淋漓的背部。有时也会在城外执行鞭刑。我至少见过一次受刑人被鞭打致死，死者是一名被指控行为不端的牧师。在另外一个案例中，一名普通的小偷被处决了，作为对其他人的警示。

温州目前几乎用鞭刑处罚一切犯罪行为，包括屡禁不止的赌博与吸食鸦片。各种公开的不得体或非法行为，甚至女性穿着被认为不得体也会受到警告，如果多次被警告就会遭受鞭刑。（温州，2月14日）

《飞行员在迫降中受伤：事故发生在距温州 13 英里处》，《北华捷报
及最高法庭与领事馆杂志》，1934 年 4 月 11 日

飞行员在迫降中受伤：事故发生在距温州 13 英里处

据星期二收到的进一步详细信息，按照南京海军部的计划，许成棨（C. C. Hsu）先生驾驶中国国产水上飞机"江凤号"（Kiang Feng）在星期天（4 月 1 日）上午从上海出发前往福州马尾。飞行途中由于发动机故障，被迫降落在浙江沿海的七里镇（Chileechin），此地离温州城 13 英里。

昨天上午，受海军部海军飞机制造处（Naval Air Establishment）处长曾贻经（Tseng Yi - ching）指派，工程师高昌庙（Kiaochangmiao）先生，乘中国航空总公司的专机赴温州视察事故现场。根据他昨天下午从温州发来的信息，飞行员许先生受伤情况并不严重，目前正在温州大同医院（Ta-tung Hospital）疗伤。

中国海军部获悉事故情况后，已从浙江象山（Siangshan）调遣军舰"楚泰舰"（Chu Tai）前往温州救援。预计这艘军舰将把许先生送回上海，以便接受治疗。

周日上午，许先生驾驶"江凤号"准备从上海到马尾做单机飞行，以测试中国国产水上飞机长途航行的可行性。他在上午 9 点从龙华机场出发，曾处长以及其他官员目送他起飞。

《温州钱庄倒闭：城市融资日益困难，补救措施无效》，《北华捷报及最高法庭与领事馆杂志》，1934 年 5 月 30 日

温州钱庄倒闭：城市融资日益困难，补救措施无效

（本报记者报道）

在我上一次的报道中，我预测由于当地贸易状况的恶化，会导致银行与钱庄出现倒闭潮，现在我可以宣布当地钱庄系统已彻底崩溃。1933 年当地已经有十多家钱庄倒闭，导致民众出现了不信任危机。当地民众开始疯狂挤兑，雪上加霜的是，中国银行驻温分行拒绝了继续给予支持。一般来说，当地的贸易商总是可以向任何一家银行寻求融资，但由于普遍缺乏的信心，大银行已经撤回了支持，由于收回贷款困难，小银行也选择明哲保身。

今年年初，永瑞银行（Yung－Nyue Bank）遭遇了不幸，这是温州最大的银行之一，它宣布负债 37 万银圆。当地银行联合会召开了一次会议，宣布立刻向支票持有人进行偿付，对储户则随后按比例进行偿付。随后就是无休止的会议，以及无数的公众抗议，也有人威胁要发起法律诉讼。紧接而来的问题是确定偿还的数额问题，储户联合起来要求偿还 80%，但这家银行只愿意还 60%。

预测到的更多倒闭

据说银行的贷款足以偿还所有存款，这可能确实是事实，但在最近不景气的状况下，银行一旦贷款出去就很难再收回。这次银行危机的直接原因是三个合伙人之一拿走了更多份额。

随后一些银行也出现了问题，还有一些银行的危机正在酝酿之中。一些银行已经暂停业务，并最终停业，剩下的六家银行将留下来满足城

市的需求。

中国银行目前正在从这些中获益。中国银行拥有大量本地居民的存款，部分钱来自钱庄，但中国银行目前相当害怕再将钱投资于当地企业。我听说中国银行转而将温州的储蓄资金投资于杭州和其他地方，而温州商业因为缺乏资金萎靡不振。温州土地与房地产很不景气，一亩地的价格只有原来的一半。温州富人以前卖地置房，现在发现房子很难租出去。鉴于银行业的形势，非专业的民间借贷迅速增长，债权人将持有债务人的财产契据，直到债务人偿还为止。但由于这种民间金融的高利息——15%以上，它从一开始就遭到政府禁止。

因此，温州的商业状况并不好，当地于是安排了一场盛大的灯节，许多乡民被吸引到城里，以促进钱的流通。灯节是与新端午节（阳历5月5日）一起结束的，这是旧节日与政府所颁布西历的融合——所以民众可以在一年当中享受两个端午节！多雨的天气将压轴戏推迟了两三天，但最终，灯笼游行在街道上蜿蜒而行，每经过一个街角都需要大约两个小时，这是该城最长的记录。成千上万人拿着形状各异的灯笼，或者燃烧着的火炬；还有人拿着鼓和钹，可以看到许多木管与铜管乐队。有人扮成中国古代历史人物的造型，有一群人踩着高跷。此外还能看到用闪亮丝绸与纸制成的龙，这条龙长40英尺，高8英尺或9英尺，通体盛装打扮，龙身扭曲，下巴愤怒地闪闪发光。这景象在晚上看来令人害怕。

这周大街上挂满了绵延数英里的遮阳篷以及色彩鲜艳的丝制横幅，每隔几码就挂着一盏灯笼。城市呈现狂欢的景象，商店大降价，窗户装饰一新。旅馆迅速挤满了人，餐馆和摊位生意兴隆，灯笼店热闹非凡。

新生活运动

这个节日正值新民族运动"新生活运动"发端，贴在每扇门上的告示，告诉人们什么是新生活运动，以及应该要做什么。其内容包括每户门前路段都要保持清洁，不准将垃圾丢到街上，关于这一点，我很高兴地告诉大家，我们看到政府已在组织城市洁净机构。此外还规定：不允许在公共场合抽烟，警察有权制止街头抽烟行为；公共场合不允许有不得体的行为，不允许衣冠不整（乞丐应该怎么办呢?）；大街上不允许乱挤乱撞，撞到人要道歉；人们应该勤洗澡、勤洗手；不许说脏话；不要举办奢侈的宴会与婚礼；等等。第一次违规者予以谴责，第二次违规者予以警告，第三次违规者罚款 5 银圆。

外侨社区最近又增加了两名海关新成员和一名白累德医院的新护士。卡萨悌（A. Casati）先生是新任海关税务司，他最近曾被派驻华南。多年以来，一直都是由外国人担任此项职务。艾尔茂（J. Elm）先生接替了原来的葛松龄（Gosling）先生担任港务长一职，葛松龄先生现已被调往宁波。伍德曼（Woodman）小姐来自英格兰威尔特郡，以前属于原始卫理公会教派。在史密斯（Smith）小姐休假期间，她正在为白累德医院的服务做准备。在偏远的温州，外国社区每增加一名成员都是一件令人高兴的大事，这些新来者也一定会受到热烈欢迎。

《来自闪电的拯救：温州海岸撞船惊心动魄的一幕》，《北华捷报及
最高法庭与领事馆杂志》，1934 年 5 月 30 日

来自闪电的拯救：温州海岸撞船惊心动魄的一幕

在暴风雨中，一道闪电避免了一场船难，挽救了 80 条生命。中国轮船
"天象号"（Tiensiang）在星期天（5 月 20 日）抵达温州外海的北天铜山
（Peitiendoong Shan），该船原本计划从瑞安驶往上海，但由于遭遇强风与强
流，船只径直向一座山崖撞去。

那闪电来的正当其时，在漆黑的夜色中，给了船长足够的亮光，使他
能看清周围情况。船长看清前方的山后，急忙改变航线，船只虽然在右舷
触礁，但也得以避免正面撞山。水进得很快，大约 10 分钟后，只有舰桥还
露在水面，船尾已被完全淹没。

船长受到高度赞扬

该船检查员陈荣（Chen Kong）先生作为代表，向本报讲述了当时的
惊险状况。他在周三下午，与 47 名船员、5 名乘客共同搭乘"大华号"返
回上海。大多数人失去了所有财物，有些人甚至丢了衣服。

"在我们鸣响警报汽笛后，几艘渔船立刻赶来帮忙，这时天开始亮了，
风暴停止了。乘客和多数船员都爬到山上干爽的地方。船头有 3 英尺的地
方还露出水面，船长、大副和其他人包括我在内，都留在船上照看船只与
堆在甲板上的行李。

当第二批渔民到来时，我们怀疑这些驾驶舢板的渔民是海盗。果然这
些人上船后就开始抢劫，他们没有武器，我们用铁棍打他们。劫掠者越来
越多，我们被迫撤退，任由他们为所欲为。海盗们抢走了一大批财物，但
他们并没有绑票的企图。"

《降雨拯救了温州庄稼：因干旱斋戒三日，白累德医院建立产房》，
《北华捷报及最高法庭与领事馆杂志》，1934 年 8 月 8 日

降雨拯救了温州庄稼：因干旱斋戒三日，
白累德医院建立产房

（本报记者报道）

就像许多其他地方一样，不只是在中国，温州也经历了痛苦的干旱季节。城市水井的水位很低，许多水井几乎干涸了。人们要穿过半个城市，从一个更深的井里获取免费的水，直到这些深水井也被嫉妒的附近的邻居上锁，他们担心自己的供水也会出问题。许多家庭不得不从乡下人那里买水，而乡下人在旱季用敞篷船从遥远的山区的溪流运水来卖。在城市外的平原上，农民们开始担心他们的水稻收成。终于几场台风带来了降雨。据说再干旱两天就可能毁掉整个收成。

这些台风确是天赐之物，因为它们带来了雨和凉风，而且几乎没有在这个地区造成任何破坏。只有轮船航运耽搁了约 5 天。

大规模斋戒的命令

当局已经命令禁止吃肉三天，表面上是因为干旱而采取的一项卫生措施，但民众认为这是一种为了祈雨而进行的宗教性质的斋戒。实际上，三天后就下起了倾盆大雨，但斋戒又延长了三天，在这段时间里只能够买到鲜鱼或几只鸡，猪肉和牛肉都禁止买卖。也许无论如何也消除不了普遍存在于当地人心中的一种看法，即雨和斋戒是联系在一起的，正是因为斋戒才会带来云和雨。在温州沿海汹涌波涛中颠簸的水手们，会知道他们的危险处境是由城里空荡荡的肉铺造成的吗？

这提醒我温州的另外一项卫生规定，动物和猪不能随便宰杀，必须在指定的地方屠宰，卫生人员会检查动物是否染病，如果染病则禁止销售。

以上这些，都是新生活运动的重要组成部分。新的鸦片管理条例也加大了惩罚力度，第一次犯判轻罪，第二次犯判监禁或判在处州修路，第三次犯判死刑。烟客在定罪之前都会被送到警察局强制戒毒，戒毒完后才会被宣布处罚。

上周两帮对立的苦力之间发生了一场严重的街头斗殴事件，其中 2 人被打死，超过 13 人受伤，一些人伤势严重。死者中有 1 人是被扔到运河里淹死的。

大约一天后在同一地点，在风灾期间，东门外的一所房子着火了，共有 10 辆手动泵消防车参与救火，房子依旧被烧毁，但周围的房子意外地完好无损。火势快要结束时，一名消防队员冒险爬上一堵摇摇欲坠的墙，结果墙体倒塌了，这名消防队员被甩进了火堆里，他虽然被抢救出来但严重烧伤。大家赶紧将他送往圣道公会医院救助，这名消防队员被送到时已经奄奄一息，他身上的皮肤除了脚底与胸口外已经全部被烧毁，最终不幸去世。

圣道公会白累德医院刚刚增设了产科部门，这是温州第一家产科门诊。产科部门拥有很多舒适的病房，可同时容纳 12 名产妇，如果需要还可以进一步扩大空间。该部门将由一名持证的助产士负责，她是一名中国妇女，必要时医院里的外国护士也会予以协助。

到医院坐月子的习惯在中国母亲群体中迅速增长，她们开始意识到狭小拥挤的房子不适合坐月子。通过引进这些更新、更好的理念，白累德医院为中国做出了大贡献。（温州，7 月 25 日）

《排外行动：国民党关闭了港口对外贸易》，《北华捷报及最高法庭
与领事馆杂志》，1934 年 8 月 15 日

排外行动：国民党关闭了港口对外贸易

　　昨天从一个可靠的消息来源得知，温州国民党批准了浙江省第三特区
行政督察专员（Special Supervisor of Civil Administration of the 3rd District of
Chekiang Province）许蟠云（Hsu Pan - yun）先生发起的排外运动，该运动
从本月开始。①

　　像香烟和化肥这样的外国商品被禁止进口，市场上持有这些外国货物
的人必须抛弃它们。许多销售商因为销售这些货物，已经被党部和警察局
抓了起来。一名销售商因为"反革命罪"仍然被扣押，一名贩售外国货物
的苦力被党部逮捕，他的货物被全部焚毁。通过以上这些行动，温州地方
党部与政府已经宣布这座通商口岸将关闭对外贸易。

---

① 本次排外运动，主要针对的是香烟，而不是全部外国货品。起因在于永嘉县党部陈
　卓生、杨雨苏等意图占据英美烟草公司永太和经理处的股份，因为索贿不成，故以
　所谓违反新生活运动之名，攻击该公司运销外国烟，许蟠云在此事中庇护了永嘉党
　部。参见陈于滨、王泽侯《十三班内幕》，《温州文史资料·第十六辑》，2002，第
　395～396 页。

《温州夏日好天气：出现干旱天气，电动防盗陷阱取得奇效》，《北华捷报及最高法庭与领事馆杂志》，1934 年 9 月 5 日

温州夏日好天气：出现干旱天气，电动防盗陷阱取得奇效

（本报记者报道）

　　一般来说，大家都知道温州的夏季很难熬，但在今年其他地方高温闷热的时候，温州的夏季却格外凉爽。7~8 月总有微风拂面，树荫下的气温低于 85 华氏度，很少会达到 90 华氏度以上。相较于往年，9 月的多风天气提早了两个星期，以至于很多人说，很久都没有这样的夏天了。

　　往年在 8 月，下午总会下雷阵雨，这种热带风暴吞没了这个地区，电闪雷鸣直至午夜，但今年鲜有雷雨。

　　暴风雨是前几年温州炎热潮湿季节的主要降雨方式，但如今雨云被吹到别处，就会留下干燥、龟裂、坚硬如岩石的土地，以及干枯的水稻。市场上粮食价格一直在稳步上升，幸运的是一周前一场台风带来了两天的降雨，在这个紧要关头，饥荒惨剧得以避免。但粮食的高价会维持到下一次收成前，温州一年会有好几次收获季节。

　　瓯江入海口的一些岛屿最近受到风灾侵袭，岛上居民多以捕鱼为生，他们说风灾将鱼全赶走了。在风灾过后，渔民们的收成自然不会很好，他们沿海岸的庄稼也被潮水淹没。更要命的是，他们还得忍受海岸地区海盗的骚扰，虽然他们因为过于贫困，也没什么东西可以被抢。

　　高财村（Kao – Choa）最近就遭到海盗光顾，海盗要求在此定居，并承诺不会骚扰村民。但村民拒绝了这一要求，他们担心会因为协助海盗而受到政府惩罚，他们请求当局提供适当保护。地方官在答复中遗憾地说，他没有钱提供保护，并指出由于该地村民已自行解散民兵，因此发生任何麻烦都必须由他们自己负责。但是村民们现在太穷了，他们支付不起民兵

费用。村民们发现自己正处于两难境地，他们必须确定在得罪海盗和得罪官员之间，哪一种选择更为明智。

新公路

新公路的建设正在稳步推进当中，通车日期也在不断延后，从一个日期推到下一个日期。因此，没有人能准确地说出到底什么时候能完全通车。我见过好几起因爆炸而伤到工人的事件，爆炸声在很远的地方就能听到。这条公路的大部分山区路段需要人工进行爆破作业。现在有一名工人正躺在医院里，他的脸完全黑了，根本认不出来，双眼也已失明。这是进步必须付出的可怕代价的一部分——这些代价通常是由罪犯付出①，同时也是完全可以避免的粗心大意所造成的。

修建新公路的另一个代价是牺牲私人财产。对于征地和拆除房屋，政府只给予名义上的极小补偿，很多情况下甚至根本就没有补偿。在街道拓宽速度很快的温州，或多或少按照既定计划，数百家商店将减少一半面积，许多商店将被彻底关闭，而且政府不会提供任何赔偿。温州是一座运河之城，运河原本在路边流淌，在许多地方，店铺横跨运河面向马路开门，所有这一切都将因为马路拓宽计划而成为过去。为了清洁、通风和安全，我们欢迎这些变化，但人们遗憾地意识到，这座古老、完整、奇特又美丽的中国城市行将远去。

建筑改良

随着马路扩建，重建工作也在进行。在过去的四年里，我看到了当地商店和公共建筑的巨大进步。以前温州没有剧院，现在已有 6 座。一座新剧院也刚刚建成，这座剧院采用混凝土结构，并且采用了类似上海大剧院的现代屋顶照明设计。在同一条街上，一家六层大商场正在筹建中，这家商场显然是为了承办上海信诚公司（Sincere Co.）与永安公司（Wing - On Co.）的业务。这条街上，交通银行的一家分行也刚刚开业，据说在开业第一天就从当地吸纳了 50 万银圆的储蓄。这些画面所反映出的景象，就像是现代主义的直线条，和丑陋的角，光亮的反面全是不整洁的、歪斜的破

---

① 这一时期的部分温州犯人会被送到工地修路。

屋。从建筑的角度来看，这种强烈的对比令人不快。

征兵

该地区已对特定年龄的所有男子实行征兵制，40 岁以上的男子免役。服役期限为 3 个月，服役满后颁发证书，人们可以重回正常工作岗位。我听说这道新命令已经是被仁慈修改过的版本，军营条件听说并不舒适，伙食也很差。义务兵穿着士兵制服，住在寺庙里，几乎没有工资。他们每天学习军事技术，进行体能训练，体能训练可能是训练中最有益的部分。目前已经可以花费 10 银圆免役，毫无疑问许多人将会通过这个方法逃役。

电动防盗陷阱

一名企图进入一所装有电动防盗设备的房屋的窃贼被电死，引起了人们的关注。这所房子的主人是一个中国人，他房子的设计很现代，可能是由于房屋新涂的油漆，吸引了夜间的"访者"共有 4 名。第一个触到电线后惊奇地发现自己竟然无法松开手，于是这名小偷开始大叫。叫声惊醒了房子里的人，电源被断开，小偷在被释放后立刻跑进黑夜。

房屋主人决定下次一定要先叫人捉住小偷，然后再切断电源。他没有等太久，上周他再次被一声尖叫惊醒。另一名小偷被这股神秘力量捕获，并正在乞求自由。但这一次房屋主人有了经验，他先去找来邻居控制小偷，然后才断开电源，但喊声已经停止，这名小偷竟然死了。

中国法律对于此种情况的界定极为模糊。据说死者家属无法通过法律得到赔偿，但他们聘请了律师，谈判的最新消息是，除丧葬费外，住户主人还将向死者家属支付约 80 银圆的赔偿金。如果上法庭解决，就一定会对原告不利吗？事实上窃贼作案的那天晚上，正是他刚从长期监禁中被释放的日子！

新生活运动的成果

虽然新生活运动并没有结束，但与开始时的声势浩大相比，现在已经很少听到相关消息。我听说官员们现在不会在公共场所或宴会上吸烟。

街道打扫得并不干净，虽然当局在每个街角都放置了垃圾箱，这项政策对于乞丐来讲简直是德政，他们现在拥有了一块能够高效觅食的宝地。

我注意到一家中国素食餐厅已经开业，在炎热的天气里为人们提供了一个吃更清洁、更卫生的素食的机会。有些素菜被做成肉菜的样子和味道，当地佛教徒一定会欢迎它。（温州，8月23日）

《车行浙江：中国花园省份的美丽乡村已开放，一场汽车之旅》，
《北华捷报及最高法庭与领事馆杂志》，1934 年 11 月 14 日

车行浙江：中国花园省份的美丽乡村已开放，一场汽车之旅

（本报专文）

正如许多媒体报道的那样，周日的典礼标志着位于杭州闸口（Zakou）的跨钱塘江公路与铁路大桥工程开建。随着这座大桥的建成，上海的有车一族将很容易前往更多的美丽景点，事实上在上周刚结束了一场值得一谈的汽车旅行。

想象一下，公园里到处是秋天的色泽鲜艳的浆果，山坡上覆盖着高大的枫树和白杨，树叶全是红色或金色，灌木丛也在深秋季节勇敢地绽放着自己最后的光彩。在大自然的美景中，触目所及皆山川溪谷，它们为这个季节增色。可以毫不夸张地讲，居住华东的外国人士，可以在这里享受到与日本传统类似的秋趣。

对外国人来讲，日本易往，浙江僻远。我们过去在上海平原度过太多乏味的岁月，现在的浙江正如盛开的花朵，愈发显得可爱！

两个美丽的季节

中国应该向世界宣传，她拥有两个美丽的季节：春日，乡村被独一无二的黄色油菜花，以及淡紫色的丁香交替铺满；秋日，山坡被杜鹃花的红色和金色染得火红，这样的景色值得跨越半个世界去观赏！

我们的旅程从杭州开始，在浙江公路局（Chekiang Highway Administration）官员的帮助下，我们在距杭州西湖 4 英里、钱塘江北岸的南兴桥（Nanshingchiao）乘上了渡轮。到目前为止，公路局还没有正式开通渡轮服务，只有一艘小型拖船拖着两艘用木板绑在一起的舢板作为临时驳船使

用。但相关交涉不是难事，很容易通过。

从南岸的江滨（Kiang Pien），到绍兴再到曹娥（Tsaogno）大概 49 英里，这一段道路的质量相当好，可以快速通过。该路段运营着一条已约 6 年的公车路线，同时这也是政府盈利的手段之一。据了解，浙江公路局已经出售这条公路的经营权许多年了，目的是为其下一步的公路计划筹措资金。

前往温州

在曹娥，有一条河通往百官（Pokwan），此地有一条铁路通往宁波。但是百官向北通往宁波的公路目前还没有完工，我们也找不到可用于车辆过河的渡轮。如果我们想要去宁波的话，就必须从曹娥南下 45 英里，然后再折向东北，从拔茅前往宁波。

这是旅途中的小问题，但宁波不是我们的目的地。如果我们一直向南行，最终将抵达永嘉（温州）。这条路确实已经完成，但在黄岩（Hwangy-en）与温州目前还没有汽车渡轮，因此也就尚未通车。鉴于这是第一次探索这条海岸大道，旅客们愿意去天台，此地大约在曹娥东南方向 78 英里处。天台山就位于前往天台主路附近的一条支路上，是一座佛教名山，山脚下有一座古庙。晚上我们在那里得到了简单而友好的住宿招待，庭院和山坡上栽有 300 多年树龄的美丽古树，清澈的小溪流过青葱的峡谷，这座寺庙真是逃脱俗世的世外桃源。

山道

然而要前往天台，就必须途经嵊县、新昌和拔茅（此地还是转往宁波的岔口），然后越过一座山脉。这条路一开始是沿着一条狭窄的山谷蜿蜒而上，最后是一条蜿蜒的山路，到达山顶的全程大概两英里半，途中还有两个陡弯。整个爬坡过程比较顺利与容易，上坡经过的山岭被称魏泽岭（Wei Tse Ling），之后山路起伏不定，然后抵达海拔较低的另一个山岭——夸岭（Kua Ling）。再行不到 10 英里，我们在天台公共汽车站看到了礼貌的欢迎人员，一名警官站在岔路口给我们指路。也许我们在这条公路上的其他地方，不能受到比这里更友好与有益的招待了。

峡谷边的 20 英里路程

清晨从庙里的锣声中醒来，天气晴朗，早早出发，为美丽的第二天奠定了基础。我们沿着夸岭和魏泽岭下山，与前天晚上一样我们经过拔茅走了大概 47 英里，很快就抵达新昌和嵊县。于是我们折向西南经过长乐抵达47 英里外的东阳。这里的乡村风景很迷人，我们穿行在山谷里，两边都是高山。秋天的旅行者，在这里能够看到赤红的乔木。这段路程没有发生什么特别的事情，但令人感到愉快。

山沟中的 20 英里路程

过东阳后，我们的车驶入更狭窄的山谷，并穿过一个小流域。通过新开通的 36 英里公路（实际上，这也使目前的环行成为可能），汽车来到永康。我们知道如果从此地继续沿着新修公路向西南行驶，就可以抵达丽水（字面意思是美丽的水域）。

为了修这段路，当局花费了至少 100 万银圆，人们不禁好奇，想弄清楚究竟为何要花这么多钱。答案很快就揭晓了，经过距永康 21 英里的青云镇（Tsinyun）后，车就不得不在从河谷山壁中开辟出的山路中蜿蜒行驶，这段路程不少于 20 英里。河在山谷底部，到处都是急流。如果在丰水期景色应该会更迷人。但也不必失望，河对岸的高山完全被竹子与秋林覆盖，山景同样令人难忘。这条公路是一项壮丽的工程，为完成这项任务，共有7 万名山东人辛勤工作。但在一些岩石最坚硬的地方，施工队还是要使用英格索兰公司（Ingersoll Rand）的钻石机。在道路的狭窄处，从上往下看似乎离谷地很近，此地只允许一车通过，但只要小心驾驶就不会有大麻烦。在如此可爱的景色中度过这么长时间，无疑是一种享受。

金华与兰溪

我们在丽水一家简陋的小客栈中过夜。由于我们明天就要回上海，因此必须要提早动身。我们在黎明前出城，飞驰于 20 英里长的峡谷中，迎着破晓的曙光，峡谷在清晨苏醒，人人都感到振奋。

车行 45 英里，我们回到永康，然后折向西北再行 28 英里抵达金华。此地以火腿闻名中国，我们在公路两边看到许多壮硕的猪证明了这一点！

金华向前新开通了一条道路，通往兰溪，我们离开金华不久就遇到一条小河，河上有驳船，我们很快得以通过。渡口并不是政府收费，但缴纳一笔60文的"赏钱"是可以接受的。去兰溪的路建在高原上，穿过连绵起伏的山麓，乡村风景相当迷人。离开金华19英里后如果向南可以通向处州，向北则是通向兰溪城。要抵达钱塘江渡口，应该是向南行驶直到右首边出现渡口为止。但由于没有提醒旅客的指示牌，我们只有在兰溪车站用比画的方式向人询问方向，最后我们才发现走错了路，我们在一开始就应该向处州方向前进。这次渡河也没遇到麻烦，清晨的阳光下，河上扬帆远航的大船令人赏心悦目。

现在我们又行驶在另一条新路上，这段路连接兰溪、寿昌与白沙。这条道路给人的感觉是从高到低，从高原地区渐渐驶向低矮的新安江（Hsing An River）河床，从兰溪出发左拐行42英里即抵达寿昌，再右拐行10英里抵达白沙，这是以村庄命名的渡口。渡船是由一名和蔼可亲的女士驾驶，她摇动船桨，长年的习惯使她轻松自如。

支路前往七里泷

越过美丽的新安江，我们唯一的遗憾就是必须要赶回上海，因而无法左转沿着新路穿过顺安、围屏前往徽州，这几乎是整个浙江风景最秀丽的路段。虽然我们不得不右转前行94英里返回杭州，但这段通过桐庐与富阳的路程，同样令人愉快。在白沙与杭州之间的一段地方，修建了一条4英里的支路，旅行者可以看到著名的钱塘美景——七里泷（Chi Li Lung）。中国有一句谚语形容七里泷"顺风七里，逆风七十里"。

我们从杭州出发，再回到杭州，共行驶超过650英里。我们在通往温州的东海岸探索了许多秀丽的山脉。我们在前往丽水的山谷中行驶了20英里，越过了金华与兰溪的高原，途经了5个渡口。

这次旅程象征着我们这些上海囚徒的自由，也预示着未来我们将收获更多美景。今后我们可能不会再走这次的路线，我们可能会先沿海岸路线到温州，随后西行至丽水，再从二十里峡出去，同时也祝愿钱塘江大桥能早日建成！

《温州抵制外货行动已经停止》，《北华捷报及最高法庭与领事馆杂志》，1934 年 12 月 12 日

温州抵制外货行动已经停止

据去年 8 月的《北华捷报》报道，温州开始抵制外国货，主要是香烟和化肥。根据最近从可靠来源得到的报告，当地一家外国烟草公司的代表最近来到温州，拜访了浙江省第三特区行政督察专员许蟠云先生，并从他那里拿到了一份官方法令，指令永嘉县立刻停止对香烟销售的任何非法阻挠。

希望这一措施能够生效并令人满意。

《来到偏远温州的新成员：新公路总体不错，新县长任职》，《北华捷报及最高法庭与领事馆杂志》，1935 年 1 月 9 日

来到偏远温州的新成员：新公路总体不错，新县长任职

（本报记者报道）

这座城市的外国小社区迎来了一些新成员。马多隆（H. C. Morgan）先生接替克萨悌先生担任瓯海关税务司职务。马多隆先生之前在扬子江上的芜湖工作。在克萨悌先生今年早些时候被任命为税务司之前的许多年，这一职务都是由来自澳门附近拱北关的中国人阿林顿（A. V. Adlington）先生担任，他取代了塔彭登先生的职务，后者现在已经被改派上海。阿林顿先生及其妻子、女儿目前都居住在城市对面的江心屿。他唯一的外国邻居是艾尔茂先生，艾尔茂先生担任港务长职务，目前在温州已居住数月。

英国圣道公会的白累德医院又增添了一名新医生——莱思（O. Lyth）医生，他来自英国。与他一同前来的还有沃尔夏（Warmisham）小姐，这位小姐来自英格兰的切希尔郡，她将于今年10月与温州圣道公会的胡宝华牧师完婚。

新公路建成

近来最重要的新闻就是农村与城市正在开展的大规模道路建设，该建设已经持续一年多，实际上已接近最后完工阶段。几年前，浙江的任何道路计划都无法得到落实，这简直是件匪夷所思的事情。计划已经写了十几年了，政府为此提高税收，但税收又总是被挪作他用。曾经有一段汽车路已经建成，但由于这是一段孤路，最终也被弃置。现在情况发生了变化，道路不断涌现，巨大的木材和混凝土桥梁横跨无数溪流。实际上，巴士已经在蜿蜒的大溪（Bowl River）河谷中试行服务。在这条河上，小轮船曾

经就是唯一的机械交通工具。乘坐轮船需要一天才能抵达青田，而坐车只需要几个小时。这条路多为开山取道，不仅风景优美，对于驾车者来讲并不危险。通往杭州的道路要经过青田与处州，在这里可以观看著名的风景区，这个风景区将被开发为旅游中心。一名来自上海的德国司机出于好奇已经完成了这条道路的环形旅行，他的评价是"总体上还不错"。

城市道路扩展

乡村道路建设已完工，政府终于要开始实施拖延已久的城市街道扩展计划。这座城市的主要街道仿佛挨了一记重拳，过去一排排的店铺，现在都成了一堆堆砖块和扬起的尘埃。老房子和老店铺被推倒的同时，它们后面 13 英尺处新的建筑在拔地而起。每个星期，老城都会发生一些变化。每次外出看到这些变化，我就会回想起那些拥挤却又古雅可爱的角落，它们的消逝令我感到悲伤。大多数建筑是在仿造超现代（ultra modern）的钢筋混凝土风格，但在不使用钢材的地方（例如窗框），木材被涂成银色。

贸易可能不景气，但对建筑工人和木匠来说却不是这样。令人瞩目的是，经济萧条伴随着的是建筑行业的繁荣。建筑行业的繁荣始于几年前，现在已经达到疯狂的程度。今天温州银行、剧院、商店和私人住宅的规模和风格，是两年前的温州人所未曾见过也不敢相信的。

新县长到来

最近的火神发威，导致了两场极具破坏性的灾难。一场大火发生在退潮时段，江堤边的一家店铺。如果当时涨潮，那么就不至于使 1200 户人家无家可归。现在天气严寒，这些灾民不得不在旷野、寺庙或任何能找到的地方过夜。当我看到两辆消防车停在一栋燃烧的大楼边时，我目击了缺水的过程，大楼的热浪烤焦了我的头发，但两辆消防车都没有足够的水源灭火。

来自政府部门的重要消息是，将有一位新县长来到温州，[1] 他将带来

---

[1] 指的是县长徐用，徐用在地方任县长期间，以精明强干著称，但也有人称其为"酷吏"。徐用在温州任职仅一年，其职务就遭到许蟠云侵夺。应一心：《徐用生平事迹点滴》，《缙云文史资料·第二辑》，文史资料委员会，1987，第 24 ~ 33 页。

大量寻找职位的随从。温州衙门将会迎来一次"大清洗"，不少人将被迫转往别处谋生。

传教士来访

由于中华基督教勉励协会总干事周志禹（Tsin Tsz‐vu）先生的到来，温州宗教界感到振奋不已。他代表当地内地会、圣道公会和自立会（Independent），组织了9天的密集的传教活动。在所有教派的教堂都举行了会议，但周末因为人数过多，所以在圣道公会教堂举行了最后一次活动，该教堂可以容纳1000人。

星期天下午，该教堂座无虚席，人们甚至只能站着听讲，门外窗外全是人，教堂大厅与走廊也挤满了人，总人数不会低于2000人。（1934年12月8日）

《温州的进步：年鉴显示虽然温州贸易衰退，但仍取得进步》，《北华捷报及最高法庭与领事馆杂志》，1935年5月1日

温州的进步：年鉴显示虽然温州贸易衰退，但仍取得进步

（本报记者报道）

我手上有一份政府的1934年年鉴①，其中包含有关于温州的内容。我要大胆地从这些卷帙浩繁的资料中挑选一些让其他地方的读者也会感兴趣的内容。这份关于过去历史的记录以及对未来的规划，表明温州的现代化在总体上是取得了巨大进步。我在前面的文章已提及道路建设。在贸易衰落的情况下，这个地区的民众在最近两三年建成数十英里的汽车公路，在没有现代机械帮助的情况下，他们仍开山铺路，遇水架桥。

城市改良

在温州，街道的拓宽计划正在迅速开展，数以百计的房屋被拆除，新的和更好的房屋（虽然房屋占地面积变小了）拔地而起。街道上的障碍物，如灌木、贞节牌坊、小贩摊位甚至乞讨者都被从街上清除了。乞讨者如果不愿服从，将会受到惩罚，甚至被监禁，许多乞讨者已经被安排参与公共工程的工作，比如城市运河的疏浚工作。加宽的街道要重新命名，我注意到当局在命名时，希望采用"孙逸仙博士"的名字来命名，以志纪念。街道市场已经搬迁到某些防火区，或搬入专门的新建市场，或搬入寺庙改建的市场。其中4座市场已经建成。温州的黄包车现在都实行了"靠左行驶"的新规定。城市的南门与北门已被拆除，许多旧传统现在已被取

---

① 原文写作 Yung-Ko-Yue，殊为难解，这份年鉴到底是何种刊物，待考。猜测极可能是实业部出版的《中国经济年鉴》。

代，如拐角设计原本是为了阻止游荡的恶鬼，现在这些拐角都被宽阔笔直、通往城市主要街道的汽车道路取代。

新生活运动的影响可以从某些卫生改革中看出来，例如在西门附近的城市屠宰场，所有的牛和猪都必须接受规定检查后才能被宰杀。

这本年鉴里有一张照片，上面展示了数百种古老的交易手段，这些手段显然被证明是骗人的。当每个店主都有自己的尺寸时，顾客怎么能确定他得到的是正确的尺寸呢？既然只有政府的衡量标准现在可以在买卖中使用，不规范行为只能被强制统一。

修复文物

我认为，新生活运动中产生的自豪感，导致当局对历史名胜古迹开始大规模修缮，温州及其周边地区的名胜古迹也得以改善。江心屿上的7层宝塔修建于1000年前的唐朝，很长一段时间，破败的宝塔上筑有鹭鸟的巢穴，塔顶斜插着荒草。如今修缮后，现在的它是一座藏红色的华丽宝塔，塔上的铃铛在微笑风中叮当作响。

农村地区目前也正在尝试进行改革。每一个小地方每年都要由当地工人修20里土路，种20亩树木。政府还鼓励民众安装电话。就像《旧约》中约瑟在埃及预言会出现七年荒年一样，[1] 当地政府也提出了一个类似的歉收援助计划，政府将建立谷仓，并强制农民缴纳粮食进行储藏，以防荒年粮铺哄抬粮价。

这本书中有一些非常有趣的统计数据，展示出社区里存在巨大的组织。那些认为中国人与外部世界完全隔离的人，当浏览这部当代出版的厚书时，可能会像我一样感到相当惊讶。这本书详细介绍了温州各地的确切贸易情况。温州曾经出口价值50万银圆的柑橘，共有6个品种，一些会出口到日本，但现在外国人更喜爱广东与台湾出产的甜柑（温州特产是苦柑），当地柑橘出口总额目前已跌到20万银圆。官方给出的建议是，种植

---

① 约瑟在埃及预言将会出现7年的丰收，和随之而来的7年灾荒。他帮法老出主意，将丰年的一半收成征收并储存，以备在荒年之用。7个丰年的一半收成，可度过7个荒年。法老信任约瑟，任命他为埃及的宰相，把一切事物都交由他掌管。在约瑟的管理下，埃及民众在荒年也能丰衣足食。——编者注

者应该放弃柑橘，转而种植更多的梨、苹果、李子和桃子等作物。

愚蠢的茶叶经销商

报告称，贸易不景气仍在持续。以茶叶为例，报告给出的理由是当地经销商坚持他们的老习惯，把劣质茶叶放在箱子里，然后在箱上层铺满好茶叶，这让客户震惊！

日本过去会为两种主要产品——菜油和木炭——专门派遣轮船来温州进行贸易，但现在不会了，唉！我想知道在温州抵制日货期间，温州商人是否比日本商人承受了更大损失，温州菜油每年出口总值约50万银圆，这对温州来讲可不是一笔小数目。

即使是渔业，情况也很糟糕，报告说是由于民众的道德败坏，整日只知道赌博喝酒。

在过去的黄金岁月，温州有1万多名渔夫在大海、江河、小溪与运河里撒网捕鱼，每年可以捕到100万银圆的渔获。今年最重的鸡可以长到5~6斤。温州当年共卖了20万银圆的鸡蛋。人们很遗憾地发现，温州纸伞不仅产量下降，而且质量也在下降。草席也一样，7块草席只能卖1银圆。青田石雕经温州销往美国、日本、俄罗斯、法国等地，虽有这样的销售渠道，但贸易仍十分萧条。显然唯一繁荣的行业是建筑行、木匠行和石匠行，因为他们忙着拆除旧商店，然后大批量地建造新商店，不是一幢一幢地干，而是一条街一条街地干！

工资仍旧很低

报告显示的工资数据（报告数据很全，甚至包括农场帮工中男性、女性、儿童各自的工资情况）都很低。一个强壮的男人可能的高收入是每年60银圆，每月6.4银圆，每天0.36银圆，这显然包括了一天的膳食。一个贫穷的工人只能得到这些数字的一半。在这个国家，女性每年的最高工资是26银圆，最低的是12银圆。10岁以上的孩子，如果情况特殊的话，可能在12个月内能挣20银圆，尽管有些孩子一年只能挣5银圆。中国人最高单日工资是1角2分，平均是7分，最低的一天只有4分，且不提供食物。乡村百姓只能靠手工业艰难度日，男人在家里制作网、粗纸、篮子、草鞋和绳子等，妇女制作草席、鞋、布、腰带、十字绣、刺绣、草帽等。

当地贷款利率飙升至20%，这是非常高的，尽管比中国其他地方低。动荡和缺乏安全感导致人们普遍不愿让没有充分回报的巨额资金承担风险，导致利率保持在高位，因此，农村百姓很难获得贷款。

根据本书记载，温州总面积为82.35万亩，其中耕地46.12万亩。其中72.24万亩地纳过税，数字表明仍有一些人没有纳过税。因此，为了征税和增加地方政府的收入，必须在该地制定一部彻底的《末日审判书》①。温州总人口约为68万人。（温州，4月4日）

---

① 征服诺曼以后，征服者英王威廉一世下令对英格兰土地进行丈量，其丈量结果被不满的封建主称为《末日审判书》。这里是借此典故，指代温州当局丈量土地时穷凶极恶。

《对烟草抵制进行调查：中国人缴获并焚毁 175 万支香烟》，《北华
捷报及最高法庭与领事馆杂志》，1935 年 6 月 5 日

对烟草抵制进行调查：中国人缴获并焚毁 175 万支香烟

新生活运动背后是一群戴着面具的排外主义者。这是昨天在上海，从
可靠政府部门那里了解到的温州目前的真实情况。

中国企业生产的香烟被允许进入温州，没有任何阻碍。只有外国制造
的香烟才受到干涉。

积极参与抵制外国香烟活动的主要是永嘉（温州）烟草公司、温州货
币兑换协会，以及新生活运动促进会，显然后者是前者的爪牙。

175 万支香烟被焚毁

5 月 18 日，货币兑换协会查获 30 只大箱和 25 只小箱的"皇后牌"香
烟，总计为 175 万支。据了解，这些货物上午被查获，当天中午时分在离
城约 15 里处被烧毁。

当地税务官员的职责是检查货物是否正确地贴了税票，他们抗议没收
行为，要求查看货物，但未被允许，没能履行职责。

当地烟草经销商怡泰公司（Yee Tsoong Distributors Ltd.，此前由英美
烟草公司直营）立刻向县长以及警察局提出抗议。直到下午 5 点，警察局
才派出 12 名警察抵达事发地，但早就找不到肇事者了。

英国副领事杰弗里先生今天将离开上海，前往温州调查此事。

日本领事馆对目前的僵局知之甚少。据说日本人在温州的利益两年前
由于一场激烈的反日运动而遭重创，他们被迫撤侨。最近一些委托给中国
商人的日本货物不允许登陆。有人认为不久的将来，也会有一名日本领事
前往温州就日本侨民重返温州进行磋商。（上海，6 月 1 日）

《温甬公路：大道上的快乐旅程》，《北华捷报及最高法庭与领事馆杂志》，1935 年 6 月 12 日

温甬公路：大道上的快乐旅程

（本报记者报道）

最近建成的从温州到宁波的公路是一条尚未为公众所知的风景路线。日本将要小心她的"桂冠"，因为日本的风景远不如这条路线。我们在早上离开温州，过河之后沿河谷绕行，逐渐爬升进山，触目所及尽是群山低谷，一块块被耕种过的梯田组成一幅幅不断变化的图景，这样的画面永远都不会令人感到厌倦。

在有些直道上，可以试着加速，但谨慎的司机很少会超过每小时 30 英里的速度。当然在陡坡上，车速通常是 10 英里或 15 英里。我自己曾是一名工程师，我非常欣赏建造这段南北贯通的公路的工程师的杰作。公路最大坡度看起来不会超过 7 度，所以在两天的行程中，我们没有遇到任何汽车故障。路面的材料很好，铺设得也相当不错，所以道路在任何程度上都不会受到雨水的影响。每年这个时候，田野里的庄稼都是金黄色的，到处都在收获。我能有机会去研究这个国家，以及这个国家的人和物产，真是一件幸事。

乘客必须通过摆渡过河，有两次我们都是通过浮桥过河，这样能够立即上岸，不会浪费时间。这次旅行我们的团队共有 7 辆巴士，一辆接一辆，每辆车都令人满意。此外，值得注意的是，这次旅行的费用是非常合理的，票价总计为 9 银圆。从温州到宁波，实际旅程不到 15 个小时。第一日的下午我们抵达了临海，在一家中国旅馆里找到了相当满意的住处。如果你不吃中餐的话，那就得自行多带点食品。我们的团队讲的是官话，而且讲得相当不错，但我们听不懂宁波话和温州话。

在拔茅，如果旅客愿意，可以安排去杭州，而不是继续去宁波。在前

往溪口的路线上，其景观很值得一看，沿途崎岖的山路也给了大家充分的机会观赏美景。各地的稻田看来状况良好，收成一定比去年好。如果沿着山路往下看，乘客刚好能看到盘旋 5 次的来路，可以看出这段路是曲折建造的，从工程角度看，这条路建得非常棒。风景如画的古桥随处可见，山中村落也错落有致。

《温州现代化：建筑章程与燃火设备》，《北华捷报及最高法庭与领事馆杂志》，1935 年 10 月 2 日

温州现代化：建筑章程与燃火设备

（本报记者报道）

本月曾创下最热纪录，现在又创下最冷纪录。整个世界好像都笼罩在秋日的蓝色与棕色里。虽然今年夏天不算太糟糕，但秋天如此寒冷实在让人吃不消。我们可以宽慰地报告说，今年这个季度虽然经历了三到四次风灾恐慌，但只有一次影响到温州附近地区，且没有造成任何损失。

度假归来，我对两个月来街道拓宽所取得的进展感到惊讶。事实上，对于两年前最后一次来这里的游客来说，现在的温州已经旧貌换新颜了——古老的木房和棚户已被高大现代风格的房子取代。狭窄的小巷已被宽阔的街道取代，道路两旁几乎全是楼房。宽敞的新门取代了狭窄的旧门。三层和四层的建筑很常见，为了保持风格的一致性，市政府不得不颁布一组规定，新建筑必须维持固有风格，并应在建设前得到检查员的批准。这是许多新建筑的占地面积过小所致。

奇特的建筑

最近，我对一家三层楼高的商店感到惊奇，它的正门宽约 15 英尺，从前窗到后墙仅深 6 英尺。像这样类似的房屋还有很多，我很好奇如果风灾来了，或是汽车发生碰撞事故，这些建筑会如何呢？又或者如果发生火灾，居民该如何逃生呢？这一切目前还没有答案。谈到火灾，政府正准备通过在主要街角挖深水井和订购现代消防车，来应对这些建筑中可能发生的灾难和破坏。

我听到消息说，为了节省开支，一些官职将被撤销，尤其是永嘉县长的职位。这个旧的机关将连同警察局局长，与另一个机关合并，该命令是

由省府发出的。

征兵仍在继续扰乱民众的生活和工作。人们有时会看到一队新兵学习出操，看起来非常拙劣和愚蠢。他们必须离开他们的家园不少于 3 个月。征兵体系虽然主要是为了国防，但可能对当地抵御土匪具有更直接的价值。今后土匪会更加谨慎地攻击村庄，每个村的壮丁都已接受过一段时间的军事训练。

土匪的威胁

这提醒了我，当地乡村经过一两年的休整后，再次受到土匪威胁。中国内地会的成员们不得不离开他们避暑的山间小屋，公共汽车也暂时停摆。目前交通虽已恢复，但局势不能保证安全。

几天前，一艘汽艇从温州开往一个大村庄，沿河往上游开约三小时的行程。他们被一群武装人员拦截，并被抢走 1000 银圆。由于船夫进行反抗，他被俘虏了，从此杳无音讯。其中一名乘客知道如何开动发动机，他于是将船开到温州，随即一队警察前去调查。

通常，坐这种小船的乘客身上很难找到 20 银圆，但此时正是各地会账的时候，碰巧有两三个城里人每年都会在这个时候去乡下讨债，当时他们刚好要返程。也可能是匪徒们掌握了情报，刻意选择了这个时机。

下星期，当地的自立会将庆祝成立 10 周年。在民族主义高涨的时期，自立会与英国圣道公会断绝了关系，并宣布独立，时至今日旧伤疤早已痊愈。庆祝期间将会召开一个为期两晚的会议，中国内地会与圣道公会的代表都将在第一场会议上发言。

自立教会

自立教会是完全独立和自治的，在过去的两年中他们使用自己的资金，在城里建起了一座教堂，同时该教会还与农村教堂保持密切联络。这些成绩都是值得称赞的，需要记住的是，只有卓越与强大的教会才敢于自立，而今天的传教事业仍旧背负着弱者的负担。

英国圣道公会外国职员的变动包括施德福夫妇与他们的儿子以及爱乐德牧师，他们将会在 11 月离开温州休假。护士史密斯将在 10 月休假归来。施德福医生、史密斯小姐和爱乐德女士都在白累德医院工作。

有一个好消息传来，现在许多传教站可以安装现代化管道，有配备煤气灶的卫生的现代化厨房。温州目前已经有了天然气工厂，由一家上海公司开设。这个工厂运转方式很简单，不需要购买化学品，也不会出现机器故障。

工厂使用的唯一燃料是普通的厨房垃圾，以及任何废物如草、蔬菜，或其他软性物质。所形成的气体比煤气安全，无毒，且燃烧温度高，该设备目前已经到圣道公会的一些住宅。包括城里中国人或外国人的住宅，在最近一两年的使用过程中都感觉不错。（温州，10 月 2 日）

《温州贸易：否认排外主义》，《北华捷报及最高法庭与领事馆杂志》，1935 年 10 月 23 日

温州贸易：否认排外主义

致《北华捷报》编辑：

先生，最近贵报有一篇文章，大意是说一些来温州寻求做生意的外国商人，会遭到来自官方的刁难。在这里我想代表温州对指控予以否认，温州从来没有，将来也不会仅仅因为政治原因就阻碍贸易的发展。正常情况下这是一个繁荣的地区，但近年来农村经济状况已接近危险点，事实上当局正不断寻求手段来改善贸易。例如，当局已做出努力消灭土匪活动，同时鼓励商人降低商品价格。事实与贵报报道相反，这里没有排外主义，最近英国与美国副领事已经访问温州，他们掌握该地区状况的第一手信息。同时他们也都对状况感到满意，我希望上述事实能打消贵报读者对温州外贸形势的疑虑。（温州，10 月 10 日）

《一些问题》，《北华捷报及最高法庭与领事馆杂志》，1935 年 10 月 23 日

一些问题

致《北华捷报》编辑：

先生，在此我要引用一封贵报 10 月 10 日刊载的信，这封信否认温州存在抵制外国商品的行为，我认为，要么是作者并不了解过去两年间温州与海门地区恶劣的商贸环境，要么是作者想要通过这封信为这个浙江重要地区外贸所遭受的严重损失表达歉意。

温州主要外国进口商品是石油、香烟和化肥。我已经亲自确认过好多次，在这三项重要商品中，目前为止只剩下石油贸易未遭冲击，温州对香烟与化肥的抵制如此强劲，以致外国香烟的进口显著下降，同时在今年甚至根本不可能运化肥进入温州。

如果温州真的没有针对外贸设置障碍，那么我要提出以下问题。

（1）为什么上海《申报》在 6 月 15 日①的文章指出，上海航运公司已经收到通知，不再向温州装运外国香烟与化肥？

（2）为什么此前在温州会发生 25 起香烟被非法没收并被公开焚烧事件？

（3）温州与海门苦力只有每天工作才能买米糊口，但他们拒绝搬运外国香烟与化肥，迫使货物退回上海，是谁在背后威胁这些苦力？

虽然最近几批受抵制货物进入了温州，但几乎无法销售。在大多数小商场，官方仍然禁止销售。而在其他销售点，虽然没有强制地抵制，经销

---

① 这则报道的日期应该是 1935 年 5 月 15 日，据报道上海方面各报馆与航运公司在 5 月 14 日接到温州急电，谓温州民众已开始对外国纸烟与肥田粉实施抵制，并且在边境组织了检查委员会与检查队，要求各方勿再采办运往温州。参见《温州抵制》，《申报》1935 年 5 月 15 日，第 10 版。

商与消费者已经产生购买洋货就需要多纳税的印象。他们被迫纳公路税或其他更多杂税，甚至每买一包货物就要向土货协会（Native Goods Promotion Association）[①] 捐 1 银圆，玉环的情况也与此类似。

我写此信是要表明，温州的外贸状况并不像温州方面说的那样好。如果温州的排外运动能够确实结束，我想不仅能够得到外国公司和中国航运业的赞赏，也能得到温州本地商人与农民的欢迎，因此从现在开始，温州的对外贸易能恢复正常。

一名航运业的观察者
上海，10 月 7 日

[①] 早在 1933 年，许蟠云就在温州地区推行鼓励土货政策，号召"有志气的温州人，应当尽量先用温州货"。参见《浙江温属物产展览会开幕》，《申报》1933 年 11 月 13 日，第 8 版。

《中国将自主造纸：能够以低于所有外国竞争者的价格销售，温州建立纸厂的方案》，《北华捷报及最高法庭与领事馆杂志》，1935 年 10 月 30 日

中国将自主造纸：能够以低于所有外国竞争者的价格销售，温州建立纸厂的方案

为了进一步增强工业自主，中国将很快建立自己的造纸工厂。一个价值 450 万银圆的工厂计划已经提交给实业部（Ministry of Industry）并获得批准，80% 的资金来自英国庚子赔款基金贷款，其余则为商股。认购股本的最后期限是 1935 年 11 月 30 日。

经过专家们的细致调查，瓯江上的马湾（Mawan）①被认为是理想厂址，此地距浙南温州大概 20 英里。工厂分为造纸厂和纸浆厂两部分，使用的机械来自英国，其资金分配预估如下：

项　　目	费用（银圆）
能 24 小时制造 35 长吨新闻纸机械总价（包括发电、运输费、装置费）	3290000
购买土地	10000
房屋及混凝土工程等	500000
预备金	100000
流动资金	600000
总　　计	4500000

机械和建筑成本随市场和汇率浮动，总价包括发电制料、纸浆与造纸等各项机器，以及运输、装置等费用。预备金为 10 万银圆，包括调查费以及派专家赴英国定制及监制机器费用。

①　厂址在今青田温溪镇马湾。

大量原料

人们常说中国的森林资源已经被破坏，虽然某些沿海省份情况确实如此，但也有例外。在龙泉、庆元（Chingyuan）、景宁（Chingning）、云和（Yunho）、松阳、遂昌、宣平（Hsuanping）、缙阳（Chinyun）、丽水和青田，上述地方拥有成片山地，存在大量适合造纸的木料。木料的主要品种是真杉（China flr）①、柳杉（liushan）②和松木。该地除供应本地所需木材外，每年还会对外输出价值约600万银圆的木材，其中2/5输出到处州，3 /5输出到温州。龙泉是输出木材最多的地方，每年的输出总值在100万银圆左右。

价格竞争

施涤华（A. G. Stewart）先生是苏格兰造纸专家，他被实业部任命为顾问并负责相关研究，尤其是制订经济方面的全盘计划。据施涤华估计，温州将纸造出来然后运到上海销售的最低成本为每吨110.64银圆，而目前中国进口的新闻纸最低价格为每吨110.94银圆，毫无疑问，这是市场"倾销"的结果。据信，外国造纸厂不可能长期维持这样的低价。即便外国造纸厂维持低价竞争，中国造纸厂也还是可以拥有0.3银圆的竞争优势，这意味着造纸厂每年可以获取3675银圆的利润。

施涤华先生还指出，中国应该与其他国家一样适当提高关税，以保护新兴产业。关于新闻纸进口关税问题，他在月刊《中国经济杂志》（*Chinese Economic Journal*）的一篇文章中这样说：

> 中国对卷筒新闻纸征收的关税是7.5%，对散令新闻纸征收的关税是33.5%，结果是散令纸进口几近断绝。目前的市面情况是进口卷筒纸，然后由上海工厂切成散令纸。如果中国能将税率予以修正，像其他国家一样按重量征税，那么必将对温州新厂大有帮助。略微地提高税率，想必也不会造成印刷公司的过分反弹。

---

① 又称家杉或正杉，英文名为China flr，学名为Obies Chenensis。参见温溪纸厂筹备委员会编《中国造纸股份有限公司计划书》，温溪纸厂筹备委员会编印，1935，第14页。

② 又称榅杉，学名为Cryptomeria，日本称之为日杉。资料来源同上。

纸厂每日产量

造纸工厂每日的新闻纸产量为 35 吨,按照每年 350 天计算,每年的产量将达到 12250 吨。中国四大报《申报》、《新闻报》(Sin Wan Pao)、《时报》(Eastern Times)、《时事新报》(China Times)每年所需新闻纸总量在 2 万吨左右,因此造纸厂产量仍显不足。

英国庚子赔款基金受托人已经就技术报告和财务问题举行了几次会议。他们已同意发放所需贷款,并将在适当时候签订合同。中国报行已经认购公开商股。中国银行、交通银行和中央银行等已经被指定处理所有相关股权交易问题。

《温州建立纸厂提案：英国庚子赔款董事会已同意计划》，《北华捷报
及最高法庭与领事馆杂志》，1935 年 12 月 11 日

温州建立纸厂提案：英国庚子赔款董事会已同意计划

由交通部部长朱家骅（Chu Chia－hua）担任主席的、第 32 次英国庚子赔款董事会常委会于本周六在上海举行。

出席的有副主席马锡尔（R. Calder Marshall）以及董事曾溶浦（T. K. Tseng）、颜德庆（Yen Te－ching）、叶恭绰（Yeh Kung－cho）、刘瑞恒（J. Heng Liu）与荆恩（W. S. King）。

常委会审议了实业部提出的在浙江温州建立造纸厂的贷款申请，决定将此事提交全体董事会议讨论。

稍晚又举行了教育委员会会议，由李书华（Li Shu－hua）博士任主席，朱家骅先生、叶恭绰先生和刘瑞恒博士列席，会议审查了关于教育的提议。

第二部分

英文
文献

ar junks cruising after pirates alon
in-Ché sea coast, it seems that th
s of Fukien and Tsichow are sti
umerous and as savage as ever.
and its consort bound from Ningpo t
ow laden with rice and sundries wer
tly attacked near Wênchow by a co
pirates, who boarded the merchant
aving ransacked everything of valu
the latter, left them with twenty-fiv
nd seriously wounded. Stri
s have been issued by the Governor
al, Tsan, for the capture of the pirate
uite a large fleet of war junks is no
ut it seems to be the universal opinio

be sent to Ta-cl
Yo-ching-hsien
f pirate-robbers
used considerat
ties of both this
chow. Some tim
does plundered two
the Yu H'uan Bay
re) which caused the
y to order one of his
against them. On
e of the bay the office
-vessel decided to an
rred a party of soldier

RIOT AT WÊNCHOW.

he *Yungning*, from Wên
ved here on Saturday, b
iculars of a riot which had
chow on the night of the
first intimation of this ri
hed up from Ningpo from informatio
lied by the *Yungning* on arrival a
port, though efforts had been made b

xpression, spread himself out over the
hole subject of the health, pestilence
amines, and topography of the place
hirty-six closely printed pages hav
iot sufficed to relieve him of his whol
urden of knowledge, for at the begin
ing of his paper he says that he reserve
he medical
ccasion; but
f which he h
ally have th
hat we sho
uch a trifle
imply
all rigl
no spec
tho gre
ie other
elsewhere,
to the saturated condition
some other such commo

cal Report
American

During a fierce gale which raged at Wen
chow about a fortnight ago, several seriou
disasters occurred, attended in many case
with loss of life. Four large junks, lade
with poles, were upset and many other
ragged anchor or sustained other injuries
whilst a great number of small fishing craf
uffered a worse fate. The villagers on th
oast showed great barbarism. Instead o
ffording succour, they busied themselve
with picking up wreckage thrown ashore
In the worst cases they even wrested th
oles away from the shipwrecked people
who in their exhausted state were made t
ield the logs to the merciless people
Owing to the unusually cold weather a
Wenchow there is considerable sufferin
mongst the poorer classes, who are no
rovided with extensive wardrobes, and
specially amongst those who have a pre

(FROM A CORRESP
Notice to mariners, also
ad to feminine sphere
markable Peak on the
avigators see on their
Vênchow, having only
nd never named, has no
e denizens of Wêncho
Hart's Peak," in recogn
ices which the Inspecto
mperial Maritime Custo
y illuminating the coas
ormal recognition of the
y the Wênchowese, in pic-nic assembled
n the 22nd March, and that being th
irthday of the Emperor of Germany, nea
o the celebration of the Queen's Jubilee
nd within measurable distance of th
atal day of President Cleveland; th
ealth of those estimable rulers was drun

ng-king, running as she n
rt of the most influential
fter trip with improved
esults, seems now to have
o that point where if more
of necessity become in
g superfluity. As has bee
the impetus given by
y means of shipment has
nt export of al
spects for tea

vastation that met ou
e river of Wênchow wa
les and miles the countr
vast expanse of wate
teads and graves, an
nds crowded with cattle
frowning background
most depressing an
We passed too quickl
by the pen. Women an
roups, doubtless talkin
sses, while the men wer
asy in their boats. In some places wher
he bridges were still standing only th
pper portion of their arches was visibl
oking like mirages—water above, belo
nd around them! Great indeed mu
ave been the downpour to have caused suc
n inundation. It was a comforting chang
o turn one's gaze from the immerse
ountry to the numberless fishermen pu
uing their calling as if no such thing
ome troubles existed. The flooded cou

Macgowa
ow recen
put down
sumption
outhwaite
ld be tra

which a reference to Mr. Don
a table on the opposite page rend

ichow as its Consul on the 12th inst.,
Parker taking leave on a new de
ure, having first secured the last instal
t of the indemnity that the authorities
ed to pay for losses sustained by
igners in the recent disturbances. To
be Mr. E. H. Parker's success in giving
ral satisfaction to foreigners and native
orities in regard to the questions raised
e riot to good luck, would be unjust to
accomplished officer. It was tact that
ted an amicable settlement

To the *Editor* of the
NORTH-CHINA DAILY NEW

IR,—Although the subject of
China was ably discussed at a l
of the Shanghai Literary and
iety the question was not so ex
reated as to preclude me from
mall contribution, assuming tha
he unacceptable to those wl
ary (but n

ically, it
think t
mature, t
where it
needed
northern
courses, a
is doubtf
ccessfully
It was u
yed by at
of Chin

R OWN CORR
ing, on en
d some stra
trawropes,

that were
ent the ever
ng. Had they resisted
would have been as use
A proposition that was u
channel has been abando
a panic was created by
quiring every family to
darins a basket of stones
as secure as if they had
protection; the authorit
solicitous for their safety
threw missiles, and other

"Street Barriers in Wenchow: An Old Custom and Present Fears," *The North – China Herald and Supreme Court & Consular Gazette*, January 15, 1916

Street Barriers in Wenchow: An Old Custom and Present Fears

(From our own correspondent)

Wenchow, January 4

A few days ago everyone here, native and foreign was surprised to see heavy wooden gates over ten feet high being erected at the ends of all the principal streets. Where the street was a long one, not only was a gate put at each end, but also one in the middle. The populous suburbs outside the city gates are being treated in the same manner. It turns out that this is the revival of an old custom called the *tung voa*, or winter protection, which has fallen into desuetude for the last twenty years.

The long winter nights are supposed to afford greater facilities to thieves and robbers, but as the last decade has not shown any special need for the revival of this custom we have to look elsewhere for the reason, and the impression has got about that while not effectively serving their ostensible purpose, the barricades might be an effective method of preventing large numbers of people massing together and rioting, which latter might ensure on the announcement of the change in the form of

STREET BARRIERS IN WENCHOW.

AN OLD CUSTOM AND PRESENT FEARS.

From Our Own Correspondent.
Wenchow, Jan. 4.

A few days ago everyone here, native and foreign was surprised to see heavy wooden gates over ten feet high being erected at the ends of all the principal streets. Where the street was a long one, not only was a gate put at each end, but also one in the middle. The populous suburbs outside the city gates are being treated in the same manner. It turns out that this is the revival of an old custom called the *tung voa*, or winter protection, which has fallen into desuetude for the last twenty years.

government.

For the last few days there has been an air of expectancy about the city. The yamens have been preparing for, and are in daily expectation of, the announcement that the President of the Republic has assumed the purple. While the general opinion here is that Wenchow with the rest of Chekiang will accept the monarchy, if not with acclamation, at least with resignation, there are quite a large number of the student class who believe that the five provinces of Yunnan, Szechuan, Kueichow, Kuangtung and Kuangsi will declare their independence.

> "Wenchow: The Orange Season and Its Riches," *The North – China Herald and Supreme Court &*
> *Consular Gazette*, March 31, 1916

Wenchow: The Orange Season and Its Riches

(From our own correspondent)

Wenchow, March 21

The orange season which is now approaching a close has been an exceptionally good one. Where-as last year the total export did not reach more than 10000 cases (the crop being a comparative failure) scarcely a China Merchants' steamer has left the port since the first week in November without carrying from 2500 to 4000 cases and in some weeks the export has reached a total of 7000 cases. The oranges are for the most part reshipped at Shanghai for Tientsin and Peking.

The Wenchow orange is peculiar and quite different from any other Chinese variety. It is large and has a thick loose skin, and with large numbers of people the liking for it is only slowly acquired, but once the taste is acquired it is preferred to any other kind. It may be pointed out that the flavour is reminiscent of the Seville orange, and it is possibly this that makes the Wenchow orange so excellent for making marmalade. Whether this could be carried out on a large scale successfully, remains to be seen.

Another of the Wenchow products that might be utilized is the gingerroot which, while produced in considerable quantity, is not exported, yet preserved ginger made from the local product is quite equal to the Canton variety.

It is reported that during the coming tea season the local producers are likely to be left severely alone by the buyers, as the amount of adulteration that took

WENCHOW.

THE ORANGE SEASON AND ITS RICHES.

From Our Own Correspondent.

Wenchow, March 21.

The orange season which is now approaching a close has been an exceptionally good one. Whereas last year the total export did not

place last year was almost without precedent. Years ago Wenchow tea had quite a good name, the greater portion of the crop going to Hankow for blending purposes, but the amount gradually diminished for the same reason as given above. The producers evidently do not see that commercially they are cutting their own throats by such corrupt practices.

The output of alum from Pingyanghsien, thirty miles south of Wenchow, is steadily increasing and as prices during the year have gone up considerably the trade is very lucrative. The alum is brought up in junks to Wenchow and transhipped to the steamers, thousands of bags being carried every trip.

Wenchow is a very conservative place and only during the last few months has the copper cent piece been in circulation. For years, owing, it is said, to the obstruction of the local banks and cash shops, there has been a boycott of this useful coin. The reason for this obstruction is difficult to find out. The obstruction having been removed, however, the number of one cent pieces in circulation is increasing rapidly.

The electric light, it would seem, has become a permanency in Wenchow. The plant, quite new, was set up nearly two years ago and during the last twelve months there has been practically no break down. The management, now entirely in the hands of Chinese, is to be congratulated on its efficient service. Over 4000 lights are in nightly use, and while the plant is capable of serving more, the company is not able to get the supplies for further installation.

In addition to the already existing Normal School the local authorities have been advised to organize a new one with a one year's course. The supply of teachers for the Government elementary schools – now called Citizen Schools is evidently not equal to the demand and the new venture is an attempt to cope with the latter. The disadvantages of this "get diploma quick" method are too obvious to need comment.

"Wenchow: Tax Disputes," *The North – China Herald and Supreme Court & Consular Gazette*, April 22, 1916

Wenchow: Tax Disputes

(From our own correspondent)

Wenchow, April 14

At Tsumen a walled city of 10000 Inhabitants, situated on the coast between Wenchow and Taichow and about the same distance from each here has been considerable difficulty during the last eighteen months on account of the attempted collection of the salt tax.

Outside the city of Tsumen the people of the villages are all

WENCHOW.

TAX DISPUTES.

From Our Own Correspondent.

Wenchow, April 14.

At Tsumen a walled city of 10,000 inhabitants, situated on the coast between Wenchow and Taichow and about the same distance from each, there has been considerable difficulty during the last eighteen months on account of the attempted collection of the salt tax.

engaged in making salt; Whadoa with 1500 inhabitants, being the most important place. Last year the people were informed that the salt officials would buy all salt and that none was to be sold to the people direct. The officials were to buy 120 chin for the price of 100 and would sell at the price of 100 chin thus netting 50 percent. The people believed that this was only another method of "squeeze" on the part of the local officials, refused to sell to the salt bureau and took the salt to the surrounding places on market days to sell to the people direct. The salt officials sent men to try to prevent the people from buying, which so incensed the latter that in the consequent matter, two of the men from the salt office were killed. This matter, it appears, was not immediately reported to Hangchow and so, when, some months later, the provincial authorities were told, they refused to take any action.

This year the official has resorted to a new method, but the people still believe or pretend to believe, that here is no high authority for the position of the tax. When the new official came to Tsumen he was supported by 50 soldiers from the provincial capital. The new plan was to collect from the buyers and not the makers: the buyers to pay 50 cents for every 81 worth of salt bought. This they refused to do as he said no business could be done on those terms. The salt official then consulted with the consulted with the Chisi of Yuhuanting and the latter had two of the chief men of Whadoa arrested. The Whadoa people retaliated a day or two later by capturing two of the Chisi's underlings and, bringing them to Yuhuanting, offered to exchange prisoners. As the crowd, 1000 strong, refused to be intimidated with blank cartridge—although they were entirely unarmed—the Chisi thought it wise to consent to the exchange. The people then quietly returned home, but being afraid that soldiers would be sent to attack their village they invited a band of tufei to help them and several skirmishes took place. one soldier and several civilians being killed.

Business at Tsumen has become completely disorganized and all the "women, children and rich people" have fled to places of safety. The latest news to hand is that a band of 160 tufei has attacked Tsumen city and burned 70 houses and that some 20 persons have lost their lives. The whole country – side is in a state of panic.

"Independence in Wenchow," *The North – China Herald and Supreme Court & Consular Gazette*, April 29, 1916

Independence in Wenchow

(From our own correspondent)

Wenchow, April 17

As soon as the news that Kuangtung had declared its independence of the Central Government reached Wenchow, it was generally thought that Chekiang would soon follow it. On the afternoon of the 14th telegram was received from Chang Tse – yang the Military commissioner in Taichow by Tai Ning, the chief military official here, stating that Taichow,

INDEPENDENCE IN
WENCHOW.

From Our Own Correspondent.

Wenchow, April 17

As soon as the news that Kuangtung had declared its independence of the Central Government reached Wenchow, it was generally thought that Chêkiang would soon follow suit. On the afternoon of the 14th a telegram was received from Chang Tse-yang the Military Commissioner in Taichow, by Tai Ning,

Ningpo, Kashing and Shaohsing had all declare their independence, and urging Tai Ning to consult with the other officials here and bring Wenchow into line. The same afternoon a conference was held at the yamen of the Superintendent of Customs, at which all the chief officials, civil and military, attended. It was finally agreed that the best possible way to maintain order in the city was to follow Chang Tse – yang's advice.

The officials, however, showed a good deal of caution and wired to the Provincial Governor asking for advice. No reply was received that day but late in the evening the chief of the water police, Mr. Chen, received a telegram from the Military chief in Hangchow informing him that Hangchow had broken off all relations with Yuan Shih – kai's government and had officially declared that no time should be lost and the Declaration of Independence was issued immediately. Next morning, Republican flags were widely displayed in the city and schools had a holiday to Commemorate the event.

It was well for immediate peace of the city that the officials took this step quickly, as, just after the declaration had been posted, a number of revolutionists arrived from different parts to inaugurate the movement. The general opinion is that much trouble would have been caused if they had found the officials not prepared to act; as it was, this undesirable body left the city almost immediately.

Some members of the Chamber of Commerce and other gentlemen of the city are trying to form a Municipal Council to co – operate with the officials in the administration of the city. Their idea, is that such a representative body would do much to insure peace. The Taoyin, however, affirms that as it was stated in the telegram from Hangchow that no new organization is to be allowed to be formed, he is not in a position, at present, to accept the proffered help. He has wired to the Governor, however, and is awaiting a reply.

"Wenchow: Government Schools Arraigned," *The North – China Herald and Supreme Court & Consular Gazette*, May 27, 1916

Wenchow: Government Schools Arraigned

(From our own correspondent)

Wenchow, May 14

The Principal of the United Methodist, Mission College, Mr. T. W. Chapman, M. SC. (Sometime correspondent of the "North China Daily News") has left the port today for furlough in England. A number of beautiful presentations made to Mr. and Mrs. Chapman show with what affection and esteem they are regarded by their students, colleagues, fellow – residents and local officials.

On Friday last a large gathering was convened by the College Y. M. C. A. to bid good – bye to Mr. Chapman. Address and odes were delivered, full of appreciation of his work. Mr. Chapman, on rising to reply, was greeted with hearty acclamation.

Amongst the speeches made, was one of perhaps wider significance than that of the local circumstances. The college orator, a youth of 20, who on one or two occasions has attracted attention by this zest in speechifying, responded to the invitation to address the gathering, and made something of a sensation by his strictures on the management of Government colleges. He said that the Methodist College was acknowledged as the leading educational institution throughout the

WENCHOW.

GOVERNMENT SCHOOLS ARRAIGNED.

From Our Own Correspondent.

Wenchow, May 14.
The Principal of the United Methodist Mission College, Mr. T. W. Chapman, M. SC. (sometime correspondent of the "North China Daily News") has left the port today for furlough in England. A number of beautiful presentations made to Mr. and Mrs. Chapman show with what affection and esteem they are regarded by their students, colleagues, fellow-residents and local officials.

district. He and his fellow – students were grateful to their principal because at this college, through his good management, the lecturers were always punctual, and put in full time at their lectures. Moreover as students they got continuity studies through the lecturers being fixed.

Then to the accompaniment of round on round of applause from the students he went on:

"But we who, have studied at Government schools at Hangchow and elsewhere know what it is. To begin with, the lecturer comes late: then, when he has taught for half an hour, he imagines he has done extremely well and dismisses the class. And that is not all You study for a short time under one lecturer when suddenly he departs and a new one is brought in. Continuity of studies is destroyed. " In considering this incident one feels that although a good discount must be allowed on account of youthful exuberance, there is nevertheless a residue of truth remaining which points to two things. The first is, that, great as the progress of government educational work has been, the com misplaces of Western school life, such as punctuality and continuity of work, have yet to become commonplaces in the schools of China. And the second is, that the feature of mission and other western educational work here, that is most helping the educational life of China, is simply its loyalty the principle of thoroughness and its utter distrust of mere showiness. And it is this feature which needs emphasis in order that this land of scholars may also become a land of schools.

"A Chinese Doctor on Typhoid," *The North - China Herald and Supreme Court & Consular Gazette*, November 4, 1916

A Chinese Doctor on Typhoid

(From our own correspondent)

Wenchow, October 24

During the early autumn the villages in the districts north of Wenchow, have suffered considerably from a disease which, from description, appears possibly to have been typhoid. Strong persons attacked by the disease might recover, but the old and the young succumbed in large numbers.

A CHINESE DOCTOR ON TYPHOID.

From Our Own Correspondent.

Wenchow, Oct. 24.

During the early autumn, the villages in the districts north of Wenchow, have suffered considerably from a disease which, from description, appears possibly to have been typhoid. Strong persons attacked by the disease might recover, but the old and the young succumbed in large numbers.

One man falling sick, called in a native doctor who was determined to take no half - measures. To keep down the high temperature he ordered cold wet towels to be applied to the head, whilst the abdomen was covered thickly with mud and earth, kept nice and cool water. At the same time the patient had to take $ 12 of rhinoceros horn during the day. And the man recovered.

The epidemic has run its course.

Harvest Methods 4000 Years Old

Just now another fine rice harvest is being reaped. The rice harvest is being reaped. The rice tubs stand in the fields or block the paths near the workers, and as the sheaves are cut, they are threshed immediately. The "Kuh" or unhulled rice, falls into the tub, and the rice - straw is thrown in a heap alongside.

"The Chinese have been using these same agricultural processes for hundreds of years, I suppose," was an observation meekly put to a native recently. "Hundreds of years!" was the quick reply, "Why, they go back to Shen Nung" (2700B. C.) . They may not go back as far as this, but at any rate, they certainly do go back a considerable period, and the Westerner hardly knows which to wonder at most, the face that these processes have continued so many hundreds, perhaps thousands, of years, practically unchanged, or the face that this same ancient system is still able to supply, in the 20th century, the needs of the vast millions to whom to eat food is to "ch'ih fan"

"Opium Smoking Rife in Wenchow," *The North – China Herald and Supreme Court & Consular Gazette*, December 2, 1916

Opium Smoking Rife in Wenchow

(From our own correspondent)

Wenchow, November 20

Wenchow has a population of roughly 80000, and it is said that the people still smoking opium here number several thousands. The magistrate is now making a vigorous campaign against them. Finding that proclamations and announcements in the Press have proved unavailing in stopping the illegal practice, he has now arrested and imprisoned a number of opium – smokers. Moreover, a report has emanated unofficially from the yamen to the effect that, with the New Year, persons found guilty of opium – smoking will be shot: if two or three had to suffer the extreme penalty it would have a "healthy" effect on the rest of the fraternity!

OPIUM SMOKING RIFE IN WENCHOW.

From Our Own Correspondent.

Wenchow, Nov. 20.

Wenchow has a population of roughly 80,000, and it is said that the people still smoking opium here number several thousands. The magistrate is now making a vigorous campaign against them. Finding that proclamations and announcements in the Press have proved unavailing in stopping the illegal practice, he has now arrested and imprisoned a number of opium-smokers. Moreover ι report has eman-

Retirement of Mr. Acheson

On November 12, Mr. James Acheson, the late Commissioner of Customs at Wenchow, left the port for England. Mr. Acheson had been in Wenchow some two and a half years and was much respected both by the foreign community and the Chinese. He is now retiring from the Service which he entered in 1874. It is noteworthy that back in the early eighties, Mr. Acheson once made the journey home on foot across Siberia. Now that he is going back home for the last time, Mr. Acheson is accompanied by the good wishes of his many friends in the China ports, who trust that his years of retirement may be as long and as happy as they are well – deserved.

"The Red Robes of Wenchow: Relics of Ming Days Sold as Old Iron," *The North – China Herald and Supreme Court & Consular Gazette*, January 27, 1917

The Red Robes of Wenchow: Relics of Ming Days Sold as Old Iron

(From our own correspondent)

Wenchow, January 13

Visitors to Wenchow are familiar with the many pieces of old cannon, some peering out from the old forts at the mouth of the river, some that used to adorn the city wall, and others that lay about on waste pieces of ground in the city. Taking them large and small there were altogether considerably more than 1000 guns. The decree has gone forth from the military authorities in Hangchow that all these useless relics of the past must be turned into as much money as possible. The whole lot has been for sale at the rate of a cent per "ching." Workmen have been breaking the cannon into pieces portable by two coolies and each steamer leaving the port has been taking a load.

These old guns have their story to tell. The later ones were brought here at the time of the Taiping Rebellion. The district had to go through hard times in order to be able to buy them and when they came, the people were proportionately proud of them. So the few who know, are now saying "K'o – sih, K'osih! To

THE RED ROBES OF WENCHOW.

RELICS OF MING DAYS SOLD AS OLD IRON.

From Our Own Correspondent.

Wenchow, Jan. 13.

Visitors to Wenchow are familiar with the many pieces of old cannon, some peering out from the old forts at the mouth of the river, some that used to adorn the city wall, and others that lay about on waste pieces of ground in the city. Taking them large and small there were altogether considerably more than 1,000 guns. The decree has gone forth from the military authorities in Hangchow that all these useless

think that the 'generals' we bought at such a cost, are at last being taken from us, and as old iron – a cent a 'ching'!"

The older guns date from the time of K'ang Hsi, when the country was still unsettled with the last rebellious adherents to the fallen Mings. In those days the cannon were called "The Great Red Robes," they were "generals," robes in red, with power to breath fire and smoke and death. Their passing now, has recalled the story of the fighting in which these guns took part, and the great slaughter of the rebel army near the foot – hills out – side the Three Horned Gate. "It was a famous victory." The canals flowed with blood and one of them became known as "The Way of the Golden – Victory," which name still continues to this day enshrining the history of those warlike times.

A Fatal Explosion

The decree mentioned above, authorizing the sale of the cannons also includes authority for the disposal of all old, useless, military stories. Hence large stocks of old cartridges belonged to the finest type of breech loading rifle used by the soldiers here.

Coolies have been at work breaking them up and separating the brass, the lead, and the gunpowder. The first day they worked actually at the ammunition magazine! The next day they moved a little further off. The third day saw another move further off still. On Friday morning, the 5th instant, the old keeper of the Temple of the Seven Holy Ones, in the western part of the city, was surprised to see a number of coolies entering the precincts carrying loads of old cartridges. Asked what they were bringing cartridges into his temple for, the men replied they were bringing them there "to sun"! Presently some 18 persons were at work taking the cartridges one by one, tapping them loose where the bullet fits into the brass in one heap, the lead in another, and the gunpowder into a third.

Some element of adventure in the work being admitted, they were getting the high rate of wage of $1 for there days and their rice! A woman was there cooking. One man who had been engaged in the first place to carry water, got some one to do the water carrying for him, and on the third day took up the more easy and lucrative employment of cartridge – breaking. It is to be regretted that he will neither carry water, which is hard, nor break up cartridges, which is easy, any more.

Twelve People Killed

By Friday evening the heaps of metal and gunpowder had grown to a considerable size, but there were still more cartridges to be dismembered. "Tap, tap – tap, tap – bang. " A cartridge had exploded, a heap of gunpowder had become ignited, and the poor coolies who, a few moments before, had been congratulating themselves on their good luck, were burnt and maimed wrecks. It is probable that three men were killed there and then. Others, rushing out of the flame, plunged into the canal at the front of the temple, or running through a side door, rolled about on a piece of flat ground seeking to extinguish the flames of their burning clothes. Gruesome evidences still remain.

The explosion severely shook the houses in the neighborhood, including some of the premises of the Roman Catholic Mission. The fire was restricted to the temple and, getting hold of the remaining cartridges, set them going off rapidly. Apparently no one was hit, though there are bullet holes in the walls of the temple. Most of the injured were carried to the United Methodist Hospital (which was besieged with "visitors" the next day) and the Sisters of Charity took in as many as they could. The gunpowder burns of some were very bad and three persons died that night. Since then six more have died, making a total of twelve deaths from this accident.

"The Man from Wenchow: A Confidence Gang Story," *The North – China Herald and Supreme Court & Consular Gazette*, August 25, 1917

The Man from Wenchow: A Confidence Gang Story

At the end of last month a wealthy visitor from Wenchow soon after his arrival in Shanghai was met by strangers who told him that an old friend of his who had left Wenchow years ago was living at 7 Mandalay Road and desired to see him to talk over old times. It was the same old " confidence game " played on countrymen in big cities in every country in the world, a game as old as cities themselves, but it was new to the man from Wenchow.

He accompanied the strangers to Mandalay Road, which is opposite the Mohawk Road entrance to the Race Club, where he was received graciously by another stranger. His friend was out, he was told, —would he sit down and wait and partake of some freshly brewed tea? It was a hot day at the end of July, and the tea was very soothing that the man went fast to sleep.

He was still asleep when he was bundled into a ricsha after dark, and when he awake the next morning in a house in Carter Road it seemed but a moment or two since he had taken, with him were the strangers, and it was then the" friend from Wenchow" was a myth. After assuring their victim that there was no hope of rescue, his captors proceeded to squeeze him for all they thought he was worth on threatening that he would never be permitted to return to Wenchow in the flesh unless he paid up.

His total funds in pocket were $ 169 and this amount he handed over, thinking it would satisfy and thankful that he had no large amount with him. But the captured a rare "bird" and were determined to pluck every gorgeous feather before liberating him. First they compelled him to write a letter requesting that $ 1000 in notes be sent to him at once. The letter was sent to the house at which he was living in Shanghai and money secured. Then they forced their victim to sign four promissory notes for $ 500 each, all payable August 17, after which he was allowed to go. All this took three days during which time the man was held prisoner.

On August 3, some days after the affair, the matter was reported to Central Police Station and the police immediately started an investigation. Such in Shanghai, where the percentage of stolen property recovered and wrongdoer arrested compares favourably with cities in other countries. On August 16 a Chinese detective of Sinza Police Station arrested two of the confidence men, one of whom had two of the promissory notes in his pocket. Last Friday, the day on which the notes were to be paid, the two had a hearing before the Mixed Court when they were remanded for special trial at a date.

"The Awakening of Wenchow: A Prosperous City Little Known," *The North - China Herald and Supreme Court & Consular Gazette*, September 29, 1917

The Awakening of Wenchow: A Prosperous City Little Known

(From our own correspondent)

Wenchow, September 23

The city of Wenchow, as the centre of a district of about two millions of people, although only two days' journey to the south of Shanghai, has not intruded itself unduly upon the notice of others. This maybe due to the fact that the people have not shown the same business enterprise as some others have done, but now we see signs of progress in several directions.

The most noticeable improvement, is the installation of the electric light. The main street in the evening now looks comparatively gay, though there are dark spots here and there, which indicate that the public spirit just there is not sufficient to pay the tax for the light. The light, seldom has "A Night Out," and for this reliability we are indebted to the manager. Mr. Hsu, We find the electric light much cheaper than the old oil lamps.

Improved Steamer Service

In the good old days, the str. Poochi was our only visitor, once in ten days,

THE AWAKENING OF WENCHOW.

A PROSPEROUS CITY LITTLE KNOWN.

From Our Own Correspondent.

Wenchow, Sept. 23.

The city of Wenchow, as the centre of a district of about two millions of people, although only two days' journey to the south of Shanghai, has not intruded itself unduly upon the notice of others. This may be due to the fact that the people have not shown the same business enterprise as some others have done, but now we see signs of progress in several directions.

now we also have the Kwangchi, both of the C. M. Co. and two others steamers belonging to two other Companies. These improved facilities seem to stimulate trade, and passengers and freights appear on the increase.

The second largest city in the district, Juean, 30000 people, is connected by canal, and two steam launches a day probably clear more than their expenses. The coming of the Standard Oil Co. and the Asiatic Oil Co. have both been within recent times, The Standard Oil Co. have two American agents here, The Anglo – American Tobacco Co. also have an agent In Wenchow. Singers' Sewing Machine Co. have a shop on the Main Street, which looks quite home – like.

New Industries

Machines for making socks, have recently been introduced, and find employment for an increasing number of people.

A well known Shanghai firm has supplied a number of people with machines for making curtains of lacework. These Wenchow people, we understand work for this firm in Shanghai, who pay them for the lace they send up to them. This is the latest industry, and it eventually may employ a large number of people.

A small glass – blowing manufactory has recently been opened. We visited it one day, and saw them making lamp glasses. The price is much cheaper than those imported, hence this industry may develop.

A steam saw mill was opened some time ago, but it has not succeeded. It may have been owing to some inexperience in the purchase of the plant, or to mismanagement. In any case there is a good deal of wood exported to Shanghai so that a saw mill under proper supervision might become a great success.

A Commercial School is being opened this autumn, which no doubt will help the people to find good positions for many of the youths of this city.

The modem and improved character of nearly all the new buildings erected in the city is an additional evidence of the increasing prospcrity of the people. The most costly and ornate building recently erected is the one put up by the Clothiers' Guild. Nearly all the new shops are in foreign style, and some of them three storeys high.

Native Arts

The Wenchow people have two industries, which are capable of considerable extension, one is the making of ornaments, carved out of soap stone, and the other wood carving inlaid with bamboo.

The soap stone is got from the mountains, about fifty miles away. Some of the Wenchow people take it themselves to Europe; we met one man in a mountain village who had travelled as far as Paris; If some firms in Shanghai had means of buying it up in Wenchow, a good profit might be made.

The same applies to the bamboo inlaid work. We have taken some to England where it was greatly valued. The people make such articles as small tables, which can be taken to pieces for export, photograph frames, trays, paper knives, etc. Many of these would bear a good profit, and still be sure of a quick sale. We have heard of one person in Shanghai, who recently ordered about400 worth from one of the best wood – carvers here in Wenchow.

Wenchow is awakening, though its trade possibilities are not yet fully realized. But to those who know the times, either foreign or Chinese merchants, there are many ways in which its progress could be increased, to the mutual advantage of capital and labour.

"Wenchow's Three Days' Independence," *The North – China Herald and Supreme Court & Consular Gazette*, December 15, 1917

Wenchow's Three days' Independence

(From our own correspondent)

Wenchow, December 5

A small party came down here a few days ago sent from Ningpo by the Southern party to induce Wenchow to join them. They first got the Yingchang, who was in charge of the modern soldiers, to join and then approached the Tungling, who after consultation with other officials consented. It is stated he was adverse to this, but the party from Ningpo said they would use bombs and start opposition to the North if consent were not given.

So Wenchow joined the South or declared its independence of the North on November 30. However, on December 2, hearing that the Southerners had been defeated in Ningpo, they revoked their decision and are now "as you were." It is to get the Wenchow people to join the South has been arrested.

All is quiet in the city.

WENCHOW'S THREE DAYS' INDEPENDENCE.

From Our Own Correspondent.

Wenchow, Dec. 5.

A small party came down here a few days ago sent from Ningpo by the Southern party to induce Wenchow to join them. They first got the Yingchang, who was in charge of the modern soldiers, to join and then approached the Tungling, who after consultation with other officials consented. It is stated he was adverse to this, but the party from Ningpo said they would use bombs and start opposition to the North if consent were not given.

"The Wreck of the Poochi: Distress in Wenchow," *The North - China Herald and Supreme Court & Consular Gazette*, January 19, 1918

The Wreck of the Poochi: Distress in Wenchow

(From our own correspondent)

Wenchow, January 12

The Tungwah arrived here yesterday, bringing, it is said, ten coffins or more, containing the bodies of some of those drowned in the recent disaster. As already reported, Mr. Hsu Ting – chao was among the victims. He was a Wenchow man: the most noted man in the whole of this district, a doctor of literature, of the old style. He managed to get into one of the lifeboats of the Poochi, but the rush for it by others was so great that the boat capsized, and the old man was drowned. This morning I saw his massive coffin, and that of his wife – they were sending the coffins up to Shanghai, in the hope that bodies might be found, – if they are not, perhaps their relatives will follow the Chinese custom and have two carved wooden figures made and clothed in funeral attire, placed in the empty coffins, and so brought back to their ancestral home for burial.

The newly – appointed Chief of Police was also among those who were lost.

Four men have returned who, after the collision, climbed up the mast, from which they were rescued by one of the boats from the O. M. S. Hsinfung. The son of one of the staff of the China, Merchants' here was also drowned; he was returning to celebrate his father's 50th birthday.

A large consignment of cloth to a local firm is said to have been worth a considerable sum; no doubt many other shopkeepers have also lost.

The loss of the Poochi is like the departure of an old friend, for that good little boat was to us what the Kiangteen is to Ningpo. For many years it was almost our only link with the outside world, for in those days we had no telegraph. The sound of the Poochi coming up the river every ten days was the sweetest music we ever heard in Wenchow, for it announced the coming of the Home mail.

The name of Captain Froberg, will probably be most closely connected with the Poochi, for he commanded her for so long a time. When he had completed 300 trips, he was presented with a large congratulatory banner by the China Merchants.

It was on the Poochi, that nearly all the foreign community, including the Consul and the Commissioner, left on July 8, 1900, during the Boxer outbreak. We hastily went on board the night before, but as word came that the people talked of pouring oil over the Poochi and setting her on fire, we left the wharf and anchored in the river, with a long row of rifles laid on the deck ready for use if required. The next morning the Poochi left. At the month of the river we met a British gunboat which had been sent to our aid, but we continued on our way to Ningpo.

It is difficult to realize that the Poochi has made her last voyage to Wenchow, and that she like many of her brave crew, has for the last time "crossed the bar." The community feels deeply the loss of so many of its members. Of the foreigners, Captain Mackie was the best known, and his tragic death is a great sorrow to us all.

Time of Sailing

As a result of the disaster, it is suggested that boats leaving Shanghai for Wenchow should leave Shanghai in the daylight whenever possible. I do not pretend to suggest what can, or cannot be done at other ports, but as an old resident, I know that boat leaving Shanghai for Wenchow, which is generally fixed for about midnight, might in many cases just as well leave at daylight the next day, and still arrive in Wenchow by the same tide.

Captain Ross, who brought the Tungwah in yesterday, did so in an ideal manner. Leaving Shanghai at daylight, on Wednesday, he entered Ningpo on Thursday morning and was out again in the daylight; he then came up the Wenchow river on the same tide yesterday morning that he would have done if he had left at midnight seven hours before. By doing this all the dangerous parts were passed in daylight. The officers got their well deserved sleep, and the ship arrived here on the same tide. Conscquently we would earnestly suggest that the Wenchow boat should not start at night unless it is absolutely necessary, but wait till daylight and by so doing lessen the possibility of accident.

"The Earthquake in Wenchow," *The North – China Herald and Supreme Court & Consular Gazette*, March 2, 1918

The Earthquake in Wenchow

(From our own correspondent)

Wenchow, February. 22

The city and district of Wenchow was in no way slighted or passed by on the memorable 13th of February; we also had our full share of the earthquake shock. The electric light wires swung violently and I saw the water in a canal moving backwards and forward in a strange way, while the earth rocked like a ship at sea. A foreigner saw the big church rock from east to west in an alarming manner. Another foreigner heard a big wall fall down, and saw a great tree sway backwards and forwards, yet he himself though walking down a street did not feel anything. Several old walls, long overdue, took this opportunity to fall.

There was a slight shock at the City of Pingyang, about 4 p. m. , in addition to the earlier one. The people say there was a lesser shock about eight years ago, and a greater one about fifty years ago, but not worse than the present one.

Troops Going South

The people of Wenchow had, before this, received a milder shock, when a

Chinese gunboat brought 500 soldiers, and since then another 500 have arrived. Their destination is a city "to the south of Wenchow," to put it vaguely. Their object, to wait there in readiness in case the Southern troops should make their way north, in the direction of Wenchow.

If the Southern troops should ever get up in this direction, then this city would have its loyalty tested again, but as we have learnt by considerable experience how to swing from North to South, according to the relative amount of pressure, we may be safely trusted to do the correct thing if an awkward situation should arise.

The O. M. S. Kwangchi

I received another shock only yesterday, when the postal notice said that the Kwangchi would be going to Foochow, while it was expected to return to Shanghai. I find two reasons are given: one, that the merchants here say it is too small, they want a larger boat; the other, that the people are vexed with the Kwangchi for not getting or trying to get the bodies of the poor people drowned when the Poochi went down. This was when the Kwangchi visited the wreck soon after the disaster. But at that time there was a heavy sea on, and the captain did the very best thing. Had he done otherwise more lives might have been lost.

Owing to the demand for ships, it may be difficult for the China Merchants to send a larger boat, which might be able to earn much more money on another route.

"Great Hallstorm in Wenchow," *The North – China Herald and Supreme Court & Consular Gazette*, May 4, 1918

Great Hailstorm in Wenchow

(From our own correspondent)

Wenchow, April 25

Three days ago, I was up country when I was caught in a storm of wind and rain of quite alarming force, my hat and cape were blown away in no time, my umbrella struggled hard to fallow, and became a total ruin—like Reims Cathedral, the roof off but the central pillar standing. But my troubles were nothing as compared with what the people in the city got, for by the time the storm had arrived in Wenchow, about dusk, it had developed into a hailstorm, of extreme violence. The storm came from the northwest, and so that part of the city has suffered the most.

It is rather difficult to get a correct idea of the exact size of these hailstones for they seem to vary, in the inverse ratio to the size of the brain of the man who describes them, but I saw one in the street, more than 12 hours after, which would be about an inch and a half long, and over an inch wide, so that we can well believe the statement of one who said there were as large as a hen's egg. The effect of all these hailstones must have been something like a squadron of aeroplanes flying low and bombing a city.

GREAT HAILSTORM IN WENCHOW.

From Our Own Correspondent.

Wenchow, April 25.

Three days ago, I was up country when I was caught in a storm of wind and rain of quite alarming force, my hat and cape were blown away in no time, my umbrella struggled hard to follow, and became a total ruin—like Reims Cathedral. the roof off but the central pillar standing. But my troubles were nothing as compared with what the people in the city got, for by the time the storm had

As to the damage done, while no houses have been completely destroyed, the walls and roofs of many have been damaged; and the number of slates broken and panes of glass is innumerable.

The Methodist Hospital has about 300 panes of glass broken, and the College more than that, the Church more than 200, and with their other properties the total will be about 1000 panes or more. A church belonging to the China Inland Mission, in the west part of the city where as stated, the storm was the worst, has been completely blown down.

Now there is a tremendous demand for glass and slates, especially the latter, which have gone up in price, and are difficult to get even at that. The dealers will even take deposit money, and then sell the tiles to someone else. Workmen are receiving double pay. Yesterday was wet, and as the rain would drip on to the uncovered bed, or into the kitchen, the misery of the people, can be better imagined, than endured. Worst of all there has been loss of life, for while the laodah of a boat was on shore having his evening meal, his boat which was near the jetty here in Wenchow, was capsized by the force of the wind, and over ten people drowned.

Inquiries are being made as to the extent of the damage done to the city, and it has been estimated that it will approximate $ 100000.

"Wenchow Letter: Standard Oil Co. 's New Property," *The North – China Herald and Supreme Court & Consular Gazette*, July 6, 1918

Wenchow Letter: Standard Oil Co. 's New Property

(From our own correspondent)

Wenchow, June 25

Last year the Standard Oil Co. 's of New York, bought a large plot of land four miles from the city of Wenchow, down the river on the north bank. The officials would not allow them to erect an Oil Tank any nearer to the city in case of a possible fire. The land purchased is about 20 Chinese mow, or more, it has a fine river front, and an excellent bund has been built, with two strong landing places.

A large tank is to be erected, also a smaller filling tank, with one godown and other buildings, it is also intended to put up a foreign – style house for theAmerican argent in charge. The Company's tank steamer will be able to come alongside the bund, and the oil will be pumped directly into the big oil tank, from which it can be repumped into the filling tank. Work has been going on for several months, but it will still require many more before all the work is fished. The whole property a large sum, but the Company naturally looks forward to getting its money back in the end, and with its new and improved facilities no doubt will do an increasing trade in this large district.

WENCHOW LETTER.

STANDARD OIL CO.'S NEW PROPERTY.

From Our Own Correspondent.

Wenchow, June 25.

Last year the Standard Oil Co., of New York, bought a large plot of land four miles from the city of Wenchow, down the river on the north bank. The officials would not allow them to erect an Oil Tank any nearer to the city in case of a possible fire. The land purchased is about 20 Chinese mow, or more, it has a fine river front, and an excellent bund has been built, with two strong landing places.

I do not know whether the putting up of this large oil tank, will tend to reduce the price of oil, the price now is about twice what it used to be, while the value of the empty tins, is about four times what it was. One empty tin is worth 35 cents, this is partly due to the fact that large quantities of lard are sent up to Shanghai in these tins, as much, I have been told, as 2000 tins.

Shanghai, we will say it is Shanghai, not only has the power to attract lard, but also large quantities of firewood, and immense numbers of eggs. This naturally increases the price for local consumption. Rice also would find its way up there, if it were not strictly prohibited, such articles as fish, chicken, and even native potatoes, have greatly increased in price, Wages are going up, in an endeavour to keep pace with the rising cost of living, and where this compensations does not take place, the people are finding it increasingly difficult to make both ends meet.

Changes in the River

The sand banks in the Wenchow River have altered a great deal in recent times; this makes it more difficult for steamers to get up. Great long sand banks now appear, even before low water, and in some places, in the highest parts, the land can be cultivated.

Sometimes a bank appears quite suddenly, as when one of the three small steamship companies built a landing stage, with a pontoon. The sand bank barely waited for the pontoon to be finished when it come alongside; moreover that pontoon was carried from its pier. The sandbank has now left, and the pontoon in expected to return, but its future term of service is uncertain. The pontoon belonging to another company higher up the river has also been carried away from its pier, but is now also being repaired. The ways of this river are hard to understand.

Four Steamers a Week

In addition to the China Merchants, who reigned without a rival for many years, we have three small companies, each sending a steamer once a week. I do not like to mention names, but one of these boats leans over on its side, to a very unusual degres. I don't profess to be a sailor, still I have seen a number of ships from both sides, but I have never seen a ship that was less upright, and I only hope it is not an indication of a future bad end. A foreign officer told me it was top – heavy, and some day would, or might turn turtle. Surely every boat carrying passengers ought to be properly inspected, and certified before being allowed, at least, to enter a Treaty Port.

This particular ship may have been, but I should be glad to know that some competent authority had inspected her, and was satisfied she was a safe and seaworthy boat.

"Wenchow's Chief Magistrate," *The North – China Herald and Supreme Court & Consular Gazette*, August 3, 1918

Wenchow's Chief Magistrate

(From our own correspondent)

Wenchow, July 27

Considering the frequent adverse criticisms of Chinese officials that one reads in the papers, and I am not in a position to say they are not merited, it is yet only fair to remember that there are some, and we hope many, who are devoting themselves sincerely to the best interests of the people under their care. Such an official, we are pleased to say, we have as the Chief Magistrate of the Wenchow District, the Dao Yung, Mr. Huang.

His father was one of the first, if not the first, to become a Chinese medical assistant in a mission hospital in Shanghai, 50 years ago.

No doubt the enlightening influences of his early home life have helped him to realize more clearly, and to discharge more faithfully, the duties of his high office.

He has issued a proclamation, pointing out the inadvisability of too early marriages and the evils of infanticide. He is in favour of unbound feet for women, and wishes to discourage an objectionable social custom in this district, which may be sufficiently described as a temporary loan, to one man, for a definite pe-

WENCHOW'S CHIEF MAGISTRATE.

From Our Own Correspondent.

Wenchow, July 27.

Considering the frequent adverse criticisms of Chinese officials that one reads in the papers, and I am not in a position to say they are not merited, it is yet only fair to remember that there are some, and we hope many, who are devoting themselves sincerely to the best interests of the people under their care. Such an official, we are pleased to say, we have as the Chief Magistrate of the Wenchow District, the Dao Yung, Mr. Huang.

riod and for an agreed sum, of another man's private property.

Mr. Huang is seeking to reform the City Orphanage, a purely Chinese institution. At present many of the foundlings are handed over to foster mothers, who "live out," they are allowed about 1200 cash a month for each child, which in the case of very young children might be expected to leave a margin of profit, but possibly not to the child.

But this system of farming out is liable to abuse, proper inspection is difficult, while it is easy for the mortality to be unusually high, so Mr. Huang wishes to erect more suitable building, where the children can live in. This will conduce to more efficient supervision.

On the recent occasion of this Magistrate's mother reaching the age of 68 years, he celebrated the event in a most useful manner. He had prepared a great number of packets of medicines, suitable for dysentery, summer fevers, and other ailments, and these were given to the poor people of the city; the total cost of these gifts is said to have been quite a large sum. But not only does he give occasional medical relief, he has a portion of his yamen set apart as a consulting room. His son is really in charge, but his wife has given much time to this good work.

Mr. Huang has two or three Chinese doctors, who take it in turn to come every day to this consulting room, and see the patients as they come in. No medicines are dispensed there, but a prescription is written out for each case, and the person then takes it to one of two or three specified medicine shops in the city where it is made up, and the medicine is then given freely to the patient, the bill being sent to Mr. Huang.

It is said that the attendance at his yamen of sick people averages about 200 per day, and the cost to him in medicines, and the doctors' salaries about $ 1000 per month.

It is understood that he has private property in Shanghai, and can thus afford to spend this large sum upon the poor people of Wenchow, but the possession of this wealth would not bring much benefit to these people if he had not the liberality to spend it, and hence one is pleased to have this opportunity of referring to one of China's officials, whose wisdom in administration, care for his people, and generosity of heart entitle him to his commendation, and show him to be an enlightened, and beneficent official, a true Father to his people.

"Robbery from the Wenchow Postoffice," *The North – China Herald and Supreme Court & Consular Gazette*, October 26, 1918

Robbery from the Wenchow Postoffice

(From our own correspondent)

Wenchow, Oct. 14

Not many days ago when the str. Kwangchi came alongside the pontoon on its return from Shanghai, a man was on board quite ready to come ashore, but alas for him a number of policemen, all unknown to him, were also ready for him to come ashore, and when he came within arm's length he was arrested, neatly caught in a tr-ap. He had just returned from a short, but up to then, no doubt, successful visit to Shanghai, where he had been trying to cash about $1700 worth of stamps which he, with three others, had stolen from the post – office employ, another had formerly been employed. About $100 in money were also stolen. The stamps have not yet been recovered—but all the four men have—which speaks well for the detective force of this city, and no doubt it will be a long time before that stamp collector pays another visit to Shanghai.

ROBBERY FROM THE WENCHOW POSTOFFICE.

From Our Own Correspondent.

Wenchow, Oct. 14.

Not many days ago when the str. Kwangchi came alongside the pontoon on its return from Shanghai, a man was on board quite ready to come ashore, but alas for him a number of policemen, all unknown to him, were also ready for him to come ashore, and when he came within arm's length he was arrested, neatly caught in a trap. He had

The First Oil Tanker

Wenchow has been visited by the str. Meinan, of the Standard Oil

Co, the first oil tank steamer to sail up this river. Now that this Company has its new property here, I expect we shall often see this trim little boat, and the coming of a tank steamer marks a further step in the progress of the city.

"Rowdy Chekiang Students: A Whole School Cleared of Pupils," *The North – China Herald and Supreme Court & Consular Gazette*, November 16, 1918

Rowdy Chekiang Students: A Whole School Cleared of Pupils

(From our own correspondent)

Wenchow, November 6

There is a very great amount of sickness in the whole of this district, and unfortunately for one boy in particular, and many in general, it spread to the Chinese Middle School in this city, a large institution of about 400 students. One of these youths became ill. It is said he asked for one of the School proctors. He, however, sent for the school doctor, who was away at the time. It is also said the servants neglected him.

When the boy became worse he was removed to another building, which his fellow students thought was not a proper place for a sick youth, and in this building the lad died.

It is reported that before he died he told at least one of his companions that he hoped the other students would get revenge for him. At any rate the indignation of his fellow students was aroused.

According to Chinese custom these students began to recall or to create little

ROWDY CHEKIANG STUDENTS.

—

A WHOLE SCHOOL CLEARED OF PUPILS.

—

From Our Own Correspondent.

Wenchow, Nov. 6.

There is a very great amount of sickness in the whole of this district, and unfortunately for one boy in particular, and many in general, it spread to the Chinese Middle School in this city, a large institution of about 400 students. One of these youths became ill. It

incidents in the life of one of these proctors, whom they accused of unkind treatment to their dead companion. It is reported that they said he had sold some of the private property of the School for himself. It was suggested that not only had the food been cooked, but also the food accounts.

Another proctor also came under their displeasure, it was even noticed that these two men came from the same local district as did the Principal of the School. This, some felt, was more than a coincidence.

At last, the Dao Yung, and the City Magistrate went to the school. They were told by Young China that it was their business to look after the city and not with school matters, but added that they would be glad to know the results of the writers' investigations. The students had pickets at the gate to stop the friends of the teachers going in; they also appointed themselves censors of the letters for the teachers.

At last, the unexpected happened: a writ came from Hangchow a few days ago that all the students were to be turned out of the school. This is translated by the youths themselves for the benefit of the general public to be that the students do not desire to study any more at such an institution so they are returning home, but the fact remains that about 360 students have left, and the School is closed. This retirement, according to plan, to previously arranged positions, sounds better than a forced retreat. Many of them have been staying in the city at restaurants and having a good time, but as their money gets used up, they will at last have to return home, and face the verdict of their fathers who were once rowdy boys themselves; but this they may forget.

There are four proctors, and matters were made more difficult, by the fact that two of them, who came from a different district from the first two, are reported to have shown sympathy with the students. However, all the four of them have ceased to be officially, also the Principal of the School will be replaced, and authority to teach for the year has been withdrawn from the other masters. The latter may be invited back later.

When the students heard they had to leave, they felt they would like to take with them a little memento of their Alma Master, so in order to avoid any distinction they practically took everything that young strong hands could take and almost looted the place, even the electric light, globes, books, fittings, etc, all have been taken or destroyed.

I am told that about 40 boys will be punished by not being allowed to come back, but that permission will be given to the others to return if they wish.

But of these 40, it is said some may be innocent, while other guilty ones may not be included and one may be sure the parents of the supposed innocent students will have something to say, while it is asserted that some of those expelled will do all in their power to induce the majority of the boys from returning, and so try to get concessions from the authorities.

Too Good to Be True

A foreigner who has been in China over 30 years told me a few days ago that a contract had been signed, about a fortnight before, for the extension of the railway from Hangchow to Wenchow. It was to be built by an American firm, and to come, not down the coast, but inland, a branch line I suppose, joining Wenchow with the main line running south.

"At Wenchow," *The North – China Herald and Supreme Court & Consular Gazette*, November 30, 1918

At Wenchow

(From our own correspondent)

Wenchow, November 21

On November 16 the Taoyin and the Official for Foreign Affairs invited the members of the foreign community, together with about 70 Chinese officials and gentry to celebrate the signing of the armistice. Refreshments were served, and congratulatory speeches made. On November 21 the foreign community gave a luncheon to the officials, and some of the gentry of Wenchow. M. Tanant, the Commissioner of Customs presided at this gathering in the Hall of the Methodist College, which was tastefully decorated for the occasion. An address of welcome was read to the Chinese guests in which appreciation of China's help in the war was expressed, and the stand taken by Germany explained. The meaning of the defeat of Germany was made clear, and the address concluded with the allies' wishes for the prosperity of China.

AT WENCHOW.

From Our Own Correspondent.

Wenchow, Nov. 21.

On November 16 the Taoyin and the Official for Foreign Affairs invited the members of the foreign community, together with about 70 Chinese officials and gentry to celebrate the signing of the armistice refreshments were served, and congratulatory speeches made. On

"Wenchow Notes," *The North – China Herald and Supreme Court & Consular Gazette*, February 22, 1919

Wenchow Notes

(From our own correspondent)

Wenchow, February 10

Wintry weather of unusual severity was experienced in Wenchow and district during the Chinese New Year's Festival.

New Year's Day dawned upon a white city, the snow lying some four inches deep; and during the day snow continued to fall. It is some 28 years since such wintry conditions were experienced in this sub – tropical port. During the first day of the 8th Republican year, Wenchow might have been a city of the dead, so quiet were its inhabitants, and so few were on its streets. It was only on the third day that the city began to awake and endeavor to make up by the noise of crackers, drums and cymbals for the repression caused by the snow and bitter cold. For Wenchow still loves the 'old customs'. The Old Year is given a – send – off by innumerable crackers, and the fires of hundreds of piles of pinewood arranged in the middle of the main streets.

WENCHOW NOTES.

From Our Own Correspondent.

Wenchow, Feb. 10.
Wintry weather of unusual severity was experienced in Wenchow and district during the Chinese New Year's Festival.

New Year's Day dawned upon a white city, the snow lying some four inches deep; and during the day snow continued to fall. It is some 28 years since such wintry conditions were experienced in this sub-tropical port. During the first day of the

"Wenchow and World Peace," *The North – China Herald and Supreme Court & Consular Gazette*, March 15, 1919

Wenchow and World Peace

(From our own correspondent)

Wenchow, February 27

A meeting of exceptional interest was held on Wednesday evening, at the house of Mr. T. W. Chapman, M. S. C, Principal of the United Methodist College. It was the first meeting of a new association called "the Society of English – speaking Chinese and foreigners," the object of which is to afford opportunities for knowing one another better, and especially for frank exchange of views on industrial, social, literary and scientific questions and on all matters of common interest. It is intended that papers will be read at the fortnight meetings, and occasional debates arranged dealing with present – day problems of world interest.

On Wednesday night two addresses were delivered on "Some Methods for the Attainment of the World's Permanent Peace," by Mr. Li Ung – bing, head of the Salt Gabelle in this port, and the Rev. W. R. Stobie. The nationalities represented at the meeting were Chinese, Japanese, British and French. Both addresses created much interest, and were followed by an equally interesting discussion.

WENCHOW AND WORLD PEACE.

From Our Own Correspondent.

Wenchow. Feb. 27.

A meeting of exceptional interest was held on Wednesday evening, at the house of Mr. T. W. Chapman, M.SC., Principal of the United Methodist College. It was the first meeting of a new Association called "The Society of English-speaking Chinese and foreigners," the object of which is to afford opportunities for knowing one another better, and especially for frank exchange of views on industrial, social, literary and scientific questions and on all matters of common interest. It is

In view of present – day problems in the Far East, the address given by Mr. Li—an ex—director of the Commercial Press, Ld. and the author of "History of China," in English, and other books—is worthy of being given in some detail as representing the Chinese outlook on the above topic.

Mr. Li said, in part:

"No war at all for the generations to come is certainly a very pleasant dream. But is it possible? The answer should be in the affirmative. It has been accepted that the war which is now coming to a close has been brought upon the world by the will of one man—that of the ex-Kaiser of Germany—and if the will of one man sufficed to bring the world into war, the will of all the civilized nations combined should suffice to give the world a peace that will last as long as the world itself lasts. By this we do not mean that the task is an easy one. On the contrary, it is very difficult and is perhaps the most tremendous one mankind has as yet to face.

"We should not let our tried diplomats and international experts do the work alone, for their work unaided by the different peoples whom they represent will fall short of the end we have in view. The question before us is a question of world – wide interest, and not only every people, but every individual, has his part to play. Now, therefore, let us see what we here in Wenchow can do to help realize a thought so sweet and fruitful of results as an everlasting peace in the world.

"The foundation of peace, I take it for granted, is nothing more than good feeling between nations. Nothing is more essential than this, and without it the work of the Peace Conference at Paris, and the League of Nations to be formed on the lines suggested by President Wilson will be all in vain. The promoters of this Society, I think, have struck at the fundamental principles of a universal lasting peace, when they say that they wish to have a better understanding between Chinese and foreigners in China through the medium of the English language. The Balkans will not play the part they did in the world's politics before the Great War, and their place is soon to be taken up by China and the Far East. The English – speaking Chinese and English – speaking foreigners in China are almost one people. Let our voices be always lifted for the cause of humanity, and let us always work hand in hand to do away with all sorts of misunderstanding so harmful to the successful and peaceful intercourse between nations. Nations may continue to be rivals, and all questions, disputes, and controversies, may continue to arise as they did in the past; but they shall, permit me to say, be settled by peaceful means, by negotiation, by arbitration, by any and every possible means, except that of war. Let there be no Balkans of the Far East and war will be impossible. What we can do in this connexion is but very little, but every bit of success we achieve brings us nearer to the realization of our great object, viz, the attainment of permanent peace.

"Our Society, therefore, is worth the support of those present. In supporting it, we are not advancing any interest of our own but those of humanity and civilization."

"Wenchow Post Office: Satisfactory Record of Progress," *The North - China Herald and Supreme Court & Consular Gazette*, May 3, 1919

Wenchow Post Office: Satisfactory Record of Progress

(From our own correspondent)

Wenchow, April 21

Great improvements have been effected in the Chinese postal service in this city and district during the past 15 months, and further advance in office efficiency and public convenience is projected.

The Head Office has hitherto been in a section of the Customs Compound, situated outside the North Gate of the city. Its position was very convenient for the receipt and despatch of mails, so far as the office itself was concerned, but not always the most convenient for the general public. A sub - office in the centre of the business part of the city has been a great aid in meeting public requirements, specially during periods of martial law when the city gates were closed at an early hour of the night.

WENCHOW POST OFFICE.

SATISFACTORY RECORD OF PROGRESS.

From Our Own Correspondent.

Wenchow, April 21.
Great improvements have been effected in the Chinese postal service in this city and district during the past 15 months, and further advance in office efficiency and public convenience is projected.

New Office Planned

There is now planned a new head office to be created in a central position of the city, which will combine all the up - to - date appointments and offices for dealing with the ever - growing business of the Chinese postal service. The now building will cost some $ 10000 and is expected to be ready for the staff before the end of the present year.

A new sub – branch office was opened at the East Gate some time ago specially to meet the needs of that important suburb, from which three coasting steamers depart every week. This office has well justified the for sight of our present postmaster, Mr. Deng Yong – yu. By his unfailing courtesy and zeal for the best interests of the public, Mr. Deng has done, and is doing, much to popularize the Chinese postal service.

The box clearances in the city when he first came to Wenchow some 20 months ago were only twice a day. Now they are cleared five times per day. In the same period the local delivery has increased from four to six times daily. At the beginning of the present year a daily rural delivery (Sundays excepted) extending some 40 li around Wenchow, has been inaugurated, and is bringing to many country people the knowledge of the cheap and efficient service which is at their disposal. Men of the type of Mr. Deng are the best representatives of Young China, and certainly are not linked on the old Conservative regime.

A Daring Robbery

An unpleasant incident happened at head office in the fall of last year. Whilst certain repairs were being carried out, a daring robbery of stamps, etc. , took place on a stormy night. The value stolen amounted to $ 1877.

The prompt action of the postmaster led to the quick arrest of four men, one of whom was a letter – carrier. The leader of this raid, however, was a local man named Dzang Lo – shang, who had within a few years blossomed into a wealthy man from the position of a coolie. Today, it is known he made most of his money in illicit opium – smuggling. Why he should have risked the position he had gained by the mad act of robbing the post office, is a moot point. The local judge found all four men guilty, and sentenced Dzang to 18 months' imprisonment, and also to refund the $ 1877. The letter – carrier also got 18 months' imprisonment. The third man was given 14 months', and the fourth man one year, whilst all four were declared disfranchised.

The wealthy prisoners appealed to the Provincial Court, which confirmed the Local Court's judgement. Once more he appealed, to the Supreme Court in Peking, and final judgement has just been given confirming the lower courts in every particular.

"Situation in Wenchow," *The North – China Herald and Supreme Court & Consular Gazette*, June 14, 1919

Situation in Wenchow

(From our own correspondent)

Wenchow, June 7

The Japanese boycott has been seriously taken up by the Wenchowese, and by active propaganda has spread to all the walled cities of the old prefecture, and is daily being preached in all the hamlets, villages and market towns.

There is a seriousness and stubbornness marking the present movement which is new in one's experience of Chinese. Organization is more in evidence; and a measure of self – restraint, thus far, that is in contrast to past days of rowdyism. To dismiss the boycott with the off – hand remark, "Oh! It is only a student's affair" is to mistake the significance of many plain facts. We who have studied the people and their language for many long years, find it difficult to smile at the "Students' Strike," which, in common with most cities, has been inaugurated here. Every care has been, and is being taken, to avoid cause of offence, apart from the buying of Japanese goods. The officials have proved themselves wise and level – head in not identifying themselves with the movement, and by taking every care against a breach of the peace.

Whilst, probably, the present boycott will end in the usual way, it will be a "milestone" in the history and evolution of China.

SITUATION IN WENCHOW.

From Our Own Correspondent.

Wenchow, June 7.

The Japanese boycott has been seriously taken up by the Wenchowese, and by active propaganda has spread to all the walled cities of the old prefecture, and is daily being preached in all the hamlets, villages and market towns.

"Placating the Cholera Demon: Elaborate Ritual at Wenchow," *The North – China Herald and Supreme Court & Consular Gazette*, November 1, 1919

Placating the Cholera Demon: Elaborate Ritual at Wenchow

(From our own correspondent)

Wenchow, October 22

One of the biggest idol – processions for many years past took place last night. It was a weird and wonderful sight even to one who had lived long in this changing yet changeless land.

In common with other parts of China, cholera was prevalent in this city, during the past summer. Further, an unusual number of small fires, originating in mysterious ways, gave rise to stories of evil and malignant spirits who were making the city the object of their special spite.

It was to propitiate these "devils" of fire and sickness, and in the hope of inducing them to leave the city, that several thousands of dollars were spent on "crackers," "candles," etc. , and over 10000 men and boys escorted thro-ugh the main streets several of the most important idols. A special bamboo – and – paper ship had been constructed to accommodate the undesired visitors (the evil spirits), and on the ebbtide was sent on its voyage down the river. The people returned rejoicing in the hope that greater peace would be their lot as a result of their zeal.

PLACATING THE CHOLERA DEMON.

ELABORATE RITUAL AT WENCHOW.

From Our Own Correspondent.

Wenchow, Oct. 22.

One of the biggest idol-processions for many years past took place last night. It was a weird and wonderful sight even to one who had lived long in this changing yet changeless land.

Boycott, Rice and Strikes

The Wenchow city people have had, from their point of view, rather an exciting and interesting summer season. First came the boycott movement, which was not only taken up with enthusiasm by the student class, but by the common people. There is a quiet but persistent loyalty to this movement even in these days.

Then came a protest against the illegal exportation of rice. That a great amount of rice was smuggled out of this port and district is a fact. The organizations which had been called into being to work the boycott took up this matter of rice leakage. They had a sharp tussle with the city authorities, who at first withstood the demands made for the better control of the sale of rice.

A general strike of shop – keepers, however, secured a victory for the people, which was celebrated by a monstrous lantern procession. No heads or bones were broken in these movements, and the people seem to have realized the power there is in their hands if only they are united and law – abiding.

The housing question is becoming a very real one to the Chinese in his city, indicating the growth of the population. Land is difficult to buy, and compared with a few years ago its price has increased from 100 to 200 percent.

Every Sign of Prosperity

The city presents every sign of prosperity in trade. New houses, semi – foreign in architecture, are to be seen in every part of the city.

Five steamers are finding it profitable to run regularly to this port—two from Shanghai, and three from Ningpo and the intervening Chinese ports.

The outlook for the autumn rice crop is the best for many years, and by heavy harvest will be in full swing.

The orange crop will not be up so that of the last two years. This, however, does not disturb the farmers, as they say it is the usual thing to have one comparatively poor season every three years.

"Fires in Wenchow," *The North – China Herald and Supreme Court & Consular Gazette*, January 10, 1920

Fires in Wenchow

(From our own correspondent)

Wenchow, December 31

One of the most destructive fires for many years past occurred yesterday in Wenchow city. Over 100 shops and a number of private houses were destroyed during the two hours the fire raged.

At least 250 families have been rendered homeless, and the loss must be very heavy.

Another big fire occurred at midnight in the southeastern part of the city; whilst in the southern suburbs yet another fire destroyed nine houses.

We have had an exceptionally dry autumn and winter thus far. City canals and wells are almost dry. Hence to fight the flames was almost hopeless. The wonder is that the fires were confined to such small areas.

FIRES IN WENCHOW.

From Our Own Correspondent.

Wenchow, Dec. 31.

One of the most destructive fires for many years past occurred yesterday in Wenchow city. Over 100 shops and a number of private houses were destroyed during the two hours the fire raged.

"Wenchow's Busy Workers: A Port with a Future," *The North – China Herald and Supreme Court & Consular Gazette*, August 3, 1920

Wenchow's Busy Workers: A Port With a Future

（From Our Wenchow Correspondent）

WENCHOW'S BUSY WORKERS

A Port With a Future

From Our Wenchow Correspondent

Wenchow has been opened to foreign trade 43 years, yet few people could pass a successful examination on its big staple industries, and would probably be "at sea" if asked any questions about the peculiar local trades which, small in themselves, yet give this port and district a marked character of its own.

Wenchow has not yet attained that success in the business world which appeared possible in the early years following its opening to foreign trade. Several reasons may be assigned for this comparative failure to make good, amongst others being: (a) the tendency to regard the port as a close preserve for a shipping company which lacked foresight, efficiency and enterprise: (b) the remarkable out – of – the – worldness of that class of the community who called themselves "business men": and (c) the lack of a few really wealthy men who could have organized the numerous rivulets of trade, and made them flow into the channel of commercial success.

Whilst prophecy is a dangerous and unreliable thing, yet, with a decided breaking away at the present time from these three setbacks one may venture on the opinion that Wenchow will make greater progress the next 10 years than she has done during the last 40.

Her trade is many – sided. In theold Prefecture the following commodities are to be found in business – paying quantities: tea, silk, oranges, cotton, wheat, sugar, eggs, lard, camphor, and alum. The day of minerals is dawning. Innumerable eyes are seeking for the treasures hidden for long ages in the hills and mountains of the district, and there is already evidence that the search will not prove vain.

Wenchow, however, has a few peculiar local trades which not only provide a livelihood for many of its people, but furnish evidence of the enterprise and skill of certain classes of the community.

Herewith a few are briefly indicated:

Soap – stone Pictures

The mining and carving of soap – stone in the Tsingt' ienhsien has long been famous, and previous to the Great War found ready sale in many Western countries. Within the last 10 years, however, a new use for certain grades of soap – stone has been found in making picture – panels illustrating scenes in Chinese history and Chinese folk – lore. Comparatively thin slabs of various coloured soapstone are inlaid on dark reddish wood with remarkable skill and artistic taste. The effect is enhanced by the soap – stone being embossed.

Pigskin and Leather

There has been a great expansion in this business of pigskin boxes, largely confined to Chinese buyers, but worthy of the attention of foreign clients in these days of costly travelling trunks. With a suitable crate – like covering, which can be hinged to prevent all trouble of opening, and which when suitably painted makes a creditable appearance, such boxes have made four journeys to Europe and are still as fit as ever for another journey. First – class boxes of this type are not dear at the cost of five dollars. There has been a recent development in the making of suitcases which is proving very successful. The writer had one made with good leather, the cost of which with foreign lock and straps was only $ 7. 50.

Square Bamboos

Known only to a comparatively few, the square bamboo is obtainable in

Wenchow. It makes an ideal walking – stick, being light and unique. In past days the British Navy, as represented by an occasional gunboat, has been the best customer for the square bamboo.

Chairs

Another modern trade which has rapidly expanded is the making of chairs of all descriptions. There is the all – wood type; the rattan – seat and back and the leather – seated chair. The kind made are suitable for dining – room, hall, bedroom, office and garden.

Rocking chairs and babies' safety high chairs are also made in fair numbers. As a rule, they are sold unvarnished, hence buyers can varnish according to taste.

Umbrellas

In conclusion one can only indicate that great quantities of Chinese umbrellas are made locally, and still find a market outside the home demand.

Paper-making

Paper-making from straw and bamboo find employment for many.

On the hills great quantities of charcoal are made, mostly for export.

"Typhoon at Wenchow: Extraordinary Rains and Flood," *The North – China Herald and Supreme Court & Consular Gazette*, September 25, 1920

Typhoon at Wenchow: Extraordinary Rains and Flood

(From our own correspondent)

Wenchow, September 11.

It is still difficult to estimate the damage caused by the great typhoon of September 3 – 6 in the Wenchow district. The plains were flooded right to the foot of the hills on every side of the city. The phenomenal rainfall, fortunately, fell within the area of the lower basins of the river and creeks. Otherwise, the disastrous floods of 1912 would probably have been repeated with even worse results.

That this is no exaggeration will be realized when the fact is stared that on the first three days of the typhoon 24 in. of rain were registered; 10 in. on the first day, 7 (1/2) in. the second day and 6 (1/2) in. on the third.

The potato crops have suffered severely. The second crop of rice will, fortunately, not suffer much.

TYPHOON AT WENCHOW

Extraordinary Rains and Flood

From Our Own Correspondent.

Wenchow, Sept. 11.

It is still difficult to estimate the damage caused by the great typhoon of September 3-6 in the Wenchow district. The plains were flooded right to the foot of the hills on every side of the city. The phenomenal rainfall, fortunately, fell within the area of the lower basins of the river and creeks. Otherwise the disastrous floods of 1912 would probably have been repeated with even worse results.

Mission property damaged

The Mission property of the English United Methodist Church has been damaged. Up to time of writing there are reports of three country churches totally destroyed, and several with portions of walls down, etc. Several villages have suffered great losses in property and lives, but full details are still lacking. The north river, known as theNan Ch'i Creek, seems to have caused the greatest loss of life, reports giving estimates of from 800 to 1500. I hope to send fuller reports in two – or three – days' time.

"Passenger Boats in Collision: Passenger Killed by Panic: None by Accident," *The North – China Herald and Supreme Court & Consular Gazette*, January 22, 1921

Passenger Boats in Collision: Passenger Killed by Panic: None by Accident

PASSENGER BOATS IN COLLISION

Passenger Killed by Panic : None by Accident

Reports reached Shanghai on Thursday giving details of a collision between two Chinese steamers. The accident happened between Wenchow and Ningpo, and as a result the Yungchuan Steam Navigation Co.'s str. Hukuang was severely holed, and after her passengers had been removed had to be beached.

Reports reached Shanghai on Thursday giving details of a collision between two Chinese steamers. The accident happe-ned between Wenchow and Ningpo, and as a result the Yungchuan Steam Navigation Co. 's str. Hukuang was severely holed, and after her passengers had been removed had to be beached.

The reports state that the Hukuang left Wenchow for Ni-ngpo at 7 a. m. on the 15th instant with over 300 passengers aboard. Shortly after midnight, while crossing the bar at Pingchai, near Taichow, she collided with the bow of another steamer, the Yungan, which was sailing from Shanghai to Ningpo. The Hukuang sustained a hole on the port side of her foredeck.

Water immediately rushed in. The passengers were thrown into a panic and terrified shouts of "Save life! Save life!" arose.

The Yungan, which was but little damaged, stood by. Shortly afterwards another steamer, the Yunchuan, which happened to be passing, hearing the distress signals immediately made for the spot. Rescue work was commenced at once, and all 300 passengers were saved. One, however, had been killed, and four seriously injured during the panic. Ten others are said to have received minor injuries.

"Wenchow and Famine Relief: Suffering Food Shortage Itself yet Willing to Aid," *The North - China Herald and Supreme Court & Consular Gazette*, May 14, 1921

Wenchow and Famine Relief: Suffering Food Shortage Itself yet Willing to Aid

(From our own correspondent)

Wenchow, April 30

Among the many efforts put forth by the cities of China to render help to the famine districts in the North, that of Wenchow is worthy of record.

For here we have a case of a district suffering itself from famine conditions and yet responding to the appeal sent forth by the United International Famine Relief Committee, Peking.

WENCHOW AND FAMINE RELIEF

Suffering Food Shortage itself Yet Willing to aid

From Our Own Correspondent.

Wenchow, April 30.

Among the many efforts put forth by the cities of China to render help to the famine districts in the North, that of Wenchow is worthy of record.

A committee comprising officials, gentry, business men and missions organized a drive. Propaganda in the form of open - air addresses and leaflets was vigorously aided by Chinese Christians. The work was not easy owing to local conditions, and the workers were often asked the question, "Why don't you assist the Wenchow people in their distress?"

The exact total raised for relief in the North has not yet been made known; but I understand the Commissioner of Foreign Affairs – who acted as treasurer – had expressed the confident opinion that fully $4000 would be available for transmission. This is a case of the poor helping the poor. Copper cents and 10 cent silver pieces were predominantly the offerings made!

Huge Increase in Prices

The conditions in the Wenchow district can be gauged when it is stated that since the failure of the autumn crops last year, over 220000 bags of rice have been imported. Never in the history of this port has such an enormous quantity of rice been imported. Wenchow under normal conditions is able to supply its own food – stuffs, and generally has a surplus to spare for other places. The typhoons and floods last year changed this, and in many of the country places great distress and suffering are being experienced. This is accentuated by the failure of the wheat crop in several districts.

Three months have yet to pass before the first rice crop can be harvested. Many on reading the report of the importation of rice will be led to the opinion that conditions have been very much eased.

Another element, however, enters into consideration. The cost of buying the rice locally is in many places 100 percent higher than it was 12 months ago. Potatoes, upon which a big population rely to eke out their scanty resources, can only be obtained at an increased cost of 400 percent as compared with normal years.

With houses destroyed; land laid waste with sand and rubble, and the loss by flood of a good proportion of their stock of foodstuffs, there are thousands of country people who cannot find the cash or credit to buy. Many respectable families are having to put pride aside and become beggars to tide them over the next three months.

Official Aid

The Wenchow magistrate is distributing free $ 5000 of rice. The other hsiens are proportionately doing the same.

The Catholic Mission has distributed several hundred bags of rice, and many private individuals have aided and are aiding to the extent of their poorer.

Mr. C. E. Tenant who has been Commissioner of Customs here for the past five years left for furlough on Thursday, April 28. He is travelling via Foochow and Southern ports, and intends to join the M. M. Mail steamer at Hongkong.

Mr. E. Alabaster who has recently returned from furlough has taken over the-Commissionership of the port. It is a great pleasure to the small foreign community here that he is accompanied by Mrs. Alabaster.

"Politics at Wenchow: Taoyin's Departure After Struggle with the Tuchun," *The North – China Herald and Supreme Court & Consular Gazette*, August 27, 1921

Politics at Wenchow: Taoyin's Departure After Struggle with the Tuchun

(From our own correspondent)

Wenchow, August 11

Yesterday, August 10, the Wenchow Taoyin left this port by the str. Ka – ho. His departure was under compulsion, and hence had none of the bustle and noise which generally are associated with the leaving of a big official.

Ling Taoyin has commended himself to the Wenchow people by his readiness to ameliorate their conditions during one of the most trying periods of food scarcity which this district has ever experienced.

Over 700000 bags of rice have been imported since last autumn, and disorders and riots have been thereby prevented.

The Taoyin has been an active member of the local famine relief committee, which, owing to the grants made by the Shanghai Chinese and Foreign Famine Relief committee, has been able to render aid to several tens of thousands of indigent families.

Politics, however, take precedence of official ability; and the fact that our Taoyin is a friend of the provincial governor (civil), has led to his banishment from Wenchow under threat of arrest.

POLITICS AT WENCHOW

Taoyin's Departure After Struggle with the Tuchun

From Our Own Correspondent.

Wenchow, Aug. 11.

Yesterday, August 10, the Wenchow Taoyin left this port by the str. Ka-ho. His departure was under compulsion, and hence had none of the bustle and noise which generally are associated with the leaving of a big official.

The Tuchun Defied

It appears that Ling Taoyin had been ordered by the governor to facilitate the election of the local members of the provincial council, but the Tuchun was opposed to the election taking place, as he is aware that there is a decided movement in his province towards self – government and that in fact a provincial constitution had been drafted.

Mr. Ling regarded the prohibition or even the delay of the election of provincial councillors as being a direct violation of articles governing the election, and determined to proceed in harmony with those articles.

This brought the military in conflict with the civil authority. Martial law was proclaimed and the Taoyin was forbidden to proceed with the elections under penalty of arrest. H. E. Ling was not to be terrorized with the result that he was forced to leave the port, having, however, the sympathy of the people. It is difficult to forecast what the next move will be.

The first crop of rice has been reaped. While being good, it has not affected the high price of the cereal. Rain is badly wanted, otherwise the later crop will prove a failure.

"Firesin in Wenchow: Opportunity for Fire Brigade Purveyors: Water Scarcity," *The North – China Herald And Supreme Court & Consular Gazette*, December 24, 1921

Fires in Wenchow: Opportunity for Fire Brigade Purveyors: Water Scarcity

(From Our Own Correspondent)

Wenchow, Chè., December 7

Since the city was supplied with electric light some seven years ago, there has not been any further progress in works of public benefit and utility, until the autumn of the present year. Two great needs have been constantly presenting themselves, but hitherto without securing any efforts towards amelioration. One is the need of better and more modern fire – fighting appliances. The other is the sufficient supply of good water for the city population.

Property is being destroyed by fires, which, in many cases, could be saved were the fire – brigades reorganized and equipped on even modest lines. The cost could probably be easily met by the contributions of property owners, plus a grant from the local officials.

It is worth the while of some Shanghai firms to investigate and suggest suitable engines, pumps, etc., for the market is capable of indefinite expansion in other cities and large towns in this Province, let alone throughout the whole country. This autumn has been one of the worst for many years as far as destructive fires are concerned. The last big fire occurred outside the East Compound wall

FIRES IN WENCHOW

Opportunity for Fire Brigade Purveyors: Water Scarcity

From Our Own Correspondent.

Wenchow, Chè., Dec. 7.

Since the city was supplied with electric light some seven years ago, there has not been any further progress in works of public benefit and utility, until the autumn of the present year. Two great needs have been constantly presenting themselves, but hitherto without securing any efforts towards amelioration. One is the need of better and more modern fire-fighting appliances.

of the English Methodist Mission; and had it not been for the concentrations of 20 "Fire – dragon Brigades," directed and aided by several foreign gentlemen unconnected with the Mission, there is no doubt the three residential houses would have been destroyed.

No Water

The second need, of a water supply for house hold purposes, is being demonstrated in a very emphatic way these days and nights. Since the middle of September there has practically been no rain – fall. Most of the wells are dry. People are having to buy water, and queues are common even throughout the night where: one or two wells are yet not exhausted.

Again, Artesian wells would not only ensure the water supply of this old city, but would tend to the lessening of disease and the saving of many lives.

The natural conditions of this city surrounded by hills promise success to the making of artesian wells, and again open up the way for business enterprise.

The people are ready to be influenced to the introduction and cost of these reforms.

A Provincial Road

In the meantime, a great road is in the making, which gives it shock to those who have travelled for long years on the two or three feet wide highways! The report is that it is to be a "Provincial Road," finally linking up with Taichow and Ningpo in the north; and with Fukien in the south. Certainly the section which has been made during the past few weeks indicates an ambitions and progressive policy. The road begins from the river bank outside the East Gate of the city, and travels from North to South. It is over 30 feet wide. Graves and portions of houses have been no hindrance in the making of the road so far; nor yet the acquiring of the necessary land.

The foreign community has been approached by the local officials to allow some 15 feet of the foreign cemetery to be made over to the Road Commission, so as to conform with their survey and plans. Or, alternatively they will provide a new and better cemetery site, and undertake the removal of all "remains," and pay the cost of everything involved!

The matter is being seriously considered by the foreign residents, but no definite decision has yet been arrived at.

"Obituary: Mr. H. E. Hobson," *The North – China Herald and Supreme Court & Consular Gazette*, April 22, 1922

Obituary: Mr. H. E. Hobson

(From our own correspondent)

OBITUARY

Mr. H. E. Hobson

News is to hand of the death, on February 25 at Iron Bridge, Shropshire, of Mr. Herbert Elgar Hobson, who was Senior Commissioner of the Chinese Maritime Customs at the time of his retirement. He was the eldest son of the late Mr. Robert Hobson, of Wellington, Somerset, and was in his seventy – eighth year.

Mr. Hobson arrived in Shanghai in August, 1861, to join the Customs Service. In the following winter the Taiping rebels were closing round Shanghai, so like nearly every other European resident he joined the Volunteers. In 1863 he went to Peking, and shortly after this, consequent on the beheading of the Taiping rebel chiefs, he was appointed Staff Interpreter to General Gordon whom he served with until the end of the campaign in 1864. For his services he was decorated with the Gordon Campaign Medal. He then rejoined the Customs, and served in one capacity or other at no less than eighteen of the Treaty ports in China. Mr. Hobson thus possessed a varied and unique experience of China.

He opened Wenchow to trade in 1877, Chungking in 1890, and Teng – yueh (Yunnan) in 1900, besides which he spent three years at Yuling on the Thibet frontier. He closed his Chinese service in Shanghai, where he endeared himself to all with whom he came in contact.

"Wenchow Notes: Chinese Customs Changes: A Missionary Deputation," *The North – China Herald and Supreme Court & Consular Gazette*, April 22, 1922

Wenchow Notes: Chinese Customs Changes: A Missionary Deputation

Wenchow, April 12

It is with regret that our small community has heard of the early transfer of our Commissioner of Customs, Mr. E. Alabaster to the port of Chinkiang.

Mr. Alabaster has only been in Wenchow 12 months; but during that period he has rendered valuable service as chairman of the Famine Relief Committee, and has ever been ready to aid and forward any of the interests of the sm-all foreign community. Every good wish will go with him and Mrs. Alabaster when they remove about the end of May.

WENCHOW NOTES

Chinese Customs Changes: A Missionary Deputation:

From Our Own Correspondent.

Wenchow, Apr. 12.

It is with regret that our small community has heard of the early transfer of our Commissioner of Customs, Mr. E. Alabaster to the port of Chinkiang.

A Successful Mission

Our port has recently been visited by Mr. and Mrs. Butler, of Bristol, England. They, along with the Rev. C. Skedeford, General Missionary Secretary, form a deputation from the United Methodist Church, and are visiting all Mission Stations in Yunnan, Chekiang, Shantung, and Chihli Provinces.

The Wenchow Mission of The United Methodists, as readers of "A Mission in China" will know, is one of the most successful, despite its woefully understaffed condition. There are 276Churches, with a roll – call of over 10000 adult members and inquirers. The College is doing a splendid work for its 170 students. For many years the Methodist Hospital has been the centre of a great and beneficient work; alleviating the manifold sufferings of a vast number of Chinese. The fact that last year 35000 out – patients, and over 800 in – patients were dealt with, will tell its own stroy of strenuous work. Hitherto, one foreign doctor has borne the burden of this great work without even the assistance of a foreign nurse; and in addition has acted as Port – doctor.

We congratulate Dr. Skedeford on the arrival of a fully qualified British nurse in the person of Miss L. Ball, and the prospect of having a colleague in the coming Autumn, when it is hoped that Dr. W. E. Plunmer, who several years ago rendered valuable services as surgeon – in – charge, will return to his duties here, which he was only forced by overwork to relinquish for a time.

British Merchants' Support

Both educational and medical missionary work are likely to be stimulated and brought to a greater degree of efficiency by the generous sympathy and support of the Associated British Chambers of Commerce. With British merchants prepared to render aid during an unprecedented trade depression, the Christian Churches will not be lacking in lesser faith or generosity.

"Wenchow Notes: Death of Miss Young of the China Inland Mission," *The North – China Herald and Supreme Court & Consular Gazette*, July 1, 1922

Wenchow Notes: Death of Miss Young of the China Inland Mission

(From our own correspondent)

Wenchow, Chê. , June 20

An old and highly respected member of the Wenchow community passed away before daylight on Saturday, June 17, in the person of Miss F. A. M. Yong, of China Inland Mission. Miss Young, at the age of 40 years, and whilst holding a good position in the British Civil Service, offered, and was accepted, for work in China in connexion with the above named Mission.

She overcame the language difficulty, and for a period of 23 years rendered faithful and effective work mainly as the Principal of a boys' boarding school. During the last six months, the C. I. M. in Wenchow has lost three valued and tried workers. The sympathy of the foreign community was very marked at the funeral service and interment of Miss Yong, which was conducted by the Rev. F. Worley. The Chinese also paid a very remarkable tribute to the deceased lady.

WENCHOW NOTES

Death of Miss Young of the China Inland Mission

From Our Own Correspondent.

Wenchow, Chê., June 20.

An old and highly respected member of the Wenchow community passed away before daylight on Saturday, June 17, in the person of Miss F. A. M. Young, of China Inland Mission. Miss Young, at the age of 40 years, and whilst holding a good position in the British Civil Service, offered, and was accepted, for work in China in connexion with the above named Mission.

Prison Reform

The officials responsible for the interned criminal classes of this district are endeavouring to improve prison life and conditions. A trial section has been recently added to the old prison and a scheme has been launched for building a new and model prison, the cost of which is estimated at $ 30000.

A dinner was recently given at the Magistrate's yamên, to which several of the leading citizens, the head of the Roman Catholic Mission, and the Chairman of the English Methodist Church Mission were invited, the object being to secure their aid and sympathy in raising funds for the project! Subscription books were distributed after the feast, and the two foreign guests were asked to interest their friends in contributing to this new and improved home for law – breakers. One of them is reported as having pointed out that such a request was rather unusual, in that in all foreign countries it was recognized as the nation's duty to provide such accommodation, and that in many other ways Missions were contributing to the welfare of China in the form of hospitals and education and in the making of good citizens. Credit, however, must be given to the magistrate and the head of the Criminal Court here, in that they are anxious to improve prison conditions, irrespective of financial aid from their superiors, and one can only wish them success.

It's an Ill Wind

The "Meitin" (steamy) season is with us, and is causing the usual feeling of limpness and lassitude among the foreign community. The Chinese, however, are hope fully looking forward to good rice crops this year. The first crop is looking splendid, and if we are spared the floods and typhoons of the last two years, there is every reason to expect good harvests this year. The orange trees are full of fruit this year and members of the Orange Guild predict that more than twice the number of oranges will be gathered in the autumn than were last year.

"Wenchow Notes," *The North – China Herald and Supreme Court & Consular Gazette*, September 2, 1922

Wenchow Notes

(From our own correspondent)

Wenchow, August 20.

The first rice crop has been safely harvested, and reports from all the surrounding districts tell of better results than the past two years. The farmers are rejoicing that typhoons have not ravaged their crops, as happened during the past two years, and they are hoping that the second crop will far excel the summer harvest. Despite the safe garnering, however, rice has not fallen, but has risen in price. The people blame the officials for allowing much rice to be exported. Eighteen months ago, over 600000 bags of rice had to be imported to meet the famine conditions here, and the man in the street is a little puzzled why thousands of bags are now being exported before the present year's crops are reaped. Wenchow has never been a rice – exporting port, and the people are suspicious that military needs are being met, rather than the famine needs of other parts of China.

Wenchow has certainly been fortunate this year in escaping the devastations of the dreaded typhoons. During the month of August, four different typhoons have been raging east, north and south of this district, but apart from a heavy rainfall during two or three days, and a much lowered temperature, we have escaped loss and damage, though for two days, plains and valleys were flooded.

The summer has been one of the coolest for some few years especially for the few fortunate ones who have been able to reside on the hills facing the city. Though only 1200 feet above sea level, the highest temperature has been 86 degrees in the shade, and often the day has been spent under conditions which made many marvel at the higher temperature registered in the more northern ports.

"Wenchow Wrecked by Last Typhoon: Six Churches and Many Houses Razed to the Ground: Terrible Losses on the River," *The North – China Herald and Supreme Court & Consular Gazette*, September 23, 1922

Wenchow Wrecked by Last Typhoon: Six Churches and Many Houses Razed to the Ground: Terrible Losses on the River

(From our own correspondent)

Wenchow, September 16

A typhoon of the most devastating character known to the oldest resident here struck the port with startling suddenness on Monday. All communication with the outside world was cut off, as the wires were down north and south and up to today, when the str. Yushun, which had called in from Foochow, left, they had not been repaired.

Sunday, September 10, was a gloriously fine day, with no suggestion of the impending calamity, but at 2 p. m. on Monday it was evident that a very severe typhoon was traveling towards Wenchow. At that time the barometer was going down fast, the reading being 29. 556. At 8 : 30 p. m. , it had fallen to 28. 56 and the city and district were being laid in ruins. It has been officially

WENCHOW WRECKED BY LAST TYPHOON

Six Churches and Many Houses Razed to the Ground: Terrible Losses on the River

From Our Own Correspondent.

Wenchow, Sept. 16.

A typhoon of the most devastating character known to the oldest resident here struck the port with startling suddenness on Monday. All communication with the outside world was cut off, as the wires were down north and south and up to today, when the str. Yushun, which had called in from Foochow, left, they had not been repaired.

computed that the typhoon traveled towards Wenchow at the rate of 500 miles in 24 hours and the centre must have passed, if not actually over, at least very close to us.

Str. Feiching's Wonderful Escape

The worst period was from 7 p. m. until midnight. The river craft suffered terribly. The China Merchants' str. Feiching had a wonderful escape from serious damage and the fact that she came through at all reflects the greatest credit on her Captain and officers. She was moored to a big pontoon, strongly fastened by anchors and chains, but the whole pontoon broke away between 8 and 8: 30 p. m. and, in dense darkness the ship swung up steam. She struck a riverside house broadside on and though, unfortunately, the house was demolished, the temporary holding up of the ship allowed time for her to be got under control. On soundings being taken where the ship struck, a depth of 47 ft. was registered. It was a wonderful escape.

A Government launch, with 30 men on board, was not so fortunate, for she crashed bows on into the riverside wall of the premises rented by the A. P. C. This meant her total wreck, but 28 of the men were saved through the gallant and praiseworthy efforts of Mr. Powell, the A. P. C. agent, and his servants. Another steam launch went under with five men.

The Chinese estimate that close upon 100 junks and other big craft were lost, whilst they place the loss of small boats, such as sampans, at about 1000 . It is impossible to estimate the total loss of life.

Havoc in the Dark

On shore, walls and houses were falling like packs of cards. The city was in dense darkness, owing to the electric light being early cut off by the storm. The city now presents a picture of destruction which can only be described as like that of a place that has suffered a severe bombardment. The second rice crop is badly damaged and the orange trees have likewise suffered.

The English United Methodist Church Mission has been badly hit, for the college, hospital and big church in the city have been seriously damaged. There is also news up to the present of six fine churches in the country being razed to the ground. The loss to this mission alone will total $ 20000.

"Wenchow Typhoon Losses: Worse than a Bombardment: Terrible Havoc Amongst Churches and Mission Property," *The North – China Herald and Supreme Court & Consular Gazette*, September 30, 1922

Wenchow Typhoon Losses: Worse than a Bombardment: Terrible Havoc Amongst Churches and Mission Property

(From our own correspondent)

Wenchow, Che. , September 21

On September 16 the Rev. J. W. and Mrs. Heywood left Wenchow, both broken down in health, the former through overstrain borne for many years, but at last beyond the limits of human endurance, the latter through the incidence of an internal complaint which demands surgical attention in the homeland. Thirty – two years ago, Mr. Heywoood came to this port and until nearly 11 years ago spent half his period of Chinese service in Ningpo Paucity of workers demanded his supervision of the work from this port during the last two years, and his superintendence of 150 churches in the Wenchow district and the strain of trying to cope, in addition, with the general work of the Mission in Ningpo, has proved too much for a frame already debilitated by recurring attacks of bronchitis during recent winters. Owing to a much more

WENCHOW TYPHOON LOSSES

Worse than a Bombardment: Terrible Havoc Amongst Churches and Mission Property

From Our Own Correspondent.

Wenchow, Che., Sept. 21.

On September 16 the Rev. J. W. and Mrs. Heywood left Wenchow, both broken down in health, the former through overstrain borne for many years, but at last beyond the limits of human endurance, the latter through the incidence of an internal complaint which demands surgical attention in the homeland.

accentuated lack of workers in this greater work here, Mr. Heywoood, whose furlough was due last spring, was trying to continue a year longer.

Unparalleled Destruction

The pathos of his experience is intensified by the impact of the typhoon of Monday night, Sept. 18, which has caused damage in and around the city such as has never, it is said, been witnessed here before. Scores of large junks and lorchas and over 70 lighters have been sunk, together with a Japanese steam launch and a small steamer, in the vicinity of the city, and many hundreds of smaller craft have perished. The loss of life thereby cannot be estimated, and others have lost their lives through falling houses and landslides. There was one case of a hill – side overwhelming five houses and destroying the 27 inmates.

I was in Hartlepool on and after the day of its bombardment of the Germans, and with my family was under fire in Scarborough during its second bombardment, when a German submarine sent some 30 shells into and over the town. Today, Wenchow presents a spectacle of devastation like bombarded Hartlepool intensified a hundred times. A million dollars will not nearly cover the loss in this city and suburbs alone, and to this must be added probably some hundreds of thousands of dollars in loss on the river, to say nothing of that in the country places, through destroyed buildings, trees, bean, maize and cotton crops, as well as fields denuded by the floods of their soil and crops.

Several Churches Ruined

In the Wenchow Methodist Mission alone, up to date, 10 churches are reported totally collapsed, and many others with walls partially collapsed and needing retiling, and a great fortune must lie in the making by tile and brick makers and lime – burners. Where tiles were from six to seven hundred a dollar they are now only 150 to the dollar. Labour, too, is much more costly. This mission station of the United Methodist Mission needs at the very least $20000, or nearly £3000 sterling to repair and rebuild. One little church destroyed four miles outside the city, was put up 12 or 15 years ago for $450; it will need over $1200 to put up that church, of the same size and style, and so with the others, in proportion, some of which accommodated up to 400 or 500 people. The compound wall of the college, surrounding a large extent of ground, has fallen for half its length, so also with the Mission compound wall, and that of the boys'

school. The large city church, accommodating 1000 people, is so seriously damaged as to be too dangerous for use.

Unfortunately, the funds in hand are always insufficient to meet even much
lighter demands than a catastrophe of this magnitude entails and while our people, poor as they are, mostly are extremely generous at such times, yet it is beyond them now that in their own dwellings and property they have similar disasters
to face. Nevertheless, our Chinese pastors and members have already formed a
court of investigation and arrangement to deal with the problem with local
help. One of our Chinese women brought me $2 out of her $5 monthly wage and
another $3 out of her $6 monthly wage to help the distress.

How a China Merchants Steamer Weathered the Storm

The suddenness with which the typhoon of September 11 broke at Wenchow
was responsible for much of the loss of life and property along the water front,
according to the officers of the China Merchants' str. Feiching which has just arrived at Shanghai from that port. Although the glass was falling fast on Monday afternoon it was not anticipated that the storm would break for another 24 hours,
and the Feiching was working cargo until 5 p. m. A torrential rain was falling and
the weather was squally with an exceptionally high tide, but the wind kept the
freshet upstream for some time.

At five minutes to eight the storm came in a great burst. The forward moorings of the Feiching tore away from the pontoon, but the stern moorings held and
the vessel drifted round but held until the wind shifted and brought down the full
force of the freshet like a mill race. Nothing could stand against that and in spite
of the heavy anchors and chains of the pontoon and the ship's anchors, both were
carried down stream together.

It was pitch dark so that rescue work was practically impossible. The Feiching picked up a couple of sailors clinging to the masts of a dismantled junk, and
another two who managed to climb up on the pontoon.

The Tale of Loss

Dead bodies are still floating on the river and as they come in and put in coffins, piled up along the shore. Over a thousand houses were destroyed. It was estimated that 58 junks could be saved, but the number totally lost cannot be computed. Some 150 cargo boats were a total loss. A Japanese motor schooner was

wrecked with a loss of 15 lives, a survivor who floated to shore on a bit of wreck-age explaining that a gigantic wave swept through the living quarters on the after deck and carried everyone overboard. The high tide flooded the city, and the decks of passing boats were seen to be level with the roofs of the houses along the bank. One junk was left stranded on the top of a house as the water receded.

When the Feiching returned to Wenchow to re – moor the pontoon it was im-possible to get even a sampan for some hours as what small craft had survived the blow were harvesting the salvage. The local officials are handling relief work as best they can but have applied to Peking for aid.

"Terrible State of Wenchow: Torrents of Rain After Typhoon: Widespread Destruction in Town and Country," *The North – China Herald and Supreme Court & Consular Gazette*, October 14, 1922

Terrible State of Wenchow: Torrents of Rain After Typhoon: Widespread Destruction in Town and Country

(From our own correspondent)

Wenchow, October 5

Since my communication of September 21 reporting the recent typhoon, we have had a deluge in this city and district which has added very considerably to the damage and distress. Many houses and buildings in the city, already partly damaged or demolished in part, have now either completed their demolition or have suffered the falling of insecure walls. People have been rendered desperate by this double calamity and some whose houses have now collapsed have be-en known to go out into the open and stand there under the pitiless pouring heavens, utterly indifferent to and apparently rendered oblivious of the need to seek other shelter, in stony despair.

News in the city is to the effect that a town of several thousand inhabitants

TERRIBLE STATE OF WENCHOW

———

Torrents of Rain After Typhoon: Widespread Destruction in Town and Country

From Our Own Correspondent.

Wenchow, Oct. 5.

Since my communication of Sept. 21 reporting the recent typhoon, we have had a deluge in this city and district which has added very considerably to the damage and distress. Many houses and buildings in the city, already partly damaged or demolished in part, have now either completed their demolition or have suffered the falling of insecure walls. People situated on the river bank about 100 miles west of Wenchow has been swept a-way, and today I hear that in the Pingyanghsien in the south of this prefecture and containing the largest plain in this district, the water stands from five to seven feet deep on the plain, making it impassable to pedestrians. One missionary has had to return from an intended three weeks' tour of his stations there, unable to proceed because of the floods. A young Chinese pastor sent to investigate the condition of damaged property belonging to his church, speaks of the crops in the hsien he visited standing black amid the flood.

The highest officials of the Prefecture have been calling on some of the foreigners today. After calling on the writer and explaining their errand they repaired to the R. C. Mission, thence to the Commissioner of Customs, to ask the cooperation of the foreigners, as was done last year during the stress of flood and famine, in forming a joint committee for the consideration of measures of relief, and means of organization for its distributing.

Great tubs of rice congee are being carried round the streets here from which the very poor are allowed to take a portion. The temples are being filled with the homeless from city and country, and one hears of recently well – to – do people now being outcast, their only shelter now some temple.

One of the great trees in the city brought down in the general ruin, destroying a house in its fall, was bought the other day by a man for $ 17. It cost him $ 90 to have it sawn into logs and it is uncertain whether or not he will be able to find the money to have the logs carried to his home.

The China Merchants str. Feiching, kept in port here for 16 days by the typhoon on her last trip, has already been detained this trip eight days and is not expected to clear for three days more. Her boilers have been going all day long, and day after day she has been apparently keeping her propeller going to resist the tremendous current, the more so as she has had to support the pontoon tied to her side like an immense incubus.

"Wenchow Typhoon: Storm Disaster Increased by Flood and Pirates," *The North – China Herald and Supreme Court & Consular Gazette*, October 28, 1922

Wenchow Typhoon: Storm Disaster Increased by Flood and Pirates

(From our own correspondent)

Wenchow, October 21

The most pressing news here just now is still connected with the recent typhoon. One cannot yet escape it, for every part of this di-strict has its own story to tell. Only yesterday an old acquaintance of the writer came up from the islands around Bullock Harbour, out at sea, and told of such raging floods on small islands as one expects to hear of only on the mainland, save in the case of tidal waves. In one island village the rain flood rose so high that the inhabitants had to find safety in the upper rooms. The consequent distress here and along the coast seems to have led to a great increase in the number of pirates who come from the local islands and the Taichow district.

The chairman of the Wenchow Chamber of Commerce, Mr. T'ang, and one of the local merchants were appointed at the recent committee meeting of the Relief Society to go to Ningpo to consult with the executive there as to measures of relief, and this after soon a meeting of Chinese and foreigners was held at the

WENCHOW TYPHOON

Storm Disaster Increased by Flood and Pirates

From Our Own Correspondent.

Wenchow, Oct. 21.

The most pressing news here just now is still connected with the recent typhoon. One cannot yet escape it, for every part of this district has its own story to tell. Only yesterday an old acquaintance of the writer came up from the Islands around Bullock Har-

former Brigadier – General's yamên to hear the report and to organize locally， as in other places for the collection of funds and of information as to the condition of the various stricken parts of this country， as well as for the future distribution of relief.

"Interest of Shippers in Wenchow Trade: More Vessels Calling at Port: A Strong Bid by Japanese," *The North - China Herald and Supreme Court & Consular Gazette*, November 4, 1922

Interest of Shippers in Wenchow Trade: More Vessels Calling at Port: A Strong Bid by Japanese

(From our own correspondent)

Wenchow, October 21

A slight increase has been noticeable lately in the number of steam craft coming to this port. Apart from the usual weekly visits of the three small steamers connecting with Haiman, Chusan and Ningpo and the C. M. S. Fei-ching from Shanghai, which has been here for a week this trip, we have had Che Kuang Hua (Chinese) from Shanghai and the Un-kai Maru (Japanese) from Yokohama, and another somewhat smaller steamer has made its appearance. The Japanese seem to be making a bid for more trade with Wenchow. We hear of a Japanese turpentine factory outside the South Gate; a three - masted oil - engined ship trades between here and the south (Amoy), said to be owned by Chinese but flying the Japanese flag; a small launch, sunk in the typhoon, the Hanyang Maru, ran down the river and for 20 miles up the Yohling coast with passengers; and the Unkai Maru, a more ambitious - looking steamer, took away a cargo of charcoal to Yokohama, her

INTEREST OF SHIPPFRS IN WENCHOW TRADE

More Vessels Calling at Port: A Strong Bid by Japanese

From Our Own Correspondent.

Wenchow, Oct. 21.

A slight increase has been noticeable lately in the number of steam craft coming to this port. Apa t from the usual weekly visits of the three small steamers connecting with Haiman, Chusan and Ningpo and the C.M.S. Feishing from Shanghai, which has been here for

deck being filled also with bundles of the samecommodity.

Week by week the number of junks and lorchas coming into and lying off the city increases visibly, as also the flying to and fro of the smaller craft and sampans, while on land carpenters are busy on every hand and wooden walls are taking the place in many houses of the brick of former days. Temples are busy, in some instances being the homes of numerous people who are forced to beg for a subsistence; in others the busy appearance is due to the number of devotees seeking the help these shrines profess to supply, one of the most popular being the Temple of Neptune on the hill over which runs the city wall, overlooking the river and the distant sea. In two months time the China Merchants S. N. Co. hope to have their pontoon in order again.

"Wenchow Notes: A Long List of Accidents: Boom in Sea and River Trade," *The North - China Herald and Supreme Court & Consular Gazette*, January 20, 1923

Wenchow Notes: A Long List of Accidents: Boom in Sea and River Trade

(From our own correspondent)

Wenchow, Chê., January 5

The past few months have been fruitful of accidents of various kinds in the city and neighbourhood. Fire broke out in one of the best streets in the city, claiming a few dwellings, among them a large modern bootshop. A gunpowder explosion in a house some time ago caused the death of several of the inmates, and of a girl who was passing at the time. Another explosion recently is said to have blown off a man's head, while about a week ago the capsizing of a boat bringing passengers and others from a steamer, which, according to one account, had got on a sandbank, and according to another was anchored in mid - stream, caused the loss of 12 lives by drowning, the boatman being among the missing.

River and sea - trade in connexion with this port seem to in an increasingly prosperous condition, judging by the increase in the visits of steam craft. Last week, the Japanese steamer Daishin Maru tool away a supply of charcoal. The Chinese steamer Shengli has paid us another visit, yesterday another Japanese steamer came in, and today two small steam launches have come into port. The

WENCHOW NOTES

A Long List of Accidents: Boom in Sea and River Trade

From Our Own Correspondent.

Wenchow,, Shê., Jan. 5.

The past few months have been fruitful of accidents of various kinds in the city and neighbourhood. Fire broke out in one of the best streets in the city, claiming a few dwellings, among them a large modern bootshop. A gunpowder

Chinese captain of one of the three Chinese steamers which coast between here and Ningpo died about a fortnight ago. These steamers had their pontoon washed away in the great typhoon, and for three months have had to discharge cargo and passengers from midstream. The pontoon has been renewed and is again being used. These three steamers ply between Ningpo and Wenchow, calling at several ports on the way, with the regularity of the London and English east coast passenger steamers, and we hear of foreign passengers preferring to travel that way, catching the Shanghai steamer at Haimen, which is said to provide as good foreign accommodation as any of the regular steamers to and from this port, whilst the fare is more reasonable.

Mr. Lampert, of the A. P. C., has left. The China Inland Mission has just welcomed one of its workers. Miss Eynon, or her return from furlough, and is expecting an early addition to the staff of foreign workers, while the Methodist Mission is looking forward to receiving the Rev. A. H. Sharman in the course of a few weeks, after an absence of three and a half years.

"Exciting Encounter with Pirates: Police Boat's Smart Work: One Boat Sunk, Another Taken,"
The North – China Herald and Supreme Court & Consular Gazette, February 17, 1923

Exciting Encounter with Pirates: Police Boat's Smart Work: One Boat Sunk, Another Taken

(From our own correspondent)

Wenchow, Chê. Febrrary 7

A former resident of Wenchow, if returning to the port at the present time would, to judge by the increase in the number of steam craft trading there, at once say that a very considerable increase had taken place in the export trade of the district. One morning no fewer than seven such craft were to be seen there, and on a recent trip outward the str. Hsin Fung met four steamers making for Wenchow.

EXCITING ENCOUNTER WITH PIRATES

Police Boat's Smart Work: One Boat Sunk, Another Taken

From Our Own Correspondent.

Wenchow, Chê. Feb. 7.

A former resident of Wenchow, if returning to the port at the present time would, to judge by the increase in the number of steam craft trading there, at once say that a very considerable increase had taken place in the export trade of the district. One morning no fewer

Of the seven vessels mentioned above three were Japanese, among them the Dai Shin Maru, the Ralph Moller flying the British flag, the Sing Li and the Kuang Hua, flying the Chinese flag, and a Chinese police boat, the Yung Ping, with 13 pirates on board who had been captured outside of Chinhoi.

It seems that the Yung Ping after leaving that place saw four junks sailing away in company under such suspicious circumstances as to justify a closer inspection and they were found to be in the possession of pirates, who, on the Yung Ping preparing for action, placed the crews about the bulwarks. The police boat then rammed and sank one of the junks, and captured another. Many of the pirates jumped overboard and two junks got away. The Yung Ping was under fire from the pirates and had a valuable compass badly damaged. She then made for Wenchow with the 13 captured pirates on board, who, an informant said, had the appearance of being opium smokers and the offscourings of the coast.

One explanation given of this increased steamer traffic is that so many junks were destroyed in last year's typhoon that steamer companies are finding an opportunity of getting some of the trade of the port. Recently the str. Kenli came from Wuhu with 11000 bags of rice to be sold at a somewhat cheaper rate than has been prevailing for some time.

Temple Festivities

During the last three or four months a large amount of money has been expended by the Chinese in renovating the damaged temples of the city. Among them the very popular temple on the Hill of the Altar of the Sea has had some $5000 or more spent on extending and beautifying it; much if not all of which has been given by a well known member of the Wu family living in the vicinity of the North Gate. This gentleman is also credited with a resuscitation of public worship in some of the neighbouring Buddhist temples, and it is said that among the men who attend these public services are some who attend because it is expected of them, otherwise it might be reckoned offensive to the promoters. Part of these services consists of preaching.

For many days prior to and after the reopening of the Sea Temple great numbers of people were to be seen visiting the fane, on the opening day especially the crowds being very large. At night a firework display was given on the hill, visible to all parts of the city. For more than a month daily theatrical performances are being given at the Fire God Temple at the foot of the same hill, which is part of the city, and as these are given in the open air, the people crowd to them in great numbers especially on the finer nights.

The Bund of the island fronting the city "Heart of the River," （江心） which was partly destroyed in the typhoon, has been repaired, thanks to the energy and initiative of our Harbour Master, Mr. Christophersen, who got the rice merchants who store the Wuhu rice in the temples on the Island to subscribe towards that necessary object.

> "Wenchow Notes: The Passion for Old Customs: New Appointments: Increasing Japanese Trade,"
> *The North - China Herald and Supreme Court & Consular Gazette*, April 28, 1923

Wenchow Notes: The Passion for Old Customs: New Appointments: Increasing Japanese Trade

(From our own correspondent)

Wenchow, Chê., April 21

Wenchow – the city mild and peaceful – moves, even if it does, so slowly and sedately; it responds to the dynamic influences of the age, even while showing unequivocal signs of a resuscitation of interest in and observance of customs and beliefs handed down from remote generations. The modern student may, in the presence of the foreign teacher, try to assume the attitude of a supercilious agnostic, but people and merchants and others crowd more than ever to the popular temples at the season of T' sing Ming and perform the ancient ceremonies at the graves with apparently greater devotion. "The old order changes," it is true, "yielding place the new," but so much of the old order is firmly embedded in the heart and life of the people at large, and for anything that gives any promise of conserving the old faith and the ancient customs, these still are not wanting those willing to give generously. Some time ago the Wu family gave thousands of dollars for the renovation of a temple which is now completed. The picturesquely sinuous avenue leading up the hill to that temple is being well repaired with fine blocks of granite, which are already half - way up,

WENCHOW NOTES

The Passion for Old Customs: New Appointments: Increasing Japanese Trade

From Our Own Correspondent.

Wenchow, Chê., Apr. 21.

Wenchow—the city mild and peaceful—moves, even if it does, so slowly and sedately; it responds to the dynamic influences of the age, even while showing unequivocal signs of a resuscitation of

through the munificence of a lady of the neighbouring city of Jui – an.

The outdoor staff of the Customs has recently undergone changes, Mr. West's departure to Newchwang having now been followed by that of the much esteemed harbour master, Mr. Christophersen, who has gone via American and London on furlough overdue two years.

Many expressions of regret have been heard, for during the three years of this, his second, appointment to Wenchow, Mr. Christophersen has earned the hearty goodwill and respect of the community. Mr. Coxall has followed Mr. West, and Mr. Ryden, accompanied by his wife, has succeeded Mr. Christophersen. Mr. Coxall's prowess at football has been mentioned and we look to see him giving more than a few points to the students on the Methodist College field, some of whom are keen, but are much in need of coaching.

Japanese steamers continue to trade, mostly in charcoal, with the port, and seldom a week passes without seeing one or more of them anchored off the city. One report now gives the number of resident Japanese here as over 50, and another says about 100. In the eastern suburb a factory is being built by or for Japanese. It is still in course of erection, there being three structures, one a single storey, the second a double – storied one, and the third a neat little painted wooden bungalow with brick pillars for the manager, Mr. Ling, a Fukienese. The two former buildings are for the production of canned beef, mutton, yan – mei and loquats, intended, according to the people on the spot, for outport trade. Asked as to whether or not Japanese were associated with the enterprise, the answer was "No. Fukienese and Wenchowese." The factory and bungalow are at the side of the new motor road where it ends near the river bank.

"Determined Boycott at Wenchow: Students out in Force to Examine Luggage: A Customs Protest:
A Principal's Wisdom," *The North – China Herald and Supreme Court & Consular Gazette*, May 5,
1923

Determined Boycott at Wenchow: Students out in Force to Examine Luggage: A Customs Protest: A Principal's Wisdom

(From our own correspondent)

Wenchow, Chê., April 21

The students from many of the schools and colleges of Wenchow have been active during the week in carrying on the Japanese boycott. A meeting for 1000 people was convened at the hall of the Merchants' Guild on Sunday afternoon, April 15, and about 500 assembled, mostly students, with some merchants and others. As the place of meeting proved too small even for that reduced number, they requisitioned the large Central Church of the United Methodist Mission, without seeking permission, the Sunday scholars having dispersed a short time before, and the building, which easily accommodates 1000 people, being empty at the time. There were various speakers, the more popular, so a young preacher said, being those who appealed to the militant feelings of the audi-

DETERMINED BOYCOTT AT WENCHOW

Students out in Force to Examine Luggage: A Customs Protest: A Principal's Wisdom

From Our Own Correspondent.

Wenchow, Chê., Apr. 21.

The students from many of the schools and colleges of Wenchow have been active during the week in carrying on the Japanese boycott. A meeting for 1,000 people was convened at the hall of the Merchants' Guild on Sunday after-

ence. The young preacher tried to emphasize the fact that all destruction of goods in the end would only mean inflicting injury on their own country, and exhorted them not to speak of the Japanese as enemies, while still insisting on the necessity for the abrogation of the treaty and the cancelling of the Twenty one Demands.

Search parties were organized by the students to visit the steamers and Customs, and to keep an eye on the luggage of incoming and outgoing passengers. Their activities, probably not less because of the participation of unauthorized idlers, soon began to interfere with the efficient conduct of the work at the Maritime Customs, which necessitated the Commissioner writing to the official for foreign affairs, who wrote to the Taoyin, and he in turn issued a stamped proclamation to the several principals of the schools, asking that the Maritime and other Customs be avoided, but neither specifying which places might be searched nor exhorting to desist.

Some Sound Advice

The acting Principal of the Methodist College, when approached by a deputation of his students, pointed out to them that, however much the students or the Principal himself might dislike the measures of the Japanese, yet the 1915 treaty still stood, and those who seized Japanese goods or prevented people trading with the Japanese were lawbreakers, and in the event of personal trouble coming upon any student for participating in the active boycott, the Principal could take no action on behalf of any such student to protect him. It was further indicated to them that China's greatest need was not a change in her external relations, but the united effort of merchants, students and people in securing official integrity, administrative honesty and fidelity and a united country; that if the students expended their boycotting energy on dishonest officials and administrators, it would be more effective in securing good results; and that, so long as China's internal state of dissension and incapacity continued, so long would she expose herself to the machinations of unscrupulous persons.

No student under 18 years of age is allowed to be a member of a search party and no resident student is allowed to go to any meeting at night or to take part in any party engaged in boycott work at night, on pain of dismissal. Students living in the city, at their own homes, may of course represent resident students at night, and report next day. Only six representatives many function for the day, and these are rotatory.

"Wenchow Notes: A School Excursion in Holiday Weather: The Japanese Boycott," *The North – China Herald and Supreme Court & Consular Gazette*, May 19, 1923

Wenchow Notes: A School Excursion in Holiday Weather: The Japanese Boycott

(From our own correspondent)

Wenchow, May 6

The Middle Schools here, in Wenchow, are having their inter – term holiday. Between 70 and 80 of the students and teachers of the Methodist College (I – Wen – Hsioh – Tàng) marched out with banners flying and to the roll of the bass and the rat – tat – tat of the kettle drums en route for a week's outing some two or three days' journey to a part of the P'ing – yanghsien among the mountains famous for its rock scenery.

WENCHOW NOTES

A School Excursion in Holiday Weather: The Japanese Boycott

From Our Own Correspondent.

Wenchow, May 6.

The Middle Schools here, in Wenchow, are having their inter-term holiday. Between 70 and 80 of the students and teachers of the Methodist College (I-Wen-Hsioh-Tàng) marched out with banners flying and to the roll of the bass and the rat-tat-tat of the kettle drums *en route* for a week's outing

So far the weather for the excursion, four days of which are past, has been ideal for such an outing, reminding one of the typical English May Days of one's far away boyhood – brilliant sunshine, azure skies flecked with snow – white cloudlets, cool breezes, to moderate the sun's heat, the multitudinous flowers smiling in their gorgeous holiday attire, and the fresh green of the young spring foliage giving restfulness to the eyes tired with the blaze of incessant sunshine. The rain, too has been considerate of the holiday makers, coming in its downpour during the night.

But the Japanese boycott is not overlooked, and provision has been made for relays of students to continue their propagandist activities, which, however, does not apply to export of Chinese produce of Japan. Three Japanese steamers have loaded here this week with very full cargoes of charcoal, the str. Daishin Maru, the Sanchoh Maru, and the Chokai Maru; the second one is still in port busily loading up.

Our correspondent recently reported that about 80 fugitive soldiers from the armies fighting in Fukien had reached this port and had then been transhipped. The report now goes that about 2000 soldiers (Northern), who have been stationed here some time have now been sent south to Fukien in connexion with the fighting in that province, and that others are being sent from further north to take their place here.

An Exchange of Troops

May 12

The troops have now come to take the place of the Northerners now in Fukien. They are Chêkiang men, and have little of the stalwartness and muscle of those whose place they have taken. Not a few tombstones are to be seen on the city hills marking the last resting place of Shantung and Chihli soldiers to whom the climate and conditions of Wenchow have proved too trying.

The plains around the city are now mostly submerged, the "water dragons" busily pumping the canal water into the fields which are at present being sedulously planted with the fresh young rice plants. Side by side with this transplanting work is going on the cutting down and threshing of the spring wheat and the rape seed, most of which is now in. Building work goes on more slowly just now, the call of the spring activities of farm life taking builders back to their ancestral plots for the season.

Among some illicit merchandise recently seized here by the Customs authorities were some of old fashioned spears and blades that used to be a common sight on the shoulders of the Chinese braves in the earlier years of one's residence in Wenchow. They were being brought from Shanghai to be sold here as old iron.

"Welcome Rainfall at Wenchow: A Godsend for the Farmers and the Crops: Proposed New A. P. C. Building," *The North – China Herald and Supreme Court & Consular Gazette*, June 9, 1923

Welcome Rainfall at Wenchow: A Godsend for the Farmers and the Crops: Proposed New A. P. C. Building

(From our own correspondent)

Wenchow, May 24

Empire Day finds the foreign community sweltering and limp in Wenchow's speciality – muggy weather. Thunder and lightning, which have been the concomitants of the season for some days, have given us heavy and sometimes protracted thunder – showers, affording but temporary alleviation. A temperature of only 80 in the shade, in perpetual vapour, feels at the time no less uncomfortable than the highest register of the days, and atmospheric pressure in these conditions appears to be twice its normal amount, and some would perhaps put it at a higher figure. At any rate it seems so and even one's spirits feel the impact of the physical. They are to be envied, the mercury of whose disposition is beyond the reach of those forces and laws which affect the mercury in the barometer.

As a rule, there is a plethora of fires in the after part of the year, but recent weeks have witnessed four or five fires. Happily the premises affected – shops and houses – were few, one fire a week ago doing damage to four fish shops at

WELCOME RAINFALL AT WENCHOW

A Godsend for the Farmers and the Crops: Proposed New A. P. C. Building

From Our Own Correspondent.

Wenchow, May 24.

Empire Day finds the foreign community sweltering and limp in Wenchow's speciality—muggy weather. Thunder and lightning, which have been the concomitants of the season for some days, have given us heavy and sometimes protracted thunder-showers, affording but

the North Gate facing the Customs and Post Offices, only the width of the road being between, the harbour master, who lives on the island, was called over to the mainland, and he and other members of the staff secured the important documents in case the fire spread; fortunately it was soon under about two or three in the morning and the Customs premises were kept intact.

The rain has been especially welcomed, as owing to the unusually dry spring the fields were becoming parched and the young rice was not being transplanted, and with last year's scarce harvest the outlook was indeed portentous. With a better supply of water, farmers have been very busy transplanting, and firewood has become 20 percent. dearer, as many of the firewood boats are laid up or otherwise engaged, their owners being in the fields.

Since last writing, Mr. and Mrs. Cance and family, of the B. A. T. have removed, the first named being transferred to Hangchow after a residence of seven years in the port. Mr. and Mrs. Cance are well known for their hospitality, and his familiar figure will be missed by many, as he was so frequently travelling in the different parts of this prefecture. Messrs Hopkin – Rees and Squires have paid a visit of several days in connexion with the business of the A. P. C. , which firm it is said is meditating the erection of premises north of the city on the banks of the North River (Nanchi) a tributary of the Wenchow River. On the way hither they had to tramp about 40 miles (120 li) one day to reach their destination for the night, rather than be held up on the road in the vicinity of bandits.

The latest fire which destroyed a building is said to have brought down the agents of a shipping firm in Shanghai, interested in insurance as, according to report, the fire took place on the night of the day when the place was insured.

One of the Chinese officials here, whose wife is residing in Shanghai, is building a house for himself and family in Hart Road, Shanghai. The site bought is about four mow, and the price paid is Tls. 4000 a mow.

Shipping Collision

A collision occurred at Haimen between the str. Kwangchi and the str. Yungning, the latter being slightly damaged. This has delayed the departure from this port of the latter vessel, which was beached the other day (May 27) below the East Gate suburb to examine her propeller. The small oil – driven vessel which plies to Amoy, and used to fly the Japanese flag, came into port on her last trip under the Portuguese colours.

At an examination held lately in one of the Middle Schools here the Chinese master set for subject for the Chinese essays "Discuss method of boycotting Japanese goods," and "Whence came the Japanese boycott?" for two of his classes. A vendor of Japanese rubber boots was caught by some students, dressed by them in red with some of the said boots suspended round his neck, and he was thus paraded through the streets.

"The Typhoon Arrival at Wenchow: Tendency to Travel Northwest to the Yangtze," *The North – China Herald and Supreme Court & Consular Gazette*, August 11, 1923

The Typhoon Arrival at Wenchow:
Tendency to Travel Northwest to the Yangtze

(From our own correspondent)

THE TYPHOON

Arrival at Wenchow: Tendency to Travel Northwest to the Yangtze

Shanghai was in no immediate danger on Tuesday from the typhoon announced by Siccawei to be approaching our coasts.

At 10:30 in the morning it was signalled to be travelling towards Wenchow, but the warning gun was not fired, the typhoon being too far off to endanger shipping around the Yangtze mouth. Very rough weather however, in the estuary throughout the day was reported.

By 4:30 in the afternoon the barometer at Siccawei had fallen nearly one – tenth of an inch since the same hour on Monday, when it stood at 29.72 in. The pressure was 29.69 in. at Siccawei at 9 a. m. yesterday, after which it made an appreciable fall. By tiffin time the mercury had descended to 29.63 in. At five o'clock, when ricshas on The Bund were being blown about by a wind that was increasing hourly in force, the barometer was down to 29.62 and still dropping.

A River Tragedy

On Tuesday afternoon shortly after 3 o'clock a Chinese boat loaded with coal had considerable difficulty with the cross winds and the unfavourable tides and although the crew managed to get the craft near to the foreshore in front of the Public Gardens a sharp and sudden blast of wind caught it broadside on and shortly afterwards the waves washed over it. The added weight of the water on the original load of coal proved too much for the boat and it sank completely out of sight, though when the ebb of the waves rolled over the stern, one could see the post to which the rudder had been fastened. All loose wooden materials and much that was broken by the rolling water soon floated away and the crew, none of whom had difficulty in getting off, were kept busy with long poles and nets hauling the debris to the pontoons. Further up the stream sampan men and river women caught the smaller pieces for firewood.

It was an exciting time, for crowds soon gathered and as the No. 1 shouted his orders and gesticulated vigorously. Everyone knew what he desired to be done except the men to whom he was giving orders. In a few minutes the tide rushing up river covered even the sternpost. The rudder was saved intact while the immense yuloh was kept from being battered to pieces against the bunding. About an hour later determined efforts were being made to draw the sunken vessel in towards the shore, probably more to keep it from getting further into the stream than to salvage it immediately. Heavy chains were fastened to the forward end and a lighter one was attached to the stern, to which block and tackle were hooked — semi − nude coolies working in the water to make the lines fast. A dozen or more coolies applied their strength from the Public Gardens and gradually drew the heavy weight in toward the shore, and when last seen had made considerable headway, but had not pulled it close enough to be visible above the waters.

In case the worst should happen, yachtsmen had their craft removed from the vicinity of the Foam to safer anchorages before sunset. There were few sampans along the French Bund and in fact all smaller craft had disappeared from the usual moorings by the evening.

A Low Barometer at Kiukiang

Although the preliminary warning was issued at 9. 30 a. m. on Wednesday, the typhoon continued during the day to bear some hundreds of miles to the westward of Shanghai, and by the evening the port was believed to be out of danger.

Very heavy squalls were experienced in local waters, the wind, even in the Huangpu, rising to the force of a gale.

The glass remained almost stationary at about 29. 73 in. throughout the day, while the centre of the typhoon remained well to the westward. After landing on Monday night in the neighbourhood of Wenchow, it recurved, bearing northwest or north – northwestward towards the Yangtze. An early message from Kiukiang stated that the barometer there was down to 29. 55 in. , the low pressure being accompanied by a northeasterly wind of almost hurricane force.

There were no casualties or damage to property as a result of Monday night's high wind.

"A New Venture at Wenchow: Public Garden for Children: Missionaries on Holiday: A Series of Transfers" *The North – China Herald and Supreme Court & Consular Gazette*, September 1, 1923

A New Venture at Wenchow: Public Garden for Children: Missionaries on Holiday: A Series of Transfers

(From our own correspondent)

Wenchow, August 18

The port is empty of its missionary community save for the perennial presence of the indefatigable Dr. Stedeford, of whom it might be said, so constant is his presence in the port and exacting his duties:

"Men may come and women go

But he goes on for ever."

Mr. and Mrs. Schlichter and family and Mr. Thompson, all of the C. I. M., and Mr. and Mrs. Stobie, of the U. M. M. are having a change away from the district, while the remainder of the C. I. M. foreign staff have this year joined with the U. M. M. staff in spending the hot weeks of the season at the bungalow of the latter.

The beginning of the summer witnessed the completion of a second bungalow built by the Commissioner of Customs immediately behind the other, and at the

A NEW VENTURE AT WENCHOW

Public Garden for Children: Missionaries on Holiday: A Series of Transfers

From Our Own Correspondent.

Wenchow, Aug. 18.

The port is empty of its missionary community save for the perennial presence of the indefatigable Dr. Stedeford, of whom it might be said, so constant is his presence in the port and exacting his duties :—

beginning of the season his family took up residence there. So conveniently are these bungalows placed, relative to the city, and 1400 feet up, that one is able to make the journey up and down daily by chair to business, and the missionaries are able to keep in contact with their Chinese workers. Mr. and Mrs. Barling, C. I. M. , left last month for furlough in England, and Miss Scott, C. I. M. has bidden farewell to the district, finding a sphere of work elsewhere.

The Rev. A. H. Sharman, U. M. M. , reports a severe clan feud in one of his West Brook circuits the opposing parties being armed and fatalities ensuing. The body of one of the slain was found by some of the opposing force, a spear was stuck through it, and it was thus carried away suspended between two carriers' shoulders.

Merchants and educationalists are making a show of enthusiasm for the renovation of society and have founded an association called "The Association for the Reformation of Society. " Mr. Tung is chairman, and on July 19, made a speech to a goodly audience at the San Kan Temple. The Primary School teachers of Wenchow have formed an association for mutual assistance in the form of an agreement not to allow any new teacher to take charge of the Primary Schools save in the case of the death of a head, or of the establishment of a new school.

On July 26 a number of Wenchow students held a meeting at which some of them presented the tragedy of the student Dzang So on the stage of the Little Temple.

The writer has received news of a new venture in Wenchow in the shape of the first public garden for children, the managers of which are well - educated and enthusiastic, public spirited gentlemen.

"Wenchow Awakes: Summer Lethargy Over: Typhoons, Student Enthusiasm and Prophets of Woe," *The North - China Herald and Supreme Court & Consular Gazette*, September 29, 1923

Wenchow Awakes: Summer Lethargy Over: Typhoons, Student Enthusiasm and Prophets of Woe

(From our own correspondent)

Wenchow, Chê. Septmber 22

Once more Wenchow can live and move and breathe with some degree of comfort and relief. No longer does one see its inhabitants or not a few of them—taking their nights' rest in the open, on the flat of their backs, with knees drawn up to their utmost height and their bed a wooden form six inches wide by about three feet long, or on the stone coping of the canal sides or the stone railings of its bridges. It is still possible in the day time to see its hardy ricsha coolies taking a siesta on a narrow plank stretched over one of its stagnant and fetid canals. But night is no longer a bedlam of voices of the many who in the hot summer nights make their bed in the streets. For the more bracing autumn evening breezes have begun to blow and blankets can now be used at night and when that condition of the climate has been attained the people seek the shelter of their houses for the night.

Typhoon Destruction

The recent two typhoons which came with an interval of only three days, have again caused considerable damage. Four hundred feet of the compound wall of the U. M. College has again been blown down. Last September witnessed the same thing, and the wall was rebuilt in the early part of the year only to be blown down again this following September. Truly the rhyme re typhoons holds good here: "September, Remember!"

The archipelago surrounding Bullock Harbour some eight or ten miles beyond the Wenchow river mouth, and known here as T－sa suffered extremely in last year's great typhoon, and it is said that in that part it was even worse this year. Many of its people are in a very indigent condition in consequence, and living and labour have become unusually expensive, the people being always dependent very largely on the importation of rice, timber, building materials, and many necessities from the mainland. The plain surrounding Wenchow was a vast lake, in parts five feet deep, or, as one who saw it said, it was all river.

That section of the foreign community which sought the cooler atmosphere during the hot season on the Bungalow Hill across the river, and those who went further afield in search of the same pleasanter conditions, in Mokanshan, Chefoo or even Shanghai have now returned, and with them Miss Moler of the C. I. M. has comeback from furlough in the U. S. A accompanied by Mrs. Banks of the same country who is taking up work in the same mission.

The Young Idea

The colleges and schools have once more become hives of industry for the many seekers after knowledge among the youth of Wenchow. The Methodist College bids fair soon to have over 200 students on its rolls, 194 having already enrolled in spite of stricter regulations, and others are yet to come in. 122 are living in, necessitating the buying of over 20 extra beds besides extra forms for the chapel. It is a really splendid sight to see the almost crowded chapel of the College filled every morning for the opening service with bright－eyed youths from 15 to 25 years of age, whose cager faces and often close attention make it no little－pleasure to address them. The acting principal takes the opportunity of addressings this gathering himself every morning, and finds pregnant occasion to deal from the Christian standpoint with current questions such as the Japanese boycott and its mistakes—the boycott has happily been suspended—the Japanese earthquake the chaotic condition of their native country, international relations, false prophets, etc.

Best Way with Scaremongers

The dark prophecies of the men from Szechuan have been printed and distributed here, but it is reported that the printer has been incarcerated by the authorities.

A recent fire has destroyed over 40 shops just inside the South Gate on both sides of the main street. Only the city wall prevented the conflagration spreading to the Southern suburb.

Our last piece of news is to the effect that Mr. Wolff of the B. A. T. is leaving us for Shanghai and then for Home. Some of us at least will miss his jovial presence, and we wish him the best that can be for him.

"Troop Movements in Chekiang: Cruiser and 5000 Men in Wenchow Last Week but No Fighting Yet," *The North - China Herald and Supreme Court & Consular Gazette*, January 19, 1924

Troop Movements in Chekiang: Cruiser and 5000 Men in Wenchow Last Week but No Fighting Yet

（From our own correspondent）

Wenchow, Chê., January 13

Probably in all its history Wenchow has not seen so many steamship arrivals in one week or as many soldiers for many decades.

Yesterday there were 11 steamers in port, among them being the French gunboat Algol and four large Japanese steamers. The latter are buying up all the charcoal they can secure and the demand has raised the price to such a figure that one hears that at least one of the four steamers is having to leave port without any cargo.

Last week a Chinese cruiser made its second visit to this port bringing another detachment of soldiers from Hangchow. No fewer than 5000 soldiers are reported to have been in Wenchow, and hundreds of river boats have been engaged to take men and stores up to Chichowfu about 90 miles up the river where fighting has been expected for sometime past. So far, however, though there have been plenty of rumours yet no definite news has come of any actual fighting there.

Talk in the city here is to the effect that if Gen. Lu Yung – hsiang will go a-way from Chêkiang no one else will begin fighting a somewhat different story from what has appeared in the "North China Daily News" recently. Others say that there is no likelihood of fighting now peace has been declared, but that in the south of the province Gen. Sun has brought 10000 men over the border from Fok-ien and will not retire until the local inhabitants have paid him $ 50000 as pay-ment for the troops for the time they have been there.

1500 Homeless in City Fires

The dry season here with its accompanying high winds, has brought an unu-sually large number of disasters in the way of fires. A fortnight ago the writer was in the small city of Tsingtien nearly 40 miles up the Wenchow river from this city and saw the ruins of a considerable section of the city caused by a fire about a month earlier which had rendered homeless about 500 families.

This beautiful little city by the side of a swiftly rushing, clear mountain stream is set in a narrow valley by towering mountains which confine the winding river as in a series of long narrow lakes. But the confirming offer of the hills which enhances the beauty of its situation is the cause of its frequent undoing, for in the flood season the waters become pent up and submerge the entire city at time. Thus in 1912 in spite of its strong and towering walls it was washed out save for about 20 buildings and very many lives were last, one girl of 15 being carried down the river among the wreckage for 50 miles down to the sea and washed up on an island out off the Coast several miles further away. In the big typhoon of 1922 the city again suffered badly again. The place where the writer's boat anchored under the city wall for the week – end used to have twice as great a depth of water as is necessary to float the great Atlantic liners. Today the rafts-men pole their craft over its shallows, filled from time to time with the ever roll-ing stones which the recurring floods bring down in immeasureable quantities so filling the bed of the river as to cause the annual flooding of that city to the depth of several feet.

The village of Whuzoedin in the Suian prefecture, south of Wenchow, was also visited by fire about a month earlier, and reports say that at least about 1000 families suffered grievously. Foreign oil and lamps are said to have been the cause of the fires.

$ 12000 Worth of Opium Burned

A couple of days ago there was in public burning of from $ 10000 to $ 12000 worth of opium which had been recently seized. Before long there will be another burning of some two or more catties also seized.

"Ningpo Steamer Wrecked: Pingyang Piled Up on Haimen Rocks During Voyage from Wenchow: No Lives Lost," *The North – China Herald and Supreme Court & Consular Gazette*, March 22, 1924

Ningpo Steamer Wrecked: Pingyang Piled Up on Haimen Rocks During Voyage from Wenchow: No Lives Lost

(From our own correspondent)

Wenchow, March 9

Since last writing telegrams have been received here announcing the loss of one of the Chinese steamers which has been trading with this port from Ningpo with great regularity every week for several years.

Said to be an old gunboat, the Pingyang was the most comfortable of the three Ningpo steamers for travel. About a month ago she left Wenchow for Ningpo via Haimen and Chusan as usual on the Friday. A few days after, telegrams were received reporting her loss in the vicinity of Haimen, one to the effect that 200 lives were lost, another that while no lives were lost, pirates had looted her cargo.

A young Chinese told me that his brother had been among the passengers at the time of the accident, and had returned home. His report was that the vessel ran on the rocks in a fog some four or five hours out of Haimen, on the way to Ningpo, that two hours later she slid back and sank losing all cargo and baggage, but that no lives were lost as a great many small boats came and took the

NINGPO STEAMER WRECKED

Pingyang Piled Up on Haimen Rocks During Voyage from Wenchow: No Lives Lost

From Our Own Correspondent.

Wenchow, Mar. 9.

Since last writing telegrams have been received here announcing the loss of one of the Chinese steamers which has been trading with this port from Ningpo with great regularity every week for several years.

passengers and crew off. This is the second mishap within a short time that has happened to Ningpo steamers.

Rumour was current recently that the str. Kwangchi was to resume her sailings which had been dropped before the New Year, between Wenchow and Ningpo, she having been chartered last year from the China Merchants' S. N. Co. for the trade by another Chinese company. Friday, however, her usual day of arrival here, did not witness her arrival and it was said that she had lost $ 20000 last year, that if the other Ningpo companies would reimburse her to that amount she would not give up the trade, that the Yungchuan and Yungning companies were willing, but that the Pao Hua Co. refused. There has also been a rumour that a rival steamer of the China Merchants' was to start the run between Shanghai and Wenchow, but so far no such steamer has been forthcoming.

Pioneer Wenchow Missionary

The str. Feiching which has been laid up in Shanghai for overhauling during the past six weeks has resumed her sailings, and among her passengers will be Rev. W. R. and Mrs. Stobie, and Miss Stobie, who are returing to England by way of Canada. At the kind invitation of the Commissioner and his wife a large party of the foreign residents met at the home of the Commissioner on Tuesday evening to bid them formal bon voyage.

The Rev. A. H. Sharman, who succeeds Mr. Stobie in the Chairmanship of the Wenchow Methodist Mission, will for several mouths look after nearly 170 churches, besides superintending the rebuilding of churches destroyed in the typhoon of September, 1922. It is 27 years since Mr. Stobie and 23 years since Mrs. Stobie first arrived in Wenchow, and the former has seen the Mission increase in that time from about 90 to 270 churches, the erection of a large hospital and of a Middle School which has now enrolled 242 students under the able principalship of T. W. Chapman, M. S. , whose name as an educationalist is widely know among Chinese far beyond Wenchow and its adjoining prefectures. Over quarter of a century ago that middle school existed in embryo in the house of Mr. Stobie and consisted of a few Chinese boys gathered together to learn English among whom was a diligent and bright little fellow who is now Dr. Timothy Lear of Peking.

27 Years Ago and Today

Today the appearance of the city presents a marked contrast to 27 years ago in the widening of considerable portions of the main street, erection of very many foreign and semi – foreign buildings, mostly occupied by Chinese, the more foreign appearance of many of the shops the kind of merchandise offered for sale in those shops, foreign tinned goods, flour, foreign clothing and foot and headwear, foreign lamps, foreign tools, the large number of shops selling clocks and watches, and many another foreign articles which 27 years ago would have been "anathematized". "Hundreds of rieshas ply on its narrow streets, the electric light makes night more pleasant to the student of Chinese, telephone wires stretch through the air in all directions. Two different lines of telegraph now connect us with the world outside, so that no longer is it true to say, as an old resident said in those far off days of one who came to Wenchow describing the difficulty of getting away again, "One coming to Wenchow is as a frog in a well." Foreign style umbrellas too and even walking sticks are numerous, though there is still a good trade done in Kittysols. A merchant, who does a business in Kittysols of about 30000 exported annually told me yesterday that thousands of Kittysols are sent to America and that about 300000 are exported annually hence.

One of the greatest changes is to be seen in the street where I live, a change which 25 years ago it seemed impossible would come about so soon. Whereas then that little street was crowded with opium dens, to – day not one is to be found, though also opium does still find its way here and some opium smokers are still to be met with. But to one who has seen such a change as this, who has seen and known what a frightful incubus, what a dreadful curse and bondage this one habit was, and sees things now there comes inevitably the feeling of certainty that China can and that China will sooner or later and probably sooner, throw off her other weights and snap her other falters, and rise free and strong and kindly and noble to take the place that is awaiting her in the progress of the race to its destined heights of world wide, liberty, brotherhood and righteousness.

"Thefts in Wenchow Mission: Exciting Capture at Methodist College After Many Depredations," *The North - China Herald and Supreme Court & Consular Gazette*, May 17, 1924

Thefts in Wenchow Mission: Exciting Capture at Methodist College After Many Depredations

(From our own correspondent)

Wenchow, Chê., May 5

A series of thefts extending over a period of six months and aggregating a total value of nearly $500 culminated with the capture of the thief of a few days ago. The thief had the advantage of knowing the College from the inside, having been a student for a few months until he was expelled nearly four years ago. He has since been expelled from two other educational institutions. The time chosen for most of his depredations was service time on Sunday afternoons when all the students were absent from the dormitories. Then entering the students' rooms, he would take off his own outer garments and clothe himself in as many robes as he could conveniently carry, reassume his own outer robe and with as much money as he could lay his hand on quickly make good his escape.

His capture was rather dramatic. One of the teachers was making a search for missing articles and went into the assembly hall with a lantern. The thief evidently hearing him enter, stepped out of one of the windows on to the outer ledge and pulled the window after him. This was a very precarious position being only a few inches wide and at least 20 feet from the ground. Unfortunately for the thief the light inside threw his figure into relief and he was seen from another part of the College. After that his apprehension was only the matter of a few minutes. With 30 students who had suffered considerable loss and nearly 200 more of their sympathizers on his trail there was not much hope of escape. The accompaniment of noise might have led the uninitiated to think that a borde of bandits were attacking the city. The students enjoyed themselves immensely in their search for any accomplices, even going on to the roof with lanterns. The thief confessed all and the students finally consented to accept half the value of the stolen property from the father, a man in poor circumstances, and the thief was set free after three days in charge of the police.

Wenchow Consulate Closed

Wenchow has just had a visit from H. B. M. Consul, Mr. Handley Derry, who has been the guest of Mr. C. W. S. Williams, Commissioner of Customs. The Consulate here is about to pass into the hands of the Customs Service, which has already been renting the building for some years. We have had no resident Consul here since 1900, but there are still people in Wenchow who look upon the British Consulate, picturesquely situated upon Conquest Island, opposite the city, with gratitude as their place of refuge in that exciting year.

The Electricity Plant

It is with feelings of thankfulness that thousands of people in this city received the news of the arrival of the new electric light plant this week. The first plant was installed by Andersen, Meyer & Co. in 1912 and while the number of users was limited the light was very good indeed. The Chinese company that owns the plant however has for years been adding light after light until all have become so dim as to be of little value. The new plant—a 4000 kilowatt—will probably be large enough for some years to come. The plant is of German make and the cost $ 30000.

"H. M. S. Bluebell at Wenchow: First British Man – of – war in Port Since 1913: Safe Conduct for Salt," *The North – China Herald and Supreme Court & Consular Gazette*, July 5, 1924

H. M. S. Bluebell at Wenchow: First British Man – of – war in Port Since 1913: Safe Conduct for Salt

(From our own correspondent)

Wenchow, June 22

For the first time since 1913 the port of Wenchow had the honour of having a British gunboat in harbour for three days last week. After expecting her several times and being disappointed H. M. S. Bluebell came up the river last Thursday and cast anchor opposite the city. The city wall on the river side soon had its crowds of Chinese gazing at the unusual sight. During practically the whole of the gunboat's stay the weather was most unpropitious—over two inches of rain falling on one of the days—but in spite of that many of the foreigners of the port took advantage of the Commander's invitation to visit the ship. A football match was arranged for the members of the crew and although the ground was by no means in good condition the game was thoroughly enjoyed.

The occasion of the gunboat's visit was in connexion with the Salt Ga-

H.M.S. BLUEBELL AT WENCHOW

First British Man-of-war in Port Since 1913: Safe Conduct for Salt

FROM OUR OWN CORRESPONDENT.

Wenchow, June 22.

For the first time since 1913 the port of Wenchow had the honour of having a British gunboat in harbour for three days last week. After expecting her several times and being disappointed H.M.S. Bluebell came up the river last Thursday and cast anchor opposite the city.

belle. Fukien having taken charge of the salt revenues of that province, two laun-ches of the Salt Administration were in danger of being annexed by the Southern Party H. M. S. Bluebell (Commander Smithwick) was detailed as escort of the launches to a zone of safety. Probably partly on account of the action of the neigh-bouring province to the South, Wenchow is to be raised to the position of a sub – office of the Hangchow administration of the Salt Gabelle, with a foreigner in charge. Mr. Reiss, who is at present in charge, is visiting the outlying parts of the prefecture, but whether this is a substantive appointment or not is uncertain.

> "Autonomous Chekiang: The 'Constitution': No Votes for Women: Money and Brains Male Quali-fications," *The North – China Herald and Supreme Court & Consular Gazette*, July 12, 1924

Autonomous Chekiang: The "Constitution": No Votes for Women: Money and Brains Male Qualifications

Wenchow, Chê., June 30

The Draft Constitution for Autonomous Chekiang is causing considerable interest in Wenchow among businessmen and students. The Civil Governor's mandate for the election of three members from this prefecture to sit on the provisional deliberative council for five months has been obeyed. The Chambers of Commerce of the six

AUTONOMOUS CHEKIANG

The "Constitution": No Votes for Women: Money and Brains Male Qualifications

FROM OUR OWN CORRESPONDENT.

Wenchow, Chê., June 30.

The Draft Constitution for Autonomous Chêkiang is causing considerable interest in Wenchow among businessmen and students.

hsiens each choose two men and these 12 elected one of their number to represent them on the council. Mr. Tang Kang, President of Wenchow Chamber of Commerce, was elected. The Educational Association and the Agricultural Association proceeded in the same way and Mr. Hsu Te – ming and Mr. Tsai Kuan – fu, a former secretary of the Provincial Council, were also elected.

The new constitution seems to be thoroughly democratic in conception—all officials from the Governor down to the minor local men, are to be chosen by the people.

The franchise is not to be extended to women, much to the disappointment of a considerable number of women students. The qualifications for the franchise are very much the same as under the former régime—partly dependent on person's education and partly on his financial standing.

The Egregious Students

The shameful feature surrounding the resignation of the Principal of the 10th Chekiang Middle School is the method by which it has been brought a-bout. Former Wenchow students now living in Peking wrote many letters to the Peking and Shanghai Chinese newspapers point – out the unfitness of the man for his position. All the man's foibles and weaknesses were laid bare and he was told that the only decent thing for him to do was to resign. This being unavailing the same former students got some influence to bear on the provincial Board of Education and finally a resignation was extorted.

"Wenchow's Trade Held up by Bad Access： Customs' Recommendations for Much Needed Improvements and How to Find the Money," *The North – China Herald and Supreme Court & Consular Gazette*, August 9, 1924

Wenchow's Trade Held up by Bad Access： Customs' Recommendations for Much Needed Improvements and How to Find the Money

(From our own correspondent)

WENCHOW'S TRADE HELD UP BY BAD ACCESS

Customs' Recommendations for Much Needed Improvements and How to Find the Money

FROM OUR OWN CORRESPONDENT.

Wenchow, Chê., August 2

The rapidly increasing trade of Wenchow makes more and more evident the inadequate and undignified approaches to the North Gate, the five – turn approach into the city, the inadequate and insanitary condition of the river – front demand immediate attention. At times the North Gate entrance—incidentally also the fish market—is so full of cargo that it is with difficulty that the pedestrian can make his way from the city to post office, customs house or steamer.

The Customs authorities have suggested to the local officials that some structural improvements should be made and have suggested. (1) The improving of the North Gate jetty; (2) The making of a broad straight approach from the jetty into the city; (3) The improvement of the river front by more adequate bunding. These suggestions have been discussed by the District Council and considerable interest evidenced.

The chief question was how to raise the necessary funds. The Customs authorities made certain suggestions, the chief of which was a charge of 5 percent. of the duty exacted on imports and exports and offered to collect this at a charge of 5 percent. of the sum collected for expenses. A special Committee was appointed by the District Council to consider the whole matter and report. This Committee has made the following suggestions to the Council.

1. —The acquiring of private property, the work of building wharfs, and and the improving of the river front shall be undertaken by the Executive Committee. The Committee shall make suggestions which must be brought to the Council for sanction. In the matter of construction of the Customs' godown and bunding the river front the Executive Committee shall cooperate with the Commissioner of Customs.

2. —In the purchasing of private property the Executive shall estimate the value in accordance with the "Regulations for the acquiring of Private Property."

3. —Competitive estimates for the construction work shall be obtained and brought to the Council for consideration.

4. —The work shall commence when the collection of the proposed dues is carried out.

5. —The collection of the dues shall be delegated to the Customs authorities and an allowance of 5 percent. of the total collected be allowed for salaries and expenses.

6. —A charge shall be made on imported goods only. All exports shall be exempt.

7. —The money so collected shall not be used for any other purpose than city improvements.

When the Customs' report for the year 1923 is taken into consideration it is evident that after allowing for the usual fluctuations in trade, a sum of at least 50000 Hai – kwan taels could be obtained in five years, and in Wenchow great improvements could be made with such a sum, provided, of course, the money is spent on the improvements.

"Southern Chekiang and the War: Disposition to Meet Fukienese Invader: No Appetite for the Conflict," *The North – China Herald and Supreme Court & Consular Gazette*, September 27, 1924

Southern Chekiang and the War: Disposition to Meet Fukienese Invader: No Appetite for the Conflict

(From our own correspondent)

Wenchow, Chê., September 18

A strategic point on the Chekiang border was occupied by the Fukien troops under Gen. Sun Ch'uan – fang to their great advantage. It was hoped that this would be the position to be occupied by the first line of defence of the Chekiang troops, but Fukien got there first. Three lines of defence have been taken by the troops in this district. The first on the south bank of the river at Pingyanghsien, the second on the Flying Cloud river, on the south bank across from Juian city, and the third about 33 li from Wenchow on the main canal joining Wenchow and Juian. The number of soldiers on the three lines is, however, very few, probably not numbering more than 1500 altogether and the opposing force is no greater. There has been no battle up to the present.

The main part of the Fukien army has gone northwest to join issue with the Kiangsi troops and they have crossed the border of Chekiang in three places; at

Taishun on the way to Kinging, at Fuling or Pucheng on the way to Lung –
chuan and from the Kiangsi border towards Chuchowfu（衢州）. Whether the
object of the Fukien troops, who are on the way to Lungchuan, is to come
northeast on the way to Chuchow（處州）and thence to Wenchow or to turn
north to join the Kiangsi troops, is not known yet; the former is considered the
most likely.

Beyond a small number of gendarmerie, Wenchow city is without defend-
ers. If the Fukien troops break through the three lines of defence the local officials
have decided to give a gracious welcome to the new military officials.

War Chest Contributions

September 19

$ 15000 was contributed by Wenchow to the Chêkiang war chest 10 days a-
go. Yesterday a further request for $ 30000 was considered by the city fathers. It
was decided to offer $ 15000 now and another $ 15000 in a month. News is just
to hand that Lungchuan has been taken by the Fukien troops. But this must be received with a certain amount of reserve. News is also to hand hat the Kiangsi
troops are in possession of Chuchowfu but this also has not been confirmed; and
the Chekiang troops retiring to Kinhua.

There is a good deal of dissatisfaction felt in the south of Chekiang in regard
to Marshal Lu. He is not a Chekiang man and is fighting for his own hand and the
province is to suffer. The only soldiers in the south here are provincial soldiers,
none of the national army has been sent to offer any resistance to Fukien. By joining the Chihli party the officials and people feel that the province may be saved
from the horrors of war. It seems not unlikely therefore that the southern part of
Chekiang will throw in its lot with the Chihli party at no distant date.

Lu's Expulsion Well Received

September 20

From a state bordering on panic, the people of Wenchow were yesterday lifted to a state of rejoicing. From only thinking of places of refuge for themselves,
and places of security for their valuables, the minds of the people are once more
turned to buying and selling and the ordinary daily tasks. About 3. 30 yesterday
afternoon telegraphic news came through of the political change at Hangchow, of
a new provincial governor, a new tuchun and the casting forth of Marshal Lu.

Chekiang is to be saved the dire penalties of civil war and whether Marshal Lu is able to join Chang Tso – lin, taking with him the remnant of his army, or join forces with Sun Yat – sen, or retire into obscurity is of profound indifference to the majority of the people this district.

"News from the Outports: Wenchow Rejoicing too Soon: Arrival of the Fukienese Invader," *The North – China Herald and Supreme Court & Consular Gazette*, October 11, 1924

News from the Outports: Wenchow Rejoicing too Soon: Arrival of the Fukienese Invader

(From our own correspondent)

NEWS FROM THE OUTPORTS

WENCHOW REJOICING TOO SOON: ARRIVAL OF THE FUKIENESE INVADER

Southerners Ordered to March on "Independent" Taichow, Shao-hsing and Ningpo: The Press Gang at Work

FROM OUR OWN CORRESPONDENT.

Wenchow, Chê., Sept. 27.

The Wenchow people began to

and lastly, in the interval between the leaving of the Chêkiang troops

Southerners Ordered to March on "Independent" Taichow, Shaohsing and Ningpo: The Press Gang at Work

Wenchow, Chê. , September 18

The Wenchow people began to re-joice too soon.

Altho-ugh the news that both the Chekiang and Fukien sol-diers had orders to retire was true, it was soon evident that affairs were not to be arranged so easi-ly. The Sz Ling at Wenchow maintained that he had received no such orders from his superior officer and would continue to oppose the Fukien troops. All kinds of wild rumours again spread over the city and a further exodus of the people, chiefly women and children, began. It is estimated that fully seventenths of the people have fled. Certainly the place has a most deserted appearance and at times is like a city of the dead. The shops are mostly closed and shuttered and very few people are in the streets.

On the 22nd the Sz Ling issued a long proclamation. In this he indicated that he was simply maintaining a defensive attitude and was not acting in a treacherous manner. He spoke of bitter fights at Lungchuan and other places on the 14th and 15th instant and how they owed their defeat to the treachery of the people of the districts who gave the enemy all the information they could. The Sz Ling then went on to mention the cruelty and savagery of the Fukienese and their killing of the wounded. (N. B. All other reports speak most highly of the treatment of the people generally by the Fukienese troops) .

"Lungchuan was looted for three days. " the proclamation continues, "and Wu Fung – yen, a wicked fellow, has been appointed Magistrate. The people were ordered to pay $ 20000 a month for the expenses of the soldiers. This is a warning to those who have a mind to welcome the Fukieness soldiers. I have been incompetent. I am to be blamed, but I will be revenged for the humiliation. It is right, however, that you should know about the barbarities of Sun Chuan – fang's armies. "

Orders Not to Fight

Not long after the issue of this very interesting document Ha Sz Ling did receive his orders not to fight. Some difficulty has arisen because the Fukien soldiers on the south advanced one mile for every mile the Chekiang soldiers retired. This appeared too much like a defeat for the Chekiang soldiers and they wished to offer resistance, but found themselves in scarcely a position to do so. The machine – guns were found to have some part of their mechanism missing and were useless. The big guns they were afraid to use, as one had exploded at Chuchow and they were considered more dangerous to those behind them than to those in front. The Sz Ling is commandeering all the craft he can get to take the Chekiang troops away. Three steamer loads have already left, their destination being given as Haimen, Ningpo or Shanghai. Probably all will have left by tomorrow (September 30) and the Fukien troops will make an entry into the city. Pingyang was occupied two days ago, Juian is being occupied today and the 70 li from the latter place will be made today and tomorrow.

French and Japanese Gunboats

A French gunboat, the Craonne, arrived here on the 24th and its presence has done much to allay the fears of the people. A Japanese gunboat is expected to arrive today. The Captain of the Craonne has landed a guard for the protection of the French property in the city and has offered to do all he can to protect all other foreign property should the necessity arise.

There is no doubt that for some time the people here have been in a state bordering on panic. They feared three things; first that the Chekiang troops before they retired would make a demand for money which, if not met, would mean they would try and get it in loot; second, that the Fukien troops entering the city as a victorious army would be given the old – time privilege of three days' "freedom" before being called to order by their officers; and lastly, in the interval between the leaving of the Chekiang troops and the entry of the Fukien troops, the lawless element in the city, increased by all the bad characters in the district would try and loot the city. The special fear was of a secret society called locally the Ching Ong Poa（Clear Red Band）.

It was reported that over 2000 short daggers had been sold by one blacksmith and when the police in disguise visited the place they found 40 of these daggers. The black – smith was arrested and the daggers confiscated. The magistrate later sent word to all iron workers that anyone found making such weapons would be shot.

The Fukienese Arrival

September 29

By the evening of the 27th all the Chekiang troops with the exception of those who were disbanded because they had lost their guns and some who deserted—had left for the north. All the steam craft in the port had been commandeered and a peaceable exit was made. Preparations were then made for the welcoming of the Fukien troops. The barracks and temples that were to lodge the troops were decorated with flags and lanterns. A feast of 24 tables was prepared for the officers and a large number of pigs slaughtered for the feeding of the soldiery. By noon yesterday the troops began to arrive from Juian. Some came by boat and steam launch, but many marched the whole 70 li. The majority of them seemed ill – clothed, weary and miserable and had none of the appearance of a victorious army. After their arrival the city began once more to assume its usual aspect. Shops were opened, the people who had sought refuge in the churches and Red Cross centres returned to their homes. People appeared in the streets again and the general trend was citywards.

Panic and Press Gang Again

September 30

H. M. S. Hollyhock arrived in port at noon yesterday from Swatow. Capt. Peace together with the Commissioner of Customs called on the new military official, the Sz Ling, who assured them that everything would be done to insure the safety of foreign lives and property; that there was no further cause for alarm and that the city had now returned to its normal state. The day was not over, however, before things were very far from normal. News had been received that Taichow, Ningpo and Shaohsing had declared their independence of the Hangchow authority, and that the troops here were therefore to march on Taichow. Men are being impressed into service. Ricksha coolies and chairbearers have entirely disappeared from the streets! Some taken, some hiding in fear. Long gowns no longer insure safety. One method employed is to rip off the skirt of the long gown and thus transform the wearer into one available for service. There is not much doubt that many of the troops are opium – smokers and as opium is relatively cheap in Fukien there has been difficulty in supplying the demand for the drug here. The "long gowns" are often allowed to go free on the payment of a bribe which provides the means of obtaining opium. Later in the day the Sz Ling issued a proclamation saying the "press gang" had been at work without his sanction and he had issued orders that its work was to discontinue at once. At the same time the local authorities have promised to provide 500 carriers when the military authorities need them. The advance (to Taichow) is delayed pending orders.

"Ningshin Pirated off Wenchow：$ 80000 Haul of Sycee and Valuable Cargo：Ship Taken to Pirates' Lair," *The North – China Herald and Supreme Court & Consular Gazette*, October 11, 1924

Ningshin Pirated off Wenchow： $ 80000 Haul of Sycee and Valuable Cargo： Ship Taken to Pirates' Lair

NINGSHIN PIRATED OFF WENCHOW

$80,000 Haul of Sycee and Valuable Cargo: Ship Taken to Pirates' Lair

That the comparatively long spell of freedom from piracies on a large scale on the China coast does not mean that the pirates have gone out of business was rudely emphasized on Tuesday, when news was received in Shanghai of another daring attack, as successful as any previous piracy and accompanied, as is almost invariably the case, by bloodshed and loss of life.

That the comparatively long spell of freedom from piracies on a large scale on the China coast does not mean that the pirates have gone out of business was rudely emphasized on Tuesday, when news was received in Shanghai of another daring attack, as successful as any previous piracy and accompanied, as is almost invariably the case, by bloodshed and loss of life.

The latest victim is the San Peh S. N. Co's str. Ningshin, a vessel well – known in Shanghai and trading regularly between this port and Foochow and other places on the coast.

The Ningshin left Shanghai on Thursday last, under the command of Capt. Torgersen, with a large number of passengers, a considerable amount of cargo and a quantity of sycee, all for Foochow. The voyage was without incident until Friday when, as the vessel was approaching Wenchow, 34 pirates, who had shipped as passengers, took charge of the ship and made prisoner most of the crew, including the master and chief officer, both foreigners, and all of the bona fide passengers.

The pirates tool complete charge of the ship, which was navigated to Bias Bay, a notorious pirate strong – hold and rendezvous not far from Hongkong, where 30 chests of sycee, some mails, consignment of piece goods and a considerable amount of booty which had been taken from the helpless passengers, was landed. Having got their booty safely ashore, the pirates abandoned the Ningshin, which made for Amoy, at which port she is stated to have arrived on Tuesday. She was expected to arrive at Foochow on Wednesday and no doubt will be back in Shanghai in a day or two.

Quartermaster Killed

No first – hand information is yet available, but there seems to be no doubt that, when the pirates first attacked the ship, some sort of resistance was shown by the crew, and that in the ensuing struggle a Chinese quartermaster was killed and another Chinese sailor wounded. The pirates would, as usual, be well armed.

The value of the booty secured by the pirates is not definitely known in Shanghai at present. It is understood that the loss in sycee alone amounts to about $ 80000, which is covered by insurance, while, according to one telegram which has been received privately, the pirates' total haul is in excess of $ 150000.

A rumour is current that some members of the crew of the Ningshin were working in collusion with the pirates, but this will not be possible of confirmation or otherwise till the ship returns to Shanghai.

The Ningshin is a typical China coast vessel of about 2000 tons. She was specially built to withstand the heavy weather that is met with in the China Seas, and is stated to have been owned originally by the Hongkong, Canton & Macao Steamboat Co. , of Hongkong. She was acquired by the San Peh Co. some six years ago, when she underwent structural alterations to conform to the requirements of trade between Shanghai and Foochow.

"Anti – Opium Move in Chekiang: High Sounding Resolutions and Huge Processions: Will They Check the Smoking," *The North – China Herald and Supreme Court & Consular Gazette*, December 20, 1924

Anti – Opium Move in Chekiang: High Sounding Resolutions and Huge Processions: Will They Check the Smoking

(From our own correspondent)

Wenchow, Chekiang, December 11

A great Anti – Opium Crusade has been carried on for some time now in Wenchow. Since the advent of the Fukien Troops opium smoking has been on the increase and it was felt by many responsible persons—both native and foreign that something should be done to check the growing evil. All interested were asked to meet together at a small hall opening on to one of the Mission compounds in the city to consider ways and means. This was the beginning of the "Resist the Poison" Society the local branch of the Anti – Opium Society. Several meetings have been held and a large number of rules and regulations drawn up, of which the following are the most important:

Purpose. To prohibit the planting and growing of opium. To stop all import, export and smoking of same.

ANTI-OPIUM MOVE IN CHEKIANG

High Sounding Resolutions and Huge Processions: Will They Check the Smoking

FROM OUR OWN CORRESPONDENT.

Wenchow, Chêkiang, Dec. 11.

A great Anti-Opium Crusade has been carried on for some time now in Wenchow. Since the advent of the Fukien Troops opium smoking has been on the increase and it was felt by many responsible persons—both native and foreign that something should be done to check the growing evil. All interested were

Duties 1. Thorough investigation of all conditions in regard to the drug.

2. Propaganda by means of public speeches, newspaper articles, circulars and pamphlets.

3. Bringing all possible influence to bear on local authorities to prohibit the growth and use of opium.

4. Co – operation with the Central Association in Shanghai.

Members' Pledge. Members promise:

1. Not to be involved in any way with the growth, sale, export, import, manufacture or smoking of opium.

2. To do all in their power to persuade others to dissociate themselves entirely with the drug.

3. To help organize other Anti – Opium Societies in other places.

4. To help in the investigation of conditions and influence and report to the Society.

Funds. Funds are to be contributed voluntarily by Officers and Members.

On Sunday, December 7, the Society organized a monster Procession. It is estimated that over 3000 took part. Hundreds of small flags with suitable mottoes were carried and leaflets distributed. Drum and fife bands and bugles supplied the necessary music. From a spectacular point of view and from the point of view of organization there is no doubt that it was a great success.

Many speeches have been made, many characters written, much paper used, many miles walked and much tea drunk, but one wonders whether the results will be at all commensurate with the amount of energy and time expended in the formation of the society.

"Poppies not Grown in Chekiang: Encouraging Report from Wenchow: Trade Improved and Fewer Bandits," *The North – China Herald and Supreme Court & Consular Gazette*, March 28, 1925

Poppies not Grown in Chekiang: Encouraging Report from Wenchow: Trade Improved and Fewer Bandits

(From our own correspondent)

Wenchow, Chê., March 20

Previous to 1915 Wenchow was a great opium – growing district. Vast areas in all the hsiens comprising the Prefecture could be seen at this period of the year covered with the poppy.

It is worth recording that go where one will; along waterways; across plains and valleys; or the less frequented tracts amongst the innumerable hills of this part of Chekiang not one sign of opium growing can be found. For 10 years this district has been loyal to the edict forbidding its growth, and there are no indications that the farmers will revert to its growing.

Wheat is now grown in ever increasing quantities; and this year's spring crop is promising to be a good one.

Opium smuggling goes on apace Fukien province is credited with being the chief area of supply. The fact has to be stated that there are many employed in this traffic, and a vast number of people addicted to the drug. The Wenchow Anti –

POPPIES NOT GROWN IN CHEKIANG

Encouraging Report from Wenchow: Trade Improved and Fewer Bandits

FROM OUR OWN CORRESPONDENT.

Wenchow, Chê., Mar. 20.

Previous to 1915 Wenchow was a great opium-growing district. Vast areas in all the *hsiens* comprising the Prefecture could be seen at this period of the year covered with the poppy.

Opium Association is proving itself to be something more than a name, and has secured support from all the officials and leading gentry.

Within the last two months, new officials have been appointed to every yamên in this city. It may be significant of the times that these new appointments are merely "acting." Co – incident with these changes has come a period of greater confidence in peace, resulting in many signs of business activity and increased prosperity. The rivers and canals are free from acts of piracy, and the hill districts from banditti.

Our port still ranks as a minor. Its progress is slow, but sure. Last year's Customs returns show a further increase in revenue, and given a continuance of peace, there is no reason why trade returns should not steadily increase.

The Salt Gabelle authorities have decided to make Taichow and Wenchow a separate district for administrative purposes. Hitherto there has been the one administrative centre for Chekiang province at Hangchow. I understand that Wenchow has been chosen as the new centre.

After a period of 10 years, the Chekiang Federation Council's annual meetings will be held this year in Wenchow. It has been arranged for the Council to open its sessions on April 24, and it is expected that its business will be completed by the 27th.

"A Popular Official of Wenchow: Deputy Commissioner of Customs Transferred to Ningpo," *The North – China Herald and Supreme Court & Consular Gazette*, April 25, 1925

A Popular Official of Wenchow: Deputy Commissioner of Customs Transferred to Ningpo

(From our own correspondent)

Wenchow, Chê., April 14

After three years residence in this port as Deputy Commissioner of Customs, Mr. C. A. S. Williams left to – day to take up his new appointment as Chief of the Ningpo staff.

In this land of comings and goings, it is no little thing that an official should gain high esteem and sincere respect from all classes of the community. The sincerity of the regrets of both Chinese and foreign residents was very marked; and rarely has one witnessed such a genuine and hearty "send off" as Mr. Williams got to – day. This port has made steady progress during the past three years, and has been fortunate in having an official of the type of Mr. Williams during this period. Mr. Bernadski, of the Nanking Customs, is appointed Acting Commissioner for Wenchow, and is expected to take up his appointment during the present month.

Other changes in the Wenchow staff are: Mr. Camiade for home leave, and Mr. Coxall transferred to Yochow.

A POPULAR OFFICIAL OF WENCHOW

Deputy Commissioner of Customs Transferred to Ningpo

FROM OUR OWN CORRESPONDENT.

Wenchow, April 14.

After three years residence in this port as Deputy Commissioner of Customs, Mr. C. A. S. Williams left to-day to take up his new appointment as Chief of the Ningpo staff.

"Church Work in Chekiang: Chekiang Christian Federation Council Meetings in Wenchow," *The North – China Herald and Supreme Court & Consular Gazette*, May 16, 1925

Church Work in Chekiang: Chekiang Christian Federation Council Meetings in Wenchow

(From a Correspondent)

CHURCH WORK IN CHEKIANG

Chekiang Christian Federation Council Meetings in Wenchow

FROM A CORRESPONDENT

It may be suggested that Federation and Comity are not prominent these days in the programme of Protestant Missions in China as they were 20 years ago, without the implication being made that they have not a very real place in the polity of most Christian Missions.

The advocacy of Dr. Cochrane has borne much good fruit, especially since the Shanghai Conference of 1907. A more friendly co – operation between Missions has been in evidence for many years which has tended to greater efficiency, absence of overlapping, and a steady extension of church activities.

The province of Chekiang has been one of the loyal upholders of the Federation Movement, and year by delegates have assembled in various cities for conference.

Eleven years ago Wenchow had the pleasure of entertaining the Council, and on April 24 of the present year this old world city once more was the place of meeting. Twenty – five delegates were present, representing the following socie-ties: C. M. S. , Presbyterian North, Baptist North, London Mission, C. I. M. , and United Methodist Church Mission.

Three Strenuous Sessions

It was a disappointment to the local committee that a greater test of Wenchow hospitality was not called for. At a welcome meeting, held in the U. M. C. Mission compound on the evening of April 23, the visitors were made to feel quite at home. The following morning, the Council settled down to business entailing three strenuous sessions each day, Friday and Saturday; and a closing meeting on Monday, April 27. The retiring President, the Rev – Nyi Liang – ping (C. M. S.) gave an inspiring address in opening the Conference, after which the election of officers resulted in the following being elected: President, the Rev. J. W. Heywood, U. M. C. M. ; Vice – president, the Rev. Nia Ts – shi, Presbyt. N. Secretaries, (Chinese) Yin Ji – shung; (English) Rev. A. A. Coni-bear. Treasurer, Rev. Bau Tsih – ching, Bapt. N.

The Treasurer's report revealed the finances of the Council to be in a healthy condition. New and amended rules were agreed upon, the most important being the change of name to "The Chekiang Christian Church Association"; meetings to be held every two years, and not annually as hithertofore; and restricted num-ber of delegates from affiliated missions.

Questions dealing with such problem as ancestral property and rights; opi-um, church, property, and the anti – Christian movement in the province, were dealt with at length and in a marked spirit of toleration.

The Church More Chinese

Perhaps one of the most interesting and most closely debated subjects was a resolution introduced by one of the Chinese delegates on "the Church in China becoming more Chinese in both doctrine and polity. " The discussion revealed that whilst in externals many changes were desirable and would probably be effec-ted in due time, the essentials of the Christian religion would remain the same. No vote was taken on this question, which was debated with openness and fairness by both Chinese and foreign representatives. The pulpits of the C. I. M. , and U. M. C. M. in Wenchow city were occupied on the Sunday morning by ap-pointed delegates; and in the afternoon a united meeting of city Christians, numbering over 1000 was held in the city church of the U. M. C. M. and over 800 students and teachers listened to a cultured address given by the Rev. Bau Tsih – ching at the English Methodist College.

The social side of the conference was not neglected, two garden parties and two Chinese feasts providing that easement from conference atmosphere which is so much appreciated by the average delegate.

The Wenchow Council meeting was a success in every way, and will prove a challenge to Hangchow where the next meeting will be held in 1927.

> "Level – Headed Wenchow: Utter Failure of Newspapers and Agitators to Stir Mob Passion," *The North – China Herald and Supreme Court & Consular Gazette*, June 12, 1926

Level – Headed Wenchow: Utter Failure of Newspapers and Agitators to Stir Mob Passion

(From our own correspondent)

Wenchow, June 2

May 30, so far as this outport is concerned, proved to be one of the quietest and most peaceful days of the past 12 months. Many rumours and forecasts of what was to happen on this date had been prevalent during the month and seeds of distrust and hatred had been profusely sown by the native press, and by speeches week by week; but somehow these efforts seemed to bear very little fruit.

Official Restraint

Several reasons may be assigned for this comparative failure to stir up mob passion. First of all it is only fair to acknowledge the temper and attitude of the local officials as being emphatically for peace and goodwill. They have given rein to the young student class, but have never ceased to

LEVEL-HEADED WENCHOW

Utter Failure of Newspapers and Agitators to Stir Mob Passion

FROM OUR OWN CORRESPONDENT

Wenchow, June 2.

May 30, so far as this outport is concerned, proved to be one of the quietest and most peaceful days of the past 12 months. Many rumours and forecasts of what was to happen on this date had been prevalent during the month and seeds of distrust and hatred had been profusely sown by the native press, and by speeches week by week; but somehow these efforts seemed to bear very little fruit.

govern and restrain at the right time. Their policy has been one of allowing a certain amount of "steam" to escape believing it would conduce to safety.

A second reason for our immunity from serious local troubles may be found in the increased prosperity of shopkeepers and traders generally within the city during the past 12 months.

There are many outward and visible signs of this in all parts of the city. The umbrella trade has had a boom year. The leather – bag industry has become a huge one. While living costs have considerably advanced, there has not seemed any money stringency amongst the people. Good trade is undoubtedly one great influence in preserving the peace of a Chinese city.

Then, it is due to the Wenchowese to acknowledge their level – headedness. They have a good record of over 40 years without an anti – foreign riot. The leading gentry and the heads of various Guilds give a good lead to the people in inciting to peace and in pursuing it.

...

The wheat crop has been safely harvested and proved a good one in all districts. The rice fields are now gloriously green with promising young stalks which show that a good beginning of this all important cereal crop has been made.

H. M. S. Petersfield arrived here on May 20, and left for Ningpo before noon on May 30.

"News from the Outports: North and South at Wenchow," *The North – China Herald and Supreme Court & Consular Gazette*, March 19, 1927

News from the Outports: North and South at Wenchow

(From our own correspondent)

Wenchow

This Treaty Port has had the experience of being "host" to both Northern and Southern troops, and incidentally has found it to be a very heavy burden financially. The levies ma-de upon this city and district will come not far short of $ 1000000.

This, for the time being, has been regarded as an insurance against the more costly, and disastrous losses that fighting and looting would cause, and has more or less, been given without grumbling, except in the cases of certain wealthy men who have found the glint of the bayonet to be more persuasive than the glitter of their silver.

Northerners' Good Conduct

The coming of the Northern troops was the signal for a great exodus of the people, so well had propaganda done its work to instil fear and distrust in all that was associated with the name of Sun Chuan – fang. Some 18000 men were billeted in Wenchow during a period of 14 days, but caused little trouble beyond making shop assistants and food caterers work a little harder, for which they paid quite

NEWS FROM THE OUTPORTS

NORTH AND SOUTH AT WENCHOW

Peace and Well Behaved Soldiers Under Northern Troops: Violence and Seizure of Buildings Under Southern:

FROM OUR OWN CORRESPONDENT

Wenchow. This Treaty Port has had the ex-

found it more healthy to live away from his home: of which the sequel will be found below.

as generously as the average peaceful citizen. They scrupulously respected all foreign persons and property, and did not interfere with the varied work carried on by the Missions. During their occupation of the city, the local Student Association and the Kuomintang leaders ceased their bitter tirades against all British plus Sun Chuan – fang, and took a well earned holiday. This quietness and peace were as deceptive as the centre of a typhoon.

The Northerners departed for Taichow and Ningpo, and the Chinese refugees returned to their homes.

Lying Out – Lied

The local "Reds" with renewed strength after their vacation began once more their propaganda, and even out – lied their previous lies! The Southerners were coming. With their advent would be ushered in the Millennium. Rice would be obtainable 30 ching for the dollar. No one would be short of money. The revenues be short of money. The revenues of both foreign and native Customs would be placed at the disposal of the people. There would be no rich, for all would have a common purse. And to emphasize these "truths" the energetic speechifiers put up caricatures of Marshal Sun and the hated foreignner and fired shots at them. Get rid of these enemies, and all these things so speciously promised would be realized.

What wonder the people longed for the coming of the "Southern" troops, despite the fact that they were truly "Northern" men who had turned traitors in the adjoining province of Fukien?

There was no exodus when the first hundred arrived. Flags galore greeted the advent of the 17th. Division of the People's Army as they arrived day by day by land and sea. Then were seen the usual corps of trained agitators and propagandists with their loads of printed matter. Every vacant wall, telegraph, and electric standard were covered with their unscrupulous statements and inflammatory incitements. Vile pictorial posters greeted the eye on the main streets. Speeches in mass meeting and on the streets became more anti – foreign and anti – Christian.

A So – called Christian Preacher

Incitement to murder was not lacking. To the everlasting disgrace of one prominent speaker who claims to be a Christian preacher and a member of the N. C. C. , it is creditably reported that he called upon his hearers "to knife to

the bone" a well – known local citizen who had long been a member of the Chekiang Provincial Council. This Councillor was warned, and found it more health-
ily to live away from his home: of which the sequel will be found below.

The outcome of all this was the commandeering of the College and schools of
the United Methodist Church: their city church and Sunday school: and also the
church and Girls' School of the China Inland Mission for the purpose of billeting
soldiers. This, despite the fact that only 3000 troops were then in the city, and
the Northerners had previously found ample accommodation in Chinese buildings
when numbering over 10000.

Some Missionaries Removed

Before this plain warning was given that the position of foreigners was likely
to become untenable, 10 men, women and children of the missionary community
had left the port. Despite an assurance given to the Commissioner of Customs by
Gen Tsao Wan – shun of the 17th Division that "all foreign residents at Wenchow
would be fully protected by him, and that no churches, schools and private residences which were under the control of foreigners would be occupied by soldiers," it was considered the wiser policy for the members of the U. M. Church,
and the C. I. M. to withdraw for a time. In all, 23 adults and six children have
left Wenchow, all being British subjects with the exception of four Ameri-
cans. Dr. Stedeford and Dymond of the U. M. Church Mission decided to carry on
as long as possible their fine hospital work. For the last few years over 40000 patients have been treated annually. Further, as port doctor, Dr. Stedeford considered it his duty to stand by the Customs staff.

So long as Gen. Tsao remained in Wenchow …, the city remained fairly
quiet. At the end of February, the General left for Taichow and Ningpo, leaving
only a few hundred soldiers in the city.

Mob Law At Once

On March 4, the Kuomintang held a big mass meeting which was intensely
anti – British. Overthrowing the Customs, boycotting British goods, stopping all
Mission work, and denunciation of Tsie Hue – sang — the Provincial Councillor —
were the subjects of their agitation. Afterwards a procession went around the city.
They stopped outside the Customs House and broke a few fanes of glass and the
gate, but they were stopped from going further by their leaders. At the Native

Customs they broke a lot of furniture and assaulted the Chinese Assistant. Another lot composed mainly of workmen and coolies, went to the Councillor's house and literally smashed it up. The furniture was broken into small pieces, and all clothing torn to shreds; the doors, windows, and all woodwork were torn down, even to the roof. The mob came without any warning and the family escaped by the back door.

Further, the whole city was placarded with incitements to "overthrow" the Christians and their "foreign religion."

That further trouble was brewing seemed almost certain from the action taken by the mob on March 4.

The foreigners still residing in Wenchow are: the two doctors, two married and two single members of the Customs Staff and one Catholic Sister (British): two married American Missionaries and three children: the Commissioner of Customs (Mr. Bernadsky) his wife and six children, and two Russian lady helpers: and several French Catholic Missionaries and Sisters.

"Clearing Wenchow of Communists: Chinese Authorities Active Against Radicals," *The North - China Herald and Supreme Court & Consular Gazette*, April 23, 1927

Clearing Wenchow of Communists: Chinese Authorities Active Against Radicals

Shanghai, April 19

According to a Wenchow telegram dated April 17, received in Shanghai this morning, the Chinese authorities there are endeavouring to clear the town of radical elements and have arrested several communists belonging to the Kuomintang Provincial Headquarters and the General Labour Union.

The telegram adds that 24 Japanese, including 10 women and children, and 30 Formosans reside in the town at present. Toho.

CLEARING WENCHOW OF COMMUNISTS

Chinese Authorities Active Against Radicals

Shanghai, Apr. 19.

According to a Wenchow telegram dated April 17, received in Shanghai this morning, the Chinese authorities there are endeavouring to clear the town of radical elements and have arrested several communists belonging to the Kuomintang Provincial Headquarters and the General Labour Union.

"The Bolshevizing of Wenchow: Determined Effort on Carefully Prepared Line of Action: Poison Well Implanted," *The North – China Herald and Supreme Court & Consular Gazette*, May 14, 1927

The Bolshevizing of Wenchow: Determined Effort on Carefully Prepared Line of Action: Poison Well Implanted

Some six years ago, the writer was confidently asked to make inquiries throughout the Wenchow district, as to whether there was any evidence of Bolshevik teaching or influence amongst the Wenchowese. One must confess that such a request caused not only surprise but a measure of amusement. With over 30 years' intercourse with all classes of people, the idea that there was any likelihood of good soil being found in the cities and country towns and villages of the old prefecture was about the last which would present itself. Nevertheless, an investigation on the lines suggested would be worth while, if only to confirm one's faith in the futility of any such movement gaining a hold on a people who had impressed the alien in their midst as being of the peaceable, contented and industrious order.

...

Russian Bribery

The growth of the movement in this section of southeast Chekiang, as known by one observer, may be of interest and possibly may enlighten some of the darkened minds which still refuse to admit the agency of Moscow in the present upheaval in China. A few months previous to May 30, 1925, evidence that Bolshevik propaganda was finding recruits in Wenchow city was not lacking. One of the three native newspapers changed its policy, and, finding official indifference to its pronouncements a safeguard, gradually assumed its place as an out – and – out advocate of Russian methods. ···

By the middle of June, 1925, a more open advocacy of Soviet policies boldly was being proclaimed. What had been done secretly hitherto to began to be published at street corners and through the agency of innumerable pamphlets. ···

The Gentle N. C. C.

It was at this time that your correspondent was told with a tone of certitude by a Chinese, a member of the N. C. C. that it would not be long before expropriation of all foreign property would take place. Further, he was kind enough to inform me that the horrors of the Boxer year would pale in comparison with the sufferings which would come upon all those connected with the British and all British Christian churches! That he was out to do his best to accomplish these results, numerous pamphlets from his pen, which were broadcast in walled cities, towns and villages, testify beyond doubt. Needless to state, he had to resign his position as pastor, but it is an irony of the constitution of the N. C. C. that he remained as "honourable" member of that important Council.

Yui Ji – sung, the man referred to, became a Red of the Reds; and in passing it is interesting to note that at the present time a reward of $ 100 is offered for his arrest by those who are endeavouring to clean up Wenchow extremists.

The Bolshevik Strategy

The procedure pursued in Bolshevizing the Wenchow district may be stated under the follwing heads:

I. The Students' Association was captured by specious promisses and a mixture of perfervid Nationalist appeals and the seductions of the Muscovite Utopia.

II. Youngsters were incited to rebellion against their parents. Leninism was of far greater importance than the teaching of Confucius.

III. Canton became the Mecca of these students. Great numbers were induced to enter the Whampoa Military Academy, not merely for the military training, but to become experts in Bolshevik propaganda. Many of these youths had no future before them other than positions which would be worth $10 to $20 per month, whereas they were assured of all expenses paid for 13 months, and the promise of being sent back to their native places as young Mandarins, with salaries ranging from $50 to $150 per month. "The Wenchow man never moves" was a saying not long ago. It can no longer be said of the Wenchowese for, apart from the foregoing, there is another fact which gives one "furiously to think," and which may well come under the next heading:

Ⅳ. Moscow has taken the place of Canton in the affections of many Wenchowese. Take these two evidences out of many which might be given: In the Tsingtienhsien alone, over 1000 men, mostly agriculturists, have gone to Russia; one village, totalling 52 families, has 48 of its menfolk in the delectable land. Last year, a young farmer had to borrow $300 to pay his expenses to Moscow. Within six months, the loan was repaid, and, further, he was able to remit $400 to his family with the promise of several hundred more before the end of the year. And the powers that be in Peking are just awaking to the significance of this drift over their border!

Ⅴ. One other indication of the growth of Bolshevism in the Wenchow district needs to be recorded. For the past two years there has been the quiet penetration of villages by groups of two or four men, whose mission it has been to prepare the soil for the definite founding of Peasants' Unions.

······

"Raid on Communists at Wenchow: Arrest of Teachers and Students in United Methodist Church College:
One Executed" *The North – China Herald and Supreme Court & Consular Gazette*, June 11, 1927

Raid on Communists at Wenchow: Arrest of Teachers and Students in United Methodist Church College: One Executed

(From our own correspondent)

Wenchow. June 1

With secrecy and suddenness, over 100 soldiers were ordered to raid the United Methodist Church College on May 21, for the purpose of rooting out Communistic activities.

The search lasted from 4 p. m. to 11 p. m. , and resulted in the arrest of five teachers and students. The Principal was away from the city, and so escaped arrest.

The following day the five men were brought up for trial. Four of the prisoners were released; but a young student named Tsa Ning – gyi, a native of the market town Doa'o Chian was shot at 10 p. m.

Needless to state, the College has been evacuated both teachers and students of the "Ao Hoe School" who had been in forceful occupancy for three months.

It is interesting to note that the seizure and occupancy of Mission Colleges and Churches are not proving in some cases, to be quite as "glorious" as was anticipated by a certain section of the Nationalists.

RAID ON COMMUNISTS AT WENCHOW.

Arrest of Teachers and Students in United Methodist Church College: One Executed

FROM OUR OWN CORRESPONDENT

Wenchow. June 1.

With secrecy and suddenness, over 100 soldiers were ordered to raid the United Methodist Church College on May 21, for the purpose of rooting out Communistic activities.

To be proscribed and a price put on one's arrest after such a proof of hatred of the foreigner; let alone the risk of having to face a firing squad at all hours of the day and night must be rather disturbing. It must be a very minor matter of disillusionment for some of these youthful confiscators to find the financial burden to be too heavy, and so they must "close down" as is reported to be the case at the Ningpo Methodist College!

A new kind of recruiting has come into action. Conscription of young lads of 15 or 16 years of age is being enforced. When the str. Hoean left Wenchow on her last trip, she had 300 young recruits on board, in mufti, who were duly shepherded on arrival at the Kinleeynen Wharf, and taken to the city.

"In Wenchow after Seven Months: No Anti – Foreign Bitterness, Thanks to Evacuation of Port,"
The North – China Herald and Supreme Court & Consular Gazette, October 1, 1927

In Wenchow after Seven Months: No Anti – Foreign Bitterness, Thanks to Evacuation of Port

(From our own correspondent)

Shanghai, September 23

The following report upon conditions in Wenchow has been compiled by our correspondent who recently paid a visit to the port after an absence of seven months.

Very little first – hand news has been possible from this outport during the past seven months owing to the withdrawal of most of the foreign residents during this period. For one considerable portion of this time, apart from a few Japanese it may be, there were no foreigners resident in Wenchow. Missionaries, merchants, and Customs staff, all had left the port.

The wisdom of leaving this place for a time cannot be questioned as it has made possible a return without bitterness, and without any very serious incident to liquidate. Despite all the propaganda of extremists and Wenchow had more than its fair share of their incitements the bona fide inhabitants of the city were not won over to rabid anti foreignism. It can justly be said of them that they maintained the good name they have had for many years.

The Black Months

March and April were the black months. Official authority was usurped by

IN WENCHOW AFTER
SEVEN MONTHS

No Anti-Foreign Bitterness,
Thanks to Evacuation of Port

FROM OUR WENCHOW CORRESPONDENT

Shanghai, Sept. 23.

The following report upon conditions in Wenchow has been compiled by our correspondent who recently paid a visit to the port after an absence of seven months.

various committees and unions. Then followed a period of gradual suppression of "wild men." Some were shot; others were imprisoned; and many sought safety in Ningpo and Shanghai. Churches which had been sealed or taken possession of by unions or mushroom schools, were handed back to the missions and services were once more regularly held.

The fine middle school of the United Methodist Church Mission is, however, still occupied by a rival school whose main reason for such occupation is that if they do not take possession of the buildings some other school will! This school was raided last June by troops seeking evidences of Bolshevik propaganda. Several teachers and students were arrested, and after investigation, one student was executed. Despite this, the same lot of teachers are in possession of the college buildings and the Principal's house. The latter has been practically looted by these so – called eductionists. Many non – chritstian Chinese regret this blot on the city's good name, for none of the missionary compounds have been occupied or the houses looted.

Outwardly Peaceful

Conditions in the city these days are outwardly peaceful. The country people come in freely with their produce, and all the shops are open and seem to be doing a fair business. Reports of the rice crops are not good. The prospects for the autumn crop being up to average are poor. Already rice has had to be imported, and prices have advanced.

Local banditti are having an innings. Almost every hsien is suffering from this pest. The people from the hill – districts say the robbers are local men and not ex-soldiers.

Very few troops are stationed in the city. At the present time, three parties are recognized as having authority in the city and district, viz: The local Nationalist Committee; the Peasants' Union; and the Workers' Union.

If conditions continue to improve, it is hoped that Consular permission will be given to live in the port.

"Conditions Peaceful in Wenchow: Arrival of Troops and Equally Hurried Departure," *The North - China Herald and Supreme Court & Consular Gazette*, October 15, 1927

Conditions Peaceful in Wenchow: Arrival of Troops and Equally Hurried Departure

(From our own correspondent)

Wenchow, October 4

Two or three weeks ago, we were able to report that very few troops were stationed in Wenchow or its near neighbourhood. Wednesday, and Thursday of last week, however, saw the arrival of 3000 soldiers who had mostly come from up river. The district from which they had been drafted was Chuchow. (Chê.) They arrived in Wenchow with every sign of a hurried and rough journey. The China Merchants' steamer, Haean which happened to be in port, and two Ningpo boats, the Pingyang and the Yungning, were commandeered by the military authorities. Tt was reported that Foochow was the place where the troops were being sent; but to the mystery of many people, Ningpo was their destination.

Seventeen hundred were crowded on the Haean, and the rest on the two small coasters. They left Wenchow on Friday morning, and arrived in Ningpo Saturday where they were disembarked.

There does not appear to be any special need for these troops in Ningpo, as conditions are so favourable and quiet as to allow the return of all former residents. Some of the men seemed to be sure that their ultimate destination would be Hangchow.

CONDITIONS PEACEFUL IN WENCHOW

Arrival of Troops and Equally Hurried Departure

FROM OUR OWN CORRESPONDENT

Wenchow, Oct. 4.

Two or three weeks ago, we were able to report that very few troops were stationed in Wenchow or its near neighbourhood. Wednesday

For the time being, the two boats which the China Merchants' S. S. Co. have been regularly running to Wenchow, are held up in Shanghai by a strike of go-down coolies.

Conditions in Wenchow continue to be peaceful. One of the leading scholars in the city declared the other day that the local people had "lost face" by driving out the foreign residents; and that they desired them to return.

"Conditions in Wenchow," *The North – China Herald and Supreme Court & Consular Gazette*, October 22, 1927

Conditions in Wenchow

To the Editor of the "North – China Daily News."

SIR, In your esteemed paper (either September 22, 23, or 24.) I have read with pleasure some lines about Wenchow. It was said that, owing to the departure of all Europeans, this port had remained peaceful for seven months. It is quite true

CONDITIONS IN WENCHOW

To the Editor of the
" NORTH-CHINA DAILY NEWS."

SIR,—In your esteemed paper (either September 22, 23, or 24.) 1 have read with pleasure some lines about Wenchow. It was said that, owing to the departure of all Europeans, this port had remained peaceful for seven months. It is

that, from Easter untill the middle of May, they were of foreigners in Wenchow, some Japanese excepted: all had left for Shanghai. But I am surprised your correspondent (an old Wenchow resident, I suppose) ignores that from that date three European Fathers from the Catholic mission had returned there. They were soon followed by six European Sisters of Charity, who immediately took up their work in the Jean – Gabriel Hospital and in the Municipal Orphanage. It is needless to say that the population was sympathetic, and since our return I have never heard a hostile word.

In the interior of Wenchow (the region of Chuchow), I have been told that the German or Swiss missionaries of the C. I. Mission remained at their post. A Spanish Father belonging to the Catholic Canadian Mission refused to leave, and the other four fathers returned to Chuchow after an absence of a month and a half.

Your worthy correspondent affirms also that all the churches have been occupied: it is true that some of them were used, for some time, for union clubs, etc. , but so far, the Catholic Church, College and its premises have remained unoccupied. We trust the same peaceful conditions will continue.

I am etc. ,

J. Prost.

Wenchow, October 6, 1927.

"United Methodist Mission College, Wenchow," *The North – China Herald and Supreme Court &*
Consular Gazette, September 15, 1928

United Methodist Mission College, Wenchow

UNITED METHODIST MISSION COLLEGE, WENCHOW

This fine building has been illegally occupied by a Chinese school
for more than a year and a half. Despite urgent orders from
Nanking and Hangchow, the Wenchow city magistrate declines
to assist in making restitution.

This fine building has been illegally occupied by a Chinese school for more
than a year and a half. Despite urgent orders from Nanking and Hangchow,
the Wenchow city magistrae declines to assist in making restitution.

Wenchow Scoffs at Authority: Mission Premises which Magistrate Refuses to Allow Missionaries to Use: Home of a Communist School

In spite of repeated assurances by officials of the local government and
Nanking that the Nyie Vang College and principal's house of the United Methodist
Mission in Wenchow would be returned immediately to their rightful owners after

having been occupied by a native school, strongly suspected of communism, for more than a year and a half, the premises are still held by Chinese. Orders have either been ignored or pretexts for continuing to occupy the premises have been trumped up by the illegal possessors, apparently with the connivance of the local city magistrate Recent reports seem to show that the return of the property is as far away as ever.

A year and a half ago the buildings were taken over without permission by the principal and members of a school known in Wenchow as Ao Hae, whose communist activities have long been suspected. Near the end of May, 1927, the school was raided by the military and half – a – dozen teachers and students were arrested as suspected communists. One of these was executed the day following by the authorities, and the school dispersed.

Communists Again in Possession

In the early autumn of 1927 the school reopened, one again appropriating the mission buildings, and since that time all efforts to have them ejected have been brought to nothing, mainly through the obstructive methods of the local magistrate and the apparent inability of the Nationalist authorities to enforce their order that the premises be immediately evacuated and restored to the mission.

In addition, the school is still suspected of being a hotbed of communism, a Wenchow merchant declaring that over 60 of the students and teachers belonged to that subversive party. That the school is certainly inclined against law and order is shown by the reported declaration of the teachers of "again stirring up trouble and hounding out the foreigners if pressure were brought to turn them out of the college." This threat is not regarded with much concern by foreigners, despite the fact that communism has taken deep root in the Wenchow district.

Government Orders Flouted

Orders for the return of the premises to the mission were issued by the Nationalist Government early in May, but nothing has yet been done. All the local officials save one seem to be willing to carry out the instructions of the Government, but this one, the Wenchow city magistrate, seems to be able to prevent action.

More recently the mission was advised to go and take back their premises, turning out the present occupants. This, however, was not a task for the missionaries, but the City Magistrate refused any assistance in the matter. On the contrary, we are informed, he wrote asking that the 'Ao Hae school be allowed to continue in the mission college until the end of February, 1929. The Commissioner of Foreign Affairs in Wenchow then advised the mission authorities to call on the magistrate and discuss with him personally how and when the college would be returned.

And this in spite of orders from the Provincial Government at Hangchow and the Central Government at Nanking that the college was to be handed back immediately!

Mr. J. W. Heywood, chairman of the United Methodist mission, called upon the Magistrate, however and failed to obtain any action. For more than an hour the official ignored the main issue, the return of the premises, and sought to extort a promise that the mission would consent to a continuance of the occupation of their prmises. This, of course, was impossible, and the situation remained exactly as it was before.

More Subterfuges

After this it would appear that further pressure was brought to bear on the recalcitrant Magistrate, for the mission authorities received a request from him that the 'Ao Hae School be permitted to remain in the mission buildings util October 25. The principal of the 'Ao Hae School had, according to the communication received, rented a building of 40 rooms, but these badly needed repairs which would take quite two months.

Upon investigation it turned out that there was no truth in this excuse. The house mentioned as being the one rented by the school was not in nearly such a bad condition as had been made out; four or five days' work would have made it fit for habitation. There were no signs of workmen about making repairs, and also the proprietors of the building denied that they were prepared to lease more than half of it to any one. The whole story appeared to be a tissue of lies.

A further application to the magistrate has brought about no action. In the meantime, the 'Ao Hae School has reassembled and according to the latest news, is still in session.

"Peaceful Days in Wenchow: Good Crops Bring Content and Prosperity to E. Chekiang," *The North – China Herald and Supreme Court & Consular Gazette*, September 29, 1928

Peaceful Days in Wenchow: Good Crops Bring Content and Prosperity to E. Chekiang

(From our Wenchow Correspondent)

Wenchow is gradually but surely reverting to its calm and peaceful days. Favoured by its geographical situation, and the fact that it lies off from any of the main roads used by troops, we have been spared many of the unfortunate experiences of other cities during the past six months. Very few soldiers have been in evidence this present year; and what few there have been can be credited with decent behaviour. As a consequence, the city has shown signs of business prosperity; and so far as the people are concerned, the heavy and black clouds of last year have almost disappeared.

Another and important factor in stabilizing conditions is the good rice harvest which was reaped in the first crop. Such an abounding harvest has not been reaped for 20 years. Whereas the people were only getting from nine to twelve ching of rice for the dollar during 1927; this year they are rejoicing that one dollar will buy 20 ching and over. The same good news can be reported of the potato crop. Moreover, the second crop of rice is also promising to be a bumper one, and the local papers forecast that prices will be even lower. Despite this favoura-

PEACEFUL DAYS IN WENCHOW

Good Crops Bring Content and Prosperity to E. Chekiang

FROM OUR WENCHOW CORRESPONDENT

Wenchow is gradually but surely reverting to its calm and peaceful days. Favoured by its geographical situation, and the fact that it lies off from any of the main roads used by troops, we have been spared many of the unfortunate experiences of other cities during the past six months. Very few soldiers

ble outlook, the officials are prohibiting any exportation; threatening severe penalties to those who disobey. This assurance that the rice – bowl will be well filled has a wonderful effect in creating a more peaceful and cheerful atmosphere.

A New Public Park

In harmony with the innovations being made by many cities, Wenchow is demolishing a portion of the city wall. The section being pulled down faces the east, and lies between what has long been known by foreigners as "Bonnie Corner" and the Northern Ting. It is projected to make a public park by including land which lies outside the wall as far as the wide canal which forms the moat of the eastern wall, and a large plot of land inside the city which formerly has been cultivated for vegetables. It should make a very attractive park for the people when completed.

The Japanese boycott is being enforced here as in other places. The procedure is as in other districts. No untoward incidents have taken place. The Customs Staff has been peacefully and efficiently functioning under a Japanese Commissioner, an American Harbour Master, and a tide – waiter of Russian nationality.

Coercion of Communists

In the hilly country districts banditti are constantly being reported. The local officials, with the magistrates of the different hsiens, have concerted measures for their control and suppression. Recently a conference was held in Wenchow by all the Magistrates concerned, and as a result there is hope that this trouble to the out – lying towns and villages will be overcome.

That there is still an active party of Communists in this districts cannot be ignored. Five suffered the extreme penalty a few weeks ago, and since then many known leaders have felt it wiser to retire to the islands off Wenchow Bay and other places. The officials are keenly alert to this danger, and to their credit it must be said they are taking all possible precautions to maintain all possible in the city and the country side.

This makes it all the more puzzling that repeated orders to return the College property of the Methodist Mission are not yet carried out. So long as Nanking and Hangchow are ignored, it is not only the foreigner that doubts the stability of law and order, but also the respectable and law – abiding citizen. It is to be hoped that this wrong will soon be righted.

Escaping the Typhoon

Wenchow was fortunate in escaping the full force of the last typhoon. Last Thursday night was the most threatening time when a very strong north – northwest wind raged for a time, and the barometer fell to 29.23. Heavy rains were experienced, and floods were caused up river. There is hope that the outstanding crops will not have suffered much, as the second harvest is not reaped until the end of October.

"Terrible Fire at Wenchow: Brigade Helpless: Damage Put at $500000," *The North – China Herald and Supreme Court & Consular Gazette*, November 3, 1928

Terrible Fire at Wenchow: Brigade Helpless: Damage Put at $500000

(From our own correspondent)

Wenchow, Chê., October 23

One of the most destructive fire for several years ravaged an important area of Wenchow city last Sunday night. Breaking out in a paper – colouring shop, situated in the East Gate Street, known locally as the K'oa – loh – foa, it spread to the main street of the city. Both sides of these important streets went up in flames; and at one time it seemed likely that an immense business section would be destroyed. The flames leaped both roads and canals. Shop after shop, and house after house, went up in spectacular flares that illumined the whole city. For two hours and a half the fire defied the efforts of the local fire – brigades, which, unfortunately were deprived of more than half of their strength owing to many machines being under repair by special order of the officials.

The Chinese estimate of damage done by this fire is $500000. Only some five or six shops and houses were insured.

TERRIBLE FIRE AT WENCHOW

Brigade Helpless: Damage Put at $500,000

FROM OUR OWN CORRESPONDENT

Wenchow, Chê., Oct. 23.

One of the most destructive fires for several years years ravaged an important area of Wenchow city last Sunday night. Breaking out

"The Adventures of the Cassum: Almost Capsized in Heavy Swell: Refuge in Wenchow," *The North - China Herald and Supreme Court & Consular Gazette*, November 24, 1928

The Adventures of the Cassum: Almost Capsized in Heavy Swell: Refuge in Wenchow

THE ADVENTURES OF THE CASSUM

Almost Capsized in Heavy Swell: Refuge in Wenchow

An exact account of what happened to the str. Cassum, formerly H. M. S. Woodlark, which was reported last week to be in trouble while on her way from Shanghai to Hongkong, has been given us by Capt. Mather, master of the C. N. S. Sinkiang, who encountered the Cassum some 60 miles north of Wenchow.

Interviewed by a representative of the "North - China Daily News," Capt. Mather recounted how, on the morning of Saturday, the 10th instant, he saw a vessel "surging along" on his port bow some distance away. On coming nearer to the vessel in question, he was able to see that the vessel was making signals by displaying numerous flags. Two messages could be made out. These were "Can you give us coal?" and another "Report us to Shanghai." Capt. Mather replied "Follow me to an anchorage." He then made for a spot behind Shetung Island and there dropped anchor.

Speed Down to Three Knots

The Cassum later came alongside the B. & S. steamer and Capt. Knight explained his predicament. He said that he had had a very rough time and, although given to understand by his owners that the Cassum could make 13 knots had only been able to accomplish six knots in the very best circumstances. On many occasions his speed had been little more than three knots. Capt. Knight attributed this to the quality of the coal he had been supplied with at Shanghai and the two captains had a short conference in regard to the position. As a result of this conversation, it was decided that the best course was to make for Wenchow and take in bunkers there, as, although the Xinjiang could give the Cassum coal, no useful object would be achieved when the vessel was so near to Wenchow and, moreover, the transfer of coal during the heavy swell which was running would have been a slow and tedious operation which in all probability would have meant another night's anchorage for the Cassum in an unsuitable spot. The vessels therefore proceeded on their respective ways, Capt. Mather at once sending a wireless message to H. M. Consulate at Shanghai reporting the position of the Cassum in accordance with the request of the Cassum in accordance with the request of Capt. Knight.

Barren Bay is situated behind an island known as Bella Vista and it was in this spot that the Cassum almost came to grief. It was later when the ships were in a position north of Shetung Pass that signals were exchanged which subsequently resulted in a conference while at anchorage behind Shetung Island.

Fortunate Not to Crash

In the course of the conversation, Capt, Knight said that, owing to the quality of the coal, his engineers had been quite unable to keep a head of steam, with the result that positions of difficulty had repeatedly been encountered. Hugging the coast as the Cassum necessarily had to do, it was essential that complete control be possible at all times, as, with the heavy swells running and with strong winds, the light ship drawing only four feet needed the maximum of power in dealing with the various situations which arose in the course of the trip.

"We all but capsized in the swell and then the wind drove us towards the rocks and we were fortunate in not crashing," said Captain Knight.

Capt. Mather thought that the Cassum would only proceed on her voyage from Wenchow to Hongkong in daylight and would select suitable anchorages to spend the hours of night. As is now known, the vessel remained in Wenchow for five days due no doubt to the inability of Capt. Knight to obtain suitable bunkers and his observation of weather reports.

Departure from Wenchow

Mrs. W. C. H. Knight，wife of the commanding officer of the str. Cassum，informed the "North – China Daily News" on November 18 that she had received a telegram from her husband saying that he had left Wenchow on November 15.

"A Chinese Paper Making Scheme: Plan to Set Up a Factory at Wenchow in Chekiang," *The North - China Herald and Supreme Court & Consular Gazette*, December 22, 1928

A Chinese Paper Making Scheme: Plan to Set Up a Factory at Wenchow in Chekiang

With a view to driving Japanese paper out of the market and meeting demands from various Chinese newspapers, an ambitious scheme has been formed by various local merchants, including Mr. Yu Yaching, Wang Yi – ting, Hsu Shib – ching, Fong Chu – pa. S. S. Fung and others, whereby a factory, the first of its kind in China, for the manufacture of paper will be established.

It is proposed to establish this factory in Wenchow, Chekiang, as that city is situated in a district where there is a considerable amount of timber and where communications are convenient.

An agreement has been concluded by the promoters and the Chekiang Provincial Government and this provides for monopoly for a period of 30 years, in return for which 6 percent of the profits will go to the provincial government concerned. Furthermore, the company will be exempt from all taxes for a period of ten years.

A committee has been formed with Mr. King Han, a returned student, who specialized in paper manufacture, as director of the company.

A CHINESE PAPER MAKING SCHEME

Plan to Set Up a Factory at Wenchow in Chekiang

With a view to driving Japanese paper out of the market and meeting demands from various Chinese newspapers, an ambitious scheme has been formed by various local merchants, including Mr. Yu Yaching, Wang Yi-ting, Hsu Shih-ying, Sze Liang-say. Ching Zung-ching. Fong Chu-pa. S. S. Fung and others, whereby a factory, the first of its kind in China, for the manufacture of paper will be established.

"Wenchow College Given Back: After Two Years: Everything of Worth Stolen," *The North – China Herald and Supreme Court & Consular Gazette*, January 19, 1929

Wenchow College Given Back: After Two Years: Everything of Worth Stolen

（From our own correspondent）

WENCHOW COLLEGE GIVEN BACK

After Two Years: Everything of Worth Stolen

FROM OUR OWN CORRESPONDENT

Wenchow, Chê., Jan. 12.

After being occupied for almost two years, the College buildings of the United Methodist Church have been restored to the Mission.

Wenchow, Chê., January 12

After being occupied for almost two years, the College buildings of the United Methodist Church have been restored to the Mission.

It is significant of some official minds that the written instructions to the Magistrate's Deputy contained the phrase, "The College which was lent" How those who "borrowed" the fine property of the Mission regarded the duty of returning it as they found it, may be judged by the following facts.

1. The College and Principal's house has been practically looted. Rooms have been cleared of furniture, and equipment.

2. Not even one small bottle, let alone one of the valuable instruments in the Science Laboratory, has been left by the invaders.

3. All the electrical fittings have been ruthlessly cut down, and thoughfully taken away.

4. The condition of the whole of the buildings was indescribably dirty and filthy.

5. Many windows were deliberately broken before the students left the compound.

One regrets to report these things; but to hide the facts of the case would not be to the welfare of this country. There is a class of men and youths who pose as being the "lovers of their country"; but who under the guise of teachers and students are really its enemies.

The College buildings were returned to the Mission on the 11th instant.

For some months past the Nanking Government has been trying to get these buildings restored to the U. M. C. Mission and repeated orders to this effect have been sent to the Wenchow authorities. But hitherto local resistance had been too strong.

"Mission Property at Wenchow: Returned to Owners After Clean Looting Throughout," *The North - China Herald and Supreme Court & Consular Gazette*, April 20, 1929

Mission Property at Wenchow: Returned to Owners After Clean Looting Throughout

(From our own correspondent)

Wenchow, April 9

After negotiations covering a period of over 12 months the College property of the United Methodist College, Wenchow has at last been restored to its legitimate owners. For months in spite of orders from the Foreign Office at Nanking the local authorities allowed the governors of the ' Ao He public school to retain possession of the premises which they had "annexed" early in 1927. At long last, however, when it was evident that the Mission authorities were determined to leave no stone unturned to get possession of their own premises an arrangement was made between the Wenchow Commissioner for Foreign Affairs and the usurping school for the premises to he returned in February.

The buildings have certainly been given back but they have been to a very great extent denuded of furniture and fittings. Desks, forms, tables, books, registers beds, locks, electric light fittings, almost all gone. Of the chemical and physics apparatus worth $ 3003 not a single 2oz. bottle is left. From the Principal's house pictures chairs, rugs, linen, crockery etc. most of which were in tin - lined locked boxes - have disappeared. The total loss at a very conservative estimate from the whole College premises is $ 1000. No compensation has been given for any of this.

It is hoped that the College will reopen in the autumn. Repairs are well in hand and new furniture in being made but it may be necessary for the first session to limit the number of students 100 or 150, although since the extensions were made in 1924 there is accommodation for 300 students.

As far as is consistent with the aims of the Mission the College authorities are trying to meet all the requirements of the Government in regard to Private Schools—under which heading Mission schools are included. If they find themselves so hedged in by regulations that the very purpose of the College's existence is threatened, the whole matter of Missionary educational work will have to be reconsidered.

"Era of Prosperity for Wenchow: Unprecedented Conditions: Improvements Follow," *The North - China Herald and Supreme Court & Consular Gazette*, May 4, 1929

Era of Prosperity for Wenchow: Unprecedented Conditions: Improvements Follow

(From our own correspondent)

Wenchow, April 23.

Wenchow seems to have entered upon an era of unprecedented prosperity. Never during the last quarter of a century has trade been so brisk. Every fire—and in the past there have been many—sees old shops and houses replaced by modern buildings of much greater size and importance. Streets gradually are being widened and show the modern plate glass fronted shops to much better advantage. Instead of the one small steamer of 20 years ago arriving every ten days, Wenchow now has its regular five steamers a week and many others coming at irregular intervals. Under all these conditions, it is not to be wondered at that the city is to have its park. Wenchow like another famous city, is built on seven hills and the land between two of these, to the east of the city, is being used for the new park. The city wall between these hills has been taken down and the gently rolling ground, part of which formerly was a cemetery, is to be provided with flowers shrubs, pavilions, lakes and bridges, for the delight of the people.

Possibly the sanitary condition of the city will be considered later. Many of the canals have been blocked for years and their stagnant water and decaying re-

ERA OF PROSPERITY FOR WENCHOW

Unprecedented Conditions: Improvements Follow

FROM OUR OWN CORRESPONDENT

Wenchow, Apr. 23.

Wenchow seems to have entered upon an era of unprecedented prosperity. Never during the last quarter of a century has trade been so brisk. Every fire—and in the

fuse, together with the open cesspools still to be met with all over the city, are breeding places for all sorts of diseases. Rarely a year passes without its cholera outbreak, which sometimes attains terrible propertions.

A Modern Theatre

During the last week or two, Wenchow has been favoured with a visit from a theatrical company from Shanghai. To pay to see a theatrical performance is an innovation. Usually one goes to the temple, taking one's own seat sometimes in the form of a very high trestle which raises one a good three feet above the crowd and has just as many hours of enjoyment as one can spare time for, quite free of all cost. The new company brought a considerable quantity of stage property and scenery and is giving a series of plays dealing with current events.

One can see Chiang Kai – shek seated in a room fitted with modern office furniture, transacting the affairs of the nation. One play, dealing with Tsinan, shows in a very realistic manner the Japanese committing all sorts of barbarities which, according to a Chinese eyewitness, are thoroughly appreciated anu behaved in by the enthusiastic audience. The entrance prices are 10 and 20 cents and $ 1500 a month is needed to meat all expense of the company.

A Hold – up

One evening recently a wealthy merchant was held up by armed men at his own residence and threatened. with dire penalties unless he immediately provided his captors with a large sum of money ($ 20000) . He was allowed to go upstairs to get the money and managed to make his escape through an upper window. He ran for the police, —but, by the time they arrived, the robbers had decamped, taking whatever they could lay their hands on.

Pirates Active

pirates still are very active about the mouth of the Wenchow river. In some cases, their vessels are fitted with old cannon and the crews number as many as 100. Steamers are fairly safe from these robbers, but the junks often suffer heavily.

Several armed robbers have been caught recently and executed.

"Chekiang Bandits Captured: Formidable Band with Strong Hold on Island," *The North – China Herald and Supreme Court & Consular Gazette*, July 13, 1929

Chekiang Bandits Captured: Formidable Band with Strong Hold on Island

(From our own correspondent)

Wenchow, July 4

The island of Pien San at the mouth of the Wenchow River was invested on July 1 and about 160 bandits were either captured or killed. Pieh San is an island about eight miles long and one broad with a very rocky coast and only two narrow entrances capable of being easily defended. the total number of the band is said to be 268 and all are armed with very modern rifles and automatics.

The depredations of the band at sea were conducted from "borrowed" junks and as the same junk was rarely used for more than two days, the authorities had great difficulty in apprehending them at sea. Before venturing forth on a new raid the band invariably consulted the idols and also inquired in which direction, north, south east or west, fortune would come. to them. This time the oracle played them false as, on emerging from their fastnesses on Pieh San, they found gunboats awaiting. In the resulting melee about 160 were either

CHEKIANG BANDITS CAPTURED

Formidable Band with Strong-hold on Island

FROM OUR OWN CORRESPONDENT

Wenchow, July 4.

The island of Pien San at the mouth of the Wenchow River was invested on July 1 and about 160 bandits were either captured or killed. Pieh San is an island about eight miles long and one broad with a very rocky coast and only two narrow entrances capable of being easily defended. The total number of the band is said to be 268 and all are armed with very modern rifles and automatics.

captured or killed and the remainder managed to regain the great caves which have proved such a good retreat in the past. It can only be a matter of time, however, before they. are all captured as hunger will finally drive them out into the open.

"Distress Round Wenchow: Failure of Rice Crop: Three Typhoons," *The North – China Herald and Supreme Court & Consular Gazette*, August 24, 1929

Distress Round Wenchow: Failure of Rice Crop: Three Typhoons

(From our own correspondent)

Wenchow, Che. , August 15

The almost total failure of the early rice crop is causing already deep distress in many parts of the prefecture. It has been an inordinately wet summer even for Wenchow and blight and want of sun so seriously affected the early rice crop that prices went up with a leap. In a very short time the price went up from 11 pints to the $1 to 8 pints and the price is still going up.

We have experienced three typhoons already and while the wind has seldom reached gale force the rain has been excessive: During the last one the rain came down almost continuously from August 7 to 14 and the plain on which the city is situated became one great lake with houses and embankments appearing above the surface. All the canals in the city overflowed and many of the streets were inundated. It was impossible to go through any of the gates of the city without wading through deep water. It will be many days before the plain can assume its ordinary appearance even if we have fine sunny weather.

DISTRESS ROUND WENCHOW

Failure of Rice Crop: Three Typhoons

FROM OUR OWN CORRESPONDENT

Wenchow, Che., Aug. 15.

The almost total failure of the early rice crop is causing already deep distress in many parts of the prefecture. It has been an inordinately wet summer even for Wenchow and blight and want of sun so seriously affected the early rice crop that prices went up with a leap. In a very short time the price went up from 11 pints to the $1 to 8 pints and the price is still going up.

In some of the country districts the poor people have been reduced to such straits on account of the rice failure that raids have been made on the richer people's houses to get the necessary food on which to live.

The second rice crop is in great danger of failure also unless the weather greatly improves. A month's sunshine is necessary to redeem the crop from failure.

"A Case of Arson at Wenchow: Telephone Exchange Destroyed: Communists Suspected," *The North - China Herald and Supreme Court & Consular Gazette*, September 14, 1929

A Case of Arson at Wenchow: Telephone Exchange Destroyed: Communists Suspected

(From our own correspondent)

Wenchow, Chê., September 7

On Sunday evening last a very serious fire occurred at Wenchow. The telephone exchange was completely burnt out. The whole business is wrapped in mystery, but all the evidence points to the fact that it was a deliberate case of malice, and intended to hamper the officials in the discharge of their duties. Three people were in the building at the time, but managed to escape without injury and can give no explanation of the occurrence.

The general impression is that it is the work of the Communist party, but whether there is any real justification for the accusation it is difficult to find out. Fearing that this may only be the beginning of an attempt to interfere with all the public services, the Electric Light Company have established a special guard to protect their property. The Telephone Company have been. ordered to have the telephones in working condition within three weeks, but it is doubtful whether the work can be done in the time.

A CASE OF ARSON AT WENCHOW

Telephone Exchange Destroyed: Communists Suspected

FROM OUR OWN CORRESPONDENT
Wenchow, Chê., Sept. 7.

On Sunday evening last a very serious fire occurred at Wenchow. The telephone exchange was completely burnt out. The whole business is wrapped in mystery, but all the evidence points to the fact that it was a deliberate case of malice, and intended to hamper the officials in the discharge of their duties. Three people were in the building at the time, but managed to escape without injury and can give no explanation of the occurrence.

"Cholera Epidemic in Wenchow: Serious Outbreak Decreasing: Methodist School Reopened," *The North – China Herald and Supreme Court & Consular Gazette*, September 14, 1929

Cholera Epidemic in Wenchow: Serious Outbreak Decreasing: Methodist School Reopened

(From our own correspondent)

Wenchow, September 4

Cholera has once again appeared in epidemic form in Wenchow. As far as can be ascertained, it seems probable that it has been brought from further south. Pingyanghsien, 30 miles to the south, is reported to have the epidemic rather widely spread and a daily launch communication between that city and Wenchow, via Juian, makes the rapid spread of the disease easy. The first cases in Wenchow were heard of about a week ago in the South Gate district and since then the epidemic has spread rather rapidly. Twenty cases of the disease have been received into the Blyth Hospital (Methodist Mission) and the doctor reports the disease to be of a rather virulent type. Three of the patients have died, but the rest have reacted favourably to the saline injection treatment. Unfortunately, so many will only go to the "foreign" hospital as a last resource and in the case of cholera that has often proved too late.

Reopening of Methodist College

After being closed for 2. 5 years, the Methodist Middle School is opening again to – day. While the school has not yet ben registered, it is being carried on

CHOLERA EPIDEMIC
IN WENCHOW

Serious Outbreak Decreasing:
Methodist School Reopened

FROM OUR OWN CORRESPONDENT
Wenchow, Sept. 4.
Cholera has once again appeared in epidemic form in Wenchow. As far as can be ascertained, it seems probable that it has been brought from further south. Pingyanghsien,

as far as is consistent with the principles of the Mission, according to the regulations of the Government pertaining to Middle Schools. A Chinese board of Governors and a Chinese Principal have been appointed, while the former principal is acting as adviser. About 200 students have been received, representing only about half the number of applicants. The whole of the buildings have been renovated and new furniture made or purchased. Is it too much to hope that any portion of the large expense incurred due to destruction and "annexation" by a body of students, whose occupation of the buildings was tacitly permitted by the authorities, will ever be repaid?

"Famine Conditions in Wenchow: Crops Destroyed by an Unidentified Organism," *The North – China Herald and Supreme Court & Consular Gazette*, October 12, 1929

Famine Conditions in Wenchow: Crops Destroyed by an Unidentified Organism

(From our own correspondent)

Wenchow, October 5

Owing to the almost complete failure of the rice crop in the Wenchow district, there are thousands of families reduced to absolute starvation. In the Yotsing district and the island of Yo – wan, people are reduced to eating grass and any green stuff they can pick up. Whole families are coming in their hundreds to the city and simply becoming beggars in the streets. Some attempt is being made to look after the children, to prevent them being sold by their parents. A father sold his 13 – year – old son the other day for $ 14 and immediately the mother committed suicide by throwing herself in the canal.

The failure of the crop is due to some organism which destroyed the whole plant from the roots. No one seems to remember a similar failure, although crops have been destroyed by floods in recent years. All sorts of rumours are current as to the cause, from the wildest superstitions to approximate possible reasons. Among the latter is that it is the grub of a certain moth. Unless the real cause is found out and precautionary measures taken, the same thing may happen next year. Surely this is a matter for the agricultural department. of the provincial university to inquire into.

FAMINE CONDITIONS IN WENCHOW

Crops Destroyed by an Unidentified Organism

FROM OUR OWN CORRESPONDENT

Wenchow, Oct. 5.

Owing to the almost complete failure of the rice crop in the Wenchow district, there are thousands of families reduced to absolute starvation. In the Yotsing district

Cholera Prevalent

The situation is complicated by the prevalence of cholera in the city. Already, 400 cases have been treated at the Methodist Hospital and, although the number of deaths approaches 20 percent. , these are chiefly among the infants and the aged, besides a unmber who left the hospital too soon and against advice and returned in a few days in extremis.

There is great apprehension among the people generally that the abnormal conditions will be taken advantage of by the Communists to stir up trouble. The officials seem awake to the situation, however and, since the destruction of the telephone exchange a month ago by fire, the electric light works, the telegraph office, etc. , have been so guarded that no untoward act has been done.

"Bandit Invasion of Lungchuan: A Reward for Foreign Missionaries' Kindness," *The North – China Herald and Supreme Court & Consular Gazette*, November 16, 1929

Bandit Invasion of Lungchuan: A Reward for Foreign Missionaries' Kindness

(From our own correspondent)

Wenchow, October 12

Soldiers numbering 150 from Wenchow who had been reinforced by 200 from Chuchow, have just returned to the city from Lungchuan: having failed to come into contact with the band of about 500 bandits which has become a very serious menace to life and property in the Lungchuan district. Some time ago this band descended on the city of Lungchuan, opened the do-ors of the prison and set the priso-ners free. They then carried off the magistrate, chief of police and about 20 of the richest men of the city for ransom. One of the prisoners led some of the bandits to the home of Mr. and Mrs. Bender, the only, foreign missionaries in the city and said "Leave this house alone, the people here are good to all and treat rich and poor alike." A few of the bandits entered, and after taking a look round, left the house intact. It is reported that about 20 innocent persons suffered at the hands of the soldiers. The magistrate of Lungchuan escaped, but the others are still in the hands is of the bandits.

BANDIT INVASION OF LUNGCHUAN

A Reward for Foreign Missionaries' Kindness

FROM OUR OWN CORRESPONDENT

Wenchow, Nov. 9.

Soldiers numbering 150 from Wenchow who had been reinforced by 200 from Chuchow, have just returned to the city from Lungchuan: having failed to come into contact with the band of about 500 bandits which has become a very serious menace to life and property in the Lungchuan district. Some

Children Taken for Ransom

From many other parts of the districts come distressing stories of famine and lawlessness. Suicides, especially among women, are increasingly prevalent. At Pieh – Li a village about 30 miles directly north of Wenchow four children have been carried off by bandits and $1000 each demanded as ransom. Three of the families affected would have the greatest difficulty to raise $20 each, while the fourth could not possibly manage even half of the sum demanded if they were to sell everything.

"Shanghai Steamer Pirated: Kwangchi Seized by Gang Taken as Passengers," *The North – China Herald and Supreme Court & Consular Gazette*, November 16, 1929

Shanghai Steamer Pirated: Kwangchi Seized by Gang Taken as Passengers

(From our own correspondent)

Another China Merchants str. has been pirated. This time it is the more or less obsolete vessel Kwangchi, a vessel of 1000 tons or thereabouts, which has been for ma-ny years on various runs of the China coast. The outrage took place ne-ar a port known as Haimen, a sm-all port off the Chekiang coast and the vessel at the time of pirating was on the Shanghai – Wenchow run.

It appears that the pirates bo-arded the vessel as passengers and after carrying out their work used the ship to convey them to a small port called Shihpu and where they robbed the Bureau of Public Safety of arms and ammunition. They then left the ship which at present is in the hands of the port authorities at Shihpu. Orders have been given for the ship to sail for Shanghai.

According to wireless messages from. Haimen, all on board are safe although all valuable and clothes were taken by the pirates before they disembarked. Another report states that one passenger was wounded and that another was carried off the marauders.

SHANGHAI STEAMER PIRATED

Kwangchi Seized by Gang Taken as Passengers

Another China Merchants str. has been pirated. This time it is the more or less obsolete vessel Kwangchi, a vessel of 1,000 tons or thereabouts, which has been for many years on various runs off the China coast. The outrage took place near a port known as Haimen, a small port off the Chekiang coast and the vessel at the time of pirating was on the Shanghai-Wenchow run.

Sighted by Wing Tai

The Kwangchi left Wenchow with a full cargo and many passengers on November 5 and after being at sea for some 20 hours was seized by the pirates and the officers were forced to steer the vessel in the direction of Shihpu. Another steamer, the Wing Tai, noticed that the Kwangchi was proceeding in a direction incompatible with her sailing programme and reported the incident to the China Merchants Co. at Ningpo. The Shanghai office of the company was advised and the Chekiang provincial authorities and coastal patroling police were informed of the occurrence.

Accounts of the piracy show that after the ship was a day out from Wenchow, the pirates held up the captain, officers, and engineers and ordered the course to be diverted to Shihpu. On approaching the port, the pirates divided themselves into two parties, one remaining on board and the other going on shore.

The captain and officers were bound with cords as the vessel approached the port of Shihpu, and the pirate landing party entered the Bureau of Public Safety and obtaind a large quantity of arms and ammunition. The ship then being in charge of the first party of pirates, the second or landing party returned and commenced to search the passengers. Meanwhile, the captain, a Chinese, was instructed to leave port. Reaching a small port on the Chekiang coast, the pirates escaped in the ship's boats and took with them. one of the passengers whom they are holding for ransom. The vessel carried $ 27000 in silver, the property of the Bank of China and put on board at Wenchow for shipment to Shanghai. This prize was entirely overlooked by the pirates.

Passengers' Pitiful Stories

The following telegram was received at the Shanghai branch of the China Merchants Co: "Kwangchi arrived Haimen at 6. 30 p. m. today (Monday) and again awaits orders although police using boat to chase pirates. Capt. Tong. "

Accordingly the position resolves itself to this. The vessel was pirated, is now chasing pirates on the instructions of the "water police" and is prevented from transporting cargo from. Chekiang ports to Shanghai.

Some of the passengers who were on board at the time of the piracy have arrived in Shanghai. They told pitiful stories.

It appears that eight pirates travelling as passengers embarked at Wenchow and that soon after the ship left port held up the master and officers. The officers were bound and were told that it was not the intention to pirate the ship. The object was to rob the water police of arms and ammunition. The ship approached a small island and Capt. Tong navigating his ship under threats, brought the vessel to an anchorage. The leader of the pirate gang fired three shots in the air and immediately more than 100 men appeared on the shore and entering native boats made for the Kwangchi and boarded her Captain Tong was then ordered to proceed. They reached Shihpu at 7 p. m. on November 7 and the pirates landed – leaving a guard on the ship. There were three small cruisers and one gunboat at the latter place but in spite of these, the pirates had little difficulty in over powering the water police and those in charge of the latter vessels, and actually captured the two cruisers. Seven members of the police were killed and two were taken captive by the pirates. The gunboat managed to open fire, whereupon the marauders withdrew and again boarded the Kwangchi. One passenger on the merchant ship was killed and several wounded in the course of the engagement.

Two steamers in Pursuit

Three hours after the pirate gang left Shihpu, the strs. Tah Hwa and Chow Shan arrived at that port. The inspector of the water police commandeered the Tah Hwa and gave chase to the Kwangchi. Reaching a small harbour known as King Chin Kong, the vessels met and fire was exchanged. Apparently realizing that the time for escape had arrived, the pirates then left the ship and carried their loot to the shore in the ship's boats. They systematically searched all the passengers before doing so and collected several thousands of dollars worth of jewellery and other valuables. They also secured some $ 3000 from the compradore's safe. Passenger's state that the pursuing vessel with the water police on board refrained from firing during the disembarkment but later fired shells neither of which hit the Kwangchi. They attribute this state of affairs to the fact that it was later stated that the police were afraid of wounding passengers and crew. One passenger named Liu was kidnapped. Freed of the pirates the Kwangchi made for Haimen and later was commandeered by the water police to pursue the pirates. Some of the passengers were able to obtain passages on other vessels bound for Shanghai and arrived here yesterday.

Pirates Preparing to Fight

It is learned that the small harbour of King Chin Kong has been blockaded by men – of – var despatched by the Chekiang Provincial Government. Two war vessels of the Ministry of Navy are also expected to reach there to assist the water police in suppressing the pirates The latter have placed three gun in position on Chih Tan Hill where they have established headquarters and apparently are prepared to resist all attacks.

"Anxious Days at Wenchow: Bandits Rife in Country Round: Inadequate Resistance," *The North –
China Herald and Supreme Court & Consular Gazette*, December 7, 1929

Anxious Days at Wenchow: Bandits Rife in Country Round: Inadequate Resistance

(From our own correspondent)

Wenchow, Chê., November 25

We have just passed through a time of great anxiety at Wenchow owing to the tremendous increase in the number of bandits in the neighbourhood and the inadequate means of protection. Tales of lawlessness from the outlying districts are of daily occurrence. The whole of the district from Yotsing to Taichow is at the mercy of marauding bands of robbers who are astonishingly well – armed. The missionaries in the Chunchow area – to the west of Wenchow – in places like Lungchuan, Yunho and Sunyang are finding it impossible to do any work owing to the very unsettled state of the country and may have to withdraw for a time. The officials in the city of Wenchow have taken every precaution against bandits coming to the city in small numbers at a time and secretly, but as the total force they could rely on was only 400 armed police some anxiety was felt. A meeting of officials and merchants was held a few days ago to consider the raising of a body of volunteers for self – defence, but no definite conclusion was arrived at. The anxiety was relieved when 1500 soldiers from Hangchow via Ningpo arrived by steamer three days ago. On the same day a French gunboat arrived and is still in port but is reported to be leaving tomorrow.

ANXIOUS DAYS AT WENCHOW

Bandits Rife in Country Round: Inadequate Resistance

FROM OUR OWN CORRESPONDENT

Wenchow, Chê., Nov. 25.

We have just passed through a time of great anxiety at Wenchow owing to the tremendous increase in the number of bandits in the neighbourhood and the inadequate means of protection. Tales of lawlessness

The Cholera Epidemic

After more than three months of very strenuous work with cholera patients the Blyth Hospital staff is returning to its normal duties. In the city generally the epidemic has not been considered a very severe one, but as the vast majority of cases have been to the Blyth Hospital (Methodist) for treatment the doctors and nurses have been kept busy day and night. Altogether 998 cases have been treated and excluding those who left the Hospital without the doctors' permission only 10 percent. were fatal and of this 10 percent, the majority were infants or very old people. Unfortunately, especially at the beginning of the epidemic patients sometimes insisted on leaving as soon as they felt better but while they were still in the infectious stage and each such case resulted in further cases among their relations. The doctor considers that, owing to those who left the Hospital before their cure was complete, the total number of deaths would probably reach 20 percent. No member of the staff either foreign or Chinese caught the disease as all the necessary precautions were taken, Never in the history of Wenchow have so many people been inoculated against cholera as during the last few months.

"Chekiang Coast Bandits: Operations Round Wenchow: Difficult Country," *The North – China Herald and Supreme Court & Consular Gazette*, December 31, 1929

Chekiang Coast Bandits: Operations Round Wenchow: Difficult Country

(From our own correspondent)

Wenchow, December 20

Bandits have now been cleared within a radius of about 50 li of the city of Wenchow. A few have been captured by the soldiers and brought to the city for trial and probably execution; a few also were shot trying to evade capture but the majority escaped. The soldiers have a very hard task in all this kind of work. The whole district is mountainous and while every bypath and cave is known to the bandits, the soldiers are at a complete loss owing to their ignorance of the district. Fear of the bandits also keeps the villagers from giving information, even of they are not allied to the bandits themselves.

In several of the districts north of the city a plan tried on more than one occasion recently is to enter a school during the day – time and terrify the boys into giving particulars of themselves and their families and then taking off for ransom those whom they thought most worth while. In one case at Piehli a father had paid $ 200 on account for the ransom of his son. Unfortunately the middle man was captured by the soldiers before the money was paid over and he was imprisoned in the city prison. The father then had to pay several hundreds of dollars as security for the man and also pay the full sum demanded as ransom for his son before he could get his boy back again. The whole affair cost him over $ 2000.

CHEKIANG COAST BANDITS

Operations Round Wenchow: Difficult Country

FROM OUR OWN CORRESPONDENT

Wenchow, Dec. 20.

Bandits have now been cleared within a radius of about 50 li of the city of Wenchow. A few have

The president of one of the neighbouring farmers' Unions was suspected of not only having leanings towards communism, but of carrying on a very active part in disseminating communistic literature. He was arrested and, under interrogation, admitted that he was receiving $40 a month from some outside source for this work. He was condemned and shot a few days ago.

Thousands Become Beggars

Such is the distress in the magistracy of Yotsing that thousands of the country folk, in many cases whole families, are travelling up and down the countryside begging for sweet potatoes. The whole of the hill sides in this district where there is not sufficient water for rice is given over to sweet potatoes and while the rice has been such a failure the potatoes have not done badly in many parts, except that on account of the drought they are only about half the usual size. Potatoes have become of such value, however, that it is very difficult to beg even these. It is no uncommon thing to come across families if three to five people travelling with all their worldly belongings who have not seen their homes for weeks and who show in their faces and bodies the very difficult task they are having to keep body and soul together.

"Winter Spreads to Chekiang: Cold Unknown for 30 Years: Market Prices Soar," *The North – China Herald and Supreme Court & Gazette*, January 21, 1930

Winter Spreads to Chekiang: Cold Unknown for 30 Years: Market Prices Soar

(From our own correspondent)

Wenchow, Jan. 14

Relief Fund Raised

The lowest temperature for the last 25 years has been experienced during the last week in Wenchow. Five to seven degrees of frost has been registered each night and the day temperature has been little higher. It is unfortunate that this extreme weather should coincide with the time of such great distress and extreme poverty. A fund of $100000 has been raised to try and alleviate the sufferings of the poorest of the country people who have flocked to the city from the famine stricken countryside. Over 15000 people are living in the temples of the city entirely dependent on charity. The authorities have tried to organize relief and congee is distributed from certain centres. Rice is also distributed on presentation of tickets which are obtained: from the members of the relief committee and hundreds of little fires may be seen in temple courtyards and odd corners where this rice is being cooked. Many have to be turned away disappointed and the crush is so great that several infants have been killed. Quite a number of deaths are reported from exposure to the cold, chiefly of little children.

Three merchants have given $1000 each to provide warm clothing for the

WINTER SPREADS TO CHEKIANG

Cold Unknown for 30 Years: Market Prices Soar

FROM OUR OWN CORRESPONDENT

Shaohsing, Jan. 11.

The older people do remark that the like of such cold as we have now has not been felt for a period of 30 years. The thermometer has gone far below freezing point; the temperature of the day and night being almost identical.

refugees from lotsing of whom there are about 900 in the city. Another merchant has housed 300 women and children and is providing them with food, but in spite of all that is being done there is still very great suffering and want. The 100000 dollars is nearly exhausted and it will be April before the first crop of wheat will be ready for reaping.

"Meningitis in Chekiang: Coast Area Severely Affected: Hopes of Harvests," *The North - China Herald and Supreme Court & Gazette*, April 1, 1930

Meningitis in Chekiang: Coast Area Severely Affected: Hopes of Harvests

(From our own correspondent)

Wenchow, Chê., March 20

Epidemics and kidnapping are now, alas, the order of the day and have been for very many days in this part of the Republic. No sooner has the cholera scourge disappeared than the scourge of meningitis takes its place carrying off its many victims with even more startling suddenness and often with the accompaniment of apparently tortuous agony to the sufferers. In the city here Dr. Marrow tells me that in a fortnight he has had 20 to 30 cases of it, three or four coming in in a day. A Chinese pastor came down to the city from his country circuit, 10 or 12 miles away, last week for a supply of serum, to be inoculated as he is called out so frequently to visit stricken families. Apparently supplies in Shanghai were exhausted and the doctor had to send to Peking for it.

Bandits As Well

The pastor told the writer that, in one small village among the mountains some 20 miles north or northwest of the city, known by the picturesque name of Plum Torrent, 24 children had been carried off by the disease, that it was working dreadful havock too in a much larger neighbouring village and that in

MENINGITIS IN CHEKIANG

Coast Area Severely Affected: Hopes of Harvests

FROM OUR OWN CORRESPONDENT

Wenchow, Che., Mar. 20.

Epidemics and kidnapping are now, alas, the order of the day and have been for very many days in this part of the Republic. No sooner has the cholera scourge disappeared than the scourge of meningitis takes its place carrying off its many victims with even more startling

his own place of residence was very bad, three and four in a family being carried off by it.

This last village is in terror of bandits, who are busy in the neighbourhood. Word has come down to the city of an attack on a mountain village well – known to the writer when two local policemen were put to death by torture by the brigands. 200 soldiers were sent up there and spent ' a little time at the place of debarkation. The night they left to proceed into the interior that place had a visit from bandits who robbed one of the houses. To – day there 1s a report that the head official of the small hsien city of Tsingtien (Greenfield), 35 miles up the Wenchow river from here, has fed to this city in danger of his life from the prisones, who are said to have broken out of prison.

Good Harvest Prospects

It is a pleasing change to have to record that all round here the plains are a mass of gold as far as the eye can reach to the foot of the encircling mountains from the bloom of the sesame plant, which fills the atmosphere with its perfume. The crop seems a very fine one, as also the broad beans, and it to – day's warm, bright sunny promise cam hold out, there is every evidence of a fine harvest of wheat in six or eight weeks time. Already in places the wheat has been in ear for a week or so, and in places from two to three feet in height. If that harvest materializes it will bring renewed life and hope to many in this famine – stricken country.

Customs officers recently made a seizure on a local vessel of contraband silk and piece goods, it was computed, to the value of about Hk. Tls. 1600 to 1800. We have now a Commissioner of Customs whose advent brought some little change for the small foreign population.

Formerly a postal employee used to be sent round from the Post Office with a written notice stating the date and time of the closing of the Shanghai and Ningpo mails when the Shanghai steamer had arrived in port. That very convenient little custom has now been abrogated.

A Lonely Island's Distress

The China Inland Mission here has had another generous donation sent for the relief of their Chinese members suffering in the famine stricken parts. The Methodist Mission too keeps receiving such help also from time to time, and has been busy for some month giving financial help to its Chinese members similarly distressed. The Rev. Irving Scott is taking a second supply with him this week end to one of the most needy parts the Jade Ring Island Oity and Hsien, out at sea some 30 or 40 miles away on the way to Shanghai. The Methodist Mission has a-bout half – a – dozen societies on that island and Mr. Scott's visit will mean much to several scores of Christians there who are in very desperate circumstances. Your correspondent was asked by the Hsien Chang（Magistrate）there to visit him when down there four months ago to talk over the needy condition of his people with a view to getting into touch with one of the Famine Relief Committees in Shanghai. That official subsequently sent a very business – like and detailed re-port, stating among other that over 200 boats had been lost in the typhoon that year, several li of roads had been washed away, large' numbers of houses blown down, crops destroyed by flood, insects, drought, and typhoon, and no little life lost. Unfortunately, the place is so out of the way, that none of the relief sent for other parts has found its way there with the exception of the help given by the Methodist Mission to its members.

"Lawlessness at Wenchow: Kidnappers and Robbers: Methodist College Closed," *The North – China Herald and Supreme Court & Gazette*, April 15, 1930

Lawlessness at Wenchow: Kidnappers and Robbers: Methodist College Closed

(From our own correspondent)

Wenchow, Chê., March 3

Wenchow County is experiencing a very noticeable increase of its perennial trouble—lawlessness which shows itself, at one time in banditry, at another in piracy, and for some time now in kidnapping and holding to ransom, and is being held to large ransom in the Ts'ing – T'ien (Green Fields) Hsien among the Western hills

A Chinese member of the Methodist Church has taken a house in the city to which he has brought his family for safety from his home in the highlands of Cedar Creek to the North. In that district the brigands are very active. A message reached him from the brigands threatening to burn his home unless $1000 was paid them. He hurried up to the walled town of Maple Grove where he could with safety negotiate with the bandits. He was willing to go to the sum of $200, I have not yet heard the result of the negotiations. About a month ago I met a country Christian who told me that recently his horse had been attacked by a band of outlaws who robbed him of $250. A more gruesome rumour, which one hopes to be untrue, is that another country house in one of the Wenchow hsien was similarly attacked and a woman of the house who was too slow in

LAWLESSNESS AT WENCHOW

Kidnappers and Robbers: Methodist College Closed

FROM OUR OWN CORRESPONDENT

Wenchow, Che., Mar. 3.

Wenchow County is experiencing a very noticeable increase of its perennial trouble - lawlessness — which shows itself at one time in banditry, at another in piracy, and for some time now in kidnapping and holding to ransom, and is being held to large ransom in the Ts'ing T'ien (Green Fields) Hsien among the Western hills.

opening the door had a hand cut off by one or the other of the brigands. This is by no means unlikely. During the closing months of last year a wounded patient was admitted to the Methodist Mission Hospital too seriously injured to be saved. With a few others he had travelled up river to the city in a small boat which was set upon by armed men who put out from shore in another boat. Finding that the men had no money one of the pirates wantonly discharged his gun at the poor fellows wounding the one fatally in the stomach.

The Wenchow Methodist Mission College has been compelled to close, not for lack of students but because the experimental year under present government conditions added to local conditions made Principal Chapman M. SC. , feel that the institution could not adequately function. Our small community feels very much the loss of Principal Chapman's fine social activities, his fraternal qualities, his cheerful humour, and his hospitable spirit. Twenty – eight years of splendid and really inimitable educational work he has put in. The fine college of which he was principal from its inception in 1902 until the beginning of 1930 has now become an annex of the Mission Hospital, housing one of the foreign nurses—Miss Raine—who is to be married shortly and go to Japan, and several young Chinese nurses. This is a new venture on the part of Nurses Smith and Raine the training of Chinese nurses who will be able to sit for their certificates now that registration has been effected in Shanghai. It is intended also that a children's ward and a women's ward shall be opened. Principal Chapman left Wenchow last month for Tengshan in North China to take the principalship of the Middle School of the same mission. Many Chinese here regret his leaving, former students, and others. He has been a good elder brother to many a poor Chinese student paying fees from his private resources and helping in various ways. The poor of the Church too found in him a generous and ready helper. Among his former students are men to be found in most ranks of life, as Dr. Timothy Lee, and in the ranks of medical, business, and political life, as well as in the Ministry of the Mission to which he belongs both ministerial or clerical and educational.

On Saturday I had a visit from the Superintendent of Police of this city asking for the use of a large number of the beds of the college formerly used by the students. A large consignment of soldiers was expected this weekend, part of whom are going to help in the present fighting against the brigands in the northern parts of the country and part to be kept in the city for its protection. Seven temples are allocated: for billets, but the soldiers have not yet come.

"Wenchow's Tricky River: Adventures of Incoming Ships: Large Vessels Launched," *The North – China Herald and Supreme Court & Gazette*, April 15, 1930

Wenchow's Tricky River: Adventures of Incoming Ship: Large Vessels Launched

(From our own correspondent)

Wenchow, Chê., Aprch 4

Since last writing we have' had the C. M. S. Ka – ho in for cargo, calling in on her way down to Foochow and again on her way, back from that port to Shanghai. The same company's steamer, the Hsinchang has also made a call on the port for cargo, these in addition to the regular steamers, the Haean and the Kwangchi. One steamer making her way up this river of perennially shifting sand banks found herself aground once and again, and another about a week ago, in getting into position to be ready to take her place at the wharf, found a sand bank unexpectedly which swung her in the strong tide athwart the river, and dragging her anchor with the rising tide, was brought up, happily slowly, against a small mid – channel rock but no damage was caused. A steamer went to her assistance but was unable to tow her against the strong current. The following morning she came to under her own steam.

Within the last fortnight a wooden – hull steamer of about 400 to 500 tons has been launched here, the first of such a size ever to have been built in this port, to the writer's knowledge.

WENCHOW'S TRICKY RIVER

Adventures of Incoming Ships: Large Vessels Launched

FROM OUR OWN CORRESPONDENT

Wenchow, Chê., Apr. 4.

Since last writing we have' had the C.M.S. Ka-ho in for cargo, calling in on her way down to Foochow and again on her way, back from that port to Shanghai. The same

Communist Outrages

From the western border of this part of Chekiang comes news of serious disturbances by Communist bandits. It is reported that a battalion of soldiers sent up there some time ago has been defeated by them, their leader killed and two soldiers captured. One of the C. I. M. ladies of that district whose residence was said to have been surrounded by the brigands has been expected here for refuge, while four Chinese officials have had to fee thence Your correspondent learns that in the Cedar Creek hsien, where the bandits are still very active, their activities are being directed by a man of that hsien whose name is not printed abroad, but who is known to have been a figure in Hangchow and also in Nanking official circles but was cashiered for his known Communist sympathies. If that is really so, it may be a true rumour which is floating about that the bandits up there have on their flag the two characters for "Communist" – Kung – Ch'an.

Beggars are said to have caused a fire in one of the larger streets of this city recently which destroyed about two squares of shops and houses whereby about 100 families were rendered homeless.

Travel Dangers and Meningitis

Miss Simpson, a deaconess of the Methodist Mission, has just held, aided by her workers, a Bible and Reading Class for Women in the city. There was an attendance of over 50 for the fortnight. Many of the women coming from a long distance in the country in spite of the danger of travelling in these times. At the time of writing a second class is in session, of over 30 women and girls from nearer places in the country, who are lodged for the term of the classes in the Mission premises connected with the Central Church of the city.

A larger number would have at tended but the fear of meningitis which is still scourging the people has prevented several women from coming from a small island in the river nine – miles away toward the sea. Four or five deaths have recently occurred there from meningitis. The supply of serum having again been used up, cases of meningitis are having to return to their homes from the Methodist Hospital.

Dr. Marrow of the Methodist Mission reports more cases of meningitis admitted to hospital last week, and on the small island—" Heart of the River" (Kiang – Hsin) just opposite the north wall of the city, on which the British Consulate stands, two cases of that disease are reported among its few inhabitants.

The Bandit's Stray Shot

Last week a pitiable case was admitted to this hospital which, owing to long delay, ended fatally. A woman from near the Western part of the province referred to above, was brought from the Roman Catholic Hospital, where she had been attended to for about six days, after travelling in a seriously wounded condition for two days. Your correspondent had business in the Methodist Hospital at the time she was there and say her. She seemed then to be pretty far gone, but answered in a very faint yet audible whisper to a question as to her mishap, that she had just got up when a shot from bandits caught her. The doctor found that the pelvis was broken, and that the diaphragm also seems to have been penetrated.

"Soldiers' Search for Opium: Disagreeable Incident at Wenchow on the Taishun," *The North – China Herald and Supreme Court & Gazette*, May 6, 1930

Soldiers' Search for Opium: Disagreeable Incident at Wenchow on the Taishun

(From our own correspondent)

A member of the compradore's staff of the C. M. S. Taishun was severely manhandled by soldiers at Wenchow last week, following a search for opium. Shipping people inform us that the soldiers are carrying out unauthorized searches of vessels and that they are constantly assaulting people who attempt to reason with them.

The Taishun had been examined by Customs officials on the day in question and no opium was found.

SOLDIERS' SEARCH FOR OPIUM

Disagreeable Incident at Wenchow on the Taishun

A member of the compradore's staff of the C. M. S. Taishun was severely manhandled by soldiers at Wenchow last week, following a search for opium. Shipping people inform us that the soldiers are carrying out unauthorized searches of vessels and that they are constantly assaulting people who attempt to reason with them.

Later, a party of soldiers under a subordinate officer boarded the vessel and announced that they had come to look for opium. One of the compradore's staff asked them for their papers but, instead of producing these, the soldiers caught hold of him and gave him a severe beating.

They searched the ship from bow to stern and found that one of the passengers was smoking opium. This man was taken into custody and, incidentally, robbed of his belongings including a couple of rings, after which the soldiers went to the compradore's room and said that he must assume responsibility for the behaviour of the passengers. The compradore's accountant and a godown keeper tried to explain matters to them but the soldiers refused to listen and said that, untill the compradore paid the fine, the two men would be kept in prison. The unfortunate fellows were then taken away and, at the time the Taishun sailed, they were still being detained.

"Wharf Coolie Riot at Wenchow: Dispute as to Which Union Should Unload Steamer," *The North - China Herald and Supreme Court & Gazette*, May 6, 1930

Wharf Coolie Riot at Wenchow: Dispute as to Which Union Should Unload Steamer

(From our own correspondent)

Wharf coolies in Wenchow have declared a general boycott of the China Merchants S. N. Co. and are refusing to unload cargo destined for that port following serious trouble which occurred between two rival gangs of coolies at the company's wharf there on the 25th instant. As a result, the steamers Taishun and Kwangchi were delayed in their arrival at Shanghai.

A gentleman who was on board the Taishun when the trouble broke out, interviewed by a representative of the "North - China Daily News," said that, contrary to reports appearing in the Chinese press to the effect that half a dozen men had been killed, only two or three persons received minor injuries.

When the Taishun arrived at Wenchow', our informant said, coolies who were members of the Seamen's Union were engaged to unload the cargo, which consisted of rice, from the ship and move it to the company's godown across the bund. As they were carrying out their duties, a rival coolie gang operating under the title of the "Firewood Labourers Union" attempted to take over the job but the members of the Seamen's Union refused to allow them to do so. The former then attacked the latter with clubs, iron bars, hooks and other instruments and the latter put up a sturdy resistance. A member of the compradore's staff went out for the purpose of mediating but he was set upon by the "firewood" coolies and given a severe beating, after which he was bound with ropes, kicked and removed to headquarters from which, fortunately he escaped later.

The police intervened and arrested several of the ringleaders of the rival gang and this appeared to infuriate the members of both gangs, who then joined hands. They tried to storm the police station and to rescue their leaders and this resulted in a free – for – all – fight in the course of which several shots had to be fired into the air to quieten the maddened crowd. Seeing that it was useless to try to capture the police station, the gangs then turned their attention to the Taishun and tried to force their way on board but they were prevented from doing so by the police and the ship's staff.

During the trouble, several hundred bags of rice were stolen and the compradore of the ship is being held responsible in this connection, though, says our informant, the matter had absolutely nothing to do with him.

A general strike was later declared by the wharf coolies, who posted a huge sheet of red paper on the side of the Taishun declaring a general boycott of the China Merchants S. N. Co. and announcing that they would refuse to move cargoes from the company's ships.

Mediators later got to work and the cargo was removed to the company's godwns but the matter is still unsettled. Meanwhile, the Taishun aid the Kwangchi were held up on their return to Shanghai.

"The Wheat Crops Stem Famine: Plucky Resistance to Bandits: Three of a Band Shot," *The North - China Herald and Supreme Court & Gazette*, May 13, 1930

The Wheat Crops Stem Famine: Plucky Resistance to Bandits: Three of a Band Shot

(From our own correspondent)

Wenchow, May 3

In these bad times it is comforting to hear that inveterate and proverbial grumbler, the farmer, state that the Wenchow wheat harvest is good. In spite of damp days, men and boys and girls are busy cutting and threshing. Being his people speak of it as if there was little or no food value in it. Nevertheless it is largely saving the situation, temporarily at least, for many, many families who have long been on the brink of starvation.

THE WHEAT CROPS STEM FAMINE

Plucky Resistance to Bandits: Three of a Band Shot

FROM OUR OWN CORRESPONDENT

Wenchow, May 3.

in these bad times it is comforting to hear that inveterate and proverbial grumbler, the farmer, state that the Wenchow wheat harvest is good. In spite of damp days, men and boys and girls are busy cutting and threshing. Being his

The number of steamers, Chinese and Japanese, that for weeks have been plying to and from this port, in addition to the regular steamers, indicates a very large increase of business over what there was 20 or even 10 years ago; and this is confirmed by the continued erection of large foreign - style houses and business premises shooting up all over the city and suburbs. Some of the steamers are engaged in bringing to this port rice for which the inhabitants are paying a dollar for six and seven pints. Extra cargo space has had to be supplied because of cargo to be exported, and the Japanese steamers whose white banded funnel are not a familiar sight on the river are engaged mostly in the charcoal transport trade.

But grim tales still pour in. A coolie, formerly in the writer's employ, went up country last month to his married daughter's home amid the mountains to try and buy rice where last year's harvest was not quite so bad in most places nearer the sea, but could only secure $3 worth. He reported an attack by a band of over 30 brigands on a household fortunately possessed of arms. Three of the marauders were shot and the rest fled. A week or so ago a party of 10 soldiers of the city are reported to have ordered a sampan man one evening to take them over the river. An altercation arose and the soldiers beat the man very seriously injuring his arm. He took them across to a sandbank which, he told them in the dusk, was the mainland, and when they got out to walk up what they took to be the sandy shore, he went off, leaving them marooned. The rising tide overwhelmed them and eight of the party were drowned.

The Rev. Irving Scott, of the Methodist Mission, who was attending the district meeting of the circuit in the seaside city of Yoh – ts'ing (Clear Music) relates that party of bandits invaded that city, the few armed police having fled, and liberated the 20 odd prisoners in the jail, of whom only two were recaptured shortly afterwards. A few days ago a soldier, a very poor Wenchowese, who had been induced to join the army, or the section of it at present here, having become dissatisfied at receiving no pay and frightened by the officers' harsh treatment of the men, deserted and sought concealment in the New Canal Street. A hue and cry was raised. He was retaken, brought back and punished not only by a dreadful beating, which left him more than half dead, but also by the cutting off of one of his cars.

Toward the end of April the picturesque little walled town of Crystal Lily sending its smiles over its clean pebbly front and swift – flowing cliff opposite, and itself lying sheltered at the foot of the mountain, was horrified by the murder of the local Ts'un – Chang, who, in the discharge of his official duties, had framed a charge against some of the bandits who happened to be of his own clan and town. Two of the bandits went into his house and shot him through the head. The daughter – in – law is at present in the city here laying a complaint of murder against them.

Owing to the close proximity of large numbers of bandits, probably Communists of whom this city is said to contain many, a large party of whom—one report says 300—at—tacked the village of Hsinchiao (New Bridge) three miles from Wenchow city, on the night of April 30, killing one policeman and carrying off three or four of the inhabitants; this city is now under military law, shops have been ordered to close at dusk, soldiers parade the streets and question suspicious looking passengers. The city gates have augmented armed guards, the commander's residence is said to be defended by cannon and evening gatherings are being suspended. The military here who were sent from further north some weeks ago and said to have been sent to be out of the way because they are some of Feng Yu – hsiang's men, are said to be a bad lot of men, and it is feared that if things go wrong with Chiang Kai – shek's forces these men will play havoc in this place. A report has spread here to the effect that the bandits, supposedly Communists, of the Nan – Ch'i district, north of Wenchow, are desirous of making their way to the hsien city of P'ing – yang, and of joining up with similar bands to attack and take possession of that city. Six miles beyond Hsinchiao referred to above, is the large village of Djuchi at the head of valley eight or nine miles long. A former divisional commander, a reputed millionaire and possessor of thousand mows of land, has built himself a large residence in that village. He keeps a guard of 40 young fellows whom he has armed, so it is said, but that has not prevented him from receiving a command from the neighbouring brigands of Zie – Shi to supply them with about 80 tables of wine. Having no son, a nephew lives with him, though at present the uncle, finding it too perilous a place to stay in, has gone to Shanghai with his secondary wife and left the principal wife at home with the nephew.

Last night, May 2, soldiers patrolling the streets could be heard from our houses challenging passers – by, and a member of the Customs staff reports that there was a clash between soldiers and Communists just outside the East Gate, and saw the flashes of the firearms. There is no confirmation up to this evening of that rumour. A walk, this evening, on the city wall overlooking the. river, showed the C. M. S. N. Co. 's steamer, Kang – lee, at anchor in midstream with about score' of men in uniform on her, as though on guard, and the Sai Shun at the wharf in place of the same company's' steamer, Kwang – chi, which left for Shanghai earlier in the day. At 6 p. m. the unfamiliar sight was seen of the shops closed just outside and under the busy North Gate. The 10 soldiers referred to earlier of whom eight were drowned are said to have had their arms with them, as though they had secretly gone off either to loot on the north bank of the river, or to join the bandits in the northern part of the county, that they beat the boatman for not taking them over more quickly, and that he purposely misled them as to the sand bank being the mainland. There seems every reason, from the activities of the military about the city these days and nights, to believe that the authorities sense a very imminent danger.

"Martial Law at Wenchow: Special Precaution Against Bandit Activities," *The North – China Herald and Supreme Court & Gazette*, May 20, 1930

Martial Law at Wenchow: Special Precaution Against Bandit Activities

(From our own correspondent)

Owing to the activities of the bandits and the pirates, martial law is being very strictly enforced by the Wenchow authorities. The curfew hours are between sunset and daybreak and, even during the daytime, people are being held up in the streets and searched. After 6 p. m. , all means of communication are cut and nobody is permitted on the streets without special permission.

All wharves and places of importance are being very closely guarded and it is impossible for ships to enter or leave port after sunset.

As a result of these precautions, no vessels have been coming to Shanghai or leaving this port for Wenchow and, it is reported, no fewer than 2000 persons who had intended to go to the southern "port are marooned here. A number of foreigners" are said to be among these and they accordingly have been forced to cancel their passage.

MARTIAL LAW AT WENCHOW

Special Precaution Against Bandit Activities

Owing to the activities of the bandits and the pirates, martial law is being very strictly enforced by the Wenchow authorities. The curfew hours are between sunset and daybreak and, even during the daytime, people are being held up in the streets and searched. After 6 p.m.,

"Bandits of S. E. Chekiang: A Series of Towns Stormed and Raided," *The North – China Herald and Supreme Court & Gazette*, June 3, 1930

Bandits of S. E. Chekiang: A Series of Towns Stormed and Raided

(From our own correspondent)

Wenchow, Chê., May 27

During the second week of this month the town of Fung – ling (Maple Grove) in the Nan – Chi (Cedar Creek) district of this county was attacked by more than a thousand bandits, 20 to 30 of whom were reported killed in the fight. Maple Grove is a town of several thousand inhabitants with a good wall surrounding it. Its inhabitants are hardy mountaineers and rugged Christians. I understand there were two attacks, one at 9 a. m. , which seems to have been beaten off; then later in the day, through, it is said, the collusion of about 20 men of the place in league with the enemy, a second attack was made which resulted in the attackers getting into the town about 4 p. m.

Several of the inhabitants were also killed, 13 houses and five temples burned and other mischief done. A man who had run into the Methodist Church there, evidently for security, when he reappeared at the door with a carving knife in his hand, presumably thinking the attack had drifted to another quarter, was shot by bandit. A few days later a number of the soldiers stationed in this city were sent up against the marauders' who since then have made a wide detour to the west by way of the county of Chuchow and found their way to the busy walled town of

BANDITS OF S. E. CHEKIANG

A Series of Towns Stormed and Raided

FROM OUR OWN CORRESPONDENT

Wenchow, Che., May 27.

During the second week of this month the town of Fung-ling (Maple Grove) in the Nan-Chi (Cedar Creek) district of this county was attacked by more than a thousand bandits, 20 to 30 of whom

Pingyang, about 34 miles south of Wenchow.

The soldiers seem to have made some captures in Cedar Creek as there were several executions of bandits last week in the city and heads exposed at the gates. The military are also reported to have destroyed the village of Ng – ts'i in Cedar Creek, the home of the notorious leader of the bandits who have now for long been committing such depredations.

Having made their way, to the number of over a thousand, to Pingyang, these bandits from Cedar Creek attacked the town on Saturday, the 24th. A letter to hand from Miss Eynon of the Pingyang China Inland Mission to the Rev. F. Worley, of Wenchow, superintendent of the Mission, gives some particulars of the occurrence. All (that is the Rev. and Mrs. Barling and child, and Miss Eynon and Lange, all of the C. I. M.) are safe, though they had experienced a very anxious time. The attack took place on Saturday at the West Gate where there was heavy fighting. The ladies were not molested at all. (These two ladies live outside the city wall). On Sunday Mr. Barling was able to send a card to them saying that they were all right. They stated that over 200 bandits had been killed and a very thorough search was being made for stray bandits. At the time of writing on Sunday all was peaceful. Other particulars of the incident given this morning to your correspondent by his secretary, who has been much in touch with the yamêns here, is to the effect that over 100 bandits were killed, 100 rifles taken, one soldier killed and six wounded, and that the attackers had retreated south.

Last week the city was startled by the news that the village of Djiae – o – Ka in Lich'i had also been attacked by a very large band, who had carried off two women, and burned two small launches and had tried to seize the Ch'ing – T'ien launch and fired on it, but that launch had managed to get away by cutting the tow rope joining it to its complement of passenger boats: It got to the city with a hot hole in its hull. It was also rumoured that numbers of these bandits were in hiding on the north bank of the river, ready to join with these who would come down by launches, to make an attack on the city on Sunday last. Nothing of the sort has eventuated, however, so far as this city is concerned, and at the time of writing it has a more peaceful atmosphere than for months past.

But from every quarter come tales of rapine and incendiarism and bloodshed. I have just resumed my pen after being interviewed by a colleague who is now being interviewed by a pastor from a populous valley 12 miles up the river, who has come down with the news of raids on villages in his circuit in which many people lost everything. This man is on his way to see the military commander about the danger to another village there which it is feared will be attacked in a very short time. He tells of five Chinese Methodists in the place attacked who have been robbed in this attack of all their belongings.

"Ghastly Scenes in Wenchow: Horrible Stories of Public Executions," *The North - China Herald and Supreme Court & Gazette*, July 8, 1930

Ghastly Scenes in Wenchow: Horrible Stories of Public Executions

(From our own correspondent)

Wenchow, June. 25

One feels in writing so unintermittently of rapine that not only to an editor, but to oneself, must come the sense of satiety with such effect as to make the continued reception and writing of such incidents an utter adherence. And yet, here as elsewhere, these are the things just now that are most powerfully infringing on the daily life of multitudes, and multitudes more are experiencing with no less poignancy the secondary results of such impacts.

Business suffers and must suffer for so much money is lost to these innumerable bands of marauders who often use "method in their madness," mulcting the victims of their murderous onslaughts in $50, $60, $100, and more dollars a household in a village according to their reputed or imagined financial condition.

A country shop - keeper in a small village up among the mountains, when down in the city four days ago, told me that he had just lost $300 in a visit by bandits to his place. He was seeking a secure place in the city for four boxes of his goods and chattels. Three of the women attending the Summer School for 50 women and girls being held just now by Miss Simpson and her workers of the

GHASTLY SCENES IN WENCHOW

Horrible Stories of Public Executions

FROM OUR OWN CORRESPONDENT

Wenchow, June 25.

One feels in writing so unintermittently of rapine that not only to an editor, but to oneself, must come the sense of satiety with such effect as to make the continued reception and writing of such incidents an utter adherence. And

Methodist Mission asked leave at the weekend to return to their village homes 12 or 15 miles away as word had come that these homes had just been rifled by bandits, households not of well – to – do people, but of the ordinary hard working small farmer.

Education suffers for country schools are visited and boys carried off for ransom. Agriculture suffers—what is the use, is the question being put in some places now, of reaping when our grain will be taken by those who have not sowed. Social progress suffers, civilization in China is getting an unspeakable, an immeasurable, one hopes a not irremediable, set – back by this nation – wide onset of murder, bloodlust, rapine and vengeful fury.

Gentle Art of Execution

Two gentlemen called on me last week. One had just seen a sight the description of which matched anything of the many revolting descriptions of mediaeval callousness. Two bandits had been caught, one beheaded, the head tied to the neck of the other, who was thus led to execution, and the two heads then exposed on one of the city gates.

In this city in full view of the writer's house is a very picturesque hillock, some 300 or 400 yards away. We here speak of it as Pavilion Hill. The city wall runs over its eastern shoulder. The crest some 150 to 200 feet high is crowned by neat little pavilion with its stone pillars and connecting stone seats supporting hexagonal curved roof of fluted tiles.

Open to all the winds of heaven this pretty little pavilion gives views of sea and island, river and plain, city and mountain, rice – filled fields and smiling villagers. Immediately below is a swelling cluster of restless bamboos folding in their embrace a tripled – terraced Buddhist temple looking westward over the entire city and seeming to brood in unending and patient, yet anxious, meditative watchfulness over its fortunes. Below and around it are the green tree clad slopes open in places and one of these open spaces just below the temple has lately time and again been the place of execution of captured brigands.

On Wednesday June 4, as I was writing on my upstairs verandah I was surprised by the sound of a short sharp volley and looking up saw a squad of soldiers on the green just below the temple, and a few paces in front what looked like huddled little heap of blue. The glasses revealed this to be a human being lying prostate clad in the ordinary blue cotton garments of a countrymen. Soon crowds were hurrying up the hill, apparently all conditions of people, well – dressed women, and fathers leading neatly dressed little girls of 6 or 7 years of age to see the sight. On – lookers spurned aside with the foot the clothes of the victim evidently desirous of seeing the wound. This went on for a couple of hours perhaps when two coolies brought a plain looking coffin, the corpse was bundled into it and they carried it away.

A few days later the sound of two shots again caused me to look at the hill and it seemed from the vast crowd that in summer's many hued garments covered the hill from almost its base to the pavilion summit, to be a gala day, but they had just looked on the shooting of two more brigands, and even as looked a soldier with a broad sword two feet long knelt on the sward and swinging his weapon apparently over the same object invisible from the house. He dealt a succession of blows one! two! three! Then a pause of a few seconds to shift his position to get more purchase four! five! And raising himself he walked a few paces carrying by its: short, half – cut hair a human head. Laying it down he wiped his weapon on and with the grass while another soldier strode forward picked up the head and walled away, probably to expose it at one of the gates.

"The Development of Wenchow: Chekiang Officials Plan to Expand Trade," *The North – China Herald and Supreme Court & Gazette*, August 12, 1930

The Development of Wenchow: Chekiang Officials Plan to Expand Trade

(From our own correspondent)

With a view to improving the commence of southeastern Chêkiang, and increasing the exports of Chekiang, as well as expanding the shipping trade along the Wu River region, officials of the Chekiang Provincial Reconstruction Bureau have resolved to develop Wenchow by dredging the Wu River and constructing a railway between Wenchow and Lanchi.

A number of engineers and experts were sent to Wenchow on August 5 to make investigations and work on the development of the port is. expected to be commenced within a month.

THE DEVELOPMENT OF WENCHOW

Chekiang Officials Plan to Expand Trade

With a view to improving the commecre of southeastern Chêkiang, and increasing the exports of Chêkiang, as well as expanding the shipping trade along the Wu River region, officials of the Chêkiang Provincial Reconstruction Bureau have resolved to develop Wenchow by dredging the Wu River and constructing a railway between Wenchow and Lanchi.

Wenchow is one of the chief ports in Chekiang and at present seven vessels owned by Shanghai companies ply regularly between that port and Shanghai. However, the port is not as large as could be hoped because no means are available just now for the rapid transportation of native products from southern Chekiang to other places or vice versa. In view of this, the "Shunpao" says, officials of the Chekiang Reconstruction Bureau recently decided to develop the port.

Initial development work to be undertaken by officials of the Bureau will consist of dredging the Wu River so that large vessels may enter Wenchow directly instead of calling at Yungkia, which is to Wenchow what Woosung is to Shanghai.

Officials of the Chekiang Reconstruction Bureau also propose to construct a railway from Lanchi, in south Chekiang, to Wenchow to facilitate the transportation of Chekiang products from the interior to the coast. These products include timber, charcoal, hams, woodoil, paper, all of which are well – known in Chekiang and which, if exported, should help considerably to improve trade and commerce.

"News from the Outports: More Executions at Wenchow: Batch of Sixteen Shot Just Recently" *The North – China Herald and Supreme Court & Gazette*, August 19, 1930

News from the Outports: More Executions at Wenchow: Batch of Sixteen Shot Just Recently

（From our own correspondent）

Wenchow, August 6

NEWS FROM THE OUTPORTS

MORE EXECUTIONS AT WENCHOW

Batch of Sixteen Shot Just Recently

FROM OUR OWN CORRESPONDENT

Since last writing—June 25—a considerable number of executions of bandits and communists has taken place, on Pavilion Hill, totalling to date something over seventy, the last batch twelve in number being shot on July 31. Among this last party were a woman said to have been a propagandist and her 19 year old son. A few days prior to that a batch of sixteen were shot, soldiers going up to each one as he knelt on the grass and shooting him. In most, if not all cases the victim had to be shot again in the same fashion. It seemed the height of cruelty that for several minutes those captives whose turn came last, had to endure the sight as they knelt others being shot ere their turn came. In the case of the last executions a little more of the spirit of civilization, or perhaps the desire to appear so, to foreign eyes was manifested in that the bodies were wrapped up in matting before being roped to the carrying pole to be taken away.

The troops are still engaged among the hills but it seems with very varying success. They are apparently too few for the work in hand, and are said to be much inferior in ability to the Northern soldiers, some of them Feng Yuhsiang's former men, who were stationed here for a short time until about two months ago. ⋯Still they appear to be making a brave effort in spite of being sadly out-numbered, and about a month or so ago made a very important capture, the de-tails of which I heard just today from an informant who says he knew some of those concerned.

The capture was of the leader of the Communists of this district, a young highlander from a very large village just over 30 miles north of Wenchow city. During more than 30 years your correspondent spent many a day and night in that village whose inhabitants have for a longer time than that had a reputation for pugnacity and clan feuds of a ferocious quality. They do, however, make staunch Christians when once they have been won. The communist leader re-ferred to was a young man of reputed great ability who graduated in the Normal School here.

His family was poor, the father owning ten mow of land and he sold five mow to enable his son to proceed to Russia where he is said to have graduated, and where he seems' to have been more firmly indoctrinated in Communism. The report goes that he never helped his parents who had made such sacrifices for him, and on his return to his native country of Wenchow he was the hands through which the Russian money went to help on the work of Communist propa-ganda.

Several weeks ago the young man Chin Chia – chu by name came down to Wenchow, and stayed with a relative who keeps a rice – shop near the South Gate. A school girl is said to have told the authorities of his place of temporary residence and soldiers were sent to apprehend him. He endeavoured to defend himself with a revolver but it missed fire and the soldiers closed in on him and secured him. He asked them why they should do this as Communism was what would benefit soldiers. But it was of no avail and he told them they could shoot him.

His end came in the usual way on the hill here in the city. But the impor-tance of that capture is said to lie here, that he and his next in command, Ho Kung – mien, whose native village of U – ch'ih, I reported in the "N. – C. D. News" as having been burned by the military, had arranged in their plan of cam-paign first to attack and take Wenchow, then proceed up river and take the city of Chuchow, then across country to Hangchow. With the ablest leader put out of the way there does not seem now much likelihood of the realization of that plan.

Another report given me today is to the effect that the soldiers in the small walled town of Piehlien（Crystal Lily）in the Neihsichi district between 20 and 30 miles to the N. N. W. have recently suffered a very serious reverse at the hands of the bandits there, several of them having been killed, their billets in that town destroyed and arms taken, besides coolies whom the soldiers had commandeered from the city here for portage, being also taken away by the bandits. The billets for: the Northern soldiers when in Piehlien were in the Church and premises of the United Methodist Mission but no word has been received of any harm to those premises, from the pastor – in – charge. This rumour is most probably untrue; it has no confirmation.

Another item of news received recently was that in another part of the country several tailors had been carried off by the brigands and were ordered to make two thousand military uniforms for them.

One of the lady workers of . the Methodist Mission very desirous of resuming prison work among the female prisoners in the city got the Chinese Secretary of the Mission to write a letter requesting the officials' permission. . The Secretary took the letter in person and presented the letter, at the same time enlarging on the good nature of such work, its aim being to try and reclaim the fallen and to help them to become worthy citizens of the nation, a work and aim which the official would be glad to help and give opportunities for. He replied that he himself acknowledged this, but that the local Tang – Pu, was anti – Christian and would be hostile to the work. To the question as to his own attitude and feeling toward Christianity he represented himself as not inimical to it, but he could not ignore the Tang – Pu. However he would write to headquarters at Hangchow and if they were willing it would be allowed here. Asked why the Roman Catholic Sisters were allowed to do such work the reply was that they did not teach their religion but exhorted the prisoners to be good and also treated any sick. His only reply when told the Methodist worker would do the same, also dispense to the sick and sometimes bring little food, dainties and the like, was that he would write to Hangchow.

"Unrest Rife Near Wenchow," *The North - China Herald and Supreme Court & Gazette*, September 23, 1930

Unrest Rife Near Wenchow

(From our own correspondent)

Wenchow, September 16

The past week has witnessed the return of Mrs. Scott of the Methodist Mission to the port after an absence of about six months spent in England. She was met by her husband in Hongkong, the Rev. Irving Scott.

Our little foreign community will soon be having its number increased by the arrival of new members to the Mission and by the return of some on furlough. The Hospital is to have another English fully trained nurse, a young man who has finished his College course is now on his way to join the staff in the General work, Miss Dcidge B. A., is about to return for educational and other work, Dr. and Mrs. Stedeford are also expected, to return about the end of the year, bringing their infant son, who has appeared on the stage of life during their furlough. It is mooted, but no information so far, that a young doctor is to accompany them, to join the medical staff.

This with the following makes brighter reading for Wenchow people than has characterized the Wenchow reports for a long period now.

On Sunday I was speaking to a Chinese friend of many years, who is a well - to - do farmer living in a secluded little village in the side of a miniature valley up among the beautiful tree clad hills of West Brook. It is known to a few foreigners by the delightful name of Plum Torrent. High up above most of the terraced houses of the hamlet stands his well built and comfortable home, overlooking vil-

UNREST RIFE NEAR WENCHOW

FROM OUR OWN CORRESPONDENT

Wenchow, Sept. 16.

The past week has witnessed the return of Mrs. Scott of the Methodist Mission to the port after an absence of about six months spent in England. She was met by her husband in Hongkong, the Rev. Irving Scott.

lage and valley and facing a high steep hill up whose flank we have raced together in "The years beyond recall", when he would show me the remains of the circular wall on the summit to which the inhabitants were wont resort to for defence, when rumours of an approaching enemy were brought, in the days of the T'ai Ping Rebellion.

For years he has been a local preacher in the Methodist Circuit to which he is attached, and the leader of his village church. The village is situated in the very heart of the bandit country, and as men in his position socially are especially subject to the personal attentions of the bandits, he considered it expedient to live for several months in the city here with his son, who is a hospital assistant. His attendance at the Sunday services at the city church was marked with great regularity, but latterly he was missing for a few Sundays, then returned to his accustomed place two Sundays ago.

Asked the reason of his absence he said he had been to his home again. Probably the harvest season had necessitated the risk of the return. He said things were peaceful in his home village but that the vicinity was as disturbed and dangerous as ever. He had had the misfortune to fall into the hands of a band of the marauders on his way. They searched him, took his money and his watch, and were searching his wallet when they came across a book in it. It was his Chinese copy of Bible Daily Readings. Replying to their questions that it was such, "Oh" they said, "you are a Christian. Well, Christians do us no harm," and returning what they had taken from him, they let him go.

A few months ago an Adventist pastor had a similar experience. His shoes were taken from him, and continuing to search his person, the bandits came across a badge he wore. When told it was the badge which the Adventists pastors are said to carry with them, the leader of the bandits, learning that he was a Christian pastor, gave him a better pair of shoes than those taken, and let him go. One sighs in vain for the pleasure of describing normal conditions in this more lightsome aspect, but it is the Saturnine aspect that in these days has the more forcible and constant impact.

Though carried out in a different part of the city, executions still go on. Yesterday eight bandits were executed. One day last week seven, another day three, another day two. Wang Wen – han, the commandant of five prefectural cities in Chekiang, is here just now, so that the military have not now to send to Hangchow for authority to execute prisoners as his word is said to be authoritative.

On the 9th. of the month one of the largest villages in West Brook about 20 miles away was attacked by large force of bandits. The local press gives the figures as between 60 and 70 houses destroyed and four or five of the people killed. One of my informants said that the bandits used hand bombs—probably incendiary bombs. There was only a small force, about 40, of soldiers there at the time. Another report says a very serious attack was made about ten days ago on the town of Chin – Yun in the west, and that of the $ 17000 loot taken there was a sum of Government taxes which had been collected by the District Magistrate.

"Merchants' Strike in Wenchow: Opposition to Increased Taxation on Merchandise," *The North - China Herald and Supreme Court & Gazette*, November 25, 1930

Merchants' Strike in Wenchow: Opposition to Increased Taxation on Merchandise

(From our own correspondent)

The Wenchow authorities' decision to increase, from 20 to 30 percent, the tax on merchandise shipped to and from Wenchow by native merchants has resulted in a strike and the merchants have instigated the wharf coolies to join. The result is that all vessels calling at that port are unable to load or unload their cargo.

On November 17, the Wenchow authorities announced the increase but the merchants refused to pay according to the old scales. They (the merchants) then stopped shipping goods affected by the tax to other places from November 17. Representatives called on the authorities and requested them to abolish the proposed increase, but the latter were firm in their attitude and refused to comply with the request.

As some merchants were found to be secretly paying the new tax and shipping goods to other places, the merchants decided to prevent this and instigated the wharf coolies to join the strike, with the result that all vessels calling there are unable to load or unload their Kwangchi returned to Shanghai from Wenchow on Friday, bringing no cargo.

Many local native firms having business relations with Wenchow merchants are affected, as a large quantity of cargo ordered from Wenchow is being held in the southern port on account of the wharf coolies' strike.

MERCHANTS' STRIKE IN WENCHOW

Opposition to Increased Taxation on Merchandise

The Wenchow authorities' decision to increase, from 20 to 30 per cent., the tax on merchandise shipped to and from Wenchow by native merchants has resulted in a strike and the merchants have instigated the wharf coolies to join. The result is that all vessels calling at that port are unable to load or unload their cargo.

"Good Crops in Chekiang: Many Missing Sold in Famine Times," *The North – China Herald and Supreme Court & Gazette*, December 2, 1930

Good Crops in Chekiang: Many Missing Sold in Famine Times

(From our own correspondent)

Wenchow, Chê., November 10

Since the writer's last news of this port and district was mailed—September 16—he has been absent from the district for some time and though banditry is not terminated, he was pleased to find that there was and still is a very considerable diminution of it, and in some parts, where it is yet carried on it is said to be by a very small bands who prey on single households. Executions are still taking place, but the scene is shifted to a hill inside the South west corner of the city at the Three Horn Gate. An English woman just recently arrived in this city, married to a Chinese belonging to this part of the country whom she met and married ten years ago in London, he being vendor of soapstone and other Chinese curios there, has had horrifying introduction to life in this country. The rooms they took are in the part of the city where the executions of bandits and communists now take place, and being very near, these rooms look right on the scene of these tragedies. Up to a few weeks ago these had been in full view no fewer than 27 executions. The explanation of the transfer of the scene of the executions, given to your correspondent, was that there was a much used well at the foot of the hill on whose side about 40 yards above and away from the well the captives were shot, and the people using the well complained that the well was being tain-

GOOD CROPS IN CHEKIANG

Many Missing Sold in Famine Times

FROM OUR OWN CORRESPONDENT

Wenchow, Chê., Nov. 10.

Since the writer's last news of this port and district was mailed—September 16—he has been absent from the district for some time and though banditry is not terminated, he was pleased to find that there

ted by the blood of the victims percolating through the soil. People however are still using the well.

A new comer

A fortnight ago, our foreign community had its numbers augumented by the arrival of Rev. W. Roy Aylott of the Westcliffon Sea, a young man fresh from college, who has joined the staff of the Methodist Mission. He has already applied himself to the study of the language, written and spoken, and is charmed with the beauty of the surroundings, with the homeliness of the many Chinese who have already greeted him, and with the merry character of the bright faced Wenchow boys and girls. Nurse Petrie Smith of the Methodist Hospital has gone to Shanghai for a thoroughly well – earned change after two strenuous summers in the trying conditions of her profession here as evidenced by the excerpts from the report of Dr. W. A, N. Morrow. "The months of September and November (1929) inclusive were rendered very strenuous by the admission of a large number of cases of cholera to the hospital···four times that of the highest attained in any other year, it is worthy of note that although there are hospitals in the city run by Chinese, these showed less than hundred cases among them. This is to be ascribed to the excellent results obtained at the hospital during the epidemics of 1926. " (Dr. E. T. A. Stedeford was then in charge) 971 cholera cases were' admitted, a recovery rate of approximately 80 percent, was obtained, "This figure being arrived at by addition of 9 percent, to the death rate recurring at the hospital···not single case of cholera occurred amongst the hospital staff. "

Nurse Smith had as colleague Nurse Raine married and now living in Yokohama. But during the dysentry epidemic of this year she has had no trained nurse with her. The statistics for the last tabulated year will show something of the responsibility which has been hers.

Out – patients 37920

In – patients (male) 2610 (female) 1263

Operations (major) 239 (minor) 529 "About one – third of the cases are medical and include ··· cases the following: Tuberculosis, malaria: beri – heri. typhoid, dysentery (amoebic and bacillary) meningitis, diphtheria, diabetes, diseases of heart, lung, kidney and liver. "

"Wenchow Teachers' Strike: Merchants' Refusal to Pay Another Levy to Meet Salaries," *The North-China Herald and Supreme Court & Gazette*, December 16, 1930

Wenchow Teachers' Strike: Merchants' Refusal to Pay Another Levy to Meet Salaries

(From our own correspondent)

WENCHOW TEACHERS' STRIKE

Merchants' Refusal to Pay Another Levy to Meet Salaries

FROM OUR OWN CORRESPONDENT

Wenchow, December 3

Talking with the head of one of the schools in this city this morning, I was told that to-day all the schools in the Yung – Chia Hsien here, which includes Wenchow city have closed down—all that is except Mission Schools. The reason for this step is related to some happenings of three or four years ago during the troublous times when North and South were fighting. A Fukien general and his troops passing through the city demanded a large sum of money from the inhabitants and this the merchants had to meet. During the recent famine the Yung Chia merchants of the city gave the writer a place on this Relief Committee and I know that they contributed tens of thousands of dollars in relief. In these and many ways much money has been drained out of the people.

The teachers in the schools of the Yung Chia district not being paid by the Educational authorities as they say they were promised, have now gone on strike and have closed all the schools and are refusing to be used. The local Education Bureau had, it seems, suggested to the Provincial Board that another levy should be made on the people through the merchants to pay the teachers. The merchants goaded to desperation by these continuous levies and exactions have replied that they will close down business rather than submit, so the Provincial authority has advised that the levy be not made.

This has its repercussion on the teachers who accuse the Bureau of perfidy and as that "servant of the people" (sic) replied to the deputation of teachers that he could not help himself, that he could only act on the instructions of the Provincial Board, they replied that they would close the schools. Asked what would be done in the case of any of the people inviting a teacher for their children privately, my informant said that the teachers he was talking with responded that they would prevent such teaching.

A Youth's Revenge

The local press—Chinese—has during the last few weeks been publishing correspondence and articles animadverting against the Seventh Day Adventists' Day Schools. Some of this correspondence I have read in those newspapers. It is said that in order to keep the schools open as Mission Schools the name of the schools was changed to "Theological Schools."

Another report goes on to say that a student had a difference with the principal because of carrying on correspondence with a girl pupil of the school which resulted in the youth's dismissal, and it is assumed that this youth is making use of the local Chinese Press to "get his own back again." A press representative writes of paying visit to the school in question, of the absence of Sun Yat – sen's portrait, of the religious pictures or texts to be seen in the school, of the many hours given to teaching and learning hymns and scripture, of the illegal character of the school and much more that one may expect from those Chinese who are inimical to Mission Schools in China.

My latest news is that the whole of the pupils—over a hundred boys and girls have left, and added to this that one pupil, the son of a pastor refused to leave the premises saying they belonged to the Church members and they would run the school.

Repentant Bandits

One, happily, hears little or nothing just now of banditry in the district, which is probably mostly owing to the fact that, as reported in the Chinese press here, there has recently been an accession to the numbers of the Chinese army by the turn over of several hundred bandits and their leaders to the official fighting forces. Hu Hsieh – Wei of Nan – Ch'i in this prefecture, a bandit leader is the first reported to have been received into the army with 84 bandits and over 40 rifles. Earlier in the year his brother a graduate of Russia, was executed here, being the leader then and much of his home village was destroyed by the military. Next comes Hsieh Wenchow of P'an – K'eng in Nan – Ch'i with 25 bandits and over ten rifles. Lastly and somewhat later comes Tong Tsoh – kuang of Nei Hsi Ch'i with over 400 bandits. This last force joined up on November 13, the leader being given a captain's rank. A further Evidence of more promising serenity lies in the fact that the whole staff including ladies of the C. M. have returned to their station of P'ing Yang nearer the Fukien Border.

Return of Miss Doridge

The Methodist Mission has now received into' its midst Miss D. Doridge B. A. , returned from furlough in England, she has already resumed her duties in her flourishing school, which by the way, is not affected by the other educational disturbances. Miss Doridge was given a great reception by her pupils who lined up in two long ranks inside the entrance and as she passed between them they simultaneously bowed to her with inimitable Chinese gracefulness. The walls were pasted with coloured scrolls recording in prodigious expressions her prodigious abilities and her prodigiously numerous virtues. The main room was festooned with coloured streamers and the children gave a concert and speeches in the welcome. The tiny tots among the girls gave a very enchanting exhibition of dancing and of recitation to the accompaniment of graceful physical evolutions. So charmingly did these tots do their part, and wholly devoid of self consciousness, that one under the charm of the remembrance feel under constraint to say that if there are such things as fairies, they must be tiny Chinese girls. Miss Doridge replied to these and other speeches from visitors, after' which whole school, staff and visitors were photographed.

Miss Doridge will now devote part of her time to the development of Christian Endeavour work and Sunday school work in the city and neighbouring, and hopes to find opportunities of getting into touch with the older girl students in some or other of the city schools. Nurse Fieldsend, who travelled with Mis Doridge from England, has now made acquaintance with the scenes of her future work in the two palatial hospitals of the mission, and to this end is already at work with a Chinese teacher on the language to fit herself, in addition to her other duties, to assist in the training of Chinese probationer women nurses of whom several here have now been received for training.

"Bandits Around Wenchow: Mission Bungalows on Hill Despoiled: the Drug Pill," *The North - China Herald and Supreme Court & Gazette*, January 6, 1931

Bandits Around Wenchow: Mission Bungalows on Hill Despoiled: the Drug Pill

(From our own correspondent)

Wenchow. December 8

On Saturday, December 6, your correspondent with a small party of English ladies and gentlemen, paid visit on foot up the 1300 feet of hill to the north of the Wenchow river to see in what state the bungalows belonging to the Methodist Mission were left after remaining unused for more than a year because of the danger from roving companies of bandits some of whom had paid the buildings a visit some months ago, broken in a few windows, taken a few things, and left the remainder of the furnishings as being of no monetary value to them and inconvenient for transport. The Chinese caretaker, whose dwelling is near told me that on the preceding Saturday bandits had again appeared and had carried off six or seven men from two villages at the foot of the bungalow hill and were still holding them to ransom, few thousand dollars being demanded for their redemption. All the hill folk in the vicinity of the Bungalows of whom there were several families—and the inhabit—ants of a neighbouring hamlet had fled at the approach of the brigands.

Sharp Talk to Teachers

One is pleased to report that the strike of the teachers recorded in one's last communication very speedily came to an end, very ignominiously, if rumours are correct, to the teachers. It appears that a representative of the Provincial Educational Bureau, was sent here to look into the matter, and he seems to have spoken in no uncertain tones to those who represented the teachers at the interview. Banging his hand on the table he accused the teachers of lack of patriotism, bidding them consider the trying conditions through which the country was passing. He told them that it was self interest that was tainting them, that their consciences were darkened by money. Finally he told all those unwilling to teach to write down their names and they would be dismissed and others appointed in their places. None, however, came forward—they were cowed and thus ended the short - lived strike. Once more as one goes along the streets one hears the voices of the scholars in their singing classes or at their recitation. One feels that had similar firmness been manifested in the discipline of the student body throughout the country from the first much of the loss and misery that have come to so many in China would have been mitigated if not quite obviated.

Back from Furlough

On Thursday, December 11, Dr. E. T. A. Stedford and his wife returned from furlough in England and were given warm welcome by the whole staff of the Mission of which he is a member. The glistening eyes and smiling faces of Chinese men and women who also came to welcome them at the wharf testified to the sure place the doctor holds in the esteem of very many in the veneration too of not a few Chinese. Furlough has been a time of tragically mixed experience for the Doctor for while it has meant the return of the Doctor and his wife with a promising son of some months of age, it has also meant to him the double sadness of the loss of his father. Rev. J. B. Stedford whose death was soon followed by that of the Doctor's mother. The Rev. Dr. Stedford, was a minister of very many years standing in the Methodist Church, who had filled the presidential chair for more than one term and who was held in high honour for his faithful service, his excellence as a preacher and his intellectual attainments.

A Convenient Method

On December 13, a detachment of some 120 soldiers was sent down from Wenchow to the Sui - an Hsien over 20 miles south, to attack some bandits who were raiding in that part. The bandits, however, had fled, but instead of following them up the soldiers came back here. A Chinese to whom I told this replied that that was what they did on occasions like that! Not particularly anxious to get to close quarters, they go to the place designated find the bandits gone and come back and say to their superior officer that they went to the place as told, the briands had fled, and so they come back themselves having done their duty.

The Drag Pill Trade

From information supplied to the writer in relation to a questionnaire on the narcotic situation here by the National Anti – opium Association it has been ascertained that there is quite considerable trade in opium, morphine, red pills, golden pills and white pills, that opium was introduced here about 90 years ago, the other drugs about 20, that opium is supplied from Fukien, the other drugs from Shanghai, that approximately 4000 catties of opium are imported annually at an estimated value of about $ 640000, that there are about 1000 retail dealers, all Chinese, most of whom are in the East Gate Suburb, that there are about 8000 addicts, most of whom belong to the wealthy class, that about 1/10 become habitues through illness, the rest through pleasure, and that the worst effects are produced by the pills and by morphine.

Wide Range of Fines

My informant, who made personal investigation at the office of one of the institutions established to combat the narcotic evil, tells me also that there are several institutions in the city for curing addicts who when cured receive certificates of cure. Some officials fine addicts from $ 30 to $ 1000 according to their financial standing, while other officials give sentences to addicts of imprisonment from 30 days to three years. Some of the officials and some people of influence are said to be themselves addicts, and it was suggested that if these were publicly punished, and those officials who give assistance to and countenance addicts and vendors degraded, it would have a more salutary and deterrent effect. Nanchi to the north of Wenchow is reported to be growing opium extensively, and the Nanchi bandit chief who was recently received with his men and arms into the army and given an official standing is in the way of receiving money from growers to secure his protection and patronage of their interests.

Dr. Marrow of the Methodist Hospital is again having quite a number of cases of bullet wounds, several of whom the writer saw when visiting the hospital a few days ago.

"New Comes to Wenchow: Dr. Dymond's Arrival to Replace Brother," *The North – China Herald and Supreme Court& Consular Gazette*, January 27, 1931

New Comers to Wenchow: Dr. Dymond's Arrival to Replace Brother

(From our own correspondent)

Wenchow, January 13

Since last writing, the medical staff of the Methodist Hospital has been increased by the advent of Dr. Elmlie Dymond who with his wife arrived from England on January 2. Dr. Dymond has nobly taken up the place of his brother, also a medical missionary who after a short term of service here was transferred to Yunnan to take up the medical work of the late Dr. R. P. Hadden who died at his post, of disease contracted in the pro – section of his professional duties. His young successor soon and similarly fell a victim to disease.

Dr. and Mrs. Dymond have received a most hearty welcome by the staff of the mission whose work in two hospitals will afford ample scope for his professional ability.

These brothers have a fine ancestry behind them, their father Rev. F. J. Dymond also in Yunnan having been the almost lifelong comrade – in – arms of the late Rev. Sam Pollard the inventor of the Miao dialect script into which the latter had turned parts of the New Testament thus giving to a whole tribe the beginning of a literature. The Rev. F. J. Dymond after 45 years in China almost entirely in Yunnan is due to return home to England in the spring of this year. A sister of the doctor's is also on the China Mission Field, after serving for a time in Yunnan,

NEW COMERS TO WENCHOW

Dr. Dymond's Arrival to Replace Brother

FROM OUR OWN CORRESPONDENT

Wenchow, Jan. 13.

Since last writing, the medical staff of the Methodist Hospital has been increased by the advent of Dr. Elmlie Dymond who with his wife arrived from England on January 2. Dr. Dymond has nobly taken up

and now married into the China Inland Mission.

Too Old for Bandits

I was speaking to an old pastor of the mission this afternoon, over 70 years of age, who has sted fastly continued at his post in spite of bandits, among the mountains of this county. In the prosecution of his work, he has encountered them but they have not molested him. In answer to a question, he replied that he was too old for the bandits to want him. He tells me that in his circuit banditry is still rife, and that when taking morning service at one of the village churches word was received those bandits were coming. He refused, however, to leave and announced that he would take the afternoon service as usual.

On Friday, January 2, a village just across the river from Wenchow was attacked by a party of 40 bandits who carried off eleven people. From a neighbouring village several people have come into the city to be safe from the marauders. A few days ago, a pastor informed me that in his district 700 soldiers were endeavouring by an encircling movement to round up bandits who were said to have 17 captives in their custody in that part. I have heard no further news.

Searches for Contraband

An officer of one of the steamers plying between this port and Shanghai told me recently that steamers are held up away down the river and searched for contraband by the Chinese cruiser, Chao Hua which has been in these parts for some time. A custom's official told me also recently, that when searching for contraband on a vessel here, a soldier threatened him with his revolver. The latter it appears was keeping guard over the smuggled goods. The local press—Chinese—records the closing of the likin in this area in both its departments, the T'ung chuen – chu and the Yang Kwang Chu, that the Hsien Chang had issued a proclamation telling the traders that they were not to pay duty now to the likin, and that the property of the closed likin establishment was to be placed in his charge. At the Maritime Customs I had it confirmed by a foreign official that the adjacent likin office was closed.

Bitter Cold Felt

Wenchow has for several days now been in the grip of keen frosts, canals having half an inch of ice on them. Walking home from the country the other day, a country man apparently a farmer of the ordinary type said in passing, "Even the vegetation is wilting with the cold," and one fears from the sight of the withered looking vegetables that there will be considerable loss to the farmers on these crops for s far as the eye could reach over the miles of plain covered with luxuriant crops of the broad leaved vegetable common to this part, the leaves were pendant and curled in apparently devitalized apathy.

"The Weather at Wenchow: A Chinese Convert's Question," *The North – China Herald and Supreme Court& Consular Gazette*, February 9, 1931

The Weather at Wenchow: A Chinese Convert's Question

(From our own correspondent)

Wenchow, Febuary 9

Wenchow is just now experiencing an excess of meteorological variability. January saw days of keen frost which caused much of the profuse vegetation in the fields to curl up and wither under its blighting power, but being speedily, succeeded by days of genial sunshine, there was a resulting rapid convalescence and today the fields present an aspect of satisfying plenty.

February has a similar meteorological tale to tell of days and nights when during the former fires in the house seemed to be a first necessity and those whose youthful pride scorned, such things, as bedsocks might be pardoned for envying those who put comfortable nights before pride and cold feet.

Then came a Sunday of such mildness that one discarded winter clothing, for light autumn wear, nevertheless a quiet walk of no more than a mile on level roads, produced profuse perspiration. Yesterday saw slight snow on the hills, to – day is so different that the least degree of unaccustomed physical exercise means damp underclothing. After a night of cold and damp follows a day of such warmth and sunshine that by afternoon tennis nets are up and old men who should know

THE WEATHER AT WENCHOW

A Chinese Convert's Question

FROM OUR OWN CORRESPONDENT

Wenchow, Feb. 9.

Wenchow is just now experiencing an excess of meteorological variability. January saw days of keen frost which caused much of the profuse vegetation in the fields to curl up and wither under its blighting power, but being speedily succeeded by days of genial sunshine there was a resulting rapid convalescence and to-day the fields present an aspect of satisfying plenty.

better are induced to play in shorts.

A Convert's Puzzle

And as in the sphere of the physical so it is in other—shall we say metaphysical spheres. Here too we have alternations fluctuating between the sublime and the ridiculous. Coming home from church one morning, recently a Chinese middle aged convert but recently baptized, a man in very humble circumstances, called out as I was passing him. "Sir, sir! there is a matter I am wanting to ask you. I have been reading through the Bible and I can find no answer to what has been troubling me. We human beings, you and myself, for instance have surnames, but I cannot find that God has a surname. Can you tell me what God's surname. "

"We," your correspondent replied, "have had our surnames handed down from our ancestors, we need surnames to distinguish us in address. But we are taught that God is self existent, omnipotent, all seeing, all knowing, eternal unlike ourselves. He has no ancestry, He has no like and so no need for such names as we have to distinguish Him from His fellows. He has no fellows. But the names that Jesus called Him by is the one we may use in addressing Him "Our Father who are in heaven!""

A week or two ago a maternity patient in the Methodist Mission Hospital gave birth to triplets—a great marvel to the local Chinese who came in hundreds to see the three infants when the news was noised abroad.

That there are not a few Chinese parents even non – Christians who desire that their children's moral training shall not be neglected during the period of intellectual nurture and discipline has been evidenced quite markedly in the reopening this week and last of the Methodist Lower Primary Mixed School.

There were some tens of vacancies in the school to be filed – up, caused by the graduation into the Higher Primary at term end of those whose period of tuition in the Lower School was completed. More than three times the number made application for entrance, and the school is filled to its utmost capacity. Parents freely confess that they have taken their children away from other schools because of the lack of this higher tone, and are more than willing to have their children receive Christian instruction rather than that their offspring should have an education divorced from ethical and disciplinarian culture. One cannot but believe that throughout this vast country there are great numbers of non – Christian parents who would be glad to see the religions liberty restored to Mission Schools which was once enjoyed by them.

Bandits and Pirates

Banditry is by no means at an end in many parts of this country. A note in my diary of February 2, runs thus " L – told me that banditry is still very very bad in Jade Ring Island, a village there recently had ten homes burned down and several people carried off by brigands. About four days ago an hotel – keeper of this city was murdered by bandits in Inner Westbrook of which he was a native. It seems that earlier in these troubles, he was employed by the military to guide them in their operations against the bandits there. Recently he had business requiring, his attentions up there the bandits learning where he was staying, collected a force of about 100 men, surrounded the place, caught him and put him to death. "

The same may be said of piracy—it is still being carried on. Yesterday morning February 8, the C. M. S. Co's steamer the Kwang – chi left for Shanghai. She was back here early in the afternoon, I went down the office and both there and on the steamer itself, I was told that when she got outside the river, the guard of 12 soldiers carried by her found 12 pirates among the passengers, and these were at once brought back by the steamer and handed over to the authorities. Today the Kwang – chi has again assayed to reach Shanghai.

"Methodist Mission Meeting: Wenchow Gathering Well Attended by Young Delegates," *The North –*
China Herald and Supreme Court& Consular Gazette , March 31, 1931

Methodist Mission Meeting: Wenchow Gathering Well Attended by Young Delegates

(From our own correspondent)

Wenchow, March 13

The Methodist Mission has just held its annual meetings for this district, attended by nearly, 200 delegates, some coming from churches 2 to 3 days distant. A very pleasing and encouraging feature of the gatherings was the large number of young men who represented their churches in town and country. Over a period of 34 years the writer has no recollection of so many members still young being representatives of these meetings. Day after day for nearly a week the rain fell, but the smiling faces in the meetings spoke of "sunshine in the soul. " That the church has still wonderful virility is evidenced by the fact that notwithstanding famine, pestilence, universal rapine incendiarism, murder and ⋯ menace during the past year, and in spite of some lapses and nearly a hundred deaths the membership is only eighty below the preceding year. It was heartening news too for mission workers to hear of districts, though not all, so free from banditry that the foreign missionaries were advised that they might once more itinerate there. One large village of only a very small Christian communion is without a place of worship this year as the house hitherto used was burned down along with others by bandits. To –

METHODIST MISSION
MEETING

Wenchow Gathering Well Attended by Young Delegates

FROM OUR OWN CORRESPONDENT

Wenchow, Mar. 13.

The Methodist Mission has just held its annual meetings for this district, attended by nearly 200 delegates, some coming from churches 2 to 3 days distant. A very pleasing and encouraging feature of the gatherings was the large number of young men who represented their churches in town and country. Over a period of 34 years

day Wenchow is exulting with all local vocal nature in the enjoyment of its 3rd consecutive day of spring sunshine.

Miss Simpson's Narrow Escape

It is a great change here to be able to report that several members of the missionary community are now up country. Mr. Chow of Shanghai is here for a few weeks as Christian Endeavour Deputation to some of the missions. He has had very large and appreciative audiences in the large Methodist City church, at the annual meetings referred to, and is now in the south of the district on the same work. News has just been received from Miss Simpson and Miss Dridge of that mission who are in the same part holding Bible classes masses for women for C. E. work that the former had a very narrow escape from what might have been a very tragic accident. Arrived at her destination by canal steam launch, she had engaged a riesha. The coolie soon got into a quarrel with another, and in his anger let loose his hands, the vehicle up – turning on the edge of the canal. Miss Simpson managed to get hold of a post as she overhung the edge of the canal but could not extricate herself. A Chinese who fortunately saw her predicament came and liberated her.

"Naval Brush with Pirates: Attempt to Attack Wreck Near Wenchow Repulsed", *The North – China Herald and Supreme Court& Consular Gazette*, April 7, 1931

Naval Brush with Pirates: Attempt to Attack Wreck Near Wenchow Repulsed

(From our own correspondent)

Nanking, April 1

Messages received at the Ministry of the Navy report that a miniature battle was fought between the gun – boat "Chukuan" and a gang of pirates near Wenchow, on the Che – kiang coast yesterday.

The gunboat which had been standing by to protect the salvage work for a Norwegian steamer, which recently foundered near Wenchow, suddenly encountered at three o'clock in the afternoon a large band of more than 100 pirates riding in junks who were approaching the derelict vessel for the purpose of plunder.

The naval men immediately brought their machine guns into action against the pirate boats, which returned the fire with their rifles. For several hours the encounter continued until the pirates were finally overwhelmed by the naval gunfire—Kuo Min.

NAVAL BRUSH WITH PIRATES

Attempt to Attack Wreck Near Wenchow Repulsed

Nanking, Apr. 1.

Messages received at the Ministry of the Navy report that a miniature battle was fought between the gunboat "Chukuan" and a gang of pirates near Wenchow, on the Chekiang coast yesterday.

"Waishing Wrecked Near Wenchow," *The North – China Herald and Supreme Court & Consular Gazette*, August 18, 1931

Waishing Wrecked Near Wenchow

(From our own correspondent)

Wenchow, August 14

Battered by the sea, pillaged by pirates and worn and weary with fatigue, 43 survivors of the wreck of the I. – C. S. Waishing arrived in Shanghai yesterday morning as passengers aboard the C. N. S. Kuangtung, bringing with them narrowing tales of the night's battle with the typhoon which drove their ship ashore at Namkwan Bay last Monday morning.

WAISHING WRECKED NEAR WENCHOW

Aug. 14.

Battered by the sea, pillaged by pirates and worn and weary with fatigue, 43 survivors of the wreck of the I.-C.S. Waishing arrived in Shanghai yesterday morning as passengers aboard the C.N.S. Kuangtung, bringing with them narrowing tales of the night's battle with the typhoon which drove their ship ashore at Namkwan Bay last Monday morning.

Both passenger's and members of the crew of the ill – fated craft were included among the rescued brought here by the Kuangtung, which was the first vessel to arrive at Nam – kwan Bay, near Wenchow, in response to the S. O. S. broadcast after the disaster. When the Kuangtung left the scene of the wreck after rendering all the aid possible, the Waishing was high and dry on the rocks, with her master, Captain T. Hughes, and a skeleton crew still aboard, awaiting the arrival of the salvage str. , Yusto Maru, due there at noon yesterday. The H. M. S. Sepoy also is steaming at full speed from Hongkong to protect the wrecked vessel from further depredations by pirates.

Due to the seamanship and coolness displayed by Captain Hughes and his officers, only one life was lost in the disaster and the pirates were prevented from stripping the survivors of all their possessions and absolutely looting the ship. As it was, Mr. R. B. Symington, third engineer of the Waishing, made a determined effort to save the one man lost, a Chinese assistant to the compradore who was drowned when a ship's boat, loaded with men, was driven against the cliffs and smashed to pieces in the seas then raging. Although he had gained safety, Mr. Symington unhesitatingly dived back again, seeking to reach the drowning man. It was only with great difficulty that the other members of the boat's crew succeeded in dragging the engineer ashore when the Chinese had been swept beyond hope of rescue.

According to the stories told by the survivors, Captain Hughes, when first advised of the typhoon's presence in his vicinity, immediately headed into Namkwan Bay, a bottle – necked harbour recommended by the maritime authorities as a typhoon refuge. With everything mutable lashed down and two anchors out, the Waishing rode the typhoon all Sunday night, the disturbance having hit the vessel at dusk.

Shortly before morning, however, it was seen that the anchors, out to the last, link of chain, were dragging, although the vessel had steamed at full speed into the teeth of the gale in order to relieve the strain. Having but little cargo aboard, the Waishing was high out of the water and the wind, blowing with terrific force, was driving her directly on the rocks.

Noticing a sandy beach just around a rocky head, Captain Hughes made a determined effort to beach his craft there where she could have been salvaged with ease. However, the Waishing did not have sufficient power to make any headway against the gale and at eight o'clock Monday morning she struck with terrible force. Fearing that the vessel would break up if the typhoon continued, Captain Hughes ordered a boat lowered. The wind however, drove the small craft on the rocks.

A breeches – buoy was improvised and by this means the remainder of the passengers and crew, with the exception of those who volunteered to stand by the ship, were sent ashore safely.

Hardly had the ship struck when the petty pirates who live in that vicinity swarmed about the ship and survivors, making off with everything they could lay their hands on. When these men became more menacing Captain Hughes formed a perimeter camp ashore and gathered with men therein, mounting guard with the one revolver that had been salvaged.

In the meanwhile, when the ship first struck and the main radio apparatus went out of commission, S. O. S was sent out on the auxiliary batteries. This message was picked up by the Keelung Radio Station, at Formosa, and relayed to Hongkong and other ships at sea. This resulted in the Kuangtung, Captain Hodgekiss, who was about 100 miles away teaming to Nankwan Bay at full speed. The Kuangtung arrived at the entrance Monday night but could not enter until Tuesday morning.

Arrangements were made for the newly arrived vessel to bring the main body of the survivors to Shanghai while additional arms were landed for the protection of the men who were to stay by the hip.

August 16

Reports were received in Shanghai yesterday that the steamer was heeling to the threat of destruction.

A skeleton crew was left on the vessel when she went aground and additional supplies were despatched to them yesterday by the steamer Fooshing. H. M. S. Sepoy and a Japanese salvage vessel are standing by.

"Air Operations Against Reds: Wenchow Inhabitants' Mixed Feelings," *The North – China Herald and Supreme Court& Consular Gazette*, September 1, 1931

Air Operations Against Reds: Wenchow Inhabitants' Mixed Feelings

(From our own correspondent)

Wenchow Che. , August 18

For the space of a week this area has been under the pall of a deep climatic depression, bringing clouds, showers, squalls and little sunshine. It started with the visit of a typhoon that had drifted up from Hongkong way, and for a day or two farmers in the vicinity were fearful of the damage threatening the ripening harvest, when fortunately the storm soon lessened in velocity and did not, so far as I have heard, cause extensive damage by wind or flood. The steamer Ka – Ho on her weekly trip from Shanghai, with a full passenger list, and in addition two foreign ladies, being forced to anchor in the shelter of the islands at the mouth of the Wenchow river, was in consequence delayed some 30 hours, and eventually came feeling her way cautiously up the river late on Tuesday night.

The weather still gives promise of remaining cool. People are remarking on the unusual lowness of the temperature this Summer. Since one disagreeably hot week in early July my indoor thermometer has seldom registered over 85 percent, while just lately the mercury has found a stopping – place several points lower.

AIR OPERATIONS AGAINST REDS

Wenchow Inhabitants' Mixed Feelings

FROM OUR OWN CORRESPONDENT

Wenchow Che., Aug. 18.

For the space of a week this area has been under the pall of a deep climatic depression, bringing clouds, showers, squalls and little sunshine. It started with the visit of a typhoon that had drifted up from Hongkong way, and for a day or two farmers in the vicinity were

The aerodrome, which the Nan-king authorities gave orders to be erected near this city, is still in process of erection, although for its completion a time-limit of one month had been imposed. A large acreage of land outside the West Gate has been requisitioned for the purpose, the former owners of the land who declined the invitation of the Government to grant their property freely as a gift to the Nation, receiving a small compensation. The aerodrome is to be the base in the South, and a sister-station to the one in Ningpo. It will be employed purely for military purposes, and its immediate purpose is reported to be in the nature of a base of aerial operations against the Communist armies. The citizens do not all regard the project as a good news. Although they recognize that the presence of a military aerodrome might act as an effective defense against bandit armies, and the Red armies now retreating from the General Chiang offensive, yet there is the other consideration that the presence of a flying-station might bring Wenchow to the front in military circles, and rob us of that fortunate obscurity that has hitherto helped us to evade the path of warring armies

Pedestrians in the City on a recent day found themselves suddenly drawn up to the side of the road to witness a small procession of horse-soldiers, headed by buglers, and escorting a woman-criminal trussed in a ricksha with her crimes attached to her person in the usual way. She was exhibited through all the main thoroughfares in this manner, and then taken to her death at an execution ground outside one of the gates. This wretched woman had for many years been a trusted servant in a certain Chinese household where lived a small son of the family. One morning it was discovered by the agitated parents that the lad had mysteriously disappeared, robbers having effected an entrance and taken him away to ransom. A search resulted in the discovery of both prey and captors. Unfortunately for the woman, one of the robbers, a relation of hers, betrayed her as having opened the doors of the house for them to effect an entrance to do their work, and before long the boy who had been taken to a distant village was recovered by the police, with the capture of the servant and some of those in league with her.

"Mob Violence at Wenchow: Japanese Godowns Looted and Burned," *The North - China Herald and Supreme Court& Consular Gazette*, November 17, 1931

Mob Violence at Wenchow: Japanese Godowns Looted and Burned

(From our own correspondent)

Smashing their way through ba-rred gates and doors, a Chinese mob, led by pickets of the Anti - Japanese Association, at Wenchow, Chekiang province, on Sunday afternoon looted the shops, godowns, offices and staff residences of the Iwai Yoko Company, Ltd. and then set fire to the entire group of buildings, which were burned to the gro-und, causing a total loss estimated at well o-ver $100000. Information of the

MOB VIOLENCE AT WENCHOW

Japanese Godowns Looted and Burned

Smashing their way through barred gates and doors, a Chinese mob, led by pickets of the Anti-Japanese Association, at Wenchow, Chekiang province, on Sunday afternoon looted the shops, godowns, offices and staff residences of the Iwai Yoko Company, Ltd. and then set fire to the entire group of buildings, which we e burned to the ground, causing a total loss estimated at well over $100,000.

outrage was received here yesterday at the local offices of the Iwai Yoko Company, Ltd, at 9a Hankow Road, one of the largest Japanese importing and exporting firms operating in China, and was immediately reported to the Japanese Consulate General for Shanghai. Mr. K. Murai, the Consul General, communicated at once with the Japanese Consul at Hangchow, which is the seat of the Chekiang Provincial Government, and instructed him to register a stern protest with the Chinese authorities and advise them that they would be held directly responsible for the affair.

This step was taken inasmuch as when the Japanese community evacuated Wenchow for Shanghai on November 9, due to the threatening attitude of the

Chinese populace the premises of both the Iwai and Suzuki Yoko Company, another large Japanese firm, were placed completely under the supervision of the Provincial Government. An acknowledgment of the letter and acceptance of the responsibility was received in reply from the Chinese authorities.

For some time past Wenchow has been the headquarters for considerable anti – Japanese propaganda, the Japanese report, and the evacuation of the town was deemed necessary to avoid a clash between the two nationalities. Several days ago, the Shanghai office of the Suzuki Company was notified that its premises at Wenchow, which also contain considerable merchandise and property, had been left unguarded through the arrest by pickets of the Anti – Japanese Association of the Chinese watchmen who had been left on guard. The Chinese authorities had been notified by the local Consulate – General of this occurrence but the news of Sunday's outrage arrived before a reply could be received.

According to the brief description of the affair telegraphed here, the attack on the Iwai Yoko buildings followed a large anti – Japanese meeting at Wenchow on that day. Pickets are said to have harangued the crowd, which numbered over 5000 and, after urging it to "wipe all traces of the Japanese off the face of the earth," led a dash at the barred gates. With no opposition to halt them, entrance was soon effected and when the premises were completely looted of all property, they were given over to the flames.

Chinese soldiers and police are reported to have watched the proceedings without attempting to interfere and, when, the local fire brigade responded to the alarm, efforts are alleged to have been confined to seeing that the blaze did not spread to adjacent Chinese structures. It is feared here that if the Suzuki – godowns and offices have escaped damage so far, they may be the next target for anti – Japanese violence.

"Students Busy in Wenchow: Comparative Quiet but Much Activity," *The North – China Herald and Supreme Court& Consular Gazette*, January 19, 1932

Students Busy in Wenchow: Comparative Quiet but Much Activity

(From our own correspondent)

Wenchow, Che, December 26

While during the last few months in other places there have been violent anti – Japanese student disturbances, the city of Wenchow has in comparison enjoyed security and quiet. That is not to say that the local student organizations are not of sympathy with the National student bodies, but only that their nationalistic enthusiasm and anti – Japanese exuberances have not so far gone beyond the official activities permitted by the local authorities.

STUDENTS BUSY IN WENCHOW

Comparative Quiet but Much Activity

FROM OUR OWN CORRESPONDENT

Wenchow, Che., Dec. 26.

While during the last few months in other places there have been violent anti-Japanese student disturbances, the city of Wenchow has in comparison enjoyed security and quiet. That is not to say that the local student organisations are not of sympathy with the National student bodies, but only that their nationalistic enthusiasm and anti-Japanese exuberances have not so far gone beyond the official activities permitted by the local authorities.

The students have not been idle. They have been in close cooperation with the National Salvation Society, organizing the boycott, and in the schools bringing the military element, already not inconspicuous, to the fore. Thus every school is now organized on the lines of a military camp, and as an enrolling station for student squads of boys who enlist voluntarily as young soldiers, and drill together with dummy rifles. A bugler has replaced the school bell to announce changes of classes.

In the libraries, spread on the conspicuous tables and hung along the walls are maps and books dealing with the Manchurian situation, all detrimental to Japan. In the street outside a placard displays pictorially, and with lavish use of the crimson colors, some of the substances of this library literature. Every now and again there are short holidays in the senior middle schools so as to enable the students and staff to propagate the facts or some of the facts of the situation to the illiterate by means of public meetings, and also to make a tour of the shops confiscating or sealing up all goods made in Japan. Even the wee mites of the primary schools have done their bit. One hardly knew whether to laugh or to cry at the not infrequent sight of little fellows, probably not yet advanced beyond the third National Reader congregating together at street corners with the avowed intention, as I gathered from their baby speeches and slogans, of urging their unpatriotic elders to go to war. These same children were all wearing the arm badge of national humiliation. Finally, and most funnily, all are now in khaki uniform.

One result of the boycott has been to make money scarce. Shopkeepers with their money sealed up in unsaleable Japanese goods have been borrowing at a rising scale of interest from the money – shops, who are themselves getting into difficulties, and will have no relief as long as the situation is prolonged. Even if the banks come to the aid of the smaller money concerns money will continue to be scarce, with interference to trade, and disaster to many businesses.

There have been a few incidents, absurd and serious, connected with this boycotting.

An incident with some humor in it suggests a revival of the old English stocks, or the pillory. A Wenchow man discovering that a certain shop was selling Japanese goods by subterfuge, threatened to disclose the fact. Later he agreed to sell them a promise of silence for $ 60.

All this was somehow discovered by the police. The result was that the shop lost all its Japanese goods, in addition to the $ 60, and the blackmailer was first fined, and then condemned to the tub for half – an – hour every afternoon. This tub was thereafter at each appointed time set in the public square before the Mandarinate, the occupant standing in it up to his armpits enjoying to the full, no doubt, his sudden conspicuous notoriety.

"A Cinema for Wenchow: Competitor to Poor Shows at the Temples," *The North - China Herald and Supreme Court& Consular Gazette*, March 22, 1932

A Cinema for Wenchow: Competitor to Poor Shows at the Temples

(From our own correspondent)

Wenchow, March 1.1

There were a number of foreign missionaries and Christian Chinese gathered at the Wenchow wharf of the C. M. S. Haean on March 11 to bid bon voyage to Mr. and Mrs. G. L. Wilkinson and their two sons on their departure for their second furlough to America. Mr. and Mrs. Wilkinson who hail from California have served 14 years in the Wenchow Mission of Seventh Day Adventists, and at the conclusion of a year's furlough will return to resume the superintendency of that Mission. The family will sail direct for America from Shanghai on March 18.

Local conversation, (it is at any rate amongst the young people) is now chiefly concerned with the opening this week of Wenchow's first real cinema. The opening had been arranged for the New Year week but had to be postponed owing to the non - arrival of films from Shanghai. Now with peace a Shanghai the new cinema has started of with a promise of a weekly programme, and the novel thrill of western films. The building, being of cramped size, with hard seats, and a small gallery near the ceiling, would be scorned by Shanghai landers; but it will feel palatial to the patient Wenchowites who on any night off have formed a habit of going for entertainment to one of the two temples where two ancient machines night by night unwound with wearying slowness poorly illumined Chinese films.

Wenchow, throughout the troubles at Shanghai, has remained quiet, though anxious. Rumours have been wild, fanciful and frequent. One daily heard that Japanese battleships were waiting to find a pilot who would betray the channel of the difficult river and bring them to the City. Quite as assuredly one heard that enemy bombing planes were on the way to destroy us.

Special news bulletins were issued twice daily containing wireless, and telephone news, and rumours galore. At one time we were for a long period without Shanghai newspapers. Since our only trading outlet is by sea – route, the delays and stoppages caused to the steamship services with Shanghai has been a cause of anxiety to local merchants.

Another hindrance to local tradehas been the blockade on money. It was risky sending silver or notes to and from Shanghai on the few steamer's in service. Shortage of silver dollars once caused a flutter when the banks were reported to be short of silver and a rush followed to exchange notes for dollars or even small coins. In reply the banks gave assurances that notes had not depreciated, and that if the rush for silver did not cease they would be obliged to close their doors. With the increasing renewal of the steamship services, the money care, as well as other annoyances has dwindled away.

Bandits Around Wenchow: Missionaries' Lucky Escape: Merchant Brigands," *The North – China Herald and Supreme Court& Consular Gazette*, May 17, 1932

Bandits Around Wenchow: Missionaries' Lucky Escape: Merchant Brigands

(From our own correspondent)

Wenchow, May 1

The China Inland Mission in Wenchow are losing some of their foreign staff whose furloughs are due. Mr. and Mrs. F. S. Barling are already on the way to England where they will go to Dover, Mr. Barling's home town. They arrived in China in 1915. Mr. Barling has been in charge of the C. I. M. work in Pingyinghsien, where his wife serves the community in the dispensary which she superintends. Miss G. I. F. Taylor of Wenchow whose particular work lies with the Chinese women will be leaving for England within two weeks, after seven unbroken years of strenuous work.

The same mission nearly lost their foreign superintendent last week in circumstances not so happy. He was all but captured by bandits. Travelling to the city of Jui – an on the Jin – an River, he and a Chinese pastor, being overtaken by the turn of the tide, put in to the bank and secured there for the night. Soon after nightfall a sampan approached and tied up just above them. There some features about this boat that struck Mr. Worley as suspicious, and he ordered the boatman to row further away. Immedicitely the sampan followed them. Moreover,

BANDITS AROUND WENCHOW

Missionaries' Lucky Escape: Merchant Brigands

FROM OUR OWN CORRESPONDENT

Wenchow, May 1.

The China Inland Mission in Wenchow are losing some of their foreign staff whose furloughs are due. Mr. and Mrs. F. S. Barling are already on the way to England where they will go to Dover, Mr. Barling's home town. They arrived in China in 1915. Mr. Barling has been in charge of the

silhouetted against the night sky a figure could be seen running along the shore o-vertaking their boat.

The boatman tried to row faster but could make little speed against the current. Suddenly they collided with another boat, and Mr. Worley was alarmed to see that it was but one of a flotilla of sampans each crowded with standing men. The river previous to darkness had not contained a single boat. When they collided the bandits made no move, not being sure that this was the correct boat, and the pause gave them time to push off into mid – stream. But directly the man running on the shore had arrived at the spot he signalled to the boats and they all gave chase, some heading up stream, and others downstream to cut off escape. The missionary boat, however, made for the opposite bank, where, on grounding the two preachers leaped ashore and ran.

This manoeuvre had not been reckoned for by the enemy and they had placed no guards on the shore. For a long time in bright moon – light the two searched vainly for a road that would lead them to Jui – an. Every road led to the river edge, and concluding at last that they had entrapped themselves on an island, they hid in a field of barley, and lay all night on the bare earth not daring to move or speak. Near dawn some men passed near enough to be heard complaining that the fugitives were not to be found anywhere.

Stiff, but otherwise uninjured the two fugitives rose at dawn from their unusual beds and again set about finding their way home. They came across an old villager who fortunately looked unsuspicious, and they asked him where they were. He explained that the island was not an island, but a peninsular made by a bend in the river. He also assured them, in reply to a query, that the district was undisturbed by bandits, and safe to travel in. I understand that this intelligence was received by Mr. Worley and his companion with no little surprise. Eventually they arrived home unharmed.

This nasty incident has served as a useful proof to other foreigners that banditry is not only not on the decrease, but that it seems to be improving in organization. On examination the affair reveals the existence of a widely spread organization, having leadership, rules, signals, codes, and practised with methods. Local rumours have something to say about these bandit bands which is interesting though impossible to verify, since the people themselves repeat these rumours without much real proof and on the evidence of mere suspicions.

According to popular talk, these bands, consisting of men who, lawful citizens by day, become bandits after dark, are secret clubs whose premier usefulness is to stand for the protection of the individual members, and to inflict brutal revenge on the members' enemies. It follows that such societies because they are secret must be a greater menace than the ordinary mountain marauders. One cannot be certain that one is not at any time in the company of a ruffian. Nor can one rely confidently on the assurances of country villagers when they tell the traveller that their district is free from bandits. They do not know it as a fact themselves. Their own neighbours maybe bandits sometimes.

Manifestly it is impossible for government soldiers to attack this kind of bandit, unless they chance to alight on a midnight prowl, which is unlikely, and therefore the military pay their own spies and informers. With spies acting for both sides there must be an atmosphere of suspicion and fear throughout the countryside. It is a common thing even in the city for people to accuse one another of belonging to this or that secret alliance. Many of the recent disastrous fires in the city have been blamed, not without some reason, on to the operations of a sinister group designated as "The Black Society."

A number of soldiers belonging to the government armies which were recently defeated by the Communists in Amoy, have escaped North and found their way to Wenchow, where they intend to stay for a time.

"Thunder – Loud – Voice: Caught and Killed," *The North – China Herald and Supreme Court& Consular Gazette*, July 13, 1932

Thunder – Loud – Voice: Caught and Killed

(From our own correspondent)

Wenchow Che, June 30

It is greatly to be feared that this Season's harvest may be ruined by continued rain falling on ground already swamped to saturation after a long period of wet weather. For no less than two months rain has been falling almost incessantly, interrupted by only very occasional fine days and nights. Farmers hope that some immediate sunshine may yet be in time to avert large losses. With the rain the temperature for the time of the year is strangely low, and today, the last day in June, it is only just cool enough for summer suits.

I have previously reported on the peculiar problems presented in the countryside by the bandits, bands of whom roam the mountains in undiminishing numbers; and I recently noted the ineffectiveness of the Government soldiers to abolish them, though it is to be admitted that the presence of soldiers acts as a check on disorder in that particular district. Recently, however the military made a coup. They resorted to strategy, and the whole incident could well find a place in a story – magazine.

Lai Koe – sing colloquial, ··· was the name of a ··· chief ····. But someone one day got into communication with him suggesting that if he surrendered to the military officials they would not only grant him a free pardon but enlist him and

THUNDER-LOUD-VOICE

Caught and Killed

FROM OUR OWN CORRESPONDENT

Wenchow, Che. June 30.

It is greatly to be feared that this Season's harvest may be ruined by continued rain falling on ground already swamped to saturation after a long period of wet weather. For no less than two months rain has been falling almost incessantly, interrupted by only very occasional fine days and nights. Farmers hope

his men in the regular army making him a commanding officer. Such a thing has been accomplished more than once here, and Lai Koe – sing remembering this assented, and actually went to the city. The officials received him with an outward respect. They sent him back to the mountains clothed in officer's uniform and with soldier's uniforms and money for salaries to give to his men.

The soldiers at No – Chi then suggested an induction feast. At the conclusion of the feast which was held in a temple, they announced that they had called a photographer and courteously requested···to pose first, and they, unsuspecting, assented, stacked up their rifles in a corner, and grouped before the camera. It was the work of a second then for every soldier to stride forward and take···prisoner. It happened that a servant of the···leader was not included in the photography, and had possession of his rifle, seeing this move fired, and the report warned the remaining···feasting in a second temple. This second lot all fled out into the night with soldiers at their heels firing, and in the end some 25 dead were left of those who escaped. The leaders were taken to Wenchow and tried, and convicted. Lai Koe – sing was the first to go. This man was little more than 30 years of age, and is said to have been previously employed by the Yamen before he turned outlaw. He was now commanded to be trussed in a ricksha and drawn through the streets of the city as an example to would be evil – doers, and maybe to advertise the military. Throughout this grim journey, which ended before a firing – party outside the city wall, the···chief shouted constantly to bystanders, "I am a Communist; I am a Communist."

"Religious Films Banned: No Public Show Allowed at Wenchow," *The North – China Herald and Supreme Court& Consular Gazette*, November 3, 1932

Religious Films Banned: No Public Show Allowed at Wenchow

(From our own correspondent)

Wenchow, October 19

In view of the ban on religious films being shown in public theatres, the local mission of Seventh Day Adventists have contrived to introduce to Wenchow the well known film depicting the Life of Jesus Christ, "The King of Kings," with also some additional shorter films, by showing them off in their spacious, modern city church. Eager crowds have clamoured nightly at the church doors for the free tickets, and nightly for three weeks the building has been packed to suffocation. The preacher shouting through a large megaphone could seldom render his running explanations of the pictures very distinctly audible above the din made by the large congregation.

Cinemas of the more secular variety are on the increase here. Apart from a portable machine that wound out films in local temples a year ago there was not anything at that time that could be styled a proper cinema. Now there are two quite respectable, theatres showing Chinese films daily. In addition, a still larger building has recently been completed for the display of stage – shows, —old Chinese plays dancing, and the like, and movie films on occasion. I have heard that

RELIGIOUS FILMS BANNED

No Public Show Allowed at Wenchow

FROM OUR OWN CORRESPONDENT

Wenchow, Oct. 19.

In view of the ban on religious films being shown in public theatres, the local mission of Seventh Day Adventists have contrived to introduce to Wenchow the well-known film depicting the Life of Jesus Christ, "The King of Kings," with also some additional shorter films, by showing them off in their spacious, modern city church. Eager

the proprietors have engaged a troupe of Chinese girl actresses from Shanghai. Wenchow will quickly lose its enchanting country atmosphere now that the louder features of modern city life have found a market amongst her citizens.

The city sports were held this autumn in perfect autumn weather, and with all the success and gaiety of last years events. The children of the Junior Schools ran off their events during three strenuous days. The third being devoted to citizens excluding school teachers, and scholars. Swimming, running, pole – jumping, were favourite items. The park was a scene of holiday excitement.

Recently, the same park had another sort of decoration when a firm of silk merchants journeyed to Wenchow in search of new customers. A great feast of foreign food which necessitated a general combing out of every single cook who knew anything about foreign cookery, was first served in the Park Restaurant to some 70 guests, including among the number the City Magistrate. Then for a day or two silk – lengths of every variety and colour were spread out in gorgeous display for the public admiration of shopkeepers, salespeople, and anybody interested. We wonder if this method of advertisement is as novel as it undoubtedly is courteous.

The Middle schools are suffering through lapses in their provincial allowances. Ever since the outbreak of the Japanese – Shanghai affair all teachers have been three months in arrears with their salaries. There have been protests, but as yet nothing in the nature of a strike.

Everybody uttered some sound of satisfaction when in September, a notorious "bandit" leader was captured by soldiers in Noe – Chi, the district where the capture of Lai – Koe – Sing was effected a few months previously. Bandit La had been in Wenchow disguised. This was generally known, and it was also generally thought that the soldiers knew his whereabouts, and kept "mum". These were the same soldiers who very nearly succeeded in creating, a serious condition of affairs in this area of Chekiang which is affected by subversive political activity if at all then for the most part quietly and unobtrusively. Several thousands of these soldiers, Southerners I understand, had been quartered in the city during the summer, and there was amongst them a strong feeling in favour of communism. This sympathy would undoubtedly be accentuated by their being several months in arrears of the slender salary ordinarily due to them. The Noe – Chi Communists heard of this. They promptly sent away for a large quantity of dollars and at the same time sent representatives to Wenchow to offer the troops an increase on their regular salary and in addition an immediate first payment. The emissaries audaciously made this attempt to buy over the local military, and might well have succeeded with such tempting bait had not the officials paid the troops their salaries, and sent them away to some other area, replacing them by others of less dangerous potencies.

Meanwhile, Lu had got well away, there now developed an exciting chase over the mountains. The new soldiers would trace the fugitive to a village only to lose all trace of his whereabouts, when he would again turn up at some further spot. This happened in one particular village with sad consequences for the inhabitants. The soldiers, thinking their prey was now secure enough, made a circle round the village and approached but only to find, when they entered that Lu had already flown. As a reprisal the entire village was taken in charge. Some 200 people were put under lock and key, examined and in a few instances treated badly. Only one or two old men were allowed to go home. For I do not know how many days the prisoners were kept; but it was not until some time after they had been set free that the bandit Lu was tracked down and captured.

"Wenchow," *The North - China Herald and Supreme Court& Consular Gazette*, November 9, 1932

Wenchow

In Wenchow conditions have changed very little in the last two years. The city is just a trifle more modern. Every year several of the better kind of glass – fronted shops are added. But thousands of the old medieval hovels remain and will remain until they are burned down I mean this literally. The regulation is that when shops are rebuilt after being burned down, they must be put back some 13 feet. Thus in the main street while in the greater part of its length there is just enough zoom for two rickshaws to pass, there are wider spots here and there where a motor car could go. This is an important feature pointing to the introduction of machanical traffic. It is the only "scheme" in operation to provide for this inevitable future. A little over two years ago a public park was built by the authorities. There is also now a free city hospital for Cholera epidemics. In this there takes place every year a week of sports which is a healthy omen for the people. Cinemas and theatres have found a place here at long last. The above are all the recent developments I can think of.

As to banditry and general security, surrounded as we almost are by mountains, bandits are to be expected all times, and foreigners must receive reports of any place to which they intend to travel, as to its security. But this has been Wenchow from times immemorial should a sensational capture take place people would then say that Wenchow is now less safe than formerly. But security must not be estimated on the numbers of outrages that occur, but on the potentialities that exist for outrages. Of the former there have been none concerning foreigners; of the latter I can but remark that it is impossible to say. I only know that, ignoring the occasional ebb and flow of bandits, the general situation has not changed for the better.

"Medical Service at Wenchow: Some Recent Departures and Arrivals of Foreigners," *The North – China Herald and Supreme Court& Consular Gazette*, May 31, 1933

Medical Service at Wenchow: Some Recent Departures and Arrivals of Foreigners

(From our own correspondent)

Wenchow, May 19

The various medical services that serve this area, sometimes reveal that they have been progressing, by some striking innovation, which is not merely an innovation since it springs from the gradual advance being made in the regular work. Last year during the cholera epidemic a free city Cholera Hospital was opened to the public thus relieving the general hospital of the usual congestion at such times, and isolating the infection to one place. There are in addition some free dispensaries now open continuously for the poor. I have now to name a recent medical event that is probably unique in the history of this old city, and marks a new stage for the future. There was a public ceremony held last week in the premises of the English Methodist Mission Hospital, Blyth Hospital, at which the first nurses to graduate, numbering four, were presented with the diplomas of the Nursing Association of China. The superintendent of the hospital Dr. E. T. A. Stedeford, made the presentations, and congratulatory speeches were given by several of the city medical fraternity. The training school is in the charge of Nurses Petrie Smith and Phyllis Fieldsend.

Departures and arrivals of foreigners in Wenchow are rare events and, therefore, important. There has recently been an exchange in the Customs Serv-

MEDICAL SERVICE AT WENCHOW

Some Recent Departures and Arrivals of Foreigners

FROM OUR OWN CORRESPONDENT

Wenchow, May 19.

The various medical services that serve this area, sometimes reveal that they have been progressing, by some striking innovation, which is not merely an innovation since it springs from the gradual advance being made in the regular work.

ices, Mr. and Mrs. W. H. Tappenden having taken the position occupied the previous year by Mr. and Mrs. W. H. Tipton now on furlough in England. Mr. and Mrs. Tappenden find the city quiet after Tientsin though an improvement in scenery, and their three children think the Heart of River Island where their new home is situated, with the two old pagodas nested by gulls and herons, and the tree – covered hills, is quite a jolly place really.

The Cinema

Just about a year ago Wenchow received her first cinema palace. Within a month or two she had a second. Today there are at least four. Talkie synchronisation has just been installed in the largest of these, and I went to test the quality of the reproduction when "Ingadi" the wild nature film was being shown. Neither the pictures nor the sound were very distinct, but it was not for these reasons that the film drew little enthusiasm from the audience. "We prefer love, and adventure stories," explained a Chinese gentleman to me afterwards, "And besides, we cannot understand talkies in English. " Still, as I said, what can one expect, for less than 30 cents in the best seats!

The 10th Middle School, the largest and best equipped of the City schools held an exhibition of its work when the building was opened to public inspection for three days. Exhibits included character writing, painting, carving, and woodwork, botany, entomology, biology, physics, and chemistry. The primary section was not without more juvenile entries. Sports play was held the same week and vent off with gusto.

The united schools have also held their annual demonstration of hygiene. The idea is a commend able one, but this year it degenerated into the delivery of speeches and the distribution of tracts; this at any rate was the body of the effort. Originally, I am informed, the Scouts and Guide scholars would set to with dustpans and brushes and sweep the streets and people's houses, a more difficult method of demonstrating, but more likely to be remembered and imitated.

"New Arrivals in Wenchow: Aeroplanes and the Steamer Traffic," *The North - China Herald and Supreme Court& Consular Gazette*, November 22, 1933

New Arrivals in Wenchow: Aeroplanes and the Steamer Traffic

(From our own correspondent)

Wenchow, October 27

The foreign community at Wenchow has recently been increased by new addition to the ministerial staff of the English Methodist Mission. The Rev. Jenkins Hooper is a son of the Methodist Hanse, and has come to China direct from several year's residence at Victoria College, Manchester, where he took higher studies at Manchester University. The many places in England where he is well known include Wigan, Bristol, and Cornwall, and he has left behind him many friends in order to spend the rest of his ministerial career in Wenchow. But M. Hooper is on charmed with the beauties of his beauty spot, and too busy with the peculiarities of the dialect, to be distressed overmuch by the prospect of a long separation from Western life.

Any movement of foreigners is an event in Wenchow where foreigners total only some thirty and which number only four are not engaged in missionary work. In he earlier part of the year the Roman Catholic Mission received some additions including two priest from Poland; and the Methodist Mission again are expecting to welcome two more lady workers in 1934.

Associated with travel to and from Shanghai, which remains our only gate-

NEW ARRIVALS IN WENCHOW

Aeroplanes and the Steamer Traffic

FROM OUR OWN CORRESPONDENT

Wenchow, Oct. 27.

The foreign community at Wenow has recently been increased by new addition to the ministerial aff of the English Methodist lission. The Rev. R. Jenkins

way to the world, is the weekly aeroplane service just started, and connecting us now with shanghai, Foochow, and Hongkong. Previously the only road to Shanghai was the sea road, traversed by Chinese cargo steamers, running not too regularly, and undergoing repairs with an ominous frequency. While the fare by air, single trip remains at $ 70, there will be little competition with even such steamers as these; but the aeroplanes have brought more hope now for travel in the future. It is strange to hear machines roaring above this peaceful, medieval – like city an stranger to watch the excited capers of a population that is a stranger to railways, cars, and, until just recently, aeroplanes.

Theunfinished Road

It is again possible to report progress with the building of Wenchow's first motor road. This road to Chuchow which will link Wenchow with Hangchow, and be the first land highway to connect this city with the outer world, has been reported on by me twice before each time the plans having afterwards come to nothing. I cannot guarantee even now that this road will be finished, even though it has been begun. I am told that some ten years ago a tobacco tax was levied for new roads, and that, when the money had been received by the authorities, an inter – provincial affair arose, and the money was devoted to the purchase of arms and ammunition in a quarrel with Fukien, so that the road on that occasion never came into being. To provide for this year's project a levy was put on the populace in the earlier part of the year, on landowners of a few cents per field, on shopkeepers of $ 25 per $ 1000 capital, and on extra special demand on rich people. People are also being invited to buy investment certificates at low interest returns, but the response is not enthusiastic owing partly to lack of confidence due to the memory of previous occasions when money lent to the Government was never returned. A hopeful sign that there will be built motor roads outside the city is a declaration this week that the Government intends to widen the principal streets within the city to allow for the passage of larger traffic than rickshaws, which, with an occasional bicycle, is the only wheeled traffic to be seen.

Trade is as bad as ever, and likely to remain so until Shanghai improves. Not much is being heard about boycotting, and since the sign of the treaty in the North displayed openly in principal shops. It is, however, previous stock which was sealed up by students when the boycott began; I don't think of Japanese goods are being imported here that they could get through without some kind of camouflage. With another good harvest country people are feeling better favoured than city tradesmen, and in their favour also is a general quietening down of country banditry.

"No Pioneering for Wenchow: A General Preference for Old Styles: Roads to Open a Grand Scenic Center," *The North – China Herald and Supreme Court& Consular Gazette*, March 14, 1934

No Pioneering for Wenchow: A General Preference for Old Styles: Roads to Open a Grand Scenic Center

(From our own correspondent)

Wenchow,
February 14

It is China New Year's Day and the traditional celebrations are as animated

NO PIONEERING FOR WENCHOW

A General Preference for Old Styles: Roads to Open a Grand Scenic Centre

FROM OUR OWN CORRESPONDENT

Wenchow, Feb. 14.

It is China New Year's Day and the traditional celebrations are as animated as ever before, with crackling fireworks, drumming gongs, and crowded incense – filled temples. The streets yesterday evening were illuminated at sunset, when small red candles were set on every threshold, and wood bonfires were lighted outside every front door in the street. They were bigger than usual and in the recent dry weather constituted a serious danger to property. Should ever the Western calendar finally come to be adopted in China, Wenchow certainly will not be a pioneer. So far, only Government employees, such as the Post Office staff, keep up the first of January.

As is usual at this time, there are only a very few patients in the hospitals, where the wards have an appearance of complete desertion. No Chinese will remain away from home at New Year if he can by any means return. One of the city hospitals which has been suffering from a scarcity of custom was found quite empty just before New Year and the management has decided to close. This is a Chinese hospital that is one of the leading institutions in the district, possessing one of the finest operating theatres in Chekiang Province.

Roads At Last

There is at long last some definite news to report on road – building. Various local schemes during the past quarter of a century have failed to produce a single road, either within or outside the city, but this year in both regions building actually has commenced. The long road west to Chuchow when finished certainly will make one of the finest motor runs in China for grandeur of scenery, for it winds around the base of the steep ranges that rise out of the winding river, and is for long distances cut shelf – like out of the solid mountain granite. In the higher reaches of this river, which has its mouth beside Wenchow city, the water becomes clear, and great rafts from the mountain forests are floated over the rapids down – stream.

The city of Chuchow is reached now, and has been since time, immemorial, by hand – rowed or hand – towed boats, and the trip takes about three days. The motor car will shorten this distance by an easy two days. I was recently up in that direction and was interested to watch the blasting operations. They are performed with crude stools, in a manner dangerous to life. Numerous casualties have been brought to the Wenchow Methodist Hospital. Holes for the explosives are made by ordinary cold chisel and hammers, the refuse after a discharge being with great difficulty tumbled over the cliff into the river by the mere use of ropes and crowbars. The echoes of every discharge can be heard rumbling, among the hills for a duration of several seconds. Besides the blasting there are other great difficulties to be overcome by the sweat and persistence of hand – labour. All that carrying of vast quantities of masonry and earth must be upon the backs of men. All the small stones which will form the road surface are broken by an army of men with small hammers sitting all day to their monotonous task. Moreover, a bridge, usually of reinforced concrete must be raised over every stream, and there are streams at every few yards.

Shantung Benefits

A good deal of labour for this enterprise comes from Shantung. Some 5000 Shantungese have been employed here, and I met a number last week in the Bank of China, changing their pay – money into dollars before returning to their home Province for the New Year. They are most remarkably distinguishable from the Wenchowese by their thick wadded northern clothing, their large stature, and their ruffianly appearance.

It is a problem how the road fund will be raised at this time of languishing trade. Besides heavy assessments, public investing has been invited, though not very successfully. I understand that private capital is levied by $12 per $1000 and $150 for $10000, while there is also a special levy for the very rich. The road schemes, which are all due entirely to an order from the Provincial Capital, include the city itself, where at present there exists no other wheeled traffic than rickshaws and bicycles. A short specimen motor road now exists on the site of the old and dirty "Beggars Lane," presumably to inspire the citizens with an example of the blessings that will be brought to them by their taxes and contributions. Orders exist for the demolition of thousands of homes and shops to make way for new city roads.

A Deserted Aerodrome

When, in the autumn of last year, the Fukienese rebellion threatened Chekiang, Gen. Chiang Kaishek, decided to arm Wenchow against attack with an air base. A site was selected on the plain on the south side of the city and rolled out until flat enough for aeroplanes to ride over, although a good many farmers lost their crops of oranges, which were still partly green. Some very meagre compensation was given them, with the assurances that their patriotism (even if compulsory) had saved them from an even worse confiscation at the hand of Fukienese Communism.

For a time, until the rebellion was crushed, a fleet of bombing and fighting planes, became the daily wonder and terror of the Wenchowese, to whom war operations are, unlike many other parts of China, largely unfamiliar. Happily, the aeroplanes have now departed, but it does not seem that the airfield will be returned to the original owners.

The Rev. I. Scott Leaves

The Rev. and Mrs. I. Scott, with their two children, left last month for England, where they will make their home in Bristol. Mr. Scott is chairman of the Methodist Mission, Wenchow district, and for the last two years and more has been administering this large work without active ministerial assistance. It is much to his credit, in spite of this under – staffing, that the Church is now successfully entering the forth year of a ten – year period scheme of self – support which Mr. Scott took a leading part in initiating. The Scott family expect to return to China in the spring of 1935.

A Money Shortage

I have already referred to the dangerous condition of trade. The local banks now are beginning to reveal this, for they are all short of money. The capital of some is said to be reduced by half, and by more than half, and some of the gloomier rumour – makers are predicting a series of failures.

A Flogging Disciplinarian

The city of Wenchow has experienced an effective, if rough, method of administering discipline. The late chief of the local military bureau believed in the efficiency of corporal punishment for wrong doers, and he inflicted it without stint or mercy and with an admirable ignoring of class distinctions. He argued that fines are heavy on the poor man, and let the rich off lightly, while Chinese prisons are merely degrading, to the prisoner, thus it has been that twice at least I have met in the streets a troop of soldiers marching before them through the public thoroughfares a condemned man, with a paper hat on his head bearing the details in writing of his misdeeds, his hands chained together, and a soldier walking behind him with a leather whip, tormenting an already raw and bleeding back. Sometimes flogging was inflicted outside the city walls. Once at least, in the case of a priest accused of misconduct, the severity of the punishment all but ended fatally. Another, a common thief, was executed as an example to others.

Whippings were the almost certain correction for every kind of misbehaviour, including inveterable gambling and opium – smoking. All kinds of public behaviour at all suggestive of impropriety or illegality, even supposed indecency in women's clothing, met with a warning, and, if repeated, the lash.

"Aviator Injured in Forced Landing: Accident Occurred 13 Miles from Wenchow," *The North – China Herald and Supreme Court & Consular Gazette*, April 11, 1934

Aviator Injured in Forced Landing: Accident Occurred 13 Miles from Wenchow

The Chinese – built seaplane Kiang Feng in which Mr. C. C. Hsu, instructor of the Naval Aviation Department of Nanking attempted to make a solo fight from Shanghai to Mamoi on Sunday (April 1) morning, was forced down by engine trouble at Chileechin about 13 miles from Wenchow, along the Chekiang coast, according to further details of the accident received here on Tuesday.

Mr. Wang Chun – hung, engineer of the Naval Air Establishment of the Ministry of Navy, Kiaochangmiao, who was sent down to Wenchow by Capt. Tseng Yi – ching, director, in a China National Aviation Corporation's aero plane early yesterday morning, is visiting the scene of the accident. According to his message received here from Wenchow yesterday afternoon, Mr. Hsu, the pilot, was not in a serious condition. Mr. Hsu is being detained in the Tatung Hospital, Wenchow.

Following the receipt of information of the accident, the Ministry of Navy has despatched the warship Chu Tai from Siangshan, Chekiang coast, to Wenchow. It is expected that the warship will convey Mr. Hsu back to Shanghai for medical attention.

Mr. Hsu made the solo fight from Shanghai with Mamoi as his destination in the seaplane Kiang Feng on Sunday morning to test the feasibility of a long distance flight by a nativemade's plane. He hopped off in the Kiang Feng from the Lunghua Aerodrome at about 9 a. m. , being seen off by Capt. Tseng and several other naval officers.

"Bank Failures in Wenchow: City Financing Increasing Difficult: Only Remedies Tried as Yet Too Superficial," *The North – China Herald and Supreme Court & Consular Gazette*, May 30, 1934

Bank Failures in Wenchow: City Financing Increasing Difficult: Only Remedies Tried as Yet Too Superficial

(From our own correspondent)

BANK FAILURES IN WENCHOW

City Financing Increasingly Difficult: Only Remedies Tried as Yet Too Superficial

FROM OUR OWN CORRESPONDENT

Wenchow, May 15.
In my last report I predicted a further series of bank and money | before its own house; rubbish is not to thrown into the streets, and in regard to this, it is a pleasure to re-

Wenchow, May 15

In my last report I predicted a further series of bank and money shop failures due to local trade conditions, and it is possible now to announce the almost total collapse of local native banking. Some ten or more money shops closed during 1933, bringing upon those still maintaining credit balances the distrust of the populace. Deposits were withdrawn, and, to add to their difficulties, they were deprived of the customary backing of the local branch of the Bank of China. Generally local trading interests can always go for financial help to any of the banks, but this year, the big banks having withdrawn their local support in view of the general lack of confidence, the smaller banking concerns have lost their surest mainstay at the very time when it is peculiarly difficult to reclaim loans.

One old established money shop, the Yung – Nyue Bank, came to grief early in the year. It is one of the largest in the city, and announced a deficit of $370000. The local Bankers Association called a meeting and decided to repay holders of cheques at once, and to repay depositors later at a percentage rate. Continuous meetings since then, numerous public protests, threats of law proceedings, etc. , have followed over the amount that should be repaid. Some of the depositors have banded themselves together and are working for an 80 percent. repayment, but this Bank is offering only some 60 percent.

More Failures Predicted

It is said that in loans due to the bank there is sufficient to repay every depositor in full. This may be true, but in these days it is distinctly difficult to gather money in once it has been lent out. The immediate cause of this failure was the defection of one of the three partners with a good share of his own.

Other failures have followed this and others still are predicted. The rest of the banks are gradually winding up their affairs with a view to closing down. Probably a residue of about half a dozen will remain to serve city needs.

The Bank of China is reaping the reward of all this. It has enormous deposits by local citizens, part being money diverted from money shops, but the bank is afraid to reinvest it in local business. I have heard that this money is invested in Hangchow and other places, and meanwhile Wenchow trade languishes for want of capital. Land and property have slumped badly. The price of a mow of land is about half what it used to be, and although people with money have been selling their fields and buying houses in Wenchow, yet they find it no easy matter to earn their rent. In view of the banking situation private money lending, by non – professionals, is on the increase, the creditor holding the debtors' property deeds until repayment. But with this kind of financing such high rates of interest prevail – from 15 percent. upwards – that business is stifled at its inception.

Wenchow is thus in a sorry condition commercially, and a big lantern festival was, therefore, arranged to attract country people into the city and set money circulating. It was to have ended with the "New Double Eight" (May 5) which is the old festival superimposed by order of the Government on the new western calendar – so that the populace now enjoys two "Double – Eights," in one year! Rainy weather postponed the grand finale for two or three days, but eventually a lantern procession wound through the streets that took about two hours to pass any one point, and was the longest in the city records. Many thousands of men carried lanterns of every fantastic shape, or flaming rush torches; others carried drums and cymbals, numerous woodwind or brass bands, tableaux of old Chinese historical characters, parties of men striding on stilts, and illuminated silk and paper dragons 40 yards long in fancy dress eight or nine feet tall with twisting bodies and angrily gleaming jaws were included. It was an eerie sight at night.

During the week the streets were hung with miles of awning, silk streamers of every bright colour and lanterns every few yards. The town took on carnival colours. Shop prices were lowered, and the windows decorated. Hotels filled up quickly restaurants and stalls did good trade as well as lantern shops.

"New Life Movement"

This festival came at the time on the inauguration of the new national movement, the "New Life Movement". Announcements pasted on every door indicate what it mean and what is to be done. Every household must keep clean the road before its own house; rubbish is not be thrown into the streets, and in regard to this, it is a pleasure to report that the rudimentary beginning of a Corporation Dust Service can be seen; there must be no smoking in public, and the police have authority to snatch cigarettes from the hungry lips of street smokers; there must be no unruly behaviour in public places, or dishevelled dress (what will the beggars do about this?); no pushing without apologizing; people should bathe and wash regularly, and should be clean in language; no extravagance is the rule for feasts and weddings. Offences are punished on the first offence by reproof, on the second offence, by a warning, and on the third offence, by a $ 5 fine.

The foreign community has been added to recently with two new members of the Customs, and a new nurse for the Methodist Hospital, Mr. A. Casati, who recently was stationed in South China, is the new Commissioner of Custome. It is several years since a foreigner occupied that position. Mr. J. Elm has taken the position of Harbour Master, formerly held by Mr. Gosling, who is now transferred to Ningpo. Miss A. Woodman comes from Wiltshire, England, and belonged previously to the Primitive Methodist connection. She is preparing for service in the Methodist Blythe Hospital while Miss Smith is on furlough. Every addition to foreign society is an event and a pleasure in out – of – the – way Wenchow, and these new visitors have found a sure welcome.

"Flash of Lightning Saves Disaster: Thrilling Episode in Collision off Wenchow Coast" *The North - China Herald and Supreme Court & Consular Gazette*, May 30, 1934

Flash of Lightning Saves Disaster: Thrilling Episode in Collision off Wenchow Coast

FLASH OF LIGHTNING SAVES DISASTER

Thrilling Episode in Collision off Wenchow Coast

A flash of lightning in a heavy storm averted what might have resulted in a major shipping disaster and the loss of eighty lives at Peitiendoong Shan, off the Wenchow coast, on Sunday (May 20), when the Chinese steamer Tiensiang, driven off her course by strong winds and rough seas while on her way from Juian, southern Chekiang, to Shanghai, was heading straight towards the hill.

The flash came just in time, giving the captain sufficient light in pitch - darkness to see what was happening. With the vessel steaming on to the hill ahead, the captain lost no time in altering the course in a desperate attempt to beach her on a sand bar. A head - on collision was avoided but her right side struck submerged rocks. Water rushed quickly. In about ten minutes only the bridge remained above water, the stern being completely submerged.

Captain Highly Praised

This thrilling experience in the accident, was related to a representative of the "North - China Herald" by Mr. Chen Kong, inspector on the steamer, who arrived last Wednesday afternoon on the ss. Dah Hwa with 47 members of the crew and five passengers. The majority of the arrivals had lost all their belongings. Some had even lost their clothing.

"In response to our distress sirens, several fishing boats arrived to our help. It was then dawning. The storm had ceased. The passengers and the majority of the crew reached dry land on the hill. As three feet of the bow remained above water the captain, the chief officer and ten others, including myself, remained on board, looking after the vessel and the luggage which had been piled up on the deck by those people who occupied cabin on the fore part of the vessel.

"When the second batch of what appeared to be fishing boats, arrived on the scene, I suspected that they were pirate junks. At first a few men came on board and, as was expected, they started looting. As they were not armed, we fought them with iron bars. The looters grew in number, and we were finally forced to retreat and let them do what they pleased. The pirates left with a handsome booty. No attempt at kindnapping was made however. "

"Rain Saves Crops in Wenchow: Three Days Fast Ordered in Drought: Maternity Ward in Blyth Hospital," *The North – China Herald and Supreme Court & Consular Gazette*, August 8, 1934

Rain Saves Crops in Wenchow: Three Days Fast Ordered in Drought: Maternity Ward in Blyth Hospital

(From our own correspondent)

RAIN SAVES CROPS IN WENCHOW

Three Days Fast Ordered in Drought: Maternity Ward in Blyth Hospital

FROM OUR OWN CORRESPONDENT

Wenchow, Che, July 25.

As though in sympathy with numerous other places, not in China only, Wenchow also has been undergoing the anxieties and discomforts of a rainless season. City wells were all of them low, and the greater

A serious street fight took place last week between two rival bands of coolies, in which two were killed and over thirteen injured, some badly injured. One of the dead men was flung into a canal where he drowned.

Wenchow, Che, July 25

As though in sympathy with numerous other places, not in China only, Wenchow also has been undergoing the anxieties and discomforts of a rainless season. City wells were all of them low, and the greater number almost dry. People would walk half – way across a city to obtain free water from a deeper well, until even these would be padlocked by the jealous neighbours of the well who feared for their own supplies. Large numbers of families had to buy their water from the countrymen who bring it in open – boats during dry seasons from the mountain streams further up – country. In the plains outside the city farmers became scared for their rice crops. When eventually a couple of typhoons brought rain, it was said that two more days of drought only might have destroyed the entire grain crop.

These typhoons were indeed a Godsend, for they brought rain and cool winds without striking the district with any destructive force. Steamer traffic was held up for some five days.

General Fast Ordered

A general fast from all meats for three days was ordered by the authorities, ostensibly as a hygenic measure during drought – time, but naturally accepted by the populace as a religious precaution to induce rain. Rain actually came in torrents after three days, but the fast was prolonged a further three days during which time no pork or beef could be purchased, though fish was being sold, and it is always possible to get hold of a chicken or two. Probably nothing will ever remove the general conviction that because rain and fasting came together, therefore it is fasting that brings clouds and rain. Did sailors tossed on tumultous waves off the Wenchow coast know that their dangerous situation was caused by the empty meat – shops in Wenchow city?

This reminds me of yet another health regulation whereby beasts and pigs are not to be killed willy – nilly, but must be slaughtered in an appointed place where inspectors can examine them for traces of infection, when they will be banned from the market.

These, above, are activities of the "New Life Movement", as also are the new opium regulations greatly increasing penalties for convictions. First offence will be light, second offence heavy imprisonment or hard labour road – making at Chu – chow, and third offence the death – penalty. In any case of conviction, before passing judgment, the offender will be locked up in the police station without opium for a considerable period to break the habit, afterwards he will receive his due penalty.

A serious street fight took place last week between two rival bands of coolies, in which two were killed and over thirteen injured, some badly injured. One of the dead men was flung into a canal where he drowned.

Near the same spot a day or so later and during the typhoon a house outside the East gate caught fire and in defiance of ten hand – pumped fire engines, burned itself to the ground. Though the burnt house was surrounded by other houses they surprisingly escaped damage. Towards the finish of the fire, when a fire – man had ventured on the top of a tottering wall, it collapsed and flung him into the debris from whence he was rescued in a terribly burned condition. They brought him to the Methodist Hospital where he languished for a time before dying, although all the skin of his body but the soles of his feet and a small area of skin on his chest had been burned away.

The Blyth Methodist Hospital has just completed the addition of a maternity department to its services, the first of its kind in Wenchow. There is a very excellent set of rooms to receive a total capacity of some dozen patients, though there is room for future extension if necessary. This department will be in the charge of a certificated midwife, a Chinese woman, who, however, will be assisted when necessary by foreign members of the hospital nursing staff.

The habit of entering hospital for confinement is rapidly growing amongst Chinese mothers, who are beginning to appreciate the sad unsuitability of their small crowded houses for such occasions. By introducing these newer and better ideas, hospitals such as the Blyth are doing an inestimable service to China.

"Anti – Foreign Move in Wenchow: Port Closed to Foreign Trade by the Kuomintang," *The North – China Herald and Supreme Court & Consular Gazette*, August 15, 1934

Anti – Foreign Move in Wenchow: Port Closed to Foreign Trade by the Kuomintang

Shanghai, August 14

It was learnt from a reliable source yesterday that the Wenchow Kuomintang with the approval of Mr. Hsu Pan – yun, Special Supervisor of Civil Administration of the 3rd District of Chekiang Province, has launched an anti – foreign movement, since the beginning of this month.

Foreign goods like cigarettes and fertilizers are forbidden to land, and holders of stocks on the market have been forced to put them away. Several dealers in these lines have been arrested and detained in the Tangpu and Police Headquarters. One retailer is still detained on the false charge of "counter – revolution". A sales coolie was arrested by the Tangpu and his stock was burnt. By so doing the Treaty Port of Wenchow has been declared closed to foreign trade by the Tangpu and local authorities.

ANTI-FOREIGN MOVE IN WENCHOW

Port Closed to Foreign Trade by The Kuomintang

Shanghai, Aug. 14.

It was learnt from a reliable source yesterday that the Wenchow Kuomintang with the approval of Mr. Hsu Pan-yun, Special Supervisor of Civil Administration of the 3rd District of Chêkiang Province, has launched an anti-foreign movement since the beginning of this month.

"Wenchow's Perfect Summer Weather: Lack of Water only Drawback to Date: Electric Burglar Trap too Successful," *The North – China Herald and Supreme Court & Consular Gazette*, September 5, 1934

Wenchow's Perfect Summer Weather: Lack of Water only Drawback to Date: Electric Burglar Trap too Successful

(From our own correspondent)

WENCHOW'S PERFECT SUMMER WEATHER

Lack of Water Only Drawback to Date: Electric Burglar Trap Too Successful

FROM OUR OWN CORRESPONDENT

Wenchow, Aug. 23.

Generally noted for its uncomfortable summer climate, Wenchow has improved its reputation by giving us a perfect July and August, while of construction, which will rise to six storeys, and is apparently meant to follow the line of business of the Sincere Co. and Wing-On's in Shanghai. In the same street, a branch of

Wenchow, August 23

Generally noted for its uncomfortable summer climate, Wenchow has improved its reputation by giving us a perfect July and August, while other places sweltered in high temperatures. Tempered by daily cool breezes, the thermometer has settled below 85 in the shade, rising towards the nineties only very seldom, and as an additional kindness the September breezes have already begun blowing two weeks before they should, while everybody is saying how that they cannot remember such a summer since the year dot.

Even the daily afternoon thunderstorms keep away, and these are a regular feature of August, and break over the country with tropical violence, the lightning flickering on silently until midnight. But not this year.

These daily storms are a source of rainfall, as also the hot, moist days of previous years, and all this potential rain has been carried away in the clouds by the breezes to other places, leaving the land dry, hard like rock, and splitting, and the rice crops wilting. On the market, the price of grain has been steadily rising. Anything like famine was fortunately averted in the nick of time a week ago, when a distant typhoon brought two days of rain, but food will remain dear until the next harvest, of which there are several in a year.

Some of the rocky islands at the mouth of the Wenchow River were disturbed by the recent typhoons. These islands' inhabitants always suffer greatly since their main livelihood is derived from fishing, and they claim that typhoons drive all the fish away. Certainly, there is a poor fishing harvest after these aerial disturbances. Their crops are also buried by the great waves that burst into the fields along the seashore. To add to their troubles these people are at the mercy of pirates who infest the rock – bound coast, though their poverty must give them some immunity.

The village of Kao – Choa was recently visited by a body of pirates, who came and asked for residence, there on promise of non – molestation. This was refused by the people for fear that they would be punished for assisting law – breakers, and they petitioned the authorities to provide suitable protection. In his reply the magistrate regretted that he had not the funds to do this, and pointed out that, since the people of that part had disbanded the local militia, any trouble that occurred must be their own responsibility. But the people are too poor now to pay for a militia; and so they find themselves between two fires, and must decide whether it is wiser to offend the pirates or the officials.

New Motor Roads

The new motor roads are going ahead steadily, and the opening date no less steadily is being postponed ahead from one date to a later date, so that no one can say with precision when traffic will be introduced. I have seen several cases of injury to navies from the explosions, which can be heard booming from a long distance. Great stretches of the road have to be blasted out of the mountain – side, and the work is all done by hand. There is a man lying now in hospital with a face completely black, unrecognized and blinded. Such is part of the horrible price that must be paid for progress—and, too often, for criminal and avoidable carelessness.

Another price of new roads is the sacrifice of private property. Only a very nominal compensation is being given for fields cut into and houses demolished, and in many cases none at all. In Wenchow city, where street widening is going apace, more or less according to a set programme, hundreds of shops will be halved, and many scores completely lost, and no compensation will be offered. Wenchow is a city of canals. They lie beside the roads, and in many places shops sit astride the canals and open on to the road. All these have to go where street – widening has been ordered. For cleanliness, ventilation, and safety in fire, we welcome these changes, but one realizes sadly that it means the despoiling of one of the remaining ancient and unspoiled cities of China, and one of the quaintest and most picturesque in the country.

Building Progress

With the widening goes rebuilding. During the last four years I have seen, extraordinary progress in local shops and public buildings. There was no theatre; now there are half a dozen, and a new one has just been built which includes reinforced concrete construction; and modern roof lighting after the design employed in Shanghai's Grand Theatre. In the same road a large store is in process, of construction, which will rise to six storeys, and is apparently meant to follow the line of business of the Sincere Co. and Wing – On's in Shanghai. In the same street, a branch of the Bank of Communications has just opened, which is said to have received from local depositors some $ 500000 on the first day of opening. Perhaps this response was drawn by the frontage which is done in modernist straight lines and hard looking angels, the very extreme opposite of the light, untidy, crooked hutches and houses that surround it. Such violent contrasts are, architecturally speaking, rather disagreeable.

Military Conscription

Military conscription has been introduced into the area for all able bodied men of certain fixed ages; men of 40 and over, are exempted from service. The period is three months, for which a certificate is given, after which the bearer may return to his normal occupation. I am told that this new order is resented, and that the conditions are none too comfortable, nor the food too good. The conscripts wear soldier's uniform, live in the temples, receive next to no salary. They receive daily lessons in military science, and daily physical drill, which last is probably the most beneficial part of the training. So far it has been possible to purchase a substitute for $ 10, and no doubt many escape service by this means.

Electric Burglar Trap

Interest has been aroused by the electrocution of a would – be burglar who attempted to enter a house fitted with an electrically charged burglar trap. The house, owned by a Chinese, is in modern design, and something about it, probably its new paint, seems to be attracting night visitors; they have had some four. The first one to come into contact with the live wires found himself a prisoner and mysteriously unable to let go his hold, so he did the only other thing and called out. This woke the occupants of the house who rose quickly and disconnected the wire, immediately releasing the robber who ran away into the night.

So, it was decided that next time the current should not be cut off until somebody had been called to prevent the thief escaping. They had not long to wait. Last week the house was awakened by loud screams. Another man had been grasped by the mysterious power, and was praying to be set free. But this time they went more cautiously and first summoned the neighbours. Then the current was disconnected; but the screams had ceased, the man was already dead.

Chinese law is extremely obscure in a case of this kind. It is said that the family of the deceased could have obtained no redress by law, yet they employed a lawyer, and the latest news of the negotiations is that some $80 shall be paid the family as compensation, besides burial expenses. What would rather go against the plaintiffs, if taken to a court of law, is the fact that the burglar had only that same day been released from a long term of imprisonment!

New Life Results

Not a great deal is heard now of the New Life Movement that started with such loud gusto, although it has by no means petered out. I am told that officials do not now smoke in pubilc places, or at feasts.

The streets are not quite so well swept although the dustbins recently distributed by the authorities to prominent street corners are still doing service—especially to the beggars who find in them a very special and fruitful treasure—hunting ground. I note that a Chinese vegetarian restaurant has opened to give the opportunity for partaking of a cleaner and more sanitary vegetable diet during the hot weather. Some of the vegetarian dishes are dressed up to look and taste like meat dishes. It will probably not be received without welcome by local Buddhists.

"By Road Through Chekiang: Opening – Up of Beautiful Country – Side in China's Garden Province: A Motor Journey Described," *The North – China Herald and Supreme Court & Consular Gazette*, November 14, 1934

By Road Through Chekiang: Opening – Up of Beautiful Country – Side in China's Garden Province: A Motor Journey Described

(Special to the "N. – C. Herald")

BY ROAD THROUGH CHEKIANG

Opening-Up of Beautiful Country-Side in China's Garden Province: A Motor Journey Described

SPECIAL TO THE "N.-C. HERALD"

As described elsewhere, on Sunday, the ceremony took place which marks the beginning of construction on the highway and railway bridge to span the Chien Tang River at Zakou near Hangchow. With the completion of this bridge yet even ...

Ningpo by road if this is desired, it is necessary to turn south at Tsaogno for 45 miles, and again turn north-east at Pamao to Ningpo.

On the journey in question, however, Ningpo was not the objective. Instead it was proposed to go as far

As described elsewhere, on Sunday, the ceremony took place which marks the beginning of construction on the highway and railway bridge to span the Chien Tang River at Zakou near Hangchow. With the completion of this bridge yet even more beauty spots will come within the possibility of easy reach by the Shanghai motorist. Last week end a Shanghai car made the journey to be described.

Imagine park lands filled with the autumn tints of the candleberry, and hillsides clothed with tall maples and poplars in reds and golds of every shade and with small shrubs making their last brave show of colour. To the natural beauty of the scenes which were opened before admiring eyes, scenes of mountain and river gorge, was added the glory of the colour which belongs to this season. Indeed, it is not too much to say that the future holds for the beauty lover in East China not a little of the delight that is traditionally associated with autumn in Japan.

Japan has been accessible, Chekiang remote. Now Chekiang is opening like a flower, the more lovely because of barren years spent on the flat Shanghai plain!

Two Wonderful Seasons

China must advertise to the world that she has two wonderful seasons: a springtime when the whole countryside is carpeted with an inimitable yellow of rape alternating with the mauve of clover, while hillsides are aflame with the red and gold of azaleas, and an autumn of challenging reds and golds. Such scenes would be worth half a world of travel to see!

Starting the journey from Hangchow, by courtesy of the Chekiang highway officials, a ferry was made available at Nanshingchiao, on the north bank of the Chien Tang River four miles from the Hangchow West Lake. As yet the ferry service at this point has not come within the jurisdiction of the highway administration and for the time being a makeshift barge of two large sampans lashed together with planks laid across them is being towed across by a small tug. The approaches are nevertheless easy to negotiate and the crossing is thus readily effected.

From "Kiang Pien", the south bank of the river, to Shaoshing and through to Tsaogno, for 49 miles the road surface is splendid and rapid progress can be made along this section of the route. It has for some six years been traversed by a bus line and proved a paying proposition for the authorities. It is understood that the Chekiang Highway Administration has sold the operating rights for a period of years in order to obtain funds for the further financing of its highway programme.

Towards Wenchow

At Tsaogno, a river is crossed to Pokwan, a railway leads to Ningpo. As yet, however, the road northward from Pokwan to Ningpo has not been completed. Neither is a vehicular ferry available. To reach Ningpo by road if this is desired, it is necessary to turn south at Tsaogno for 45 miles, and again turn northeast at Pamao to Ningpo.

On the journey in question, however, Ningpo was not the objective. Instead it was proposed to go as far south as practicable on the road which ultimately will lead to Yung – kia (Wenchow). This road is, indeed, already completed, but as yet the ferry arrangements at Hwangyen and at Wenchow are not in operation, and thus the stretch is not yet open to traffic. Accordingly for a first exploration on this road to the coast, the travellers were content to make for Tientai, some 78 miles generally south – east of the Tsaogno turnoff. Tientaishan, a mountain on a spurroad off the main road near Tiental, is a famous Buddhist mountain at the foot of which is situated an old temple where simple and friendly accommodations were obtained for the night. The beautiful old trees more than 300 years of age, which are found in the courtyards as well as on the slopes of the mountain and the clear bubbling stream which flows through leafy glens make the temple a haven indeed.

Mountain Passes

To reach Tientai, however, it is necessary, after passing the towns of Chenghsien, Sinchang and the Ningpo turnoff at Pamao, to cross a mountain range. The road first winds up a narrowing valley to its head, finally beginning an ascent by a winding mountain road more than two and a half miles in length to the top, with two abrupt hairpin bends. The grading, however, is splendid throughout and the car makes the ascent with ease. This ascent is known as the Wei Tse Ling. The road then traverses the range at high level, up and down slopes, finally descending by another two mile pass on Kua Ling, to lower levels. Less than ten miles further on there awaited a courteous welcome in the bus station at Tientai and the offer of an escort on the part of a police official to show the way into the temple spur road. Perhaps in no other place in a long acquaintance with new scenes on China highways has there been so friendly and helpful a reception.

Twenty Miles Besides Valleys

Morning awakening by temple gongs and bright weather for an early start set the pace for a beautiful second day out. Retracing steps over the Kuahing and the Wei Tse Ling, just as lovely as on the previous evening, the 47 miles run back through Pamao, Sinchang and Chenghsien was quickly accomplished. Now an abrupt turn south west was made, through Changlo to Tungyang, 47 miles distant. This part of the country is attractive, generally traversing valleys with high hills and mountains in view on either side. For the traveller in the autumn the red colours of the tallow woods render even this less dramatic portion of the journey a pleasant experience.

Twenty Miles Besides Valleys

From Tungyang the road enters into narrower valleys and defiles making its way apparently across a small watershed. Another 36 miles of road newly opened (and, indeed, making the present circular tour possible) brought the car to Yung – kang. From this point it was known that, continuing on still generally south westward, it would be possible to reach Lishui ("beautiful waters") along the newly constructed road which had cost the highway authorities no less than 1000000 dollars. Curiosity was roused to discover what, indeed, had been so costly in the proceedings. It very soon became evident. Passing Tsinyun, 21 miles from Yungkang, the car soon began its winding along no fewer than twenty miles of road cut from the face of rock cliffs in a narrow river gorge. The river itself was low and full of rapids. In less dry seasons it would probably be even more attractive, but as it was, with high mountains on the other side of the river, clad in bamboos and autumn tinted trees, the scene was unforgettable. The road is a splendid piece of engineering and a monument to the 70000 Shantung labourers who were brought down to accomplish the task. Ingersoll Rand rock drilling machinery is still being used, for at some of the points where the rock was hardest the road is even yet only very narrow, and the fall to the gorge below seems very near. But, with the road controlled and only one way traffic permitted, and with due driving care it does not present undue diffculty to the traveller. It is a rewarding experience to spend so long in so lovely a scene.

Kinhwa and Lanchi

In Lishui a simple inn offered accommodation for the night. It was necessary to bestir betimes, for a long day's journey back to Shanghai loomed on the morrow. Slipping out of the city before dawn and the twenty miles of gorges towering high to the east with the breaking light upon them was exhilarating. And the gorges themselves in the early morning were inspiring.

Out again to Yungkang, 45 miles, the car turned now north west, 28 miles to Kinhwa. Famed as a city among Chinese people for its hams, the many large pigs seen along the highway would seem to prove the proposition! From Kinhwa yet another newly opened portion of road connects that city with Lanchi. It proved necessary to cross a small river by ferry soon after leaving Kinhwa, but the barge was available and the crossing quickly made. There is no official charge for ferry crossings, but sixty cents small money is considered an acceptable "cumshaw". The road to Lanchi is on a plateau, across rolling foothills, very attractive country. Nineteen miles from Kinhwa the road turns south toward Chuchow and north into Lanchi city. To reach the ferry across the Chien Tang River, however, one takes the south road till the ferry fork appears on the right. As yet there are no signboards to make this plain to the traveller and it was necessary to use tongue and civil approaches at the bus station toward Lanchi to find that the wrong turning had been taken and that it was necessary to go first toward Chuchow. Once again the ferry crossing was made without undue difficulty. The large junks with sails high to the wind on the river were a delightful sight in the morning sunshine.

And now for yet another new road—connecting Lanchi with Showchang and Paisha. In general the road runs northward down long gradual gradients, down from the very obvious upland—feeling of the plateau and to the bed of the Hsing An River, 42 miles from Lanchi the road turns left to Showchang and right toward Paisha, and ten miles further one finds the ferry at the last named village. The ferry is quickly handled by a pleasant woman who takes her turn at the oar with the ease of long custom.

Spur Road to Chi Li Lung

Across the beautiful Hsing An the only regret was that time and distance yet to be traveled back to Shanghai precluded turning left to run along possibly the loveliest run in the whole of the Chekiang province along the new road to Hweichow, through Shun An and Weiping. But turning right, the 94 miles back to Hangchow through Tunglu (and yet another ferry) and Fuyang were still most pleasant. At a point about half way between Paisha and Hangchow a new road has been constructed, four miles in length, making it possible for the traveller to see one of the most famous of the Chien Tang gorges – the Chi Li Lung, the seven mile gorge. If the wind is favourable the journey is seven li, but if not, it is seventy. So runs the Chinese proverb.

From Hangchow back to Hangchow by the circular route taken was just over 650 miles. It explored some of the lovely mountains on the road toward Wenchow and the east coast. It traversed the twenty mile gorge toward Lishui. It ran over the uplands of Kinhwa and Lanchi. It included five ferry crossings.

It spelt liberty for the Shanghai captive and betokens that there is beauty enough and to spare for the future. Later it will be possible to avoid the retracing of same steps as on the present journey and make a tour to Wenchow by the coast route and across westward to Lishui and out by the twenty – mile gorge. May the Ch'ien T'ang bridge come soon!

"Boycott in Wenchow Stopped," *The North – China Herald and Supreme Court & Consular Gazette*, December 12, 1934

Boycott in Wenchow Stopped

It was reported in an issue of the "North – China Herald" in August last that a boycott of foreign goods had been instituted at Wenchow, the products chiefly affected, being cigarettes and fertilizers. According to the latest report received from a reliable source, it appears that a representative of a local foreign tobacco company recently paid a visit to Wenchow and called upon Mr. Hsu Pan – yun, Special Supervisor of the Civil Administration of the Wenchow District, and obtained from him an official rescript stating that the Yungkia Magistrate had been instructed to put a stop to any illegal interference with the selling of cigarettes.

It is to be hoped that this measure will be entirely effectual and satisfactory.

"New Arrivals in Distant Wenchow: Verdict Generally Good on the New Roads: New Magistrate Coming," *The North – China Herald and Supreme Court & Consular Gazette*, January 9, 1935

New Arrivals in Distant Wenchow: Verdict Generally Good on the New Roads: New Magistrate Coming

(From our own correspondent)

NEW ARRIVALS IN DISTANT WENCHOW

Verdict Generally Good on the New Roads: New Magistrate Coming

FROM OUR OWN CORRESPONDENT

Wenchow, Dec. 8.

The always small foreign community of this city has received some new members. Mr. H. C Morgan replaced Mr. A. Casati as In official quarters the important news is the coming of a new city magistrate, and bringing with him the usual large retinue of place-seekers. There will be a general

Wenchow, December 8

The always small foreign community of this city has received some new members. Mr. H. C Morgan replaced Mr. A. Casati as Commissioner of Customs, and comes from his previous station at Wuhu on the Yangtze. Previously to Mr. Casati's appointment early this year there had been for several years a Chinese Commissioner Mr. A. V. Adlington, from Lappa, the Customs district around Macao, has replaced Mr. Tappenden who is now stationed in Shanghai. Mr. Adlington is staying on the "Rivers – Hearts" Island, opposite the city, with Mrs. Adlington and daughter. His only foreign neighbour is Mr. Elm, the Harbour Master who has already been several months in Wenchow.

The English Methodist Mission has received the addition of a new doctor to work in the Blyth Hospital—Dr. O. Lyth, who comes direct from England, and also Mrs. R. J. Hooper, who as Miss Warmisham came to China, from Cheshire, England, in October of this year, to marry Rev. R. Jenkins Hooper of the Wenchow Methodist Mission.

New Roads Complete

The most important news just now is the extensive road making in country and city which in progress now for over a year, has practically arrived at the final stage of completion. Four years ago, it seemed hardly credible that any of the plans for roads could come to anything definite. The matter has been on paper now for more than ten years. Sometimes taxes have been raised, and the money diverted, once at least a stretch of motor – road was actually accomplished, only to be left, because an isolated road, to waste. Things have now changed. Roads have suddenly appeared as from nowhere. Great timber and concrete bridges span innumerable creeks and streams. Motor buses have actually begun to run trial services beside the winding Bowl River which has never witnessed anything more mechanical than the little passenger motor launches that take a day to get to Tsingdie. The cars will only take a couple of hours. Most of this road has been cut out of the solid rock of the mountain slopes, if of great beauty the prospect will also be not without some danger to motorists. Roads run to Hangchow through Tsingdie and Chuchow. One may also touch the north by taking the easterly road through Ngohtsing, and the renowned mountain beauty spot Ngasa, which is to be developed as a tourist centre. The circular tour has already been made, by a German motorist from Shanghai who came out of curiosity to try the road. His verdict was "generally good."

City Street Widening

The country roads completed, the authorities are at last enforcing the long deferred threats to widen the city streets. The main streets of the city have quite suddenly come under the hard blows of the housebreaker. Where were rows of shops are now piles of broken brick and flying clouds of dust. Yet almost as quickly as these old houses and shops are pulled down others rise thirteen feet behind. Every week sees some aspects of the old city changed. It is sad to go out and miss some congested, but delightfully quaint old corner dear to one's memory. Most of the new buildings are copies of ultra modern steel and concrete buildings; and where steel is lacking (as for example, the window frames) wood is used painted silver.

Trade may be bad, but not for the builder and carpenter. One striking accompaniment of the depression is a boom in building. It began a couple of years ago, and has now reached frenzied proportions. Banks, theatres, shops and private houses—erected in size and style that the Wenchow of two years back had not seen nor believed.

New Magistrate Coming

The fire God has started at his destructive work with two fierce and devastating fires. One broke out in a shop beside a tidal canal when the tide was low. Had it been high tide there might have been saved from homelessness no less than 1200 families. Though the weather was cold these fire refugees had to spend the night in fields or temples or anywhere they could get. The water shortage came to my notice rather vividly when I saw two fire engines stationed beside a roaring building from which the heat scorched my hair, while neither had sufficient water to make a steady stream.

In official quarters the important news is the coming of a new city magistrate, and bringing with him the usual large retinue of place – seekers. There will be a general "all – change" at the Yamen, and not a few will have to find jobs for themselves elsewhere.

Missioner's Visit

Religious circles have received an awakening due to a visit from Mr. Tsin Tsz – vu, the general secretary for the China Christian Endeavour Union. He conducted an intensive mission lasting for nine days on behalf of the three large evangelical Churches in this area, the China Inland Mission, the Methodist, and the Independent. Meetings were held in Churches of all denominations, but before the end of the week it became necessary, by reason of the size of the crowds, to finish the Mission in the Methodist Church which can seat about a 1000 persons.

On the Sunday afternoon this Church was packed even to stanaing room, people crowded outside doors and windows, and overfowed into the Sunday School Hall filling both the area and the gallery. There could not have been many fewer than 2000 people.

"Progress Achieved in Wenchow: Year Book Details Improvements While Recording a Reducation in Trade," *The North – China Herald and Supreme Court & Consular Gazette*, May 1, 1935

Progress Achieved in Wenchow: Year Book Details Improvements While Recording a Reducation in Trade

(From our own correspondent)

PROGRESS ACHIEVED IN WENCHOW

Year Book Details Improvements While Recording a Reducation in Trade

FROM OUR OWN CORRESPONDENT

Wenchow, Che. Apr. 4. A copy of the Year Book for 1934 of the Government of the Yung-ko-yue which includes the City of Wen- The official advice given is that cultivators should give up oranges, and grow more bi-bo, pears, apples, plums and peaches, etc.

Wenchow, April 4

A copy of the Year Book for 1934 of the Government of the Yung – ko – yue which includes the City of Wenchow, having come into my hands, I am venturing to select items here and there from its mass of information that might interest readers living in other districts. This record of past achievements and future plans reveals the great progress being made here in the general movement of modernization. I have mentioned roads in previous articles. In two or three years the population of this district in a time of declining trade has built many scores of miles of motor roads through mountain areas, without the aid of modern machinery, although the feat required the blasting of great distances of road through solid rock, and the erecting of bridges over streams at frequent intervals.

City Improvements

Within Wenchow street widening has been going on apace, and hundreds of houses have been pulled down, and newer and better ones (though reduced in ground space) built. Street obstructions like shrubs, widows memorials, hawkers stalls, and even beggars are being removed from the streets. The beggars if persistent are punished, perhaps by imprisonment, and many have been put on the public works such as filling in or dredging of city canals. All widened streets are to be renamed, and I noticed that the new names chosen are nationalistic and tend to memorialize Dr. Sun Yat – sen. Market places on streets have been removed to certain fired roofed areas, either specially erected, or converted temples. Four at least have been already established. A new keep to the left regulation has been enforced on the rickshaws. As for the gates to the city those in the south and north have been demolished, and instead of the old conventional multiple cornered entrance designed to baffle wandering demons, there are straight and wide motor roads leading direct through to the main city street.

The influence of the New Life Movement can be seen in certain hygenic reforms, as for instance the institution of a city slaughter house near the West Gate, where all cattle and pigs must be taken to be killed under proper inspection.

The book contains a photo showing a great popular bonfire of hundreds of old trade measures, which had evidently been proved fraudulent. When every shopkeeper keeps his own size in measures how can the customer be sure that he obtains his correct measure of rice? So irregularity has at last produced enforced uniformity, since only standardized Government measures may now be bought and used in trade.

Restoring Antiquities

A great deal of activity in renovating places of historic or antique interest, and improving the noted beauty spots in which Wenchow and environs abound, results I presume from greater pride engendered by the New Life Movement. The seven storey pagoda on River's Heart Island which was built about 1000 years ago in the Doa dynasty and which has been for years a picturesque ruin inhabited only by the nests of herons, and a few tufts of gnarled bushes at the summit, is now a gaudy tower of saffron colour, with tinkling bells dangling in the breezes from the balconies.

In the country areas reforms are being attempted at least. Every small place is expected by local labour to make twenty Chinese li of foot road per year, and to plant twenty Chinese mow with trees. Telephone extension is to be encouraged. Also there is a scheme put forward for help in times of bad harvest that might have come from. Joseph's provisions for Egypt's seven lean years in the days of the Old Testament, for the plan suggests that granaries be built with an enforced contribution of grain from all farmers, for use in famine times, when shop prices soar too high for the poor.

There are very interesting statistics of the area, revealing the existence of a considerable organization in the community. Those whose idea of Chinese communal and civic life outside the international cities is strongly detrimental to the Chinese, would be, as I have been, encouragingly surprised in scanning the pages of this fat modern looking volume. Details are given of the condition of every trade in the area, with graphs diagrams picturing their exact turnover of business during the year. Wenchow used to export $ 500000 worth of oranges, of which there are six varieties, some to Japan, but now that Canton and Formosa export the more popular sweet oranges that foreigners know (Wenchow's speciality is the bitter mandarin orange) local export value has slumped to $ 200000.

The official advice given is that cultivators should give up oranges, and grow more pears, apples, plums and peaches, etc.

Foolish Tea Dealers

This sad tale of reduction in trade continues throughout the reports. Tea for example, though the reason given for tea is that local dealers persist in their old habits of camouflaging inferior tea in the packing cases with an upper layer of good leaves, so that customers are shocked away!

Japan used to send special steamers for two staple products—vegetable oil, and charcoal, but not now, alas! I have wondered whether the boycott of Japanese goods did not while it lasted inflict greater loss on the merchants of this area than on their Japanese rivals. Vegetable oils used to export to the tune of $ 500000 per year, which is a large sum for Wenchow.

Even fisheries are bad, though due apparently to the morals of those who follow this pursuit, they are said to gamble and to drink.

In the good old days over 10000 fishermen spread their nets in sea, river, stream and canal, to catch annually $ 1000000 worth of fish. The heaviest fowl of the year weighed 5 – 6 Chinese chang. While eggs fetched $ 200000. Famed from old times for her paper umbrellas one regrets to learn that not only the quantity of output, but also the quality of the work has been diminishing. So also with grass mats which sell at seven for $ 1. B'ing – Die soap – stone carvings pass through Wenchow to America, Japan, Russia, France, and in spile of such a sales area trade is depressing. Apparently the only flourishing trades are the builders, carpenters and stone masons, who are busily pulling down old shops and building new ones in wholesale quantities, not house by house, but street by street!

Wages Remain Low

Figures are (even for wages for farm hands for men, women and children respectively) low. The highest possible earnings for a strong man amount to $ 60 per year, $ 6.40 per month, and .36 per day, which figures apparently include the day's meals. A poor worker would get a minimum of just under half of these figures. A woman's maximum wage per year in the country is $ 26, the lowest $ 12. Children over ten years may, if exceptional, earn $ 20 in twelve months, though some can only earn $ 5 a year. The highest day's wage is twelve cents, and the average seven cents, and the lowest is only four cents. Food is extra. All country people eke out their earnings by home industries. Men make at home, netting, rough paper, baskets, straw shoes, and rope etc. Women make—straw mats, and shoes, cloth, belts, cross – stitch and embroidery, straw – hats etc.

Interest rates on borrowed money soar round about 20 percent. which is terrificially high, though lower than in some other places, in China. Unrest and insecurity keep the rates high by causing general reluctance to let sums of money go without ample reward for the risks taken, and thus country people have great difficulty in obtaining loans at all.

The total area surveyed in this volume is 823500 Chinese mow of land of which 461200 mow is uncultivatable land. Taxpayers represent 742400 mow of property which figure reveals a residue of property owners who do not pay taxes. Therefore a complete inventory or "Domesday Book" is to be made of the area for purposes of taxation and increasing the local government income. The entire population appears to be something like 680000.

"Investigation into Tobacco Boycott: 1750000 Cigarettes Seized and Burnt by Chinese," *The North − China Herald and Supreme Court & Consular Gazette*, June 5, 1935

Investigation into Tobacco Boycott: 1750000 Cigarettes Seized and Burnt by Chinese

INVESTIGATION INTO TOBACCO BOYCOTT

1,750,000 Cigarettes Seized and Burnt by Chinese

Shanghai, June 1

The New Life Movement is providing a mask behind which a group of anti − foreign boycotters are working. Such is the true state of affairs existing in Wenchow at the moment, it was learnt in Shanghai yesterday, from reliable authority.

Cigarettes made by Chinese firms have been allowed in to Wenchow without let or hindrance. It is only cigarettes of foreign manufacture with which interference has occurred.

The Chinese organization actively concerned in the boycott is the Yungkia (Wenchow) Cigarette & Money Exchange Shops Association, while another is the New Life Movement Promotion Society, though apparently, the principals of the latter are used as a cat's paw by the former.

1750000 Cigarettes Burnt

On May 18 the former association seized 30 large cases and 25 small cases of Ruby Queen cigarettes, amounting in all to 1750000 cigarettes on arrival in Wenchow. The seizure was made in the morning and, it is understood, these goods were burnt about 15 li from the city at about noon on the same day.

The local tax officials, whose duty was to see that the goods were properly stamped, protested against the seizure and demanded to see the goods but were not allowed to carry out their duty.

A protest was immediately made to the Magistrate and the Public Safety Bureau by the local dealer of the Yee Tsoong Distributors Ltd. (formerly the B. A. T.) but nothing was done until 5 p. m. , when the Chief of the Police sent twelve policemen to the place of seizure but by then the perpetrators of the outrage could not be found.

Mr. E. W. Jeffrey, British Vice – Consul, leaves for Wenchow today to investigate the matter.

At the Japanese Consulate, little of the present deadlock was known. Japanese interests in Wenchow, it was stated, ceased two years ago, when, owing to a vigorous anti – Japanese movement, all Japanese inhabitants were forced to evacuate. Quite recently, however, some Japanese goods consigned to a Chinese merchant were nots allowed to be landed. The view was expressed that, in the near future, a Japanese consul would visit Wenchow in the hope of successfully closing negotiations to allow Japanese to return again.

"Wenchow – Ningpo Motor Road: Pleasant Journey Along Well Laid Thoroughfare," *The North – China Herald and Supreme Court & Consular Gazette*, June 12, 1935

Wenchow – Ningpo Motor Road: Pleasant Journey Along Well Laid Thoroughfare

(From a Correspondent)

A scenic route, seemingly as yet little known to the public, is the recently completed motor road from Wenchow to Ningpo. Japan will indeed have to look to her laurels, for much of the scenery equals or exceeds what she has to offer. Leaving Wenchow early in the morning, after crossing the river, this well built motor road skirts the bay and gradually climbs into the mountains, everywhere giving an entrancing view of hill and vale, the mosaic of the cultivated plots and terraces adding much to the every changing picture which never grows tiresome.

There are some straight stretches where speed MIGHT be attempted, but the careful drivers rarely went above thirty miles an hour, and, of course, often it was ten and fifteen on the steeper grades. Once an engineer myself, I greatly appreciated the engineering skill of the Chinese engineers who have carved this useful artery from south to north. The maximum grade seems to be not over 7 percent. and the motors are kept in good condition, so that no motor trouble of any kind was experienced during the two day trip. Surfacing material is handy, and well made use of, so the roads are not affected by rains to any extent. At this time of the year, with the grain fields a golden yellow, and with harvesting going on here and there, it was doubly interesting to have this opportunity to study the country and its people and products.

The passenger has to be ferried across several stream, and in two instances crosses on pontoon bridges, but the connections at the other side are immediate and no time is lost. For this trip my party used seven buses, one after the other, and all of them were most satisfactory. Further, it is important to note that the cost of the trip is very reasonable, the fare amounting to nine dollars, Wenchow to Ningpo, and the actual travel time being under fifteen hours. The middle of the first afternoon we arrived at Ling Hai, where we were able to secure quite satisfactory quarters in a Chinese inn. For those who do not use Chinese food, other provisions should be carried. Our party spoke mandarin, and managed quite well, though not understanding the seemingly difficult Ningpo and Wenchow dialects.

At Pa Mao it is possible to arrange to go to Hangchow if the passenger desires, instead of continuing to Ningpo. The improvements along various lines at Ch'i K'ou, especially landscaping, are well worth seeing, and yet rugged nature all along the way affords ample opportunity for the sight – seer. The rice fields everywhere seemed in good condition, assuring a yield much greater than last year. Looking down the mountain at one vantage point the passenger's view intersects the road he has just traversed five times, so winding is the road, withal splendidly done from the engineering viewpoint. Old and picturesque bridges are seen here and there, as well as nestling mountain hamlets and villages.

"Modernization of Wenchow: Building Regulations and Fire Apparatus," *The North – China Herald and Supreme Court & Consular Gazette*, October 2, 1935

Modernization of Wenchow: Building Regulations and Fire Apparatus

(From our own correspondent)

Wenchow, September 16

The month that had been a record for warmth has now made a record for cold. All the world is abroad in autumn blues and browns. Autumn temperatures are by no means unwelcome, although the summer has not been too unkind this year. We are relieved to report, also, that of three or four typhoon scares this season, only one brushed anywhere near this area and no damage was wrought.

Returning from holiday I was astonished at the progress made during two months in street widening. Indeed, already Wenchow would be unrecognizable to visitors who were last here as near as two years ago—tall modern – style houses in place of the old wooden shacks and huts. Wide streets instead of the narrow lanes almost bridged over by the projective stories of the houses on either side. Wide gates instead of the old crooked devil gates. It is common to see three and four storied buildings, so common that the City Government has had to enact a group of regulations stipulating that new buildings must be of such and such a style, and should be approved by an in-

MODERNIZATION OF WENCHOW

Building Regulations and Fire Apparatus

FROM OUR OWN CORRESPONDENT

Wenchow, Sept. 16.

The month that had been a record for warmth has now made a record for cold. All the world is abroad in autumn blues and browns. Autumn temperatures are by no means unwelcome, although the summer has not been too unkind this year. We are relieved to report, also, that of three or four typhoon scares this season, only one brushed anywhere near this area and no damage was wrought.

spector before erection. This is because many of the new buildings have very small ground area.

Peculiar Building

I was recently marvelling at a three – storied shop with a frontage of about fifteen feet and a depth from front window to back wall of not more than six feet. What will happen to such buildings and there are many such, in a typhoon or when heavy motor traffic begins to rumble down the street, or how the inhabitants would escape in a fire—these are mysteries so far. As to fire, the authorities are preparing to combat possible carnage and destruction amongst such buildings, by digging deep wells at principal street corners, and by ordering modern fire – engines.

I have news that some of the official offices are to be abolished for the sake of economy, notably that of City magistrate. This old, established office is to be merged with another, together with Chief of the Police. The order was issued from the Provincial Capital.

Military conscription continues to disturb the lives and occupations of the populace. One sometimes sees a squad of country conscripts trying to learn drill steps and looking extremely raw and silly. They are required to leave their homes for a period of not less than three months. The system, although mainly for national defence, is probably of more direct value for local defence against bandits. Bandits will be more chary of attacking a village where the able – bodied males have all received a term of military training.

Menace of Bandits

This reminds me that the countryside after a year or two of respite, has again become menaced by bandits. Members of the China Inland Mission have had to retire from their summer hill bungalow and bus services came to a temporary stop. They have resumed, but the situation is by no means secure.

A few days ago a small launch that plies from Wenchow to a large village about three hours journey up river was held up by a body of armed men and $ 1000 stolen. When the boatman objected he was taken captive and since has not been heard of. One of the party knew enough about engines to bring the launch to Wenchow, when a body of police went immediately to investigate. Ordinarily there could scarcely be found $ 20 amongst the passengers of this little boat, but this being the time of settling accounts, there happened to be two or three city men who were returning from their annual visit to the country, debt collecting. The bandits seem to have selected the occasion with some intelligence.

Next week the local independent Christian Church which severed relations with the English Methodist Church during the political troubles at the time of the Nationalist rising, is to celebrate its tenth anniversary by a fortnight of special meetings. The old sores have been today largely healed, and the first meetings will be addressed by representatives from the China Inland Mission, and the Methodist Church.

Self – supporting Church

This Independent Church is entirely self – supporting and self – governing, and during the last two years has been paying off the cost of a fine, new church building erected in the city, the money having been raised locally. In addition it has associated churches in the countryside. Such a record is very commendable, though it is to be remembered that at the time of the schism only fairly well – to – do and strong churches dared to leave the parent body. This larger body today is still carrying the burden of the weaker.

Movements in the foreign staff of the English Methodist Mission include the departure on furlough in November, of Dr. and Mrs. E. T. A. Stedeford, and son, and Rev. and Mrs. W. R. Aylott, and the return from furlough in October of Miss P. Smith, (Nurse) . Dr. Stedeford, Miss Smith and Mrs. Aylott are stationed at the Blyth Methodist Hospital.

It may be welcome news to many Mission Stations that it is possible to install modern plumbing and a hygienic modern kitchen with a gas – cooker. This is made possible by means of the natural gas plant, now being sponsored by a Chinese firm in Shanghai. The plant is simple and requires no replenishment of chemical, while there is no machinery to get out of order. The only fuel is ordinary kitchen refuse, and with anything such as grass, vegetable tops, or other soft matter. The gas formed is safer than coal gas, non – poisonous, and gives a high temperature. The system has been installed in some of the Methodist houses and there are other houses in the city, foreign and Chinese, which have employed it satisfactorily for a year or two.

"Wenchow Trade: Anti–foreignism Denied," *The North–China Herald and Supreme Court & Consular Gazette*, October 23, 1935

Wenchow Trade: Anti – foreignism Denied

To the Editor of *the "North – China Daily News"*

Sir, —A notice appeared recently in the foreign press to the effect that official difficulties had been placed in the way of some foreign traders who came to the City seeking to make trade. On behalf of the City, I wish to deny that Wenchow has ever, or will ever prevent the extention of her trade for merely political reasons. Normally, this is a thriving district, but within recent years the rural economic condition has been approaching the danger point, so that the authorities have constantly sought means to improve trade. For example, efforts have been made to exterminate banditry, while tradesmen are encouraged to adopt popular prices for their goods. Contrary to reports there exists no anti – foreignism, and recently British and American vice – Consuls have visited, the district for first – hand information on the situation. They went away satisfied with the position. I hope these facts will reassure any of your readers who may have had doubts concerning the position of foreign trade in Wenchow.

Wenchow, October 10

WENCHOW TRADE

Anti-Foreignism Denied

To the Editor of the "NORTH-CHINA DAILY NEWS"

SIR,—A notice appeared recently in the foreign press to the effect that official difficulties had been placed in the way of some foreign traders who came to the City seeking to make trade. On behalf of the City I wish to deny that Wenchow has

"Some Questions," *The North – China Herald and supreme Court & Consular Gazette*, October 23, 1935

Some Questions

To the Editor of *the North – China Daily News*

SIR, —With reference to the letter which WENCHOW wrote to your paper on October 10 denying the existence of a boycott against foreign goods in Wenchow, I am of the opinion that either Wenchow is not well informed about conditions which have prevailed during the past two years throughout Wenchow and Haimen areas, or his letter has been written as a sort of attempted apology for the serious losses which have been inflicted upon foreign trade in that important section of Chekiang Province.

The principal foreign articles imported into Wenchow are oils, cigarettes and chemical fertilizers. On several occasions I have been in a position to convince myself on the spot that of these three lines of important business, so far only the oil trade has been left unharassed while the boycott against cigarettes and chemical fertilizers has been so strong that the importation of cigarettes produced by foreign – owned factories has shown marked decrease and it has been impossible to ship into Wenchow any appreciable quantities of chemical fertilizers during this year.

If Wenchow is of the opinion that no difficulties have been placed in the way of foreign trade, I should like to ask these questions：

Some Questions

To the Editor of the
"NORTH-CHINA DAILY NEWS"

SIR,—With reference to the letter which WENCHOW wrote to your paper on October 10 denying the existence of a boycott against foreign goods in Wenchow, I am of the opinion that either Wenchow is not well informed about conditions which have prevailed during the past two years throughout Wenchow and Haimen areas, or his letter has been written as a sort of attempted apology for the serious losses which have been inflicted upon foreign trade in that important section of Chekiang Province.

（1） Why did the Shanghai Shun Pao dare to write an article on June 15 to the effect that advice has been received by shipping hongs in Shanghai that no further shipments of foreign cigarettes and chemical fertilizers should be made to Wenchow?

（2） Why were 25 cases of cigarettes illegally confiscated and publicly burnt in Wenchow just prior to that date?

（3） Who intimidated the wharf coolies at Wenchow and Haimen, who are always eager to earn enough money with which to buy their daily rice, so that they refused to handle shipments of foreign made cigarettes and chemical fertilizers and thus caused the goods to be returned to Shanghai?

Although lately it has been possible to land a few shipments of these boycotted goods in Wenchow, almost no sales can be effected, as in most of the small consuming centres, sales are still officially prohibited and in other places, where no boycott is in force, the dealers and consumers are under the impression that they will have to pay extra duties or higher road taxes or contribution to the Native Goods Promotion Association, amounting to as much as $1.00 for each package sold as has actually been the case in Yuhwan.

The purpose of this letter is to show that the foreign trade situation in Wenchow is not quite as good as Wenchow likes to put it. However, I believe it will be highly appreciated not only by the import firms but also by the Chinese shipping companies, and also the merchants and farmers in Wenchow if this movement of anti – foreignism is brought to an end so that from now on import trade in Wenchow may again be carried on normally.

Shipping observer.

Shanghai, October 17.

"China to Make Her Own Paper: Capable of Underselling All Foreign Competitors: Scheme to Erect Mill at Wenchow," *The North – China Herald and Supreme Court & Consular Gazette*, October 30, 1935

China to Make Her Own Paper: Capable of Underselling All Foreign Competitors: Scheme to Erect Mill at Wenchow

CHINA TO MAKE HER OWN PAPER

Capable of Underselling All Foreign Competitors: Scheme to Erect Mill at Wenchow

Furthering her industrial independence, China soon is to have her own
paper manufacturing plant. Plans for
the construction of a $4,500,000 plant sideration the yearly production of
the mill, would mean a profit of $3,875.

It is also pointed out by Mr. Stewart
that, as practised by other countries,

Furthering her industrial independence, China soon is to have her own paper manufacturing plant. Plans for the construction of a $ 4500000 plant have been submitted to and approved by the Ministry of Industry. 80 percent. of the capital will be raised through a loan from the British Boxer Indemnity Fund and the remainder by local merchants. The last date of application for shares in the company will be November 30.

After a thorough investigation by experts, Mawan, on the Ou – kiang, about twenty miles from the city of Wenchow, in southern Chekiang Province, was chosen as the ideal site for the factory, which will consist of a paper-mill and a pulp-factory. British machinery is to be used in the factory and the distribution of the capital required is estimated approximately as follows:

Machinery to make 35 long tons newsprint per 24 hours, including power plant, all delivered and erected—— $3290000

    Purchase of land——10000

    Building and construction work, etc——500000

    Preliminary expenses——100000

    Working capital——600000

    Total—— $4500000

The cost of machinery and building fluctuates with the market and exchange rate, but the cost includes equipment for power generation, for the manufacture of pulp and paper and all necessary accessories. It also includes transportation and erection expenses. The $100000 classed under preliminary expenses is for investigation, including a trip to England by experts for the purpose of selecting machinery and the subsequent supervision of its manufacture.

Raw Material in Plenty

It is often said that China has been denuded of her forest lands and, though this may be true with regard to some of the sea coast provinces, it cannot be said of China as a whole. Suitable timber for making paper is abundant in the districts of Lungchuan, Chingyuan, Chingning, Yunho, Sungyang, Suichang, Hsuanping, Chinyun, Lishui, and Tsingtien, all of which are large tracts of mountainous country. The principal variety is the China fir, with liushan and pine coming next. In addition to supplying the local demand with timber found in these forests, China firs and liushan, valued at $6000000, are exported from these regions annually and two-fifths of this amount goes to Chuhsien and three-fifths to Wenchow. The district of Lungchuan produces the largest amount of timber, with an annual outport valued at approximately $1000000.

Comparison of Prices

Mr. A. G. Stewart, a Scottish paper manufacturing expert, who was appointed adviser to the Ministry of Industry to make a thorough study of the whole plan, especially its economic side, estimates that the mill would be capable to delivering paper in Shanghai at a cost of $110.64 per ton. Investigation into the cheapest newsprint imported into China gives the figure of $110.94 per ton. This, however, is known to be the results of dumping on the market. Foreign mills could not, it is believed, maintain such a low price for any lengthy period. Even if such prices were maintained, the China mill would show a small profit over their foreign rivals of $ 0. 30, which, taking into consideration the yearly production of the mill, would mean a profit of $ 3675.

It is also pointed out by Mr. Stewart that, as practised by other countries, the tariff might be raised a little in order to protect the new industry. Concerning tariff rates on paper imported into China, he makes the following comments, in an article which appears in this month's issue of the "Chinese Economic Journal": "The tariff on newsprint is levied at the rate of 7. 5 percent for newsprint in rolls and 33. 5 percent for newsprint in sheets. As a result of this, the import of newsprint in sheets has practically ceased. The paper is now imported in rolls and cut into sheets in factories in Shanghai. If the duty were altered, and levied on a basis of weight, as is usual in other countries, it would help the new mill a great deal. A small increase in duty could then be levied without hardship to the printing houses. "

Daily Output of Mill

It has been decided that the paper mill shall have a daily output of 35 tons of newsprint. This has been calculated on a working basis of 350 days a year and the total annual output will amount of 12250 long tons. That there is little fear of overproduction is shown by the fact that four of China's leading daily papers, the "Shun Pao", "Sin Wan Pao", "Eastern Times", and "China Times", between them consume 20000 tons of newsprint annually.

The trustees of the British Boxer Indemnity Fund have held several meetings concerning the technical reports and the financial estimates. They have agreed to grant the loan required, and the contract will be made in due course. The capital raised by public subscription will be sponsored by the local vernacular press. The Bank of China, the Bank of Communications, and the Central Bank, etc. , have been appointed to handle any transactions with regard to shares.

"Proposed Wenchow Paper Mill: British Boxer Trustees to Decide on Scheme," *The North – China Herald and Supreme Court & Consular Gazette*, December 11, 1935

Proposed Wenchow Paper Mill: British Boxer Trustees to Decide on Scheme

PROPOSED WENCHOW PAPER MILL

British Boxer Trustees to Decide on Scheme

The 32nd meeting of the standing committee of the Board of Trustees for the Administration of the British Boxer Indemnity Refund was held in Shanghai on Saturday under the chairmanship of Dr. Chu Chia – hua, Minister of Communications.

Among those present were Messrs. R. Calder Marshall, Vice – Chairman, T. K. Tseng, Yen Te – ching, Yeh Kung – cho, J. Heng Liu, and W. S. King.

The meeting had under consideration the application from the Ministry of Industry for a loan for the establishment of a paper mill at Wenchow, Chekiang. It was decided to refer the matter to the general meeting of the Board for final decision.

The Education Committee of the Board met subsequently under the chairmanship of Dr. Li Shu – hua. Dr. Chu Chia – hua, Mr. Yen Kung – cho and Dr. J. Heng Liu were present. Several educational proposals were examined.

第三部分

专有
名词

...the sea coast, it seems that th
of Fukien and Taichow are still
erous and as savage as ever.
d its consort bound from Ningpo t
y laden with rice and sundries wer
attacked near Wenchow by a co
rates, who boarded the merchant
ing ransacked everything of valu
e latter, left them with twenty-six
nd seriously wounded Stri
ave been issued by the Governm
, Tsan, for the capture of the pirate
e a large fleet of war junks is now
it seems to be the universal opinio
.... will be unsuccessful

cal Report
American

xpression, spread himself out over the
whole subject of the health, pestilence
amines, and topography of the place
hirty-six closely printed pages have
not sufficed to relieve him of his whol
burden of knowledge, for at the begin
ning of his paper he says that he reserve
he medical
occasion; but
f which he h
ully have th
hat we sho
such a trifle
He begins
district in wl
and passing
other
where,
he saturated condition
ne other such commo

Parker taking leave on a new de-
ure, having first secured the last instal-
t of the indemnity that the authorities
ed to pay for losses sustained by
igners in the recent disturbances. To
be Mr. E H Parker's success in giving
ral satisfaction to foreigners and native
orities in regard to the questions raised
e riot to good luck, would be unjust to
accomplished officer. It was tact that
.ed an amicable settlement

ug-ncng, running as she
rt of the most influential
fter trip with improved
esults, seems now to have
o that point where if mere
of necessity become n
g superfluity. As has be
the impetus given by
y means of shipment has
t export of al
spects for tea
for the Chi

During a fierce gale which raged at Wen
chow about a fortnight ago, several seriou
disasters occurred, attended in many case
with loss of life. Four large junks, lade
with poles, were upset and many other
dragged anchor or sustained other injuries
whilst a great number of small fishing craf
suffered a worse fate. The villagers on th
coast showed great barbarism. Instead o
affording succour, they busied themselve
with picking up wreckage thrown ashore
In the worst cases they even wrested th
poles away from the shipwrecked people
who in their exhausted state were made t
yield the logs to the merciless people
Owing to the unusually cold weather a
Wenchow there is considerable suffering
amongst the poorer classes, who are no
provided with extensive wardrobes, an
specially amongst those who have a pre

sent to Ta-cl
o-ching-hsien
pirate-robbers
sed considerat
s of both this
ow. Some tim
es plundered two
he Yu H'uan Bay
) which caused the
o order one of his
against them. On
of the bay the office
essel decided to an
d a party of soldier

(FROM A CORRESP
Notice to mariners, also
ad to feminine sphere
markable Peak on the
avigators see on their
Wenchow, having only
ad never named, has n
e denizens of Wenchow
Hart's Peak," in recog
ices which the Inspecto
mperial Maritime Custo
y illuminating the coas
ormal recognition of the
y the Wenchowese, in pic-nic assembled
n the 22nd March, and that being th
irthday of the Emperor of Germany, nea
the celebration of the Queen's Jubilee
nd within measurable distance of th
atal day of President Cleveland, th
ealth of those estimable rulers was dru

ny in their boats. In some places wher
he bridges were still standing only th
pper portion of their arches was visibl
oking like mirages—water above, belo
nd around them! Great indeed mu
ave been the downpour to have caused su
n inundation. It was a comforting chang
o turn one's gaze from the immense
ountry to the numberless fishermen pu
ing their calling as if no such thing a
ome troubles existed. The flooded cou
.. ..d it was pleasing

itants of the so-called "C
ave put away their store-cl
ar. The rejoicings were c
ietness and decorum, the
of nastiness was eaten,
ount of tomtomming and f
uiged in; in fact, everyth
accordance with "olo c
Year's Eve most of the
ipal thoroughfares were
ted with coloured lamps, a
re lighted in nearly all th
ty and suburbs. That this
asement did not result in
onflagration is simply miraculous,
munity is by all right-thinking
tributed to the special interve
en Tien Ta Ti, the great Lord of
Leaven, or some other benevole
hough here, as elsewhere, scoffers
und who point to the saturated cons
verything or to some other such

o the Editor of the

NORTH-CHINA DAILY NEWS.

IR,—Although the subject of re
hina was ably discussed at a late
of the Shanghai Literary and De
iety the question was not so exha
reated as to preclude me from
nall contribution, assuming that
be unacceptable to those who
ary (but not

UNICATED.)

vastation that met ou
e river of Wenchow wa
les and miles the countr
vast expanse of wate
teads and graves, an
nds crowded with cattle
frowning background
a most depressing an
We passed too quickl
by the pen. Women an
roups, doubtless talkin
sses, while the men wer

ically, it m
think the
mature, tha
where it u
needed;
northern Cl
courses, and
is doubtful
ccessfully c
It was urg
yed by an i
of China,

R OWN CORRES
ing, on enter
d some stragg
trawropes, the

that were d
ent the enemy
ing. .... they resisted th
would have been as useless
A proposition that was mad
channel has been abandone
a panic was created by a p
quiring every family to bri
daring a basket of stones.
as secure as if they had
protection; the authorities
solicitous for their safety. S
threw missiles, and others
but they were bombard

Macgowa
ow recen
put down
sumption
outhwaite
ld be tra

RIOT AT WENCHOW.

Yunquing, from Wen
here on Saturday, b
lars of a riot which had
ow on the night of the
st intimation of this ri
d up from Ningpo from information
d by the *Yunquing* on arrival a
rt, though efforts had been made by
H. Parker, British Consul, and als

which a reference to Mr. Dou
's table on the opposite page rend
ent. My views elsewhere publis

张载扬（Chang Tse – yang）

知事（Chishi）

国民学校，温州师范附属小学校改（Citizen School）

戴任（Dai Ning）

镇守使（Military Commissioner）

温州师范（Normal School）

蔡博敏（T. W. Chapman）

台州（Taichow）

楚门（Tsumen）

冬防（tung voa）

艺文学堂（United Methodist Mission College）

外塘村（Whadoa villages）

基督教青年会（Y. M. C. A.）

玉环厅，1916 年实际应为玉环县（Yuhuanting）

瓯海关税务司阿歧森（James Acheson）

红衣大将军炮（The Great Red Robes）

温州三角门，即来福门（Three Horned Gate）

得胜路（The Way of the Golden – Victory）

七圣庙（Temple of the Seven Holy Ones）

周宅祠巷天主教会（Roman Catholic Mission）

人力车（Ricsha）

上海会审公廨（Mixed Court）

许仲贤（Mr. Hsu）

普济号（Poochi）

广济号（Kwangchi）

上海轮船招商总局（C. M. S. Co.）

瑞安（Juean）

美孚火油公司（Standard Oil Co.）

亚细亚火油公司（Asiatic Oil Co.）（A. P. C.）

英美烟草公司（Anglo–American Tobacco Co.）

胜家缝纫机公司（Singer's Sewing Machine Co.）

温州甲种商业学校（Wenchow Commercial School）

绸布公会（Clothiers' Guild）

青田石（soap stone）

营长，1917 年指浙江第一师营长杨三（Yingchang）

统领，1917 年指戴任，报纸或民间一般称呼戴任为戴统领（Tungling）

"同华号"（Tungwah）

徐定超（Hsu Ting–chao）

进士（Doctor of literature of the old style）

"新丰号"（Hsinfung）

"江天号"（Kiangteen）

平阳（Pingyang）

沙洲（bank）

桥栈码头（landing stage）

浮筒（pontoon）

美南号（str. Meinan）

少年中国学会（Young China）

交涉员（Official for Foreign Affairs）

瓯海关税务司谭安（Tanant）

李文彬（Li Ung–bing）

谢道培（W. R. Stobie）

旧温州府（old Prefecture）

楠溪江（Nan Ch'i Creek）

永川轮船局（Yungchuan Steam Navigation Co.）

"湖广号"（Hukuang）

台州平礁（Pingchai）

北京国际统一救灾总会（United Inernational Famine Relief Committee）

督军（Thchun）

林鹍翔（H. E. Ling）

金宝星勋章（Gordon Campaign Medal）

好博逊（Herbert Elgar Hobson）

温州圣道公会慕道友（inquirer）

包莅茂（W. E. Plunmer）

英国商会联合会（Associated British Chambers of Commerce）

中国内地会（China Inland Mission）

内地会荣女士（F. A. M. Yong）

内地会王廉（F. Worley）

梅天（梅雨）（Meitin）

瓯柑业公会（Orange Guild）

"遇顺号"（Yushun）

"飞鲸号"（Feiching）

海和德（J. W. Heywood）

温州华洋义赈会（R. C. Mission）

洞头黑牛湾（Bullock Harbour）

永嘉商会（Wenchow Chamber of Commerce）

唐伯寅（Mr. T'ang）

厦门海门（Haiman）

舟山（Chusan）

东瓯王庙（Temple of Neptune）

伊宝珍（Eynon）

山尔曼（A. H. Sharman）

鸡冠山（Chinhoi）

"马勒号"（Ralph Moller）

"广华号"（Kuang Hua）

"升利号"（Sing Li）

"永平舰"（Yung Ping）

施开士（Cance）

"永宁号"（Yungning）

施德福（Stedeford）

司先生（Schlichter）

西溪（West Brook）

三港庙（San Kan Temple）

小庙（Little Temple）

慕传荣（Moler）

潘美贞（Banks）

法国兵舰"爱格尔号"（Algola）

宝华公司（Pao Hua Co. ）

江心屿（Conquest Island）

翰垒德（Handley Derry）

威立师（C. W. S. Williams）

协利电灯公司（Andersen，Meyer & Co. ）

英国皇家海军"风铃草号"（H. M. S. Bluebell）

永嘉县议会（District Council）

蔡经贤（Tsai Kuan – fu）

郝国玺（Ha Sz Ling）

青红帮（Ching Ong Poa）

三北公司（San Peh S. N. Co）

"宁兴号"（Ningshin）

中华国民拒毒会温州分会（local branch of the Anti – Opium Society）

浙江基督教联合会（Chekiang Federation Council）

裴纳玑（Bernadsky）

曹万顺（Tsao Wan – shun）

国民党（Kuomintang）

"红色分子"（Reds）

张焕燊（Tsie Hue – sang）

尤树勋（Yui Ji – sung）

农会（Peasants'Unions）

瓯海公学（Ao Hoe School）

蔡雄（Tsa Ning – gyi）

"海晏轮"（Hoean）

董若望济病院（Jean – Gabriel Hospital）

永嘉育婴堂（Municipal Orphanage）

仁爱会（Charity Misssion）

康乐坊（K'oa – loh – foa）

"开塞姆号"（Cassum）

皇家海军"胡特拉克号"（H. M. S. Woodlark）

牛山岛（Shetung Island）

东矶（箕）岛（Bella Vista）

虞洽卿（Yu Yaching）

王一亭（Wang Yi – ting）

许世英（Hsu Shih – ching）

方椒伯（Fong Chu – pa）

冯少山（S. S. Fung）

金翰（King Han）

披山岛（Pien San）

石浦（Shipu）

"永泰号"（Wing Tai）

鸡蛋山（Chih Tah Hill）

"嘉禾号"（Ka – ho）

"新昌号"（Hsinchang）

温州妇女圣经阅读班（Bible and Reading Class for Women）

温州码头工人海员帮（Seamen's Union）

温州码头工人柴爿帮（Firewood Labourers Union）

孙光德（Irving Scoot）

信河街（New Canal Street）

新桥（New Bridge）

"广利号"（Kang – lee）

"遇顺号"（Sai Shun）

五尺村（Ng – ts'I, U – ch'ih）

白德邻（F. S. Barling）

蘭谿，兰溪（Lanchi）

亭山，华盖山（Pavilion Hill）

金家济，金贯真（Chin Chia – Chu）

胡公冕（Ho Kung – mien）

碧莲镇（Piehlien, Crystal Lily）

地方党部（Local Tang pu）

梅岙（Plum Torrent）

基督复临安息日会（Adventist）

浙江四属剿共总指挥（Commandant of four prefectural cities in Chekiang）

王文瀚（Wang Wen – han）

缙云（Chin – Yun）

爱乐德（W. Roy Aylott）

楠溪潘坑（P'an – K'eng）

胡协和（Hu Hsieh – Wei）

谢文侯（Hsieh Wen – hou）

董佐光（Tong Tsoh – kuang）

邰慕廉（F. F. Dymond）

柏格理（Sam Pollard）

统征处（T'ung Chuen Chu）

洋广处（Yang Kwang Chu）

"楚观号"（ChuKuan）

南关湾（Namkwan）

"威升号"（Waishing）

岩井洋行（Iwai Yoko Company，Ltd.）

永嘉抗日救国会（Anti‐Japanese Association at Wenchow）

村井仓松（K. Murai）

铃木洋行（Suzuki Yoko Company）

韦更生（G. L. Wilkinson）

戴贵珍（G. I. F. Taylor）

胡宝华（R. Jenkins Hooper）

许成棨（C. C. Hsu）

水上飞机"江凤号"（Kiang Feng）

七里镇（Chileechin）

大同医院（Tatung Hospital）

曾贻经（Tseng Yi‐ching）

高昌庙（Kiaochangmiao）

海军飞机制造处（Naval Air Establishment of the Ministry of Navy）

克萨悌（A. Castati）

埃尔茂（J. Elm）

葛松龄（Gosling. G）

"天象号"（Tiensiang）

北天铜山（Peitiendoong Shan）

许蟠云（Hsu Pan‐yun）

浙江省第三特区行政督察专员（Special Supervisor of Civil Administration of the 3rd District of Chekiang Province）

信诚公司（Sincere Co.）

永安公司（Wing‐On Co.）

浙江公路局（Chekiang Highway Administration）

闸口（Zakou）

南兴桥（Nanshingchiao）

江滨（Kiang Pien）

曹娥（Tsaogno）

百官（Pokwan）

黄岩（Hwangyen）

新安江（Hsing An River）

七里泷（Chi Li Lung）

周志禹（Tsin Tsz – vu）

土货协会（Native Goods Promotion Association）

实业部（Ministry of Industry）

马湾（Mawan）

施涤华（A. G. Stewart）

图书在版编目（CIP）数据

《北华捷报》温州史料编译. 1916－1935 年 / 温州市
档案馆译编. -- 北京：社会科学文献出版社，2023.6
ISBN 978－7－5228－1637－1

Ⅰ. ①北… Ⅱ. ①温… Ⅲ. ①温州－地方史－史料－
1916－1935 Ⅳ. ①K295. 53

中国国家版本馆 CIP 数据核字（2023）第 056396 号

《北华捷报》温州史料编译（1916～1935 年）

译　　编 / 温州市档案馆

出　版　人 / 王利民
责任编辑 / 王玉敏　刘同辉
责任印制 / 王京美

出　　　版 / 社会科学文献出版社·联合出版中心（010）59367153
　　　　　　地址：北京市北三环中路甲 29 号院华龙大厦　邮编：100029
　　　　　　网址：www. ssap. com. cn
发　　　行 / 社会科学文献出版社（010）59367028
印　　　装 / 三河市东方印刷有限公司

规　　　格 / 开　本：787mm × 1092mm　1/16
　　　　　　印　张：38　字　数：673 千字
版　　　次 / 2023 年 6 月第 1 版　2023 年 6 月第 1 次印刷
书　　　号 / ISBN 978－7－5228－1637－1
定　　　价 / 188. 00 元

读者服务电话：4008918866